LEGA CULTURE

FRONTISPIECE: Mask in ivory (from *Umbangu: Art du Congo au Musée Royal de l'Afrique centrale;* copyright Cultura, Brussels).

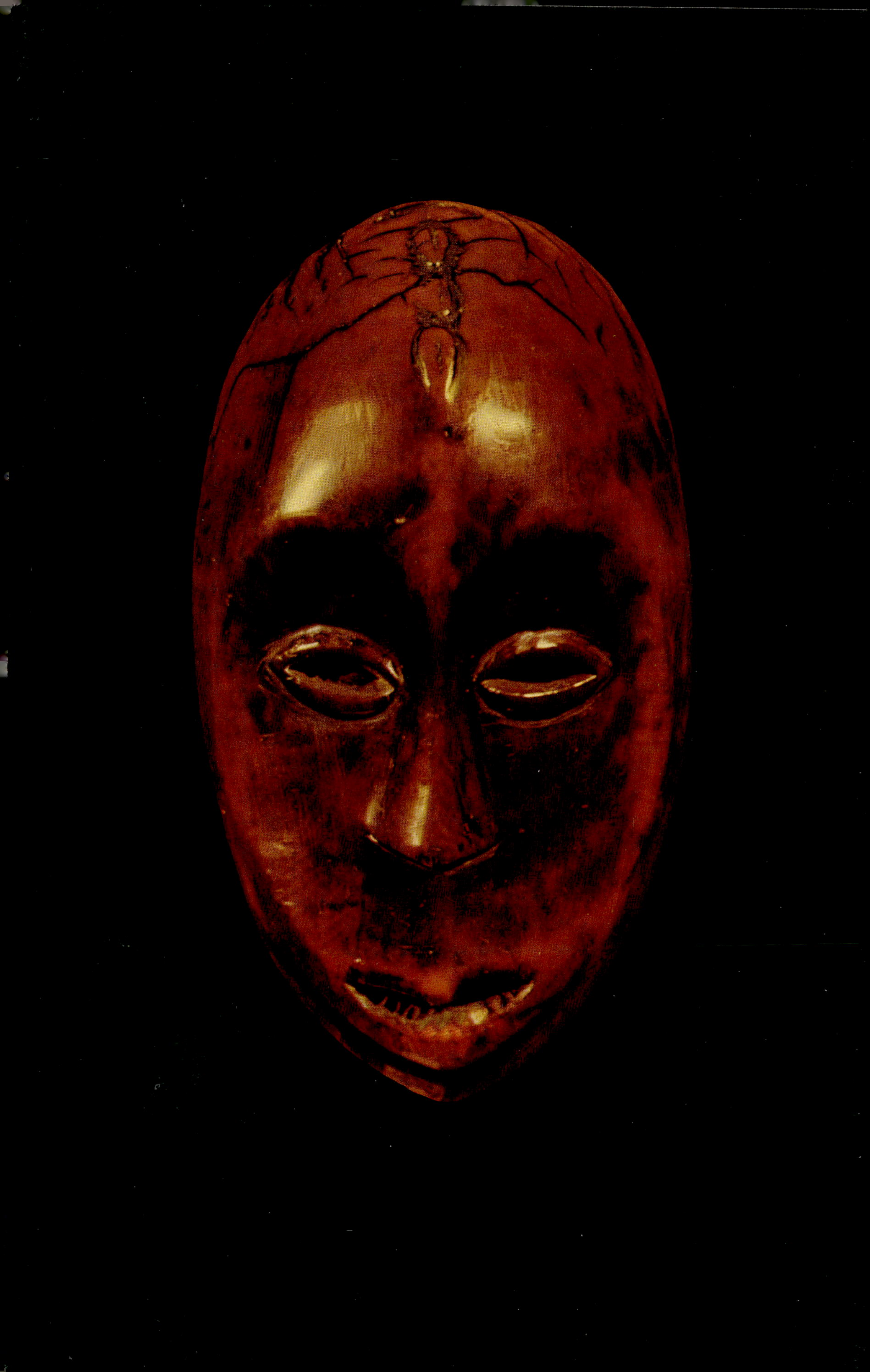

LEGA CULTURE

Art, Initiation, and Moral Philosophy
among a Central African People

DANIEL BIEBUYCK

UNIVERSITY OF CALIFORNIA PRESS
Berkeley, Los Angeles, London,

University of California Press
Berkeley and Los Angeles, California

University of California Press, Ltd.
London, England

Copyright © 1973 by The Regents of the University of California
ISBN: 0-520-02085-5
Library of Congress Catalog Card Number: 71-165226

Designed by James Mennick
Printed in the United States of America

TO LAURIE-MARIE

for her immense contribution to my work in Legaland

Musoga wane Igobo
Uwanikizie gamagu
My Good and Beautiful Gaffle
Has made me reach the intersections of the branches

Nkola ntatende
Balega ubatendezie nkola

Snail does not speak
The Balega have made snail speak

Nake mumuzegele
Na kaguma nakekutenda

Everyone in the wicker rattle
Every seed, everyone, is speaking

                                          Lega aphorisms
                                          of the bwami association

Contents

LIST OF PLATES	xi
PREFACE	xv
PHOTOGRAPHIC CREDITS	xxiii

PART 1. THE LEGA

The Name	1
Location	2
The Lega as an Ethnic Unit	3
The Language	3
The Lega Territory	5
The Genealogy	8
The Common Historical Experience	11
Environment	14
Demography	16
Relationships with Neighboring Ethnic Units	17
Internal Subdivisions	22
Cultural Subdivisions	22
Administrative Groupings	24

Part 2. Lega Culture

- Economy and Technology 26
  - Hunting and Trapping 27
  - Fishing 29
  - Gathering 29
  - Agriculture 29
  - Animal Husbandry 31
  - Food 31
  - Money and Trade 32
  - Crafts and Occupations 32
  - Village and House 34
- Social Organization 37
  - Descent, Inheritance, and Succession 37
  - The Kinship System 38
  - The Marriage System 42
  - Clan and Lineage 44
  - Political Organization 46
  - The Rites of Circumcision 50
- Religion 52
- The Arts 54
- Values 57
- Foreign Attitudes toward the Lega and Bwami . . . 58

Part 3. The Bwami Association

- Introduction 66
- Varieties of Bwami 68
- Grades, Levels, and Ritual Cycles 71
  - I. *Kongabulumbu* 74
  - II. *Kansilembo* 75
  - III. *Bombwa* 76
  - IV. *Ngandu* 76
  - V. *Bulonda* 77
  - VI. *Yananio* 77
  - VII. *Kindi* 79
  - VIII. *Bunyamwa* 81
- Origin and Distribution of Bwami among the Lega . . 82
- Membership 85
- Structure and Organization 89
  - Bwami as a Multipurpose Voluntary Association . . 89
  - Bwami as a Hierarchy of Titles 93
  - Special Statuses in Bwami 95
- Accumulation and Distribution of Food and Commodities . 107
  - The Importance of Exchange in Bwami 107
  - Types of Goods and Commodities Used in Bwami . 109

Categories of Goods and Exchanges	112
Accumulating and Distributing Goods for Lutumbo lwa kindi	114
Accumulating and Distributing Goods for Lutumbo lwa yananio	118
Conclusions	121
Bwami Ideology	123
Introduction	123
Sequence of Ideas in Kongabulumbu Initiations . . .	124
What the Lega Say about Bwami	126
What the Lega Say about the Initiate	127
Synthesis of Bwami Ideology	128
Social Functions of Bwami	132

PART 4. THE ART OF BWAMI

Range of Initiation Objects Used in Bwami	142
Natural Objects	143
Manufactured Goods	147
Artworks	149
Lega Classification of Initiation Objects	157
Usage, Functions, and Ownership and Transfer of Art Objects	166
Usage	166
Functions	169
Ownership and Transfer	181
Meaning, Configuration, and Context	184
Masks	210
Anthropomorphic Figurines	214
Animal Figurines	221
Spoons	226
The Artist	226

POSTSCRIPT	231

APPENDIXES

I. Lineages of Banasalu Clan	238
II. Initiations into Lutumbo lwa kindi in Banasalu Clan .	239
BIBLIOGRAPHY	241
INDEX	253

Plates

Frontispiece Mask in ivory
1. Lukuku, a kyogo kya kindi
2. Lusolo, a lutumbo lwa kindi
3. Mindo, a lutumbo lwa kindi, and one of his wives initiated into the kanyamwa grade
4. An initiate of lutumbo lwa kindi rank
5. Kandolo, a lutumbo lwa kindi and a great preceptor
6. A kanyamwa, in typical dress of her grade
7. A group of initiates of lutumbo lwa yananio and musagi wa yananio
8. An initiated woman of bulonda grade and her husband, a member of the lutumbo lwa yananio grade
9. A large gathering of kindi and their initiated wives
10. Two initiates: a lutumbo lwa kindi (left) and one of lower rank (right)
11. Women of kanyamwa rank conducting the wife of the male candidate into the village
12. A long row of lutumbo lwa yananio making a ceremonial entrance into the candidate's village
13. A group of kindi leading through the village an initiated woman carrying an initiation basket

14. A group of kanyamwa women carrying initiation baskets of lutumbo lwa kindi being led into the village by an initiate of yananio rank
15. Yananio initiates and women of bulonda and kanyamwa taking part in a dance performance
16. A group of drummers and singers
17. A procession of kanyamwa women proceeding in a rare rite that permits women to wear the hats of their kindi husbands
18. Two kindi dancing with wooden stools in the center of a circle of other kindi dancers
19. A kindi performing the rooftop ritual
20. Two initiates dressed as leopard men in large robes of whitened bark cloth
21. A musagi wa kindi acting as tutor for a relative being initiated into lutumbo lwa yananio
22. An old musagi wa kindi being gracefully led to the row of dancers by two close agnatic relatives
23. Display on the village floor of the contents of an initiation basket linked with kindi initiations
24. Wooden figurines displayed on the village ground during kindi initiations
25. A lavish display of animal figurines during lutumbo lwa yananio initiations
26. A display of ivory, bone, and highly polished wooden figurines during preliminaries to a lutumbo lwa kindi rite
27. Display of individually owned wooden carvings during a lutumbo lwa kindi rite
28. Four kindi dancing with three Katanda figurines
29. Four kindi dancing with three wooden figurines of the Wayinda type
30. Five kindi dancing with a representation of Sakimatwematwe, Mr. Many-Heads, during a lutumbo lwa kindi rite
31. A kindi dancing with a representation of Wayinda, the adulterous pregnant woman
32. Detail of plate 31
33. A kindi dancing with the representation of Nyabeidilwa, the woman who likes to run around to different places and is overcome by night
34. Display of wooden masks of the *lukwakongo* type
35. Display of wooden masks of the *lukwakongo* type
36. Incumbents of lutumbo lwa yananio dancing with wooden *lukwakongo* masks
37. Two preceptors of lutumbo lwa yananio dancing with the rare horned wooden *kayamba* masks in a yananio rite
38. Masks of ivory or bone fastened to a pala fence around a large wooden mask during a lutumbo lwa kindi rite
39. Masks in ivory or bone attached to a pala fence by a *munana* feather

Plates

rope, together with a large wooden *muminia* mask, during a lutumbo lwa kindi rite

40. Members of lutumbo lwa yananio wearing small *lukwakongo* masks fastened to the temples
41. A kindi preceptor, dressed in feather paraphernalia, dancing with the large wooden *nenekisi* mask illustrated in plate 38
42. Masked dancers in a lutumbo lwa yananio rite
43. Masked dancers in a lutumbo lwa yananio rite
44. Scene in a lutumbo lwa kindi rite
45. Scene in a lutumbo lwa kindi rite
46. Display, during the *nsago* rite of lutumbo lwa yananio, of shoulder bags
47. An assemblage called *kitunda kya kindi,* representing some of the attire of a musagi wa kindi
48. Display of wickerwork rattles during kindi initiations
49. Display inside the initiation hut of objects used during a lutumbo lwa yananio rite
50. Enthronement rite of a woman recently initiated to the female bulonda grade
51. Two high-ranking initiates performing a bunyamwa dance
52. Three men of low bwami rank setting out on a net hunt
53. A kindi dancing with a genet hide during a lutumbo lwa yananio rite
54. A tutor and a candidate leaning on their *mukulu* staffs
55. A kindi resting on the extremely rare wickerwork staff
56. *Lukungu* mask in ivory
57. *Lukungu* mask in bone
58. *Lukungu* mask in polished wood
59. *Muminia* mask in wood
60. *Lukwakongo* mask in wood
61. *Lukwakongo* mask in wood
62. *Lukwakongo* mask in wood
63. Human figurine in wood called Katanda
64. Human figurine in wood called Kakulu kamwenne ku masengo
65. Human figurine in wood called Bakwampego
66. Human figurine in wood with raised arm, called Kasungalala
67. Human figurine in wood called Wayinda
68. Human figurine in wood called Wayinda
69. Human figurine in wood called Kakulu ka Mpito
70. Human figurine in wood called Mutu Nyabeidilwa
71. Human figurine in wood
72. Human figurine in wood called Nkumba or Mulima
73. Human figurine in ivory, with four faces, called Sakimatwematwe or Nawasakwa nyona

74. Human figurine in ivory, with four faces, called Sakimatwematwe
75. Human figurine in ivory called Katindili
76. Figurine in ivory called Mulima
77. Human figurine in ivory, with double face, called Kakinga
78. Human figurine in ivory called Nyaminia
79. Human figurine in ivory, of the *kalimbangoma* type
80. Human figurine in ivory, of the *katimbitimbi* type
81. Human figurine in ivory called Keitula
82. Human figurine in ivory called Nawasakwa nyona
83. Human figurine in ivory
84. Human figurine in ivory called Keitula
85. Human figurine in ivory called Sakatwe
86. Double head in ivory called Sakimatwematwe
87. Head on little stool, in ivory, called Wankenge
88. Animal figurine in wood, of the *mugugundu* or the *kalimbangoma* type
89. Animal figurine in wood, with horns, of the *mugugundu* type
90. Animal figurine in ivory, representing *kimena* (crocodile)
91. Animal figurine in ivory, representing *ikaga* (pangolin)
92. Animal figurine in ivory, of the *mugugundu* type
93. Animal figurine in ivory, representing *ntumba* (aardvark)
94. Animal figurine in ivory, representing a *ngimbi* snake
95. Spoon, ivory, called *kalukili*
96. Spoon, elephant bone, called *kalukili*
97. Spoon, ivory, called *kalukili*
98. Head, ivory, called Kankubungu
99. Group of four small carvings in ivory and elephant bone, called *katimbitimbi*
100. Miniature stool in elephant bone, classified as *kalimbangoma*
101. Stool in wood with copper nails, called *kisumbi*
102. Knife, ivory, classified as *kabemba*
103. Hornbill knife in elephant bone, classified as *mugusu*
104. Scepter in elephant bone, classified as *kituta* or *nondo*
105. Ax blade in elephant bone, classified as *isaga*
106. Piece of carved elephant bone
107. Hammer in ivory, classified as *nondo*
108. Excrescence of a vine
109. Strings of shell money, called *musanga*
110. Group of natural objects used in bwami initiations

Preface

LATE IN 1951 I finished two years of intensive fieldwork among the Bembe in the highlands west of Lake Tanganyika. In the course of that research I did some work on the bwami association[1] which induced me to make further investigations among the Lega, where the association had its roots. Basically, the shift from Bembe to Lega was facilitated by the fact that the linguistic transition is a fairly easy one; the eastern forms of Lega, particularly as spoken by the Basimwenda and related clans, are very close to Bembe. In addition, the existence of a number of related groups on both sides of a loosely defined Bembe-Lega boundary enhances the sense of continuity. Finally, Lega and Bembe share many common historical and cultural features. Early in 1952, therefore, after taking a few rapid soundings among neighboring ethnic groups such as Vira, Furiiru, and Nyindu, I began my research among the eastern Lega. My prolonged work among

[1] In order to keep the italicization of foreign words within reasonable limits, I have made certain exceptions to the customary typographic rules. The word "bwami," and the names of all the levels and grades of the bwami association, are not italicized, though the names of the rites leading to membership in the different grades are handled in the usual way. Furthermore, French administrative terms, such as "secteur" and "chefferie," are printed in roman type.

the Bembe and the linkage between the two groups made easier my first contact with the Lega, to whom the character and the scope of my investigations were well known. Wherever I went I was referred to by my prized Bembe nickname "Mtoca ntaule," meaning the asker (inquirer) does not die (i.e., is strong).

The real obstacle I had to overcome was bwami itself. This voluntary association is not secret insofar as membership is concerned.[2] Most of its initiations and ceremonies, however, are closed to outsiders, as are also the special knowledge and the symbolism on which they are based. The situation was further complicated because the association had been dissolved in 1947 by a decree from the colonial government, allegedly because it constituted a threat to order and peace. Before 1947, ever since Arabs and Arabized slave raiders had operated in and around Legaland and missionaries and colonial administrators had penetrated the area, the association and its members had been treated largely with suspicion and contempt, and rarely with indulgence or indifference. Occasionally a more enlightened Belgian official would place bwami in its proper perspective, but such tolerance brought only temporary relief.

About the time I finished my Bembe studies, debates were again raging at different levels of the colonial administration concerning the validity of the ban on bwami. As always, some Belgian administrators, for a variety of personal reasons, were favorable toward the association and therefore questioned, or even regretted, the radical actions taken in the past. At the time of my research, as it happened, men of this persuasion were rather well represented at the higher echelons of the provincial government. Because of this prevailing intellectual climate, and also because of the favorable research position occupied in the Kivu Province by the Institut pour la Recherche scientifique en Afrique centrale (with which I was then associated), it was not too difficult to receive from the provincial authorities full assurances that there would be no interference with my work on bwami. In subsequent months I lived and worked with my wife in Lega villages, having little if any contact with the scattered and relatively few groups of whites—territorial administrators, missionaries, mining personnel, and a few traders—in Legaland.

Although I was well known to the Lega and had been widely accepted by them even before I started my work among them, it took about three months of intensive relationships before they decided to give me real information about bwami. Their early reticence stemmed from a number of causes. Bwami is an association and therefore, by definition, a closed body of people and knowledge. Because of persecutions and other milder interferences, the members of the association were suspicious about any

---

[2] The ethnographic present used throughout this book to describe situations and institutions relates to the period from late 1951 to 1954.

Preface

outside attempt to approach them closely. They had developed, as a protective screen in their dealings with outsiders, attitudes of reticence and feigned ignorance. Furthermore, events of the past four decades had made the Lega cautious about the motives of whites; superficial inquiries had been undertaken by a few administrators and missionaries who were eager to solve practical problems, and many traders, administrators, agronomists, and the like merely wanted to witness a dance for fun or acquire a carving for the lowest possible price. Consequently, the Lega found it difficult to take my investigations and purposes seriously. They had received little in return, except frustration, for dispensing their knowledge or giving away their artwork. And, of course, the human approach had not always been so mild. Occasionally members of the association had been raided, beaten, insulted, imprisoned, or exiled.

My difficulties, however, arose not merely from the mental attitude of the Lega, but also from deficiencies in my early methods of approach and modes of investigation. Except for the references to bwami and the Lega in Commander Delhaise's work, *Les Warega* (1909), no significant published material was available. As a student I had scrutinized the rich Lega and other Congo collections in the Musée royal de l'Afrique centrale at Tervuren. I had seen and read, in the provincial capital of Bukavu and in the relevant administrative centers of Mwenga, Shabunda, Pangi, and Kindu, all available reports and letters on the Lega in general and on bwami in particular. Some of these materials dated as far back as 1912 and formed a direct follow-up of the data recorded by Commander Delhaise in 1906. Most of these studies, based on opinions, reflections, or suggestions, gave few ethnographic facts. I did, of course, find useful hints about the nature of the hierarchies in bwami, about dances and ceremonies, practices and objects, but such information afforded little insight into useful methods for gaining a deeper understanding of bwami.

My first three months in Legaland were therefore devoted mainly to general orientation. I spent some time in a number of communities, moving out rapidly whenever I felt there was little hope of making further progress. I took censuses of villages, collected data on kinship and ethnohistory, and annotated the elaborate and detailed charts of descent groups. In acquiring this kind of information about Lega culture, I also secured substantial but general documentation about the organization, the structure, and the ceremonialism of bwami. Above all, while learning the language and picking up cultural facts, I tried to submerge myself in the Lega world through constant, but discreet, contact. Areawise, I followed a well-defined pattern of preliminary inquiries, beginning with the Basimwenda, the Bakuti, and the Bakabango in the eastern part of Legaland, where the Lega are in direct contact with the Bembe; then northward among the Beigala-Banangoma and the Bamuguba, farther northeastward among the Baliga, and northwestward among the Bakyunga. By the time I had completed my work among the Bakyunga I was more than ready to make a definite breakthrough in the study of bwami. It would be found among the western and southwestern Lega in the administrative divisions of Beia, Babene, and Bakabango in Pangi territory.

As I proceeded from the Basimwenda to the Bakyunga, enthusiasm, mutual appreciation, congeniality, acceptability, and confidence had steadily grown. This favorable climate resulted not only from the time and effort I had spent, but also from the fact that the bwami association was a more pervasive institution among the southern, western, and northern Lega than in the areas where I had begun my research. It had, therefore, proved more resistant to the onslaught of the colonial system. Gradually I became familiar with the grade system, the exchanges, the use of art objects and other artifacts during initiations, the methods of succession in and accession to bwami, the distribution of grades and initiations, the linkages between ritual communities. Quite a few initiation procedures were reenacted for me by large groups of initiates, but most of my information was gleaned from open discussions and interviews. These conversations were always conducted among rather large gatherings of initiates, never in private, and only to a limited extent did I use observational and participant methods.

In subsequent months I operated exclusively in Pangi territory, where the bwami traditions are the most strongly developed and the best preserved. I worked successively in the following areas: Baziri-Banakeigo-Banalyuba, Beianangi-Beiamisisi, Beiankuku, Banasalu, Beiamunsange, all of them in secteur Beia; Banamunwa and Banisanga-Batoba-Bagilanzelu in chefferie Babene; Babongolo in secteur Bakabango. In each of these clan groups or ritual communities I dealt with practically all living initiates of at least the two highest grades, yananio and kindi. My method of procedure required careful advance planning. For example, I would ask to be initiated into any given group I wanted to study, either alone or jointly with a Lega man designated by the initiates in the traditional way. The higher-ranking initiates, in charge of the ceremonies at the lower as well as at the higher levels, would then assemble, as agreed upon, in the village of one of the group. Large quantities of food (bananas, oil, salt, game meat, and goats) were collected for the occasion. Large-scale hunts were organized. The appropriate initiation hut was built. I paid the providers for services and food, distributing the latter according to custom during the initiations, together with Congolese money (in lieu of Lega shell money). I worked directly with high-ranking initiates, without interpreters or clerks. By the time of my main breakthrough in Pangi, however, I had availed myself of the good services of Lumbeku and Beikalantende, both of whom were members of the association and judges appointed to the *tribunaux indigènes* (so-called native courts). They were

Preface

intelligent, well traveled, and widely acknowledged as speakers. Extremely dedicated to this work, and fully aware of my needs and problems, they acted as my *hommes de confiance,* spokesmen, and intermediaries whenever necessary. With them I discussed and analyzed questions of translation, interpretation, procedure, and so on. I also benefited from the generous support of Omari Penemisenga, an able and well-liked chef de secteur in the Beia division (Pangi territory) and a strong defender and enthusiastic admirer of the bwami association.

By this time I had come to be truly liked and accepted by the Lega. Ritual communities vied with one another to have me participate in initiations in their villages. I had come to be classified as "our *mwigwa*," that is, as the sororal nephew of all Lega, a perpetual position by which members of the neighboring Bangubangu find themselves intimately linked to the Lega. I greatly benefited from this position, which carries immense prestige and bestows many privileges (see Part 2, below). (It is difficult for a maternal uncle to say no to a reasonable, or even a half-reasonable, request from his nephew!) I had received the bwami names of Mambwe (personification of a men's latrine, explained in the aphorism, "Mambwe scrutinizes the defecators"; i.e., Mambwe knows esoteric things) and of Kilinkumbi (a drum praise name for the pangolin explained in the aphorism, "Kilinkumbi, the wise animal for which danced the big ones"). I had also acquired my own slogans—"Mr. Many-Halting-Places [Isamalomengi], Yango [symbolic term for penis] is dancing on the trail," and "Progressing slowly [Kasigesige] has made chicken arrive at eleusine; progressing slowly has made seducer arrive at vulva"—which in their own way emphasize the value of circumspection, of slowness in action and decision making. In time the initiates applied to me one of their most famous aphorisms—"The little child of a mwami [is] a *nkamba* fish; in deep pools, that is where it is used to swim"—meaning that I had sought deep knowledge from them and that I had been allowed into the inner fastnesses of bwami.

In the course of my fieldwork among the Lega I worked in the following communities: some Bainyindu groups that have the bwami association, Basimwenda and subgroups, Bakuti and subgroups, Bakabango, especially Babongolo and Basitabyale, Banagabo, Banangoma, Beigala, Bamuguba, Baliga, Bakyunga, Baziri, Banakeigo, Banalyuba, Beianangi, Beiamisisi, Beiankuku, Banasalu, Beiamunsange, Bakabango/Babongolo of Kasambulu, Banamunwa, and Banisanga-Batoba-Bagilanzelu. To complete my work in each group required from eight days to more than three weeks. At the earliest stage I restricted myself almost entirely to verbal discussion, but later, in some ritual communities, I personally went through the entire cycle of initiations, from the bottom (kongabulumbu) all the way to the top (lutumbo lwa kindi). In other ritual communities I underwent only a selection of initiations, particularly at the lowest and the highest levels. The ceremonies took place in the appropriate setting at the appropriate time of day (very early morning, daytime, evening and night).

The cooperation I received from high-ranking initiates and from famed experts was exceptionally loyal. As the members of the association often stated in late evening conversations, they hoped that my findings would soon be known to top officials who, at last enlightened about bwami, would once and for all decide to let the Lega and their association alone. And, indeed, the climate was favorable for the realization of these expectations. Moreover, the basic philosophy of bwami stresses individual effort and achievement combined with an attitude of piety and temperance. The personal effort my wife and I made to live with the members of bwami, and only with them; our perseverance in the quest for the highest initiatory experience; our attitude of genuine respect and understanding—all these, sharply contrasting with a background of poor black-white understanding, greatly contributed to the success of the enterprise.

In the process of going through initiations, which cost me a vast amount of money for both services and commodities, I collected certain objets d'art, paraphernalia, and other initiatory objects (natural items and artifacts). In the pattern of the initiations, these objects, which are tokens of membership and insignia of status, are given to the initiate who achieves certain grades or levels within the association. The initiations are centered on a combination of dance, display and manipulation of objects, and sung aphorisms. My collection of these verbal texts numbers close to seven thousand. In them, and in the contexts in which they are used, is condensed the entire ideology of bwami.

By participating in my initiations and entering into discussions, thousands of members of the bwami association have contributed in one way or another to my knowledge. I am indebted to them all, yet I would like to mention especially a few spokesmen and preceptors *(nsingia)* to whom I owe probably the most, such men as Lumbeku, Beikalantende, Kandolo, Balumya, Bikenge, Kagila, Nzogu, Kaswende, Kilumbu, Bimpa, Penemisenga, Alimasi, Busile, Aliamuntu, Simbo, Mizeni, Mindo, Nyaulingu, Munyange, Kisubi, Penekenye, Kabundilila, Luzoni, Moke, and Bunzuki. Some of these were outstanding as initiators and preceptors, others as analysts and exegetes, others as advisers and counselors. Still others were able spokesmen and orators whose talent as arbiters, catalysts, and organizers was always in demand. Others were especially valuable in retracing the intricate fields of kinship relationships they used in preparing for their initiations, in soliciting commodities, in sharing goods, and so on. After many years I am still awed by the immense knowledge possessed by some of the high-ranking members of the association and am still overwhelmed by the generosity and grace that moved them to share their knowledge with me.

There are, in Lega culture, wide differences in actual ways of doing

Preface

things, clearly manifested as one travels across Legaland from east to west or from south to north. These variations are seen in the language and the social structure, in the economy and technology, in rituals and beliefs as well as the initiation system. They are caused by differences in outside contact and influence, in ecology, and in local experience, but above all, perhaps, by the very social system and the ideology itself. Each separate Lega group in the bwami association has a deep-lying instinct to do things somewhat differently from other groups, with the result that every autonomous ritual community in Legaland has some ways peculiar to itself. The structural principles on which the system operates are, of course, fundamentally the same, so that the concept of a Lega culture is a valid one. Yet possible differences in details must constantly be kept in mind. In the course of my fieldwork among the Lega I have studied all their main subdivisions, some in greater detail and over a longer period of time than others. Being thus aware of nuances and variations, I incorporate them whenever they are vital to the understanding of certain aspects of bwami and art.

My main arguments on the bwami association and on art are directly relevant to the southwestern Lega of Pangi territory, entities grouped at the time of my research in the administrative units of Beia, Babene, and Bakabango. My concern is with traditional Lega society as it had, in the 1950's, survived repeated assaults from those engaged in colonial administration, missionary activity, mining operations, and trading. The bwami association and its arts, on which this study is focused, suffered from the activities of these extraneous agencies. The association had been compelled to go underground; its membership had frequently been persecuted and prosecuted. The rich artworks either were no longer made or were produced in small quantities and were of mediocre quality. Few Western items had been admitted into the richly diversified set of initiation objects. About the only imported things I saw being used during initiations, casually submerged in the vast number of Lega items, were electric bulbs (obviously not for lighting), small madonna statues (not for worship), delicately shaped perfume bottles (not for their contents), aluminum plates, and white china dishes (not for serving food). A few modernistic carvings in mahogany ascribed to the Bausa (Mangbetu-Zande) and purchased from young men working in mining compounds within Legaland were occasionally used. The theme of the white man and his works was barely touched upon in the aphorisms sung and the interpretations given.

Bwami is an organization characterized by immense pride and greatness. Its members are men of profound wisdom and mature poise. Misunderstood and suppressed, they looked with skepticism, regret, and yet self-assurance at the pitiful conditions around them. "The hammer that remains with the children shatters the *nkoku* shell" (i.e., the land, if left to uninitiated individuals, will be ruined) and "The hunters find the *nkola* shells, but he who guards the village is master over the shells" were among the frequently quoted proverbs that gave expression to these attitudes. The initiates were not ready to discard their customs for something else because that something else, about which missionaries and other Europeans talked, was already present in their own system: "The stone [= our customs and ideas] is not heavy [and therefore to be abandoned]; inside there is something else [i.e., something that gives meaning and substance to it]."

My field research among the Lega was sponsored entirely by the Institut pour la Recherche scientifique en Afrique centrale (IRSAC) in Brussels. The idea for my undertaking a study of the Lega was first conceived by the late Professor Frans M. Olbrechts, director of the then Musée royal du Congo Belge, Tervuren. Professor Olbrechts was one of the earliest and best-informed authorities on African art, and I owe much to his stimulating influences. Over the years the vast documentation I collected in the field has been translated, classified, and partly pieced together with the help of the African Studies Center, University of California, Los Angeles, of the University of Delaware, and of the Social Science Research Council (Joint Committee on African Studies). I gratefully acknowledge their financial assistance.

Numerous colleagues in various universities, centers, and museums have given me frequent opportunities to lecture on aspects of Lega art and on the bwami association and its structure and moral philosophy. The questions and comments of both scholars and students on those occasions have been a powerful incentive for me to clarify the interpretation and presentation of data. I am especially grateful to Professors Roy Sieber of Indiana University and Robert F. Thompson of Yale University, and to many of their students. All viewpoints expressed are, of course, my own responsibility.

I am also particularly thankful for the numerous corrections and suggestions made by Mrs. Grace H. Stimson of the University of California Press, who edited the manuscript.

I am deeply indebted to governors of Kivu Province, to district commissioners of Kivu and Maniema districts, and to administrators of the territories of Fizi, Mwenga, Pangi, Shabunda, Kindu, and Kasongo for their assistance, both in personal conversations and in allowing me to consult government archives. The archives contain valuable unpublished reports and studies made by many territorial administrators since 1916.

Finally, the writing of this book was made possible by the help of Dr. Jay T. Last, connoisseur of African arts and fervent admirer and expert collector of Lega art. Without his encouragement the work could not have been finished at a time when many other academic obligations were weighing upon me.

D. B.

Photographic Credits

Daniel Biebuyck, plates 1 to 55

F. Dubus, Tervuren, frontispiece and plates 56 to 61, 63 to 65, 67 to 78, 80, 85, 87, 88, 90, 96, 98, 100, 102, 107, 109

Koninklijk Museum van Centraal Afrika, Tervuren, frontispiece and plates 56 to 61, 63 to 65, 67 to 78, 80, 85, 87, 88, 90, 96, 98, 100, 102, 107, 109

Jay T. Last, Los Angeles, plates 66, 83, 89, 91 to 94, 103, 105, 106

Museum and Laboratories of Ethnic Arts and Technology, University of California, Los Angeles, plates 95, 97, 99, 108, 110

P. T. Shima, University of California, Los Angeles, plates 97, 110

L. DuPont, University of California, Los Angeles, plates 95, 99, 108

R. D. Stewart, University of Delaware, Newark, plates 62, 79, 81, 82, 84, 86, 101, 104

Part 1 The Lega

THE NAME

The Balega (hereafter referred to as Lega without either of the classifiers *mu-* and *ba-*) are known in the earlier literature as Warega.[1] The term Lega, which in some eastern groups is pronounced as Leka and in some southern and western groups as Idega, stands out as the name of a mythical ancestor from whom most entities that identify with the Lega ethnic unit claim to be descended. A substantial number of scattered groups that no longer affiliate themselves with the Lega ethnic unit[2] are

[1] "Warega" is merely a Swahilized mispronunciation of "Balega." Delhaise (1909a, p. 22) uses the appellation Warega throughout his monograph, although he is aware that the proper term is Lega. I consistently use "Lega," without classifiers, to refer to the people (Mulega; Balega), the language (Kilega), and the country (Bulega). Some linguists spell Lega with a long vowel as Leega (see Bryan, 1959, p. 92).

[2] It is rather astonishing that neighboring groups use few nicknames in referring to the Lega; Delhaise (1909a, p. 22) says they mention the Lega either as Warega or as Mwami. The latter appellation has to do with the characteristic bwami association. Indeed, the distinctive paraphernalia worn by members of bwami give a peculiar aspect to the human environment in Legaland. According to Delhaise (*ibid.*), the Songola sometimes refer to the Lega as Bâki, people deprived of *Elaeis* palms, of which the Songola themselves have very many. The cultural separation between Lega and surrounding groups is not a sharp one, as is frequently demonstrated in this study, and this fact surely helps to account for the lack of ethnic nicknaming.

said to be descended from Lega, the ancestor. Essentially, it is his alleged descendants who make up the Lega people. Few neighboring groups use the term to refer to the people here identified as the Lega; the related Bembe currently use it to refer to their western neighbors. The Lega themselves are given other appellations by several large neighboring groups: they are called Bembe by the Shi, Baki by the Songola, Buise by the Zimba. Folk interpretations pretend that the word Lega means "sustainer,"[3] and occasionally, in line with this definition, Lega is made synonymous with Isamwati, a term that is said to mean Master-Settler-of-Problems.[4] The word Lega, now placed at the top of almost all clan genealogies, also occurs with either the singular (*mu-*) or the plural (*ba-*) classifier in a few proverbs used during bwami initiations either to mean the people in general or to emphasize the concepts of the true man, the man of poise and wisdom who represents the Lega ideal of perfection.[5] In the latter usage "Lega" underscores the contrast between the Lega way and other ways of life or between initiate and noninitiate.[6]

For purposes of internal communication the term Lega is rarely employed. Both small and large groups identify themselves, and others, under clan and lineage names or refer to groups of genealogically linked clans: Kisi, Beia, Kabango, Shile, Ikama, and the like. These names are thought to stand for the children and grandchildren of Lega, from whom groups of linked clans originated. During the colonial period, however, the term Lega became more prevalent, as Lega's descendants saw themselves more and more as a unit confronting outside forces such as neighboring peoples, the government, the missions, and so on.

Location

The Lega live in the eastern part of the Democratic Republic of the Congo/Kinshasa. Broadly speaking, they inhabit an area of irregular

---

[3] Stuhlmann (1894, p. 844), maintaining that all forest populations are called Lega, finds the term to be synonymous with *Wald-Leute*. Delhaise rejects this interpretation. Cordella's (1906, p. 975) interpretation of the name as *popolo dal vaso di terra* is based on a misreading of tones.

[4] As is shown later, these folk etymologies converge with basic philosophies held by the bwami association of the Lega.

[5] Delhaise (1909a, p. 22) indicates that the term Lega is used conversationally as the equivalent of the French *on* (indefinite pronoun). The concept is better interpreted in terms of ingroup values relating to manhood, virility, and poise. On the other hand, Delhaise (*ibid.*) correctly states that the term signifies humanity (from the Lega point of view), and, we may add, it means just people, as in the proverb, "Something big covers me; the sky hangs [as a cover] over the Balega."

[6] It must be pointed out, however, that the Lega do not customarily make explicit verbalizations about their superiority. The impact of Lega culture on adjacent sections of other ethnic units has been tremendous. Since cultural transitions from the Lega to other groups are never abrupt, differences are not strongly emphasized.

The Lega

polygonal shape, lying roughly between 2 and 4 degrees south latitude and between 26 and 28.5 degrees east longitude. Legaland covers the valleys of the middle and upper Elila and the upper Ulindi rivers.

On the eve of independence the Lega, as the result of numerous governmental reforms, were divided into three administrative territories called Mwenga, Shabunda, and Pangi. Most of the area included in the Shabunda and Pangi territories is inhabited only by Lega. Although a large part of the Mwenga territory is also occupied by Lega, its northeastern sections have other populations such as Nyindu, Rhinyirhinyi, and Hwinja, and in its southern portion a large group of Bembe overlap into Fizi territory. Surprisingly, the three Lega territories were incorporated into different administrative districts: Shabunda and Pangi into the Maniema district and Mwenga into the southern Kivu district. Both districts formed part of Kivu Province. Of all ethnic groups established in this province, the Lega occupied the largest single territory of about 50,000 square kilometers.

The Lega as an Ethnic Unit

Although the Lega are not organized into a state system, their sense of historical and cultural unity is very strong. This feeling of commonality is rooted in a common language, common historical experiences, common genealogical charts, in territoriality, and in a common set of basic institutions and values. The situation is, of course, immensely complicated. It is not easy to determine the limits of Lega culture because it overlaps with other cultures for long distances on the border lines. Legaland as shown on maps and as defined for the colonial administration and for the world of science gives a misleading idea of the cultural realities. For example, Songola, Zimba, and Bembe villages are established inside Legaland, whereas some Lega villages lie outside its boundaries. Many marginal Lega villages show the effects of cultural influences exerted by Songola, Zimba, Bembe, Komo, and Nyindu, and Lega influences have worked upon these and other ethnic groups. Furthermore, throughout Legaland one can find groups, some large, some small, which are of Lega culture without being of Lega origin; conversely, some groups outside Legaland boast Lega origin but belong to Bembe, Songola, Komo, or Zimba culture.

The Language. The Lega speak a Bantu language called Kilega (sometimes spelled Kileega, Ileega, Kelega, or Kirega). Four major groups of dialects can be recognized within Lega: the western dialects spoken mainly in the Beia and Babene administrative units of Pangi territory; the northern dialects spoken chiefly in the Bakisi administrative unit of Shabunda territory; the southern dialects used mainly in three administrative units known as Bakabango and Kama in Pangi territory and Bakabango in Shabunda territory; and the eastern dialects spoken mainly in the Bamuzimu administrative unit of Mwenga territory. The eastern dialect group can be distinguished from all the others by its widespread use of ejectives as replacements for the phoneme k.[7] The four dialect groups roughly correspond with acknowledged genealogical divisions within the Lega and with certain cultural differences and specializations.

The linguistic relationships between Lega and other languages spoken in the Kivu and Maniema districts have been discussed in earlier studies. According to Van Bulck, the Lega, together with Bembe, Vira, Leka, and Mitoko, constitute the group of ancient Bantu from the northeast. Van Bulck believed that, from certain points of view, languages spoken by Bangubangu, Nyanga, Lengola, Songola, Zimba, and Genya belonged to the same group.[8] In later studies, however, he tended to modify and reduce this group. In the *groupe du Maniema* within the *section centrale-nord* he had originally included Nyanga, Kanu, eastern Songola, Zimba, and Bembe, together with Lega, but later he restricted the group again to Lega, Bembe, Kanu, and Nyanga.[9]

According to Meeussen,[10] the Lega complex includes the following languages: Lega itself, northern Binja (or eastern Songola), southern Binja (or Zimba), Bembe, and Boyo. It may also comprise languages spoken by some northwestern (Mitoko, Lengola, Genya) and southeastern

---

[7] Cleire (1951, p. 32) draws a minimal distinction between eastern Lega idioms (Kisile and Kibembe) and western ones (Shabunda, Pangi, Kalole, and Kasese). Van Bulck (1954, p. 29) distinguishes among Ileega Imuzimu (or eastern Lega) subdivided into Ishile and Iwanyabaale (Kitutu), Kileega (Kisi) of Shabunda, and Kileega of Bakabango. These distinctions fail to take into account all the Lega linguistic and cultural subdivisions. The only succinct, but significant, study on the grammatical system of one of the Lega dialects (Banagabo of Shabunda) has recently been published by Meeussen (1971).

[8] Van Bulck (1948, pp. 228–234) insists that some of the groups included have strong links with other units. For example, he is inclined to classify Bangubangu with Boyo in another group, yet he recognizes that certain vocabulary lists compel him to speak about the Bangubangu in conjunction with the Lega. He argues that some of the lists possibly were made among certain sections of surrounding tribes that had been influenced by the Lega.

[9] Van Bulck (1954, pp. 29–31) treats Songola and Lengola as transitional between Lega and Bira-Komo.

[10] Meeussen (1953, pp. 385–391) justifies this classification on the basis of phonological, grammatical, and semantic comparisons derived from his own field research and from published sources. He also groups Ombo (or western Songola) with the Mongo languages, Bangubangu with the Luba complex, and Furiiru (Fuliru) with Shi, Hunde, Havu, and other East African languages (*ibid.*, p. 391). Guthrie (1948, pp. 40–42; 1967, *passim*; 1970, p. 12) includes Lega in Group 20 of Zone D of his large northeastern area, thus placing it closer to Songola, Zimba, Bangubangu, Komo, and Holoholo (all included in the same group) than to Bembe (Group 50). Similar separations are, in my opinion, based on inadequate ethnographic surveys and the insufficient definitions of ethnic units which underlie these linguistic comparisons.

(Holoholo) neighbors, whereas Zyoba (spoken by Vira and Sanze) has only some affinities with Lega. Meeussen also finds that Binja, Bembe, and Boyo have more resemblances to one another than to Lega.[11]

In part, the difficulties of tracing linguistic relationships of Lega with other languages stem from the inadequate definition of ethnic units in terms of ethnohistory and linguistic acculturation. Many scholars take it for granted that such groups as Zimba, Bangubangu, Songola, and so on are homogeneous entities, or that it is easy to know where the Lega end and another group begins. The cultural situation on the margins of Legaland is much more complex than the maps suggest. As shown below, the entire Lega area is characteristically surrounded by what might be called cultural buffer groups, which are either segments of Lega clans that have been subject to strong linguistic and cultural influences from neighbors, or segments of other tribes that have been acculturated by Lega groups. Because linguistic surveys are extensive, usually cover a wide area, and are restricted to one or, at best, a few checkpoints within that area, with no other culturally relevant information available, the resultant classifications are misleading. Seeming contradictions in the record could be fully understood with a broader cultural and ethnohistorical perspective. No doubt Lega, Bembe, and Kanu are closely related. Fragments of the populations identified as Songola, Zimba, Bangubangu, Kwame, and Nyindu speak dialects that have many affinities with Lega, not only because of the linguistic acculturation or common historical origin but also because of overlapping of clan fragments from different ethnic groups.

The Kingwana variant of Swahili is widely used throughout Legaland as a lingua franca in administration, education, commerce, and industry. Younger Lega speak it fluently and sometimes use the superior forms of a more pretentious Swahili. French, the official language of the Congo, was hardly known to the rural Lega.

The Lega Territory. The Lega occupy a vast uninterrupted territory whose outer limits are not sharply demarcated, since the Lega have many historical and cultural links with neighboring groups. Few "foreign" groups, representing earlier cultural strata, remain within Lega territory. Although still known under their original tribal names and still preserving some of their own cultural characteristics, they have been thoroughly Lega-ized. Chief among these widely scattered and often numerically weak groups are the following:

---

[11] The Lega restrict their observations to such statements as "Our fathers used to show us the hole of an aardvark which a Pygmy had entered and died in," and "Our fathers used to show us a tree which a Pygmy had climbed and from which he had fallen." In general, the Lega assert that one cannot speak in behalf of "those whom one has met."

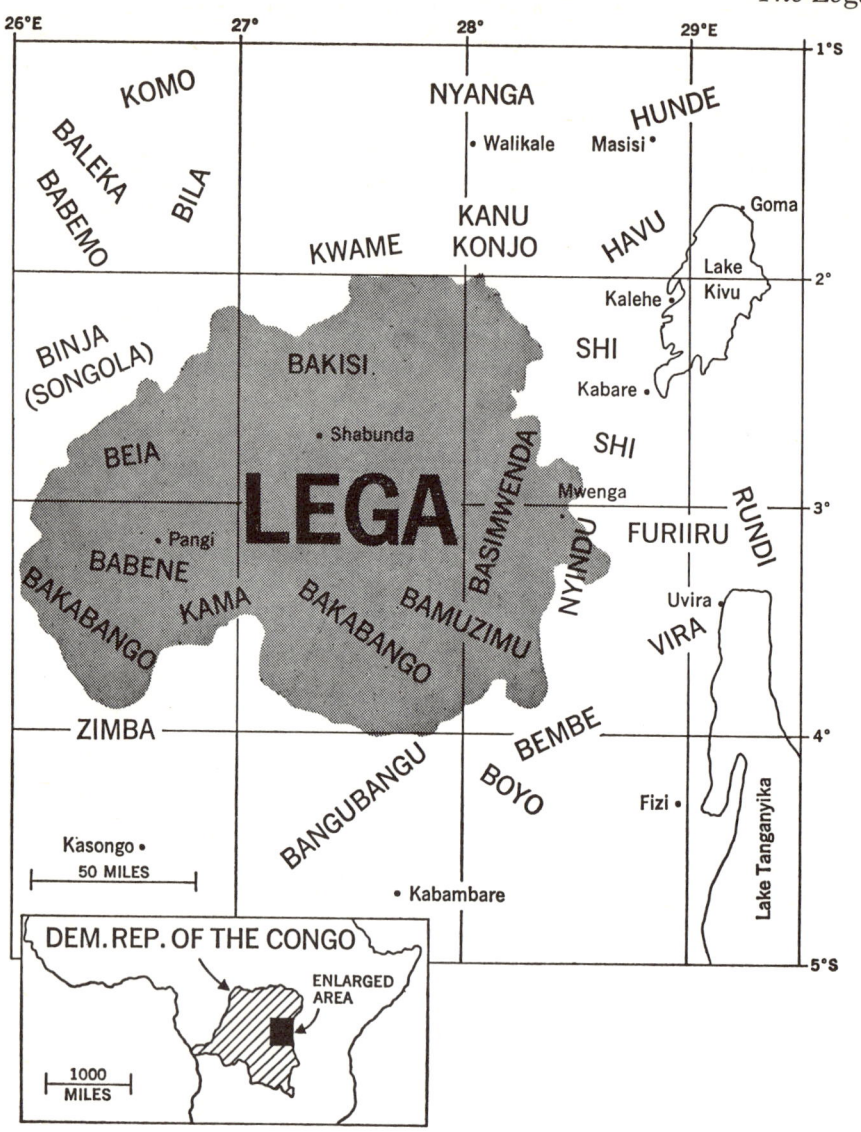

NEIGHBORS AND SUBDIVISIONS OF THE LEGA

Some riverain groups found in extremely small numbers along some of the main river courses (such as the Ulindi River) are known as the descendants of Kilimono. Originally they formed a part of the so-called Genya riverains found here and there between Kisangani and Kindu. The Lega consider them to be a different, yet friendly, people.

The Bouse, found among southern Lega groups, are a small remnant of uncertain Bantu origin exhibiting strong Pygmy influences. They are known as blacksmiths and great warriors of the past.

The Balyanga, mentioned among western Lega groups, are somewhat like the Bouse in cultural type and origin.

The Kunda, a small group found in close association with the Bakabango in southern Legaland, seem to be originally of matrilineal Luba stock.

The M'minje and Renge form a large group of Bantu people who claim to have local origins. They are found in large but scattered areas of northeastern Legaland (among the Basimwenda) and farther eastward among the Nyindu and the Bembe.

The few Twa, Mbote, or Pygmies left in Legaland are found in the eastern part and among the Baziri clan in Pangi territory. A different situation prevails among the Bembe and the Nyanga, where sizable groups of Pygmies and Pygmoids, respectively known as Mbote and Cwa, survive. The Pygmies among the Lega remain hunters and gatherers. They are not treated as a subservient people. Rather, they constitute a number of incorporated, but independent, lineages of foreign origin, and they do not exercise the ritual privileges they hold among the Bembe, Nyanga, Shi, and other Kivu populations.

The Basi'asumba, scattered among the Bembe and the eastern Lega, are of an early Bantu strain that was strongly Pygmy-ized before being exposed to Lega and Bembe culture. They engage in circumcision rituals, but they have no bwami. Living in small unstable villages, they are good hunters who practice limited hunting nomadism.

Each of these Lega-ized groups is said to have contributed specializations to Lega culture. The descendants of Kilimono knew how to make canoes and how to fish with spears; the Bouse were knowledgeable in certain hunting, warfare, and blacksmithing techniques; the M'minje-Renge introduced spirit cults and possibly the great bwami tradition. Little is said about the Pygmies and their culture, although anecdotes about specific events are widely known;[12] a direct and close linkage with the Pygmies, however, is portrayed in the genealogical recitations of the

---

[12] Delhaise (1909a, pp. 47–48), many of whose basic data on the Lega are sound, relates a legend that places Lega origins in Zimba country, south of their present habitat. The context of this legend clearly reveals that Delhaise is dealing, not with ethnohistorical records, but with imaginary elements provided by the Museme epic of

southwestern Lega. Lega is said to have married Kakinga, a daughter of the Twa, with whom he raised children who became the founders of different subgroups.

The Genealogy. The Lega have no unified genealogical chart. The four major variations of the group's genealogy, however, complement rather than contradict one another, for each one emphasizes Lega subgroups that fall within a certain geographical and historical orbit.

The most inclusive early genealogy, presented to me by a large group of influential bwami initiates of Pangi territory,[13] is shown in the accom-

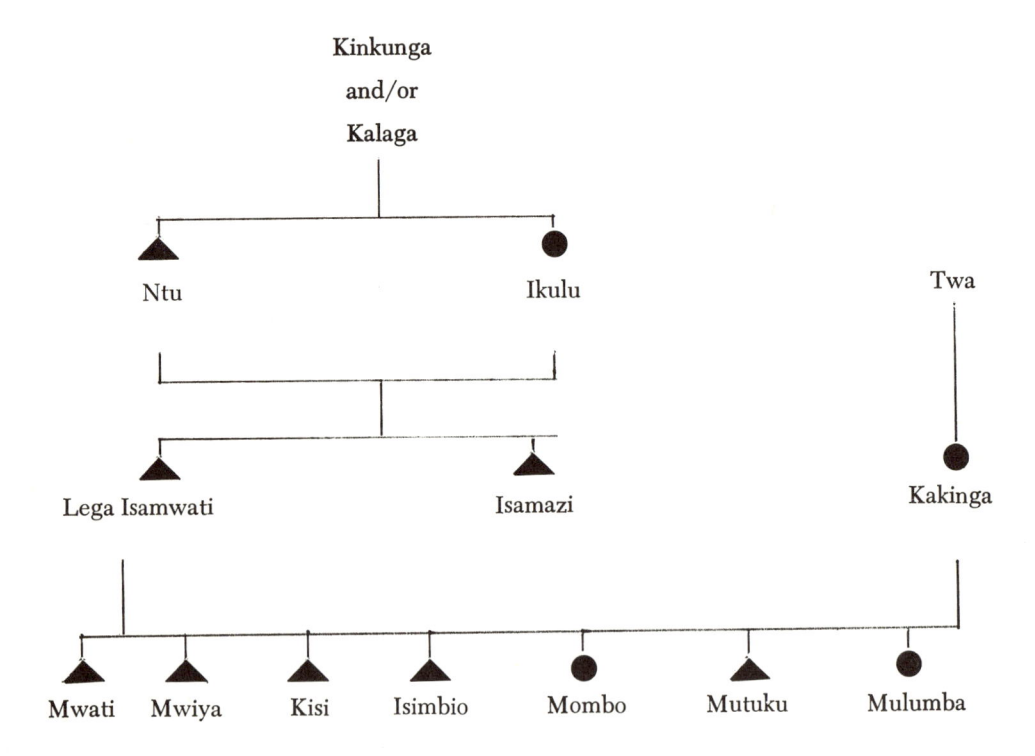

```
              Kinkunga
              and/or
              Kalaga
                 |
        ┌────────┴────────┐
        ▲                 ●                          Twa
       Ntu               Ikulu                        |
        |                 |                           |
        └────────┬────────┘                           ●
        ▲                 ▲                        Kakinga
   Lega Isamwati       Isamazi
        |                                             |
        └─────────────────────┬───────────────────────┘
    ▲     ▲     ▲     ▲     ●     ▲     ●
  Mwati Mwiya  Kisi Isimbio Mombo Mutuku Mulumba
```

---

the Lega. A few clan traditions refer, however, to early contacts with the Zimba, who at the time of the Lega immigration were mining salt in the neighborhood of Misisi (Pangi).

[13] An eminent spokesman among the western Lega gave a still more ambitious interpretation. Since he was unable to piece together all the threads of his highly symbolic discursion, however, it was rejected by most of the other spokesmen. His conception was as follows. Obeinge (interpreted as the Earth) had five children: Ngonze, Kunungu, Kisi, Kinkunga, and Kalaga. Ngonze and his son, Katima, symbolize the advent of the bwami association, "the fruit that came from above," or how wisdom (Katima-heart) grows out of ignorance. (Ngonze refers to a raffia ball or a shoulder bag; since a shoulder bag, the Lega say, has a mouth but no heart, it symbolizes the noninitiated.) Kunungu represents the foreign element. Kisi, a concept that means many things—land, country, wealth, status, and so on—and is therefore equivalent in a sense to plenitude, is the father of the Lega people. Kinkunga and Kalaga, in other

The Lega

panying diagram. Kinkunga, God the Joiner (but sometimes represented as the male element, or penis), and/or Kalaga, the Divine Messenger (but sometimes represented as the female element, or vulva), had a son and a daughter, Ntu and Ikulu. Through incestuous relationships Ntu and Ikulu had two children: Lega Isamwati, founder of the Lega world, and Isamazi, ancestor of the light-colored people, "those who," the Lega say, "have everything, ask for nothing, and have come only to kill." Lega married a Pygmy (Twa) girl, Kakinga, and by her had five sons and two daughters. Mwati, the firstborn, from whom Lega derived his teknonymous name Isamwati, died without progeniture. Mwiya gave rise to clans among the western Lega of Pangi territory; Kisi, to clans among the northern Lega of Shabunda territory; and Isimbio, to several clans among the Lega of the southern parts of Shabunda and Pangi territories. From Mutuku derived the Balega-Mitoko, who form in Ponthierville territory a separate ethnic unit territorially separated from the Lega. From incestuous relationships between Isimbio and his sister Mombo were descended a large number of clans among the eastern Lega in Mwenga territory. Finally, the Bangubangu, a separate ethnic unit living south of the Lega and in close contact with them, are said to be the descendants of Lega's daughter, Mulumba.

The basic elements of this genealogy are present among the eastern Lega, but their versions sometimes use different names of ancestors and are usually more complex, simply because their clans are more diversified. In one version (see diagram), provided by the Basimwenda (eastern Lega of Mwenga territory), Kisi refers to the same northern Lega as appear in

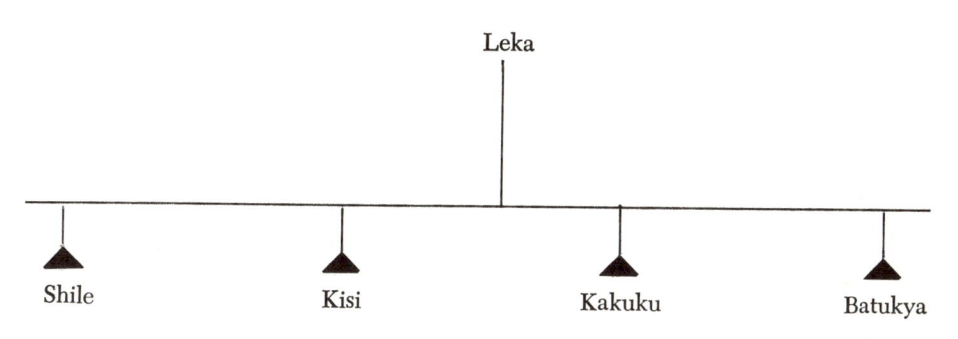

```
                        Leka
                         |
      _____|_____
      |          |                |          |
      ▲          ▲                ▲          ▲
    Shile       Kisi            Kakuku     Batukya
```

---

versions treated as divine beings comparable to the creator-god and the culture hero, are mentioned here as brother and sister of the Lega. With the help of his sister-wife Kalaga, Kinkunga created mountains, rivers, plants, and animals—that is, the Lega environment—but not the Lega. Kalaga, in a second role, brought various types of knowledge (skills, techniques, etc.) to the Lega, but not the deep knowledge that is attributable to Ngonze-Katima, creators of bwami. This interpretation, which unfortunately the informant was unable to work out, is most interesting in that it synthesizes the forces that control Lega existence: the physical environment (Kinkunga), the culture (Kalaga), a deep knowledge (Ngonze-Katima-bwami), and the human environment, divided between the non-Lega (Kunungu) and the many divisions of Lega (Kisi).

the preceding chart; Kakuka, like Mwiya in the preceding genealogy, bears on the western groups. The southern and eastern groups of Lega, however, are here distinguished somewhat differently. Most of the northeastern Lega, and some Bembe (e.g., the Lala clan), are thought to be descended from Shile, whereas most of the southern Lega (Kabango and Kuti) and a large number of Bembe clans are said to trace their origin to Batukya. A further refinement is introduced in the Moligi area by distinguishing Batukya from Nkulu. The first gave rise to Bakabango and Bembe; the second, to Babongolo, Bayoma, and several groups in western Legaland.

Despite variations in alignment and nomenclature, however, the genealogies written down in different parts of Legaland exhibit a basic unity; each recognizes within the group four subunits that correspond to what we call eastern, northern, southern, and western Lega (a simplification adopted for the sake of avoiding cumbersome Lega terminologies). Each of the four large territorial sections traces, from its own perspective, relationships with neighboring non-Lega groups. The eastern Lega are preoccupied with their connections with Nyindu and Bembe; the southern and southwestern Lega are concerned about their relationships with Bangubangu and Zimba; the western and northern groups stress their affinities with Songola, Komo, and Konjo groups. Yet these differing emphases do not modify the acknowledged genealogical unity of the Lega.

Relationships with other groups tend to be visualized more in terms of affinity and cognation than in terms of agnation. The only non-Lega groups ever considered as agnatic relatives are the Lega-Mitoko, the Bembe, and the Konjo. Relationships with Bangubangu and Zimba are interpreted in terms of cognation (the founders of these groups are said to be descended from Lega's daughter and his daughter's daughter); those with Twa, Songola, Komo, and sometimes Mitoko are interpreted in terms of affinity. In other words, Lega and his sons are thought to have married women from these ethnic groups. In this respect the individual clans, when tracing their connections within the Lega group, show wide variations in interpretation. The Beiamunsange clan, for example, which forms a part of the western Lega, claims descent from the ancestor Mwiya and his Komo wife and considers Mwiya himself as a descendant of Lega and a Mitoko wife. Similarly, many clans, in their own genealogical recitations, account for local relationships with pre-Lega or with later non-Lega immigrants. The Beiamunsange, again serving to illustrate, are in contact with a small group of remnant riverain populations that, according to oral tradition, were established before the Lega immigration and served the Lega as ferrymen. The Beiamunsange treat these pre-Lega arrivals as if they represented one of several primary lineages of which the clan is composed.

It seems, then, that the Lega are deeply conscious of their genealogical unity. Despite variations in and manipulations of different genealogical

The Lega

versions, consistency and unity mark the overall conception of the genealogical chart. From the Lega point of view, the Lega and some of their neighbors form a gigantic kinship chart in which intergroup relationships are expressed in terms of agnation, cognation, and affinity.

The Common Historical Experience. Moeller (1936, p. 10) and others place the origin of the Lega in Uganda. Their evidence, however, is not drawn from Lega oral tradition; rather, they base their conclusion on the existence of remnant groups, called Lega, living in the territory that extends from the Semliki River to the Lualaba River through areas north of Legaland now inhabited by such peoples as Komo, Nande, Nyanga, Havu, Hunde, and Shi.[14] Since these remnant groups have preserved little, if any, of what might have been a Lega-like culture, it is difficult to speculate about them. The existence of such groups is, however, beyond doubt, and it is also true that they exercise important ritual functions and have other privileges in the societies where they occur.

The most coherent Lega traditions begin at a place called Mungi-ningini, located near the Lualaba River in the neighborhood of Ponthierville.[15] From this point the Lega were dislodged by unnamed, light-skinned groups headed by Kimbimbi and Bukutu, names that might have represented real people or might have been symbols. The Lega say that Kimbimbi Sayala lured people with his impressive hat and then killed them; they sing that he was a ghost *(mulimu)* who destroyed the Lega. The Lega claim that there was never any actual fighting with Kimbimbi, but just withdrawal from him. It is unclear whether they use these symbols to refer to historical encounters between Lega and expanding Komo, Songola, and Mitoko, or between Lega and certain Mongo groups, or between Lega and a riverain population of Luba origin. (For example, it is interesting to note that among both the Mongo and the riverain group impressive hats are worn by such dignitaries as *meneganja* and *nkumu.*)[16] Still united (the Lega use *mutanda*, meaning row of related villages, to

---

[14] The traditions of contact with scattered Lega groups are lively in all these areas where dispersed groups of clans said to be of Lega origin survive. Special ritual offices are frequently ascribed to these Lega by virtue of their prior arrival in the country. Some western Lega clans trace their ultimate origin to a spot called Kitatente (lit., what does not move), which is identified as a very calm body of water (lake or swamp). It may be vaguely reminiscent of origins in the neighborhood of Lake Albert.

[15] Different subdivisions and clans sometimes use diverse place-names, such as Kilundu, Bubundu, and Kakolo, all of which point to an area on the Lualaba River between Kisangani and Ponthierville.

[16] The Banagabo clan in Shabunda territory specifically refers, under the name Kimbimbi, to the Mitoko, Komo, and Lengola. The Banangoma clan in the same territory identifies Kimbimbi with Mitoko. The Babongolo and Bayoma clans among the southeastern Lega affirm that they were chased away from the Kilundu area by Kaluba (riverain Luba) who came down the Lualaba with canoes, whereas the Lega had only rafts.

express this concept) after leaving Munginingini, the Lega spent some time, without disturbance, at a spot called Mingalangala (near the Lualaba River); from there they moved to Katundugulu, situated between the mouths of the Lowa and Ulindi rivers (two affluents of the Lualaba) just northwest of present Legaland.

From Katundugulu the Lega dispersed to the east and south, but oral records give few details of these movements. Since the Lega are not history-minded, they recount very few of their earlier experiences in their present forest habitat, except that they were torn by internal strife *(kikulula; bita bya ngabo; kasembe)* until bwami, the "fruit that came from above," was introduced among them. It is evident that the immigrant Lega encountered preestablished groups such as Pygmies and Pygmy-ized remnant groups of Bantu origin (Bouse, for example), but almost no reference is made to them. One encounter, however, is vividly recounted by the eastern Lega, the Bembe, and the Nyindu. The story, though narrated in a confusing way, clearly refers to a meeting between the eastern Lega and the unnamed preexistent group of Mwenembumbano (possibly the M'minje-Renge). Apparently it is intended to explain how several forms of bwami *(bwa ishungwe, bwa lusembe,* and *bwa kikumbu)* coexist in the northeastern corner of Legaland.

Legaland never held any special attraction for early explorers, traders, raiders, military personnel, or missionaries. Yet several trade routes and well-known centers have existed outside, but near the boundaries of, Legaland ever since the 1860's.

Arabs, Arab half-castes, and their allies, infiltrating from East Africa as ivory and slave traders, were well established at Nyangwe on the Lualaba, southwest of Legaland, by 1869 (Slade, 1962, p. 22). In time Legaland was almost surrounded by Arab centers: Nyangwe, Kasongo, Ribariba, and Kasuku on the Lualaba; Kabambare to the south; Uvira and Baraka to the east. No major centers, however, were set up inside Legaland. The deep rain forest and the eastern mountain chains were obstacles that deterred intensive penetration (Ceulemans, 1959). Yet the Lega, who frequently withdrew to the least accessible parts of the forest, felt no safety, for they were exposed to organized expeditions and to the more devastating raids of roaming bands of dissident and mutineering traders and slavers. A somber episode of this kind is known to the Lega as *esombanya* ("what causes hatred").

During much of the Congo Free State period, Legaland fell within the huge political domain in the eastern Congo which Tippo Tib and other Arabs had reserved for themselves (Ceulemans, 1959, map 2). For a time the Lega were under the domination of Munie Chabodu and Munie Mtoro, two Arabs who served as auxiliaries of the Congo Free State (Delhaise, 1909a, p. 356). Three large population centers established by the Arabs and inhabited by their aides (particularly Bakusu) existed at that time:

Micici on the Elila River, Shabunda on the Ulindi River (whose population was estimated by Glorie to be 8,000 in 1899), and Mulungu in the mountains (*ibid.*, pp. 113–114). Munie Mtoro was established in Micici, and Munie Chabodu (or Shabudu), in Shabunda (*ibid.*, p. 321, quoting Glorie). Lega auxiliaries, such as Mukoniama in Mulungu, supplied Munie Chabodu, who was responsible to the Congo Free State authorities at Nyangwe, with rubber and ivory (*ibid.*, p. 326, quoting Glorie). The expeditions of Lieutenant Glorie to crush rebellions in the 1890's destroyed this system of trading, and by the time Commander Delhaise took charge of the Lega territory, both aides had disappeared (*ibid.*, p. 321 n. 1). For decades thereafter, however, the Belgian administration had to cope with Lega and their descendants who had been elevated to chiefly positions by Arabs and Arab half-castes.

From 1892 to 1895 the Congo Free State was embroiled in bloody Arab campaigns, which were fought outside Legaland. The subsequent campaigns against mutineers of the Dhanis expeditions induced Glorie and his aides to cross Legaland from west to east and led to the establishment of government posts near Micici and Shabunda (Institut Royal Colonial Belge, 1952, map v/3). Effective occupation of Legaland did not begin until about 1902. When Delhaise, first put in charge of the Maniema district and later of Warega territory, undertook reconnaissance trips through eastern Legaland in 1906, he was visiting an area where whites had never been seen before (Delhaise, 1909a, p. 355).

Subsequently, over several decades, the Lega were administratively organized and reorganized into groupments, chefferies, secteurs, and territories. The population was not hostile, but neither was it enthusiastically cooperative. According to Delhaise (1909a, p. 355), "il faut bien reconnaître que la civilisation arabe, pas plus que la civilisation européenne, n'a eu grande influence sur eux [the Lega]." The main administrative problems resulted from the extreme fractionation and dispersion of the population (Moeller, 1931, pp. 52–66), the absence of centralized political systems, the appointment of chiefs by the Arabs, and the diffuse power of the bwami association. The misconceptions that developed about the nature of Lega society and of bwami gave rise to many unfortunate actions and decisions, which impoverished and undermined Lega society.

Christian missions were relatively late in coming to Legaland. By 1908 no mission stations had yet been established there (Slade, 1959, map 2), although the Missionary White Fathers of Africa had been on the shores of Lake Tanganyika for more than twenty years (their first mission was established in Masanze in November, 1880) and had set up a station in Kasongo by 1903 (Cornet, 1952, pp. 299–303). The first Protestant mission, the Evangelization Society Africa Mission, was established in Shabunda in 1922.

The first mining company (MGL) in Legaland was located at Kamituga (eastern Legaland) in 1923; it was followed in 1932 by Symétain in Kalima (western Legaland) and in 1934 by Minerga in Shabunda. Cobelmin started operations in Kampene and Shabunda. Large numbers of young Lega went to work in these mining centers (in some of them about half the population was of Lega origin). Many welcomed the opportunity to work in their homeland, in close contact with their own villages and with other Lega. Some of the Lega miners held jobs for short periods of time in order to realize specific objectives, such as the accumulation of money for marriage or for initiation into bwami.

The development of these huge mining establishments put heavy strains on the Lega labor force, on the traditional rhythm of their lives, and on their traditional occupations. Indeed, Lega villages were the main providers of food (bananas, cassava, corn) for those who worked in the mines. Since the Lega were not cultivators by predilection, the administration was compelled to put heavy pressure on the villages, persuading people to produce certain crops and to cultivate a set minimum of acreage. Although the Lega faithfully cooperated in the food-raising efforts, they complained bitterly that the impositions took the joy out of their lives, that the prices they received were too low, that the distances they had to carry heavy loads of food were too long, and that the new agricultural requirements disturbed their traditional patterns of land tenure and land usage. In the 1950's the Belgian administration successfully introduced intensive farming projects called *paysannats* into Legaland. Neither before nor after Congo independence (1960) did the Lega align with a single "tribal" party, as Unerga was at one time supposed to be. Their lack of political cohesion was owing mainly to the devastating experiences of the colonial era, not to any deep-rooted lack of a feeling of unity.

ENVIRONMENT

The Lega live in dense equatorial or tropical rain forest in the eastern Congo.[17] The region is one of luxuriant vegetation, characterized by giant and smaller trees, stranglers, woody lianas, shrubs, ground herbs, and many varieties of epiphytes (lichens, mosses, ferns). Several strata of vegetation provide a thick undergrowth. Numerous species of trees are intermingled in the forest, but in some areas *Macrolobium dewevrei, Cynometra alexandri*, and *Brachystegia laurentii* predominate. As one moves eastward in Legaland toward the western extensions of the rift valley, undulating surfaces give way to plateau surfaces, with peaks of

---

[17] My sources include Beaver and Stamp (1961, pp. 78–80), Delhaise (1909a, pp. 23–36), Stamp (1967, figs. 4–6, p. 71; p. 73), Gaillez (1955, pp. 282–288), Hance (1964, maps 2, 3, 5), Hargot (1955, pp. 2–3, 10–12), Richards (1952), Robert (1946), and Troupin (1956).

The Lega

6,000 feet or more. Here there are large patches of montane forest and grasslands and moist woodlands. North and west of Legaland the tropical forest becomes deeper and denser; southward it gradually merges into forest savanna mosaics and woodlands. Because of prolonged human occupation, shifting cultivation, and depredatory hunting techniques, the forest is intersected by many types of secondary formations of different ages and has suffered soil depletion to varying degrees. Fallow lands are covered with shrubs that rapidly change into new growths. Typical here are the patches of parasol *(Musanga smithii)* forests with dense undergrowth. These parasol forests are gradually replaced by secondary forest formations, where such species as *Alstonia, Canarium,* and *Chlorophora* predominate. In some areas large savanna spaces with tall grasses have replaced the forests and depleted the soils of the forest formations.

Many of these plants and trees are significant, not only in Lega technology and diet, but also in a symbolic sense. Besides the raffia palm and parasol trees, the red camwood tree *(Pterocarpus tinctorius),* and many species of latex plants (including *Brachystegia,* used for making bark cloth), such trees as *Autranella congolensis, Lebrunia bushaie,* and *Podocarpus milanjianus,* as well as many others mentioned later in this volume, are of high symbolic importance. Preference is given in the symbolic system to many species of plants found in the secondary formations. Vast numbers of raffia and wild banana trees are interspersed with other forest growth.[18]

Most of Legaland falls within the zone of the equatorial rain forest climate, characterized by few seasonal changes, constant heat and humidity, and morning mist. The average temperature is 75 or 80 degrees Fahrenheit; it is somewhat cooler as one moves eastward toward the adjacent plateau of the western rift. The average annual rainfall is 60 to 80 inches, but variations occur with changes in latitude, altitude, and vegetation cover. Thus, in a few pockets of Legaland, the average annual rainfall is 80 to 100 inches, one of the heaviest in Africa. A short dry season lasting two or three months between June and August occurs in the summer.

The Lega live east of the Lualaba or Congo River in a country that is watered by many rivers; the two dominant ones are the Elila in the south and the Ulindi in the north, both tributaries of the Lualaba. The fauna is incredibly rich and variegated, including many species of monkeys, antelopes, and rodents, as well as elephants, buffaloes, leopards, and chimpanzees. These animals play a prominent role in Lega diet and symbolism. Of particular interest for this study are some of the rarer animals, such as bongo antelope, aardvark, pangolin, warthog, dendrohyrax, hornbill, crowned eagle, flying squirrel, some species of turtles, and the giant snail.

---

[18] Delhaise (1909*a*, p. 31) points out that *Elaeis* palm trees, so numerous in adjoining forest areas, are absent from the Lega forest. *Elaeis* plantations have been introduced into many areas in the twentieth century.

DEMOGRAPHY[19]

It is fair to estimate the number of Lega at 225,000. Most of them live in the rural areas of the territories of Mwenga, Shabunda, and Pangi, and thousands have gone to work in the mining centers of Kalima, Kamituga, Kampene, Shabunda, and so on, and in commercial, administrative, and missionary centers within Legaland. Substantial numbers of Lega are found in urban centers throughout the Congo.

Before independence the distribution of population in these three territories was, according to census data provided by the Belgian colonial administration, as follows:

Mwenga: 100,091 inhabitants, 22,431 of them living in urban and mining agglomerations. Surface: 11,172 km². Density: 8.95 per km².

Shabunda: 79,184 inhabitants, 20,958 of them living in urban and mining agglomerations. Surface: 25,216 km². Density: 3.14 per km².

Pangi: 97,380 inhabitants, 35,518 of them living in urban and mining agglomerations. Surface: 13,635 km². Density: 7.1 per km².

In Mwenga territory, also inhabited by Bembe, Nyindu, Barhinyi, and Bahwinja, the approximate number of Lega in rural villages and urban agglomerations is 48,000. Most of the rural population of Shabunda and Pangi is Lega, and so is more than half the population living in the urban and mining centers in those territories. The higher density of population in Mwenga has nothing to do with the Lega; it is caused by heavy population concentrations of pastoral-horticultural groups of Shi origin in certain small sections.

The rural density in any of the three territories is considerably lower than the above figures, which include total (rural and urban) population. In the essentially rural chefferie Bakabango, in Shabunda territory, the rural density is 2.77 per km². Traditionally small villages and hamlets are widely, but fairly evenly, scattered throughout Legaland. The administrative regroupings undertaken by the colonial administration had brought together the majority of Lega villages in the neighborhood of roads which, because of the many mining enterprises, are numerous in Legaland. But

---

[19] The data given here are taken from Province du Kivu, *Document R. A., Service A.I.M.O.* (1954). I have chosen census data published in 1954 because they better reflect the demographic situation that prevailed at the time of my fieldwork among the Lega. Demographic figures for late 1958 reveal a population increase of about 10 percent for both Mwenga and Shabunda, whereas the population of Pangi showed an increase of barely 2,000.

The Lega

many remote hamlets and small villages continue to thrive away from the main population resettlements.

Relationships with Neighboring Ethnic Units

The Lega are surrounded by a rather bewildering diversity of ethnic units. Immediately to the north are Komo, Kwame, Konjo, and Tembo, and beyond them Nyanga. To the northwest and west are Songola (Ombo and Binja); to the south, Zimba (or Binja), Bangubangu (including the Tali, a transitional group), and Bembe. To the southeast are Bembe, and to the east, Nyindu (and beyond them, Furiiru and Vira) and various offshoots of the Shi.[20] The Lega thus live in the midst of a vast array of different cultural groups, forming a center around which constituent elements and offsoots of different culture clusters meet: Komo-Bira, Nyanga-Hunde, Havu-Shi, Bemba, Luba, Songye, Mongo-Mbole-Tetela, Furiiru-Vira, and Nyindu.

The Lega trace very close links with the Bembe, most of whom also acknowledge their Lega origin. The ties between Basimwenda, or eastern Lega, and Bembe are so close that many identical clan names are found in both. The boundary between Bembe and Lega is soft, with numerous transitional villages inhabited by individuals from both groups, which reveal similarities in language and culture. Although both adhere to patrilineal descent systems, they accord social importance to lineages with which individuals are linked through mother, father's mother, mother's mother, or even more remote cognatic lines. Both groups attach weight to circumcision rites and to the bwami association. Ivory and wood carvings made by Bembe for their bwami association are so similar to Lega sculptures that students of African art have always confused the work of the two groups.

The next closest link of the Lega is with the Mitoko (Balega-Mituku), who are territorially separated from the Lega by Songola and Lengola. The western Lega consider the Mitoko to be the descendants of one of Lega's sons. The *bukota* organization of the patrilineal Mitoko has close affinities

---

[20] Delhaise (1909a, p. 25) mentions only three groups of neighbors: Songola, Zimba, and Rundi. The Rundi of Burundi in East Africa are also established in the Ruzizi Valley of Uvira territory, northeast of Legaland. They are not directly in contact with the Lega. Delhaise seems to subsume under the name Rundi all pastoral populations living to the northeast of the Lega. Masui (1897, map on p. 163) situates "Uregga" in a large area of forest bounded by the Elila, Ulindi, and Lowa rivers, directly in contact to the north with the Komo, to the west with the Genya riverain populations and the Kusu, to the east with the Rundi, and to the southeast with the Ugoma (riverains of Lake Tanganyika) and the Maniema. Under the confusing name Maniema are subsumed such populations as Boyo, Bangubangu, and Zimba (cf. Borms, 1902, p. 256). Unless otherwise noted, my brief remarks on the neighbors of the Lega are based on data I collected in the field.

with the bwami association of the Lega. The Mitoko, like the Lega, assign extraordinary importance to circumcision ceremonies, and the art objects used by the *bukota* association bear stylistic and functional resemblance to those of the Lega.

The western and southern Lega stand in an unusual joking relationship to the Bangubangu, their southern neighbors. It is accounted for in the Lega genealogical chart: the Bangubangu, said to be the descendants of Lega's daughter, are treated as the sororal nephews of the Lega. The joking relationship is expressed in many forms, from permissible alienation of goods to funerary friendship. Bangubangu individuals working or traveling in Legaland are accorded hospitality and have the right to appropriate certain kinds of goods in the villages, analogous to privileges exercised by true sororal nephews. When a Bangubangu dies in Lega country, it is the custom for certain Lega lineages to provide the *museka* death payments (shell money, iron tools, or the equivalent in francs), just as when a Lega stranger dies in another Lega village. Lega lineages also share in the property left by a Bangubangu who dies in a mining center in Legaland, as, in normal Lega practice, maternal uncles inherit the *idigo* shares of a deceased sororal nephew. The Bangubangu speak a language of the Luba type with strong Songye and Lega influences.[21] The group is patrilineal. The political system, centered on seniority principles and on the *nsubi* association, shows close affinities with the petty state system, under a *mulohwe*, of the Songye and of some northern Luba subgroups, and with the Lega system which attaches political importance to a voluntary association. Circumcision rites are of the Lega type but are much less elaborate.

Relationships with the Zimba, also called southern Binja, are more distant, yet the Lega classify them as grandchildren or as the descendants of the Bangubangu. Most Zimba, like the riverain groups of Lake Tanganyika (such as Zyoba, Bwari, Homa, Sanze), are probably offshoots of the Bemba cluster, but both Lega and Luba influences are visible throughout their culture. The descent and kinship systems exhibit many traces of a matrilineal organization that was supplanted by patrilineal principles. The political system is somewhat like that of the northern Luba. The mixed character of the Zimba is best illustrated by scores of villages that are administratively incorporated into southern parts of Shabunda and Pangi territories. These villages, called Batali by the Lega and Bakudwa by the Zimba, are of Zimba origin; the Batali kinship system is of the Crow type and has borrowed circumcision rites and the bwami association, up to the ngandu grade, from the Lega.[22] Intermarriage of Zimba with Lega and Bembe is frequent.

[21] See Meeussen (1954, pp. 1–2). The Bangubangu, divided into four main groups, exhibit many linguistic and cultural differences.
[22] The Batali have a double system of circumcision. The small rites, called *kalomba*,

The Lega

The Songola are the northwestern and western neighbors of the Lega, who refer to them as Babile. They are divided into the Ombo and Binja linguistic communities.[23] The Binja or eastern Songola have close relationships with the Lega; the Ombo or western Songola are part of the Mongo group.[24] The Lega regard the ancestor Binja as a close agnatic relative of Lega himself. The Songola and the Lega carry on a fairly intensive palm oil and salt trade.[25] The patrilineal Songola use the *bwali* circumcision rites and the *nkago* magico-therapeutic techniques of the Lega type. They adhere to the bwami association whenever, as individuals, they have affinal and residential ties with Lega lineages, and the widespread *nsubi* association has many common characteristics with bwami.[26] Political authority is based on seniority and on membership in the *nsubi* association, in whose higher grades of *kilemba* and *zumbi* figurines of the Lega type are used.

The Komo, northern neighbors of the Lega, stretch northward over a huge forest area as far as Kisangani. They have a strongly developed circumcision system, and their *mpunzu* (or *mpunju*) association has several features in common with the bwami association of the Lega.[27] The two southernmost sections of the Komo, those geographically closest to the Lega, are called Babila and Bakwame; both are thought of as close agnatic relatives of the progenitor Lega.[28] As in so many other instances, they form a cultural buffer zone between the Lega and other types of culture.

---

involve the young men of only two or three villages and coincide with the killing of leopards. The big rites, called *lwira*, are cyclically held and are incorporated with the Lega circumcision cycles.

[23] I follow the divisions set up by Meeussen (1952, p. 1; 1953, pp. 385–386).

[24] Meeussen (1953, pp. 385–386; 1954, p. 1). According to the same authority, southern Binja or Zimba, and northern Binja or eastern Songola, are part of the Lega complex of languages.

[25] Liétard (1924, pp. 133–134) discusses this trade, which had reached the markets of Kasongo and Nyangwe.

[26] Moeller (1936, pp. 446–450) briefly discusses the hierarchy of *nsubi* and some of its prescriptions.

[27] See Biebuyck (1957), Galdermans (1934), and Gérard (1956). This institution is also found among the Nyanga, who, although territorially separated from the Lega, have some institutions in common with them.

[28] It is noteworthy that the Lega, in tracing historical and cultural links with these and other neighboring groups, do not mean to include all subunits that actually make up the population known as Komo, Songola, Bangubangu, and so on. They refer to specific subgroups. The interpretation of these many linkages requires subtlety and hence deserves a special study. The pattern of transcultural linkages shows how tenuous is the concept "tribe." The ethnic distribution in this area, as in other parts of the Congo, is more complex than any map could possibly show. Terms such as Songola, Zimba, Bangubangu, and Boyo are labels, some of which seem to have originated, or to have been expanded in meaning, during the latter part of the nineteenth century. See also Biebuyck, 1966*b*.

The Babila and the Bakwame claim autonomous origins, yet they are keenly aware that they share many characteristics with the Lega. The Bakwame, who occupy about eleven villages in the extreme north of Shabunda territory, are a particularly complex group. Their circumcision rites and kinship system are of the Nyanga type (the Nyanga are their northeastern neighbors), and some of their ceremonies and initiations resemble those of the Songola (e.g., *nsinga* possession dances and *kilemba* graded system of initiation) or of the Komo (e.g., the *mpunzu* association). In addition, most Bakwame have adopted the bwami initiations up to the ngandu grade. Together with their eastern neighbors, the Kanu and the Konjo, the Bakwame have a unique institution called *bubake*, traces of which are also found among some Lega and among Nyanga and Hunde. *Bubake* bears on the special mysticopolitical powers and authority that are attributed to one who, as the son of classificatory cross-cousins or classificatory brother and sister, traces both paternal and maternal ties in his agnatic lineage.[29]

The Kanu and the Konjo are two small groups living to the north of the Lega which mark a transition between Lega and Nyanga, Hunde, and Havu. Some Lega clans trace close connections with these groups. The Konjo and the Kanu are part of a more widely scattered population called Tembo, which seems to form an older substratum in areas now occupied by the adjoining Nyanga, Hunde, Havu, and Shi. Both groups are patrilineal; they practice circumcision ceremonies of the Lega type and the *mpunzu* initiations of the Komo and Nyanga type. The lower grades of bwami are also represented among them.

Both the eastern Lega and the Bembe trace numerous links with the Nyindu, a group of people living to the east of the Lega between the Shi-Lega-Bembe and Furiiru-Vira culture clusters. The patrilineal Nyindu are mostly a mixture of aboriginal groups (of M'minje and Lenge origin, but mixed with Pygmies) and immigrant offshoots of Lega and Furiiru-Vira. They are organized in petty states, each headed by a mwami selected from a dynastic clan by counselors *(bagingi)* and initiators *(bazyoga)*. Tradition has it that the first kingdom of the Nyindu was founded by Nalwindi, himself a descendant of Namuka, Father-of-Kings, who was allegedly of Tutsi origin.[30] Most Nyindu subgroups adhere to their own variant of the bwami association and have sculptures of the Lega type.

---

[29] The relationship between the parents of this individual may be a fairly close one, since they may trace their ascent back to a common patrilineal grandfather. Traditionally, at least, there was one *mubake* in every village. The initiation reaches its fullest elaboration among the Nyanga, whose ruling chiefs *(mubake* or *mwami)* are thought of as the descendants of a brother-sister or an uncle-niece marriage.

[30] See Schumacher (1950, pp. 268–269), whose theory is that the Tutsi, migrating from southern Ethiopia, took an eastern route leading them into Rwanda and Burundi, and that, both north and south of Lake Kivu, Tutsi groups infiltrated the mountainous

The Lega

A mosaic of peoples, most of them living in dense rain forests, covers a large area in the central and southern parts of Kivu Province in the eastern Congo. They have, and are conscious of having, such close cultural and historical relationships that it is impossible to separate one from the other or to clearly delineate tribal groups.[31]

In and near Legaland a wide variety of groups share a common set of institutions, perhaps because of a common origin, perhaps because of diffusion and borrowing. This common patrimony permits a clear contrast to be drawn between what I call the Lega cluster and other clusters, such as Luba, interlacustrine Bantu, Mongo, and Bemba.

Strictly speaking, the Lega cluster includes (1) the Lega living in Mwenga, Shabunda, and Pangi territories; (2) the Lega-ized remnant groups, such as Bouse and Balyanga, in Legaland; (3) the Bembe living in Fizi and part of Mwenga;[32] (4) the Kwame and some Babila (Komo) in Punia territory; (5) the Babile (Binja or eastern Songola) of Kindu territory; (6) the Batali (Zimba) of Pangi and Shabunda territories; and (7) the Kanu-Konjo on the boundaries of Walikale-Kabare-Kalehe territory. Other groups that have close connections with the Lega cluster are Nyindu, Vira, Furiiru, the riverains of Lake Tanganyika (in Bembeland), Bangu-

---

areas of Buhunde, Buhavu, Bufuliru, and Bunyindu to found kingdoms there. Schumacher also says that the royal dynasties originated with Nalwindi in Bunyindu. It is interesting to note that the dynastic clan among the Nyindu is called Baluzi, a term that Schumacher (*ibid.*, pp. 266–267) equates with Batutsi. The patrilineal Furiiru and Vira, who are in contact with the Bembe but are separated from the Lega, are organized in kingdoms under divine rulers (*mwami wa ishungwe*). Living in the highland grasslands, many Furiiru and Vira own cattle. Yet the basic aspects of their kinship are of the Bembe-Lega type.

[31] Baumann and Westermann (1948, p. 207, and map between pp. 203 and 204) include the Lega in the enormous northern Congo ethnographic circle. Interestingly enough, the Zimba are also included. Baumann maintains that among both Lega and Zimba, influences from the Luba and from the lake area populations are very strong. The Bangubangu are mentioned together with the Luba on the map of the southern Congo ethnographic circle, yet elsewhere they are referred to as an outpost of the northern Congo circle. Murdock (1959, pp. 278–282) places the Lega in the equatorial Bantu Province together with some of their neighbors, such as Bembe, Komo, Mitoko, Songola, and many other northeastern Congo peoples. The Zimba, closely connected with the Songye, are put in the Luba Province (*ibid.*, p. 285); the Bangubangu, in the Bemba cluster of the central Bantu Province (*ibid.*, p. 294); the Nyanga-Hunde, in the Rwanda cluster of the interlacustrine Bantu. These and other classifications are far from reflecting the exact cultural situation in and around Legaland because they treat these various "tribes" as homogeneous groups and fail to take into account the many overlappings that exist. The cultural picture in this part of Africa has many more nuances than general classifications reveal.

[32] Established along the shores of Lake Tanganyika, within what is now Bembeland, are a number of small groups—Zyoba, Sanze, Bwari, Homa, Ciba, and Bakwalumona—which originally belonged either to the Bemba or to the Luba clusters, but were strongly influenced by the Bembe.

bangu, Zimba, Komo, Nyanga, Hunde, Songola, and the geographically more remote Baleka-Mitoko. Each of them has, in one way or another, felt Lega influences; each shows some fundamental institutional similarities to the Lega. Among them, the Nyindu are closest to the Lega cluster.

There are many criteria to use in justifying the connections within the Lega cluster. The different populations show in their ethnohistorical records a strong awareness of a certain commonality. Whether they are forest or savanna dwellers, hunting technology is of extreme importance, not only in the subsistence economy but particularly in exchange, ritual, and symbolism. Shifting agriculture, centered on plantain bananas, is extensive; the growing of bananas, but not of other domesticated plants, is marked by elaborate technology, ritual, and symbolism. All groups are patrilineal, but accord special social significance to cognatically related lineages. Many clans are dispersed across the tribal subdivisions. The political system is of the segmentary lineage type. All groups have cyclically organized circumcision rites. All have, at the center of their social system, a voluntary association called bwami. This association, it must be pointed out, also operates among the Nyindu. An analogous institution, called *bukota, mpunzu,* or *nsubi,* is formed among other groups, such as Songola, Baleka-Mitoko, Zimba, Bangubangu, Komo, and Nyanga, which share institutional patterns with the Lega. Significantly, this type of voluntary association, wherever it occurs, is associated with sculpture. The sculptures are made of wood, ivory, and bone, are usually small, and are used mainly as emblems and didactic devices. The quantity of such sculptures is, by far, largest among the Lega. Some types of objects made for the association by Bembe, Nyindu, Bangubangu, Songola, and Kanu, and even by the more distant Mitoko, Komo, and Nyanga, are mostly so similar to Lega objects that no one has ever differentiated them. All sculptural activity among the Lega is monopolized by the bwami association; among other groups different categories of art objects are used in other rituals and initiations, and these are sometimes stylistically very different from those of the Lega.

INTERNAL SUBDIVISIONS

The politically noncentralized Lega are divided into a large number of patriclans. Some of them feel a special congeniality with one another, which is mainly interpreted in terms of agnation. These Lega clans are grouped in a few large genealogical complexes or units of related and interlinked clans. The colonial administration, in its policy of centralization and regroupment, reorganized the Lega at various levels into a number of administrative divisions.

Cultural Subdivisions. In conversations and texts, the Lega frequently use the terms *malinga* (below) and *ntata* (above). These dynamic concepts can be applied by any one group to any other group, depending on respective geographical positions. In Legaland the terrain gradually climbs from west to east and from south to north. Thus, from certain points of view, *malinga* means westward or southward and *ntata* means eastward or northward. The terms do not imply any major cultural cleavage or any form of dualistic organization.[33] Occasionally aphorisms sung in the bwami initiations use both terms, seemingly to underscore the basic unity of Lega cultural procedure, a unity that is fostered in diversity. Whenever the terms are so used, two objects, one typical of initiation among the eastern or highland Lega and one of initiation among the western or lowland Lega, are displayed under a pot or around a termite nest, with such simple comments as "An ancestor of *malinga* and an ancestor of *ntata*" or "A necklace of polished snail shell is child of *malinga;* a necklace of oblong beads is child of *ntata*."

In their elaborate genealogy the Lega establish the subdivisions recognized among themselves and assign positions to various component groups. These genealogies exist in many variations, with different names and ways of grouping ancestral linkages. Basically, however, four genealogical groupings of clans are recognized:

a. The Mwenda-Liga complex, or northeastern and eastern Lega, found in parts of Mwenga and Shabunda territories, in chefferie Wamuzimu, and in secteur Bakisi. A large number of Bembe and Nyindu clans also trace their origins within this complex.

b. The Kabango complex, or southern Lega, found in parts of Mwenga, Shabunda, and Pangi territories, in secteur Wamuzimu, chefferie Bakabango, secteur Bakabango, and secteur Kama. A number of groups established among Bembe, Boyo, and Zimba also trace their origins within this complex.

c. The Beia-Bene complex, or western Lega, found in parts of Pangi and Shabunda territories, in secteur Beia, chefferie Babene, secteur Kama, and here and there in other administrative divisions within these territories. A number of groups established among the Songola also trace relationships within this complex.

d. The Kisi complex, or northern Lega, found in Shabunda territory, mainly in secteur Bakisi. Some groups established among the Songola trace their ancestry within this complex.

[33] Delhaise (1909*a*, p. 22) maintains that the Lega are subdivided into two parts: Ntata *(gens d'en haut)* and Malinga *(gens du bas).* He acknowledges that there is no clear-cut boundary between the two, yet he asserts that the Lega situated east of 27 degrees east longitude are called Ntata. Moeller (1936, p. 40) fairly correctly notes that these are geographical notions whose application depends on the observer's point of view. The term *malinga* is sometimes used as the name for an individual who has called the initiates together for the bwami rites.

These four genealogical complexes[34] are not political subdivisions. Nor do they form complete territorial wholes, since various sections within a complex may have settled elsewhere in Legaland. Some administrative units are composed of clan segments drawn from different complexes. For example, of the six groupements recognized in secteur Kama, one consists of the autonomous Bouse; one has links with the Mwenda-Liga complex; another has links with the Kabango complex; and three are connected with the Beia-Bene complex. The collective and purely symbolic name sometimes given to a group of Lega of heterogeneous genealogical origin, such as Kama, is Banakubunga (from *kubunga,* to bring together what was dispersed).

These complexes, then, are to be considered as units of limited cultural specialization, as attested by dialectical variations in the language,[35] by patterns of kinship nomenclature, and by variations in bwami initiations. Matrimonial preferences also roughly corroborate this conclusion.

Administrative Groupings. The following administrative grouping of the Lega was established in the early 1950's by the Belgian colonial administration.[36]

   I. Mwenga territory
      A. Chefferie Wamuzimu: Lega, and some Bembe. This huge chefferie, in reality, comprises two major administrative groupements:
         1. Basimwenda of 'Alenga and the more or less related clans of Bamulinda, Babundu, Balinji, Bamugamba, Bagezi, Balobola, Basisunge, and so on.
         2. Bakuti of Longangi and the more or less related clans of Basi'umbilwa, Basi'asumba, Bouse, Bagunga, Basimbi, Balinzi, Basikasa, and so on.

---

[34] In an earlier study (Biebuyck, 1953*d*, pp. 902–903) I mentioned three such complexes, associating the Kisi with the Beia-Bene. I now prefer to keep the Kisi as a separate entity.

[35] Van Bulck (1954, pp. 29–31) roughly reflects these distinctions by recognizing, within the central Lega bloc, Kileega of the Bakisi, Kileega of the Bakabango, and Ileega imuzimu, comprising Ishile and Iwanyabaale. He makes no reference to the Beia-Bene, but in an earlier work (1948, p. 229) he mentions the Babeya, the Bakabango, and the Bakisi as separate "tribes" within the Lega of Maniema.

[36] Piron (1954, I, 529) defines the two administrative key divisions, called chefferies and secteurs, as follows: "Les chefferies sont les groupements traditionnels organisés sur la base de la coutume en circonscriptions administratives"; "Les secteurs sont les circonscriptions administratives formées par la réunion de groupements indigènes numériquement trop faibles." The administrative reorganization of the Lega, some in chefferies and others in secteurs, was based on a complete misconception of their traditional political system, which is of the segmentary lineage type. Any larger administrative grouping should therefore have been defined as a secteur, that is, as an artificial unit combining various politically unconnected entities.

B. Chefferie Itombwe: Bembe, with such predominant clans as Basim'minje, Balenge, Basimnyaka, Basyamakulu, and Basibucuma, a few scattered Lega, and remnant groups like Bambote and Basi'asumba.
C. Chefferie Luindi: Nyindu, including Batumba, Balambo, Balinzi, Basimbi, Bamishungwe, Banyemganga, Bazyoga, and some Bembe.
D. Chefferies Burhinyi and Luindja: Groups of Shi origin and some Nyindu.

II. Shabunda territory
A. Secteur Bakisi: Lega; some Kwame, Konjo, Songola, and Sengele; and the more or less related clans of Bamuguba, Baliga, Banagabo, Banangoma, Beigala, and Bakyunga.
B. Chefferie Bakabango: Lega; some Zimba (Batali) and Bembe; and about nineteen different clans such as Babongolo, Basitabyale, Bakasila, Bagalia, Bakasyele, Bakusa, Bakila, Bakabondo, Bakinkalo, and Bayoma.

III. Pangi territory
A. Chefferie Babene: Lega, and such clans as Banamunwa, Banisanga, Bagilanzelu, Batoba, Banibilila, and Banakagela.
B. Secteur Beia: Lega, and such clans as Baziri, Banakeigo, Bouse, Beiamunsange, Beiamisisi, Banasalu, Beianangi, Banalyuba, Beiankuku, Banalulimba, Banameya, Banamusiga, Banikozi, and Banamuningi.
C. Secteur Bakabango: Lega, and such clans as Babongolo, Banikinga, Banakinkalo, Banasunguli, Banalila, Balambia, and Banakasyele.
D. Secteur Kama: Lega, and such clans as Banamombo, Banakasyele, Babongolo, and Banantandu.

Segments of almost all clans are scattered in different places. For example, small fragments of Nyindu clans can be found among Lega, Bembe, and Shi. Fragments of many clans located in secteur Bakisi are also in secteur Kama, and so on.

Part 2   Lega Culture

Economy and Technology

Lega economy is based on a remarkable balance of hunting, food gathering, and agriculture. Fishing and animal husbandry (chickens, goats, sheep), though their products are of less importance than agricultural products to the diet and to the economic and symbolic system, are practiced throughout Legaland. The diet consists essentially of plantains and game meat, supplemented by a variety of tubers, grains, vegetables, and fruits—some cultivated, some growing wild—by fish, occasionally by small quantities of chicken, mutton, and goat meat, and by seasonal delicacies, such as honey, termites, and caterpillars.[1]

The Lega practice a wide diversity of crafts: carving in wood, bone, and ivory, pottery and bark cloth manufacturing, house and bridge building, plaiting and wickerwork, ropemaking, extraction and melting of iron ore, blacksmithing, manufacture of red powder, extraction of red earth and white clay, extraction of salt, and preparation of cosmetic oils. There is little specialization, except for ironworking and carving and the characteristic Lega expertise in curing, divining, and music performance.

---

[1] The precise information given by Delhaise (1909a, pp. 69–70, 119–129) about these activities was, I found, substantially true in the 1950's.

Lega Culture

Members of the bwami association, however, possess a well-recognized specialization in dance, song, use of artworks and artifacts, construction of initiation houses, manufacture of initiation objects, exegesis of meanings, and in the division and distribution of food, fees, and gifts. The local and regional flow of commodities, including artworks, is stimulated by kinship structure and bwami initiations. Trade outside Legaland is limited to a few products obtained from neighboring groups (e.g., palm oil from the Songola).[2] There are no organized markets.[3]

Hunting and Trapping. More than any other economic activities, hunting and trapping play a prominent part in Lega economy, ritual, and thought. The rain forest offers an abundance and a wide variety of game. Game meat, besides being a substantial part of Lega diet, is of extreme importance in feasts and exchanges connected with bwami initiations. The durable parts (hides, teeth, scales, carapaces, claws, nails, tails, bones, tusks, and shells) of many species of wild animals are used in large quantities as adornments, initiation objects, and status and prestige symbols. Animal actors and hunting scenery abound in the oral literature of the Lega. Similitudes, metaphors, and identifications drawn from the animal world fill the teachings that are given during circumcision rites and bwami initiation ceremonies.

The Lega use an extensive array of hunting and trapping techniques; all occupations in this field are male. Some traps and snares are highly specialized for killing elephants, buffaloes, wild pigs, and monkeys; others have a more general purpose. Fruits, manioc, and meat are used as bait in some of the devices. Most types of traps need only intermittent inspection, but *mugogo* fencing for antelopes, hedgehogs, genets, and some species of monkeys requires the trapper to be present in order to club the animal when it is fenced. *Kalungu,* an ingenious method for trapping elephants, is a combination of snares connected to a heavy suspended log in which a large iron spearhead is fixed. Acquaintance with this device presupposes elaborate secret rituals that are widespread outside Legaland,

---

[2] Delhaise (1909a, p. 70) refers to the culinary use of palm oil received in trade from the Songola. He notes also the increasing use of peanut oil, whose preparation the Lega had learned from the Arabs and Arabisés. At the time of my research, palm oil was extremely important to the Lega, particularly in the food distributions connected with bwami initiations. Palm oil was available in increasing quantities because of the continuing growth of *Elaeis* plantations in Legaland, and also because the product could be purchased in small local shops.

[3] Trading and marketing increased at a fairly rapid pace in the years following the development of mining centers in Legaland. In Delhaise's time the Lega sold rubber and ivory to Europeans for export, and sold them food products for consumption by local personnel. As time went by, there was a steadily increasing demand for food supplies. The Lega complained bitterly about certain economic, social, and physical aspects of these demands. In the 1950's many Lega embarked enthusiastically on the *paysannats* introduced by the administration.

among Bembe, Nyanga, and Komo. Individual hunting with bow and poisoned arrow is practiced in eastern Legaland for killing monkeys and wild pigs, but it has no particular social or ritual significance. *Makila* hunting with nets, spears, and dogs, which may last for only one day or may extend over several weeks *(bulambu)*, is enormously important, particularly in relation to ritual activities. Bwami initiations require large amounts of game meat, some of which may be dried, some of which must be fresh. Depending on the rites, the species of animals to be distributed are strictly specified. Young men and initiates of the lower grades organize the hunting parties, but recently women have participated in the battues. The technique of hunting monkeys with nets is remarkably efficient: within a certain stretch of forest all trees are systematically cleared away, thus compelling the animals to find refuge in a single tree left standing in the cleared space; the nets are then set up so that the monkeys can be chased into them and easily clubbed to death.

The Lega trap, hunt, or collect almost all the species of animals found in their environment. The giant pangolin *(Manis gigantea* or *ikaga)*, however, is not killed, because its death requires the performance by bwami members of elaborate ceremonies to ritually cleanse the community.[4] Game meat, like many other products, is always shared. The division and the distribution of almost all animals (to the exclusion of some small rodents, birds, etc.) are always performed by a group composed of individuals drawn from different families, lineages, or clans. The number of individuals, the categories of kinsmen and nonkinsmen, and the character of the group differ in accordance with the size of the animal and its socioritual classification.[5] Such animals as pangolin, aardvark, bongo antelope, eagle, genet *(Genetta tigrina)*, leopard, and some species of snakes, like *kitemutemu* (python) and *mpoma (Bitis lachesis?)*,[6] are usually skinned and distributed by members of the bwami association, although there are regional differences. In some areas the meat of these animals is consumed from a large bowl *(mupalia)* kept in the men's meeting room. Only older women are permitted to partake of these meats; the flesh of certain other animals, although not reserved for bwami members, cannot be eaten by women (exceptions are made, however, for old women and for female members of the highest levels in bwami). The animals forbidden

[4] Biebuyck (1953*d*) describes the distribution of the pangolin and analyzes the ceremonies connected with it. Delhaise (1909*a*, p. 80) details in vivid terms the importance of avoiding the pangolin. The pangolin is of great ritual significance to the Nyanga and holds a special place in the *nsubi* association of the Songola.

[5] Biebuyck (1953*d*, pp. 899–901) discusses some of the guidelines for division of animals among the Lega.

[6] Delhaise (1909*a*, p. 79) mentions several of these animals. According to Moeller (1936, pp. 447–448), members of the *nsubi* association of the Songola reserve for themselves such animals as python, leopard, crocodile, aardvark, pangolin, and eagle, or specific parts of them.

Lega Culture

to women include the so-called black antelope *(ntundu)*, several smaller carnivores (including civet cat and serval), sheep, and chickens; eggs as a by-product are placed in the same category.

Fishing. Both men and women engage in fishing. The wide variety of techniques range from fishing with tackle and bait to fishing with traps, from net fishing (with or without weirs) to fish poisoning or the drying out of smaller brooks. In some parts of Legaland the *lutumpu* or battue technique is prevalent: men on both shores use lianas to drag a large screen of leaves through the water chasing the fish toward a row of women wading with their nets. Some methods, like trapping and fishing with tackle and bait or with certain types of nets *(mulabo, kakila)*, are reserved exclusively to men. Others, such as fishing with pear-shaped *butilu* nets or drying out of brooks, are practiced only by women. Fish poisoning, by means of pounded *kisanda* leaves of a wild-growing liana, requires a cooperative effort by men and women. Fish, particularly catfish, crabs, and mussels, is an important ingredient in the diet of Lega groups that live in the proximity of the larger rivers (Elila, Ulindi, Kama, Lugulu). Fish is of little significance in the system of exchanges and initiations, but certain species are frequently referred to in the symbols of initiation. Skulls and teeth of such species as *Barbus tropidolepis, Clarias lazera, Chrysichthys cranchii*, and *Hydrocyon* are used as initiation objects.

Gathering. The collection of wild fruits and plants, of insects, and of building and construction materials is done by both men and women. The Lega are especially fond of certain nutlike fruits *(kembi, kige, mbala* or *Pentaclethra macrophylla)*, which they pick up from the ground rather than harvest. They gather the fruit of the *busezi (Lebrunia bushaie)* and other trees for making cosmetic oils. Termites *(nswa)* and a few species of caterpillars and larvae *(misigi, tumbalaka)* are seasonal delicacies that are collected in a joint enterprise; for example, men smoke the termites out of their nests and women gather them. Women collect *Costus lucanusianus* leaves for building and the multipurpose phrynium leaves *(magungu)*, but men gather most of the construction materials, including lianas, grasses, reeds, bark, and timber, and provide woods for carving. Red stone *(kibongo)* for making red powder, and white clay, are collected by women. Both men and women pick up the shells of terrestrial and aquatic mollusks from which shell money and necklaces are made. Honey harvesting is divided between men and women, depending on whether the honey is found in trees (bees' honey) or near the surface of the ground (honey produced by the small *lubuku* fly).

Agriculture. The Lega practice, extensively but carelessly, a form of slash-and-burn, shifting cultivation. The staple crop is bananas. Secondary crops include cassava, peanuts, corn, pumpkins, yams, taro, haricot beans, sweet potatoes, tomatoes, peppers, and sugarcane. Tobacco and leaves used for fish poisoning *(keita ka kabaka)* are also grown. Several of these crops are of fairly recent introduction. In enumerating and classifying species of crops, the Lega always distinguish carefully between "traditional" varieties, whose origins they cannot trace, and plants introduced by Songola, Arabisés (Bangwana), and Europeans. For example, they recognize fourteen traditional varieties of bananas, three imported from the Songola, two introduced by the Bangwana, and one (the red-skinned *kitika* banana) brought in by the Europeans. Basically, the Lega are banana growers. It is in terms of banana growing that their agricultural activities must be understood, since bananas play the principal role in diet, exchange, and ritual symbolism. Lega settlements are usually located some distance away from the banana fields; few, if any, gardens are found near the houses. Tobacco, for example, is frequently planted in heaps of burned trash behind the houses, though it is also grown on abandoned village sites or on the rim of a mature banana grove.

The Lega divide the agricultural year into two parts: *kilimo* and *mpombo*. The dry season, as the Lega translate *kilimo*, begins in April, the month of *kibala*. It is normally the time when the men begin the annual cycle by cutting away the forest undergrowth. Billhook knives are used for this task since the Lega, traditionally, have no hoes. The precise moment at which this activity begins depends on individual initiative, or, as the Lega put it, on relative personal laziness; some men start as late as May. Usually the work extends into May when the men begin to set fire to large trees that have buttresses and aerial roots and cannot easily be felled with axes (such trees are generically called *mizigo*). In the meantime, women cut rhizomes and shoots in mature banana groves and in June plant the shoots in the new clearings. The soil is only superficially scratched before the shoot is inserted. At this point the big trees are still smoldering at the base and the smaller trees have not yet been cut down. In July the men fell the smaller trees with axes, and the larger trees that were burned begin to fall. Women plant more shoots as new clearings are made available. These activities, in which both men and women engage only intermittently, are pursued during August and part of September. In the meantime firewood has been removed, but most of the trees and branches are still lying around in the banana grove. In October, when the new banana trees have started to grow, fire is set to the fallen trees and branches. In November women are still adding new banana shoots. Before the burning they may intersperse cassava, taro, and yams among the banana trees; after the burning they may add corn, beans, and pumpkins.[7]

During *mpombo*, the period of heavy rains *(nzogo)* lasting from November or December to March or April, there is relatively little agricultural

---

[7] Delhaise (1909a, pp. 127–128) accurately observes that the burning occurs sometime after the banana stipes are planted.

activity. Yet some Lega—those who have strength, the Lega say—may at the beginning of this period clear a new stretch of forest where bananas and manioc are planted in accordance with the techniques described above. Traditionally, all agricultural activity is centered in the banana grove. Little attention is paid to cleaning or weeding; when the plants mature and yield, the Lega simply gather the fruit. In recent decades, however, under the influence of foreigners (Arabs and their allies and Belgian administrators), the Lega have become more attentive to agricultural work. Besides banana groves with interspersed subsidiary crops, they now plant fields of peanuts interspersed with corn and pumpkin and fields of sweet potatoes interspersed with cassava. In the 1950's the Belgians introduced the *paysannats*.[8] Palm tree plantations have also been developed.

Animal Husbandry. The Lega raise no cattle, but goats, sheep, dogs, and chickens are found in fair quantities. Goats, sheep, and chickens enter into matrimonial and other exchange cycles. Goats are mandatory as sacrificial victims or as payments in certain bwami initiation rites. During the colonial period cattle were introduced in areas of high altitude. Although some Lega came to own cattle, the care of them was left to immigrant Banyarwanda and Barundi herdsmen from Rwanda and Burundi. Thus cattle began to take on social significance as an investment and as a sign of wealth and prestige. They played no role, however, in the exchanges and the initiations that are of concern here.

Food. The staple foods of the Lega are bananas and game meat, which are also the principal comestibles consumed in large quantities during initiation periods. Meat, which the Lega prefer to eat when it is somewhat putrefied, is commonly roasted in a leaf wrapping. Increasingly, however, it is boiled or baked in oil. Bananas *(magoma)*, roasted with or without the peel, are consumed with meat, fish, vegetables, or sauces. They are also boiled in water, with or without the peel, and then are eaten, or the boiled bananas may be pounded or roasted before being consumed.

Porridge is made from a flour that comes from pounded dried ripe bananas. Peanuts *(kalima)*, sometimes pounded with manioc leaves or boiled or roasted in the shell, are eaten with bananas or corn as a replacement for meat. Corn *(ibela)* is either roasted on the cob or cut off and then roasted. Or it may be pounded raw, mixed with ripe bananas, wrapped in banana leaves, and boiled. Corn is also dried, then roasted on a potsherd and pounded into flour for porridge. Most varieties of cassava *(muzongu)* are roasted like bananas, possibly after first being soaked and dried; sometimes cassava flour is mixed with ripe bananas to make a thick porridge.

---

[8] Staner (1955). After the introduction of *paysannats*, numerous interesting short studies were made by territorial administrators on the social organization and ethnohistory of specific Lega clans. They have not been published.

Traditionally the Lega prefer to eat roasted foods. Women are in charge of the preparation of meals. In good weather they cook in the open air in front of their living quarters; the hearth is formed by four slow-burning logs arranged in a triangle so that they can support a pot over the fire. This informal hearth, or *mutula,* is of great symbolic and social value. When the weather is inclement, the women cook in the women's kitchens *(lusu lwa bakikulu)* which intersect the long compartmentalized houses. Men eat together in the men's house; women eat with young children and occasional female guests in, or in front of, the kitchen.

Money and Trade. *Musanga,* a form of money used by the Lega, consists of small fragments of achatina shells which are usually perforated and strung on raffia fibers (pl. 109); the value is determined by the length of double rows of shells. Sometimes, for special purposes, the shell fragments are not strung but are presented loosely in baskets or in small bunches. Shell money is used in internal exchanges, in matrimonial payments, and as gifts and payments in bwami initiations.[9] Other exchange items that are in limited circulation as matrimonial goods are old iron tools (hornbill, ax, knife, spear), bracelets, cowries, fishing nets, goats, and dogs.

The Lega engage in external trade, though only to a limited extent, with the Songola, from whom they purchase palm oil. As palm plantations and shops develop in Legaland, local supplies of palm oil, together with peanut oil, satisfy most needs. From the Songola the Lega also buy camwood which is used in the manufacture of a cosmetic powder.[10] They import lion teeth (used as insignia by the bwami association) from southern savanna areas. Legaland has no fixed markets to promote trade and exchange between villages. Some scarce products of high value, like salt and red earth, are traded between certain clans. The elaborate bwami initiations, which at the higher levels bring together scores of initiates from different villages, promote the distribution and redistribution of goods.

Crafts and Occupations. Lega men and women engage in numerous activities that are creative or are vital to the subsistence economy. Men plait baskets, fish traps, mats, hats, rattles, and plates from the very strong and flexible *lububi* liana *(Eremospatha* sp.), and from other vines that are thought to be of inferior quality. They make ropes for hunting and fishing

---

[9] Biebuyck (1953*b*) gives a detailed description of shell money and its uses. See Dartevelle (1953) for comparative data.

[10] Delhaise (1909*a*, pp. 31, 89) mentions the existence of the *nkula* tree *(Pterocarpus tinctorius)* among the western Lega, but even there tradition has it that camwood originally came from the Songola. The Banalyuba, one of the westernmost Lega clans, used to trade iron tools and hunting nets with the Songola in exchange for palm oil. A hunting net, hanging in twenty loops from the shoulder to the hip, was worth two large pots of palm oil. The oil was used either for bwami initiations or to buy salt from other Lega clans.

Lega Culture

nets, hats, belts, and shoulder bags from the inner fibers of the bark of the *lukusa* liana *(Polycephalium poggei?)*. The technique of working in raffia *(mpeku)*, which the western Lega claim was introduced by the Banisanga clan, is not well developed in Legaland.[11] Raffia, where it occurs, is used by men as a substitute for *lukusa* rope and bark cloth to make loincloths and frames and chin straps for hats. The men make bark cloth from a variety of species of trees *(Brachystegia* and others). Many objects of relevance to bwami are made, by men, from the hides of certain animals, including belts made from bongo antelope skin or elephant hide and hats made from goat, monkey, or leopard hides. Carving in wood is also a typically male occupation. Parasol wood *(Musanga smithii)* is used for some types of carpentry such as plank doors; *muntonko (Alstonia gilletii)* is the most desirable wood. Lega carvers produce wooden drums (slit-drums and funnel-shaped membranophones), chairs (of three types), plates, troughs, mortars, pestles, bark beaters, ladles, handles, shafts, bells, and walking canes. They also manufacture a variety of objets d'art—masks, animal and human figurines, spoons, bracelets, miniature hammers, hornbill knives, knives, dice, scepters, ax heads, spearpoints, and pegs—from wood, elephant ivory, and elephant bone, and sometimes from clay, soapstone, *ntutu* (heart of dead trees), and hippopotamus ivory. Blacksmiths, whose profession is the most specialized and who sometimes also do carving, make various types of knife blades for hunting and domestic purposes, knives for trimming eyebrows, razors, needles, bracelets, anklets, hornbills, axes, iron bells, and specialized iron tools such as adzes and drills. Extraction of iron ore and salt and building of rafts and bridges are also male activities.

Women perform the domestic tasks of cooking, collecting firewood, and drawing water, and play a substantial role in agricultural activities. The collection of the multipurpose phrynium leaves is also their exclusive occupation. Women make their own brands of fishing nets, prepare camwood and red earth powders, and extract *mombo* and *ikumu* oils for cosmetic purposes. They make some pottery items (jars for oil and water, cups, and cooking pots), but their craftsmanship is not on a high level.

Certain tasks in Legaland are shared by men and women, such as the making of shell money (the men perforate the fragments) and of resin torches and the building of houses (where the men's role is more promi-

---

[11] Delhaise (1909a, p. 31) notes the occurrence of *Raphia* palms in proximity to large rivers in certain areas, but makes no mention of raffia work. On the basis of a photograph taken in the Ulindi River region in 1907, Loir (1935, p. 16) concludes that raffia weaving is known to the Lega. Loir provides evidence of raffia work among such neighboring groups as Songola, Zimba, and Bangubangu. Raffia *(mpeku)* in used in bwami as an initiation object and is also the raw material from which some paraphernalia and initiatory objects are made.

nent). Beer brewing, although essentially a male occupation, requires cooperation from the women. Unlike their neighbors, who value beer highly in their diet, entertainment, ritual, and exchange, the Lega attach little importance to this beverage. Beer is a source of dispute—"He who gives you beer gives you quarrelsomeness"—and is therefore avoided as an exchange item in bwami initiations.[12] The Lega use two kinds of light banana beer: *maku* and *kamukupi*. *Maku* is made from slices of very ripe bananas which are slowly heated over a low fire; this sweet beer is drunk within less than twenty-four hours of its preparation. *Kamukupi*, slightly stronger in alcoholic content, is made from slices of ripe bananas which are left to ferment in cold water for about two days. Other beverages, such as palm wine, are traditionally unknown among the Lega.

Village and House. The Lega village (*kyumo*) is traditionally built on a hill in a more or less natural clearing (*kilungubalo*) of primary rain forest. Trees and branches are cut down so that the part of the forest left standing forms a natural fence (*mukingo*) that will be close behind the two parallel rows of houses to be constructed. Both downstream and upstream sides (*isula*) of a village, from which trails depart into the forest, are fortified with a high fence of poles placed close together. A small opening left in the middle of each fence is closed at night by means of a set of transversely placed beams; a string attached to the beams is connected to a bell hanging from a bed in the nearest house.

A village consists of two parallel rows (*mikeke*) of contiguous huts, a plan that creates an impression of longhouses. The open space (*mulungu*) between the two rows of houses serves as a main street, a dance floor, and a public place. At one end of it is the men's house (*lusu lwa gamulungu* or *lusu lwidega*), an oval structure whose roof projects out beyond its sides. The walls are made of latticework, without bark or leaf coverings. The roof is first covered with a layer of phrynium leaves and then with a layer of *matungulu (Costus lucanusianus?)* plants. The men's house has four entrances, one on each of the four sides. There are elaborate prescriptions as to who enters through which door and as to where the village officeholders sit. The village has no granaries and no separate structures of other kinds. In the space near the village women may plant a few banana trees.

The rectangular houses (*kantamba*), built against one another under one huge gable roof, follow a basic ground plan. A middle room (*kyage*), with a front door and a back door, is connected along most of its interior sides with the sleeping rooms (*nkiko*), of which there are two or more

---

[12] Delhaise (1909a, p. 83) stresses the fact that the Lega of his time were not at all addicted to beer drinking. Beer is used in initiations by the Bembe, the Nyindu, and some eastern Lega, probably through the influence of neighboring groups—Shi, Vira, and Furiiru—among whom beer drinking is of great ritual and dietary significance.

Lega Culture

depending on the number of wives. One of the bedrooms may be connected with a storeroom *(kangwondo)* where shell money and other belongings are kept. A *kantamba* house is separated from the next one by a kitchen *(lusu lwa mukikulu)*, which cannot be entered from any of the bedrooms. The kitchen is under the main gable roof; it has no front wall, but has a back wall and a back door.

The houses are constructed in an ingenious way. The latticework walls are covered on the inside with large panels of bark, held together with lianas, and on the outside with *matungulu* or with dried banana leaves. The roof, also made of latticework, is covered with phrynium leaves arranged like tiles and kept flat with *matungulu* plants and sticks. Symbolically, the Lega see a direct relationship between the arrangement of scales on the back of the pangolin and their way of placing phrynium leaves on the roofs; thus the pangolin is praised as a culture hero who taught the Lega how to cover a house.

The furniture is very simple. Each bedroom contains one or more beds made of layers of poles covered with mats. Chairs, and also shoulder bags that contain some of a man's most precious belongings, including carvings, pipes, and medicine, are kept in the bedroom. In the *kyage* is a tablelike structure *(lusasa)* on and around which are baskets, pots, jars, cups, nets, spears, knives, fish traps, firewood, and drying bananas.

Sometimes a smaller house of similar construction is built behind the longhouse for old single people. Separate toilets for men and women are placed outside the village. Since many Lega are often away from the village for long periods while fishing, trapping, or hunting, they establish in the forest small camps that have different names: *lutanda* for hunting, *ishitu* for fishing, *lutala* for trapping. These precarious, beehive-shaped structures are sometimes covered with phrynium leaves. Small hamlets *(musumba)* in isolated parts of the forest far away from the main village are frequently inhabited by older officeholders. When inhabited by an individual who has the right of the pangolin knife (i.e., the special privilege of supervising the distribution of the accidentally killed pangolin), they may be called *mangele* or *kibagilo*. In some areas the kansilembo rites connected with bwami must be held in such hamlets.

The most important villages are those specially built for the highest bwami initiations, or kindi rites. (Initiations for the grades below kindi, except for the kansilembo rites held in the hamlets, take place in the regular men's houses.) The initiations call for the participation of large numbers of individuals who come from widely scattered villages and who may have to be accommodated for weeks. The prospective initiate and his kinsmen build a village that consists of the familiar two rows of contiguous rectangular houses (called *bituka* in this instance) divided into apartments, where participating initiates and their initiated wives are accommodated. Depending on his importance (fame), each initiate receives one or two rooms. The candidate for initiation also builds a shorter longhouse, with walls of soft parasol wood, in which his tutors and sponsors *(mukomi, kilezi, kakusa)* and their initiated wives stay. He adds a *lutangu,* a stable-like structure with a storeroom on the top in which the *kakusa* sponsor keeps the dried meat, and an *ibeza,* a building for storage of initiatory goods.

The initiation hut *(lubungu)* is built in the center of the initiation village, as befits its prime importance (see Delhaise, 1909a, photo 46). A huge single-room house, oval in shape, it has two door openings directly opposite each other and a roof strongly resembling the carapace of a turtle. The walls are covered with bark and dried *matungulu* stems; on the roof are placed phrynium and *matungulu* stems. The downstream door of the hut remains closed until the initiations are finished. Near its threshold, barring access to the door, is the *mukumbi* (a few logs placed in a square which represent the garbage heap). All dirt and dust picked up in the hut during the initiations must be placed here.

The initiation hut is divided into two parts, separated from each other by a panel *(makito)* in which there is a small doorway. Before the initiations begin, the candidate and his first wife sleep in the smaller part of the hut *(nkiko)* near the downstream door. In this room they pile up some of the goods needed for the initiations. After the initiations have started the *mukomi* sponsor and his wife sleep in the *nkiko* while the goods are being transported to the *ibeza* hut. In the larger part of the initiation hut *(kyage)* all important rites of the lower cycle of the highest grade (musagi wa kindi) take place. For the rites of the highest grade (lutumbo lwa kindi), the panel that divides the hut is removed. Sometime after the highest rites are finished, the initiation hut is destroyed. Before that time, however, while the initiate still aspires to move up from a lower to the highest kindi level, several objects are kept in the hut: carapaces of turtles and *kiselia* leaves hang from the walls; a chimpanzee skull hangs above the door opening in the separation panel; a fire drill is hidden in the roof just above the panel; a walking stick and a brush *(matakale)* connected with the kansilembo rites are also in the hut. Near the upstream door hangs a large "beard" *(luzelu)* made of dried banana leaves.

After the tutors, the sponsors, and a few initiates from nearby villages have arrived, the initiates engage in the preliminary *kamondo* dances. Afterward they prepare the *miaka,* short trails cutting transversely across the two main paths of access to the village. These trails represent a symbolic crossroads. When traveling initiates see the *miaka* they have a choice of alternatives: either to return home without pursuing their journey, or to enter the village and participate in the initiations. For kindi initiations an additional fence *(muluta)* of dried banana leaves is set up as a symbolic prohibition against violent behavior or disputes.

By the 1950's practically all compartmentalized longhouses had disappeared in Legaland, the direct result of colonial preference for the small, compartmentalized, rectangular wattle-and-daub house with a saddle roof. As early as Delhaise's time, though many traditional villages and structures were still in existence, the colonial administration was imposing regulations for more "hygienic" houses (Delhaise, 1909a, pp. 107–109; photos 41, 46). The cylindrical houses with cone-shaped roofs *(kasonge)* which had been prevalent since time immemorial among some eastern Lega and among the Bembe also had gradually been replaced by rectangular structures. Shrines for ancestors, nature spirits, and twins were rare among the majority of Lega; Delhaise *(ibid.,* p. 202) explicitly mentions only the small niches built on three poles placed in the middle of the village to house the skulls *(kalumba, kansimba)* of dead kindi. Farther east, shrines take on greater importance among the Basimwenda and the Wamuzimu, who were directly under the influence of the Bembe and some of the submerged groups.

SOCIAL ORGANIZATION

Descent, Inheritance, and Succession. Descent linkages among the Lega are patrilineal or agnatic. A child born of an unmarried or a not fully married woman (a woman for whom the minimal transfer of matrimonial goods has not been completed), however, belongs to the agnatic group of its mother, unless a special payment made by the later husband of the mother has regularized the situation. It would be hard to find in Legaland a patrilineal group some of whose members do not ultimately trace uterine linkage, more or less covered up but well remembered. Furthermore, the Lega attach extreme social importance to the respective patrilineages of the nonconnective parent (mother), grandparents (father's mother and mother's mother), and great-grandparents (father's father's mother, father's mother's mother, mother's father's mother, and mother's mother's mother). Because of repetitive marriages and the prevalence of unions between members of the same clan, cognatic relationships are frequently built into agnatic ones, resulting in particularly complex interpersonal and intergroup connections. There is constant social, economic, political, and ritual interaction among members of the various groups. Invariably, one finds lineages in Legaland which are closely aligned with one another in the territorial, political, or ritual sphere because of being linked together cognatically.[13] The implication is that the field of kinship relationships is an extremely wide one, closely connecting not only many kinds of agnates, but many kinds of cognates and in-laws as well.

The principles of inheritance also follow the patrilineal line. A man's sons and brothers are preferred heirs to most of his movable and immov-

[13] I am using the terms cognatic and cognate to designate relationships between individuals which are traced through the nonconnecting parent, grandparents, and great-grandparents.

able property. In the absence of direct and close collateral heirs, a man's uterine sister's sons are preferred beneficiaries, but their claim has to be confirmed by the more distantly related members of the dead man's lineage. This principle is condensed in the Lega formula: "If the female side makes the distribution, it means that the male side has died out." In the category of movable property, there are four classes of inheritable valuables: *bikulo:* shell money, animals, implements, and cloth; *masengo:* initiation objects and paraphernalia of bwami; *isigi:* marriage payments supplied and being supplied for a female relative; *bakikulu:* wives. In default of close agnates, and with the agreement of more distant agnates, sororal nephews can inherit, unconditionally, from the *bikulo,* the *isigi,* and the widows. Inheritance of the initiation objects and paraphernalia presupposes that the sororal nephew is a member of the bwami association of a rank identical with that of his uncle. In normal circumstances, when there are close agnatic heirs, a sororal nephew of appropriate rank frequently holds initiation objects in trust until a son or a brother of his uncle is initiated to the position left open by the latter. Finally, the estate and/or the agnates of the dead person must provide funerary payments *(idigo)* to the seven socially recognized groups of maternal uncles. Such payments comprise shell money, goats, cloth, and implements. Certain privileges connected with the organization of circumcision rites and the distribution of sacred animals are inherited patrilineally, some in an almost direct line of agnatic descent; some of these privileges can also be claimed by sororal nephews.

Succession is based on patrilineal ideology, but there is no automatic process whereby social importance, power, and authority are transferred from a man to his brother or to his son. In matters of domestic authority a man's structural position as senior descendant in the family is of decisive significance; from this point of view it can be said that succession follows the principles of primogeniture. Yet special social consideration and some sort of social priority are given to individuals who are senior by age (as opposed to senior by position in the kinship unit) and to those who are senior because they belong to an older genealogical generation. Political position in the village and in the village group is determined by character and skill and, correspondingly, by achievement in the bwami association. Succession to such positions is patrilineal, but there is no fixed rule as to priorities among the range of eligible agnates. Occasionally such a position in the local group is held by an individual who is incorporated in the group but whose remote ties with that group are cognatic.

The Kinship System. Despite regional differences in the kinship system, stemming from dialectal and structural variations, the relevant aspects of the system are basically as follows.

There are twenty-four basic kinship terms to designate father, mother, female grandparents, male grandparents, siblings and parallel cousins, children, grandchildren, great-grandchildren, great-great-grandchildren, mother's brothers, cross-cousins, sister's children (male speaker), husband, wife, spouse's juniors, sons-in-law, daughters-in-law, wife's senior brothers, husband's senior sisters, other in-laws, and parents-in-law (among themselves).

Siblings and parallel cousins are classified under one term *(mubitu)*. All juniors, however, are explicitly grouped as *muto* (junior), whereas seniors are spoken of as *yeya* (honorific term). The Lega distinguish between two types of seniority—*bukulu* (greatness) and *kubutoa* (to be born; age)—which they insist must never be confused. The first is a function of the structure of the polygynous household and, in a wider perspective, of the polysegmentary structure of lineages and clans; the second is determined by the chronology of birth. A senior by birth *(yeya)* is entitled to respect; he is sure to receive a wife before his junior by birth. It is likely that he will achieve access to the lower grades of bwami before his junior. He can never inherit the widow of a junior by birth. Authority in the family, however, is a function of *bukulu*, of one's structural position in the group. In other words, in a given polygynous household, it is the oldest son of a man's most senior wife *(mwikulu mukulu)* who is entitled to succeed to that man's position as head of the family. This principle is expressed in the aphorism, "Seniority by structural position [*bukulu*] cannot be bought." This aphorism is a condensed version of a story about a man who tried to buy, for the price of two goats, the *bukulu* position held by his half-sibling, who was a junior by birth. The latter accepted the two goats, ate them, and then told his brother, senior by birth, that he himself would remain in the *bukulu* position, which is inalienable and irreversible.

The *bukulu* position is not to be confused with primogeniture. It must be viewed in terms of the vertical structure of the group, that is, in terms of genealogical generations *(kibuti)*. Frequently, individuals born in a lower genealogical generation are older by birth than men belonging to higher genealogical generations. As the Lega put it: "*Kibuti* [older generation] encounters the children already born." The senior-junior terminology cannot be applied to persons of different generations. The members of lower genealogical generations, even if they are older by birth, owe respect to those of higher genealogical position, who are in the position of authority. It would therefore be unthinkable for a man to exercise authority in the family if his *kibuti* is still alive, unless the arrangement is publicly and mutually agreed upon. If a man of a lower generation achieves a bwami grade that is higher than that of his *kibuti*, which rarely happens, he must recognize, with special gifts, the social priority of the latter.

In the parental generation, the term for father *(tatagi)* is extended to his junior brothers and junior male parallel cousins, and the term for mother *(magi)* is applied to her junior sisters and her junior female parallel cousins and to father's junior sisters and junior female parallel cousins. The term for grandfather *(tatangulu)* is extended to father's senior brothers and senior male parallel cousins; the term for grandmother *(koku)* is applied to father's senior sisters and senior female parallel cousins and to mother's senior sisters and senior female parallel cousins. It is to be observed, however, that no joking relations are permitted with these two categories of grandmothers. The classification is ambivalent, for both types of women are thought of as mothers, even though they are classified as grandmothers. Joking is not permitted with father's senior sisters because, as the Lega say, they have carried one's father in their arms.

Mother's brothers are male mothers *(mwizio)*. The same term is applied to the brothers and male agnatic descendants of one's father's mother, father's father's mother, father's mother's mother, mother's mother, mothers's father's mother, and mother's mother's mother. It is also extended to male matrilateral cross-cousins when their father is dead. In the relationships of these male mothers, the Lega distinguish between the *idulu* and *mbusa* categories. The *idulu* category has two subgroups: (1) one's immediate male mothers, that is, one's mother's full brothers and half brothers, are referred to as *mwizio wanda;* (2) mother's parallel cousins, that is, members of other houses in her minimal lineage who are socially less significant, are referred to as *mwizio wa mubuto*. Under the *mbusa* category are subsumed the brothers, and their male agnatic descendants, of one's father's mother, mother's mother, and so on.

The tremendous social importance attached to these relationships is discussed later, in connection with the bwami initiations.[14] Here it is sufficient to point out that the *mwizio we idulu,* the brother of one's mother, is to be respected and honored as one's own mother. Because he is neither mother nor father, however, the element of authority and restraint is less strongly felt. The relationship is respectful but open; it is one of confidence. Mother's brother is a benevolent protector, a counselor, a guide; one can always depend on him; his help is permanently assured. From many points of view, the relationship is a reciprocal one. The concept is powerfully expressed in the aphorisms "Bwami, a big pack of rafters my maternal uncles have tied up for me"; "The sororal nephew is great; he is the gaffle [a short or long stick with a natural hook, cut precisely at an intersection of branches] that permits me to reach the inner sections of the branches." A man refers to his mother's brother's wife either as "wife of my male mother" or as "my wife." The relationship is without constraint, but the parties to it cannot indulge in verbal or other excesses. A sororal nephew has a conditional claim on her when his male mother dies; he may inherit her, with the permission of the lineage council, if no close agnatic relatives are left in the lineage of his mother's brother.

The reciprocal term for father and mother is child *(mwana)*. The Lega

---

[14] In Biebuyck (1954d, e) more details are given about these relationships.

have two autonomous words *(musikila* and *mukinga)* which mean, respectively, son and daughter, but the terms are not normally used; that is, they occur in specific circumstances with a pejorative connotation. The reciprocal term for grandfather and grandmother is grandchild *(muyukulu).* Joking is permitted in this relationship except with grandmothers in one's father's and mother's generation. The reciprocal term applied by all categories of *mwizio* is *mwigwa.*

The husband-wife *(iba-mukikulu)* and co-wife relationships are complex because of the interwoven principles of polygyny and female initiation. The first wife *(wa kilanga)* is in a position of authority within a polygynous household; as long as she remains with her husband, and particularly if she continues to please the elders of the village, her position is unalterable, no matter what the feelings of her husband might be. Her standing is considerably enhanced if she achieves high female rank in bwami. The fullest respect is owed her (the other co-wives call her mother), and it is practically unthinkable that she could ever turn into a rejected wife *(kigilwa).* The woman in authority is not to be confused with the preferred wife *(kalemba),* whose position is more precariously based on affection. Her social position may be strengthened when her husband manages to get her through some of the female initiations in bwami.

Two special terms *(mutenzia* and *mukamwana)* designate, respectively, son-in-law and daughter-in-law; they are also applied by a maternal uncle to the spouse of his sororal nephew/niece, and by a woman to a junior co-wife. Other in-law relationships are indicated by specific terms. *Mutokali* designates a senior brother's wife (male speaker), a wife's junior sister, a husband's junior brother, and a senior sister's husband (female speaker). The joking permitted in this relationship is expressed in verbal allusions and suggestions and in physical contact ranging to sexual relationships with a wife's junior sister. The Lega accept junior levirate but place heavy restrictions on sororal polygyny and sororate. *Mukozi* is a reciprocal term that designates relationships between brothers-in-law, whereas *mukulu* means a relationship between a woman and her husband's sisters. Under the appellation *ikolo,* the Lega cover a wide range of in-laws, such as one's sister's husband's sisters, one's junior brother's and one's sister's husband's sister, one's junior brother's and one's sister's parents-in-law, one's brother's children's parents-in-law. There is a joking relationship with the female *makolo,* but one does not marry an *ikolo* or an *ikolo's* child (*"Makolo* commit adultery with one another, but they don't marry"). *Musongi munane,* finally, is the term with which the parents of a married couple refer to one another.

In-law relationships in general, and connections between brothers-in-law in particular, are extremely critical, especially because the Lega may marry within their clans individuals to whom they already bear an agnatic relationship. In order to maintain a delicate balance, therefore, in-laws must observe a number of restrictions while at the same time maintaining maximum communication. One must eliminate all sources of possible dispute and injury with a brother-in-law, such as playing ball or trapping certain animals. One must never publicly criticize one's son-in-law; the criticism should rather be addressed to one's own daughter.

Constant communication and balance are best evidenced by the system of exchanges between the respective groups of the married couple. These begin as soon as the marriage is agreed upon and continue until after death. All goods transferred by the husband's to the wife's people at marriage, initiation, birth of children, death, and so on, are counted as *igambia;* all goods transmitted in the opposite direction, from the wife's to the husband's people, are counted as *mubigo*. When there is divorce, the return of goods *(mpolo)* consists of, besides the wife, the differences between the two sets of valuables.

Cross-cousin relationships are extremely complicated and dynamic in nature. *Mubiala,* the general term that covers such relationships in all directions, is applied to cross-cousins so long as the interconnecting mother's brother is alive. Relationships between *babiala* are friendly and devoid of constraints, but sexual relationships or marriage between real cross-cousins is excluded. Marriages with females of lines collateral to one's mother's lineage are possible, according to the often stated principle: "A man may marry one from behind [below] his mother; he cannot marry one from behind [below] his father." In some instances, as when a man marries his father's mother's brother's son's daughter, he is requested to give, in advance, a *kisanga* goat to be publicly shared by the parties concerned. Although true cross-cousin marriages are prohibited, a man may take his mother's brother's son's widow and give her to his own son. When mother's brother *(mwizio)* dies, his son is classified as *mwizio* (male mother) and his daughter as *magi* (mother). For the children of male matrilateral cross-cousins, the Lega prefer descriptive terms such as *mwana wa mubiala* or *mwana wa mwizio*. No joking is permitted with them; they are treated, as long as their father is alive, as one's own children.

The Marriage System. Lega marriages are based on the transfer of matrimonial goods (iron tools, goats, dogs, shell money, bark cloth, bracelets). Among eastern groups of Lega, as among Bembe, a large number of women in any lineage are married with goods that were obtained by their husbands through the marriage of their female agnates.[15] There are various phases (four are usually mentioned) of matrimonial arrangements before the marriage bond is established, since in the majority of marriages a

---

[15] Biebuyck (1961) analyzes the *mitamba* system of the Bembe. For other information on the Lega matrimonial system see Salmon (1951, 1953) and Wankenge (1948).

woman is never fully incorporated into her husband's lineage. The two groups of in-laws maintain close ties as long as the marriage lasts. These ties are fostered by endless reciprocal visits, gift exchanges (*mikesi*), and outright cooperation. When a marriage is dissolved, the parties meet again to settle the question of the return of marriage goods. Determining the amount of the return is a complicated procedure of adding up the goods given by the man's group and subtracting the items returned to it by the wife's kinsmen. Certain valuables, like shell money, iron tools, dogs, goats, hunting nets, bracelets, anklets, salt, and oil, are included in the count; others, like meat, fish, baskets, pots, sleeping mats, fishing nets, and chickens, are excluded from it.

The conditions under which the Lega can marry within their own clans are discussed later. Marriages between individuals linked as cross-cousins are excluded. One does not take a wife in the direct lines of descent originating with the male siblings of mother's father's mother, mother's mother, father's father's mother, mother's father's mother's mother, father's mother's mother, or mother's mother's mother. One cannot take a wife in the family groups of father's other wives. Sororate and sororal polygyny in the strict sense are not practiced (except in very special circumstances), but relationships with one's wife's junior sister are very close and are expressed in mild joking. Marriage with one's wife's brother's daughter is normally not permitted; however, one's wife may claim her brother's daughter as a spouse for one of her husband's closer agnates. A strict exchange marriage with one's uterine sister's husband's sister is also prohibited.

The Lega practice widow inheritance. A man may inherit the widow of his father (other than, and junior to, his mother), of his senior brother, of his little father (father's junior brother), and eventually of his mother's brother. Although no additional marriage payments are required, it is customary to give, on this occasion, presents of shell money and one or two goats to the father of the inherited woman. A woman who has achieved the highest female grade of bwami is perpetually married to her husband; she can be neither divorced nor inherited. Wealthy men with many wives sometimes give one of their recently married junior wives to a favorite son.

An overwhelming majority of Lega marry within the Lega cultural unit. Because of strong cultural continuities between the Lega and neighboring groups, however, many Lega living in borderline villages marry Bembe, Nyindu, Songola, and Bangubangu. The Lega like to marry within their clans and are proud when they can boast of being *kitutuma* or *mubake*, that is, when they have several categories of male mothers in their own clan. Among a majority of the eastern Lega, as among the Bembe, there is a form of preferred marriage with classificatory granddaughters, girls belonging to secondary and primary lineages that are thought to be junior in the clan structure to the man's lineage.[16] Women in a polygynous household are ranked on the basis of seniority, with the first wife *(mukazi wa kilanga)* directing the internal affairs of the domestic group. The relationships of authority are enhanced by graded membership in bwami.

Since in-law relationships are fragile and tenuous, their continuation and effectiveness are functions of subtle equilibrium and harmony. All excesses or liberties, and all situations that might cause disruption of the bond, must be avoided. Solid ties with one's wives' lineages strengthen one's position with regard to high-level achievements in bwami, for one can expect many initiation goods and even strong sponsorship to come from these lineages.

Clan and Lineage. The Lega are subdivided into clans *(kilongo)*. These named, nonexogamous, nontotemic patrilineal groupings of males and females recognize an eponymous ancestor and are usually based on about ten specifically remembered generations. The number of generations is correlated with the six distinctive kinship terms used to specify lineal agnatic relatives and with the conception of a clan as being subdivided into three levels of lineages. Gifted individuals and others who have well-known, very old men in the family or lineage may sometimes recite as many as fifteen generations, but this distinction has little relevance to clan and lineage structure.

As genealogical groupings, particularly among the western Lega, clans frequently have a partly fictive unilineal structure. In the course of time, various groups of nonagnatic relatives would be totally absorbed into a clan and assigned a fixed position in the agnatic chart as descendants of a sister of the primary lineage founder.[17] The Lega, well aware of this development, believe a clan embraces two kinds of people: the *tuminimini* (representing the true agnatic nucleus) and the *beidande* (representing the incorporated element). It is said repeatedly, "A clan [is] four hearths [agnatic elements] and a *kidande* [incorporated elements]," as if it could not be a complete unit without this additional segment. It is extremely difficult, and hardly pertinent, to try to sort out these two categories of elements. Members of incorporated units are not socially or legally inferior to the others, although the kinship system tends to treat them as members of a junior group. They can achieve the highest levels in the bwami association, yet a *kidande* cannot normally be a village headman or "master of the land" *(nenekisi)*. Moreover, he can never inherit the right of the pangolin knife or the *musimbi* or *lutala* privileges connected with circumcision ceremonies (see discussion of circumcision rites, below).

---

[16] Biebuyck, in an unpublished manuscript (1969), discusses in detail the preferred marriages between classificatory grandfathers and granddaughters among the Bembe.

[17] Biebuyck (1953a) describes the processes and techniques of this kind of incorporation and analyzes its legal implications.

Lega Culture

Clans are localized units in the sense that their membership is only partly dispersed. They are subdivided into a number of genealogical levels or segments which are of fundamental significance in the kinship and matrimonial system, in political organization, and in bwami initiations. The actual number of levels recognized for social purposes depends somewhat on the numerical strength and the degree of cohesiveness or dispersal of a group and on the amplitude of its recognized chart. Basically, however, one can distinguish three levels, which are designated by a variety of generic terms. Here the levels are called primary, secondary, and tertiary; the respective Lega terms are *bukolo, kikalo,* and *ibele.* Each lineage level is named after its eponymous founder. Thus, the Banakazigwa form a tertiary lineage segment within the Banakagela, who represent a secondary lineage segment within the Banamugila. The Banamugila constitute a primary lineage segment; they are named after Mugila, who is said to be one of the four sons of Salu, the eponymous ancestor of the Banasalu clan. A tertiary level or lineage forms a segment within a secondary one; a secondary lineage, a segment within a primary one. From primary to tertiary the number of generations steadily diminishes. The recognized distinction is based on at least one generation difference from lineage to lineage. The number of living individuals making up a tertiary lineage, however, may be larger than the number in a primary lineage.

Among the western Lega the clan is often symbolically subdivided or rearranged into four primary lineages. The number of smaller lineages within each primary lineage does not, however, correspond to any numerical pattern. As a rule, the male members of different primary lineages live in different villages; depending on the numerical strength of a primary lineage, its members may have several villages of their own. For example, the Salu clan is divided into four primary lineages: Kibondo, Lusumbasumba, Ninda, and Mugila (see App. I). Each lineage has one village of its own, except for Mugila. As it is a numerically strong group, its members inhabit three villages, the distribution being made on the basis of the three secondary lineages into which Mugila subdivides. The situation is complicated because segments within lineages sometimes scatter, to settle with or in proximity to other lineages of the same or different clanic origin. Thus two lineages may be found together because of *buninabo,* that is, because their respective male founders were the sons of two women who were sisters in one clan and were married to two lineage founders of the same or of different clans. Others may explain coresidence in terms of a distant maternal uncle–sororal nephew relationship between the founders of the respective groups.

A special bond of solidarity, expressed in ritual, in marriage, and in economic cooperation, may exist between lineages. This bond is maintained between lineages whose male founders are said to share a common mother. Throughout Legaland there are clans permanently and closely linked together either because they recognize a common genealogical origin within the Lega group, or because they recognize common ritual arrangements in the bwami organization, or perhaps for both reasons. Such relationships are usually based on geographical contiguity between groups linked by a common historical experience since the time of the Lega migrations and dispersal. In a few instances, as noted above, the bond is interpreted in terms of an ancient maternal uncle–sororal nephew connection. Ultimately all clans are interconnected because they trace their origins back to the few recognized sons and grandsons of Lega. In other words, they belong to Lega culture. The specific permanent connections of two or three adjoining clans have the more practical function of determining the existence in Legaland of organized ritual communities, or, more relevant in this context, of communities specifically organized for the highest initiations of bwami.

Lega clans are not exogamous. The prevailing principle is that individuals who are agnatic descendants in the fifth generation from a common male ancestor cannot intermarry. Beyond this point, kinship (i.e., close kinship) is finished *(mubuto uzinda)*, and marriage becomes theoretically possible. In principle, marriage within the tertiary lineage, or the six-generation group, is not permitted. Yet much depends on the territorial compactness of the lineage. If marriage does occur between fairly close members of the same clan, the special circumstances must be acknowledged by sacrificing a goat *(kinsansa)* and distributing it among all parties concerned. If two tertiary lineages whose founders are linked as uterine brothers form a territorial unit (which often happens), marriages between their members are discouraged. If the founder of a secondary lineage is said to have had sons by only one wife, an individual does not marry within the lineage. This rule may also extend to the level of primary lineages, depending on local experience and local practice.

Political Organization. The Lega form a stateless society. There are no hereditary chiefs.[18] The relatively simple segmentary lineage system, however, is strangely complicated by the hierarchically organized bwami association, whose power and authority are widespread.

---

[18] My comments on political organization differ considerably from those of Delhaise (1909a, pp. 341–347). Delhaise refers to a tradition asserting that the entire Lega group had been ruled in the past by a paramount chief, but I have found no traces of such a system. Each subdivision of the tribe, Delhaise (*ibid.*, p. 341) goes on to say, had its grand chef. The exact nature of a subdivision is not clearly specified, but the context (*ibid.*, p. 345) suggests that it comprised a number of villages whose headmen were tributary to the grand chef. Delhaise obviously did not understand the nature of a complex segmentary lineage organization.

Some of the confusion may be attributed to three different factors. First, the bwami hierarchies built into the kinship structure and the political system complicate the picture of a simple segmentary lineage organization. Second, the Arab and Arabized

The head of any family group (monogamous, polygynous, extended) who is in charge of its internal affairs may be referred to as *mukota*. In a monogamous or a polygynous family the head is the common husband and/or father. In the extended family, succession to authority is more complicated. The sons succeed to their father's position, each in his own household, with social recognition given to the most senior (by position, not by age). If father's brother is alive he automatically becomes the new head of the extended family because he is a man of the older generation.

The head of the village *(nene-* or *mwizakyumo,* sometimes *ntundu)* is, in principle, the most senior person in the older generation *(kibuti* position). This definition, of course, does not mean the oldest male in the village. Succession to office is not simply a question of structural position; it is mainly a function of what the Lega call *mutima* (lit., heart), signifying character, intelligence, and general behavior. The village headman was described to Uyttebroeck, a colonial administrator, in 1935 as a person of generosity "who watches over the people near him, who works hard, who hosts strangers, who guards his brood." The position of headman is based neither on heredity nor on seniority. Frequently, persons who are in the required seniority position are not in the authority position within the village.

Invariably, the village headman is flanked by a *sakuzinda* (junior kinsman) who acts as his counselor and substitute. A village is most commonly inhabited by the majority of male members of a secondary lineage, around which distantly related agnatic kinsmen and close or distant cognates and in-laws cluster. Two or more such villages in geographical contiguity *(mutula)* are most always inhabited by the members of a primary lineage *(bukolo),* their wives, and all cognates, in-laws, and distant agnates who have been given the right to reside there. The recognized head of a primary lineage, called *nenekisi* (master of the land), looks after the affairs of the group as a whole. He is assisted by two junior heads, *sakania* and *sakuzinda.* Again, the pattern is not absolute. Lineages of lower level which have developed into highly diversified genealogical units and numerically strong groups may have acquired their own *nenekisi.* The mem-

---

occupants of Legaland had introduced, as they also had in other parts of the eastern Congo, an embryonic form of centralization. For some time before 1895 the Congo Free State governed large parts of the eastern Congo through these Arabs and Arabized leaders and their political appointees. Some of the so-called chiefs and chiefly dynasties, recognized in later years by the Belgian colonial government in the context of the new administrative units, emerged during this troublesome period by way of intrigue and sheer accident. Finally, some of the eastern Lega clans, which are exposed to the political traditions of the interlacustrine states, have concepts of clan leadership which are not prevalent among the majority of Lega. An unpublished report written by Uyttebroeck, a colonial administrator in the 1930's, gives a reasonably accurate description of Lega political organization.

bers of different primary lineages of a single clan live in adjoining villages, and there is close interaction between the different *nenekisi*. Eventually, one of them, who has greater prestige, oratorship, and charisma than the others, acts as spokesman or primus inter pares for all of them.

The concept of *nenekisi* is a complex one. My translation as "master of the land" does only partial justice to the intricate connotations of the term *kisi*. The term obviously refers to an organized group of individuals, clustered around an agnatic core and living in a small number of adjoining villages. Such a group has far-reaching autonomy in the ritual, political, and economic spheres. Like similar terms in other Bantu languages, *kisi* implies a definite political subdivision. It is in this sense that the Lega speak about their deep attachment to their land: "Where the land is sick and where your wife is sick, where do you go? I go to where the land is sick. The land is goodness. I can marry another woman." But *kisi* also bears, as the Lega put it, on everything that there is on earth. More specifically, they mean humans, animals, the land, houses, fields, crops, artifacts, and such institutions as the bwami association and circumcision rites. The *nenekisi* is in control of all these aspects of life; he has knowledge of them and power and mastery over them. He is a man of achievement as well as a person in authority.

The *nenekisi* is selected on the basis, not of kinship principles, but of *mutima* (character, wisdom, general behavior). Frequently he is a high-ranking member of the bwami association, perhaps a kindi. Clearly, however, not all the high-ranking initiates are *nenekisi*, while some members of the middle grade (ngandu) in bwami have achieved this position. The *nenekisi*, then, is a man of outstanding knowledge and prestige, a man of impeccable morality and proven equity, who performs the role of arbiter, pacifier, and liaison officer within his own group and in its relationships with other groups. His symbol of office is *mukulu wibondo*, a well-patinated walking stick made from the median stem of a raffia leaf. Decisions reached by the *nenekisi*, in consultation with the assembly of seniors, are binding. Nonconformity exposes the transgressor to *kitampo*, a mystic sanction that can be wiped out only by payment of heavy fines and performance of an appropriate ritual. Various forms of divination (e.g., water reading) and ordeals (e.g., poison ordeal; jumping over the corpse) help to sanction the decisions reached.

The *sakania* and the *sakuzinda*, who act as aides to the master of the land, belong to different branches of the primary lineage. The *sakania* does not normally live in the same village as the master of the land, but the *sakuzinda* does. The function of the *sakania* is dependent, not on age or on kinship position, but on character. The *sakuzinda*, who replaces an absent *nenekisi* and looks after the group when the master of the land dies, is usually selected from the oldest members of the lineage. He receives the flank parts *(bitugu)* of all animals, and all turtles are brought to him.

Lega Culture

Because of advanced age the *sakuzinda* rarely leaves the village and is, therefore, its guardian par excellence. Lega cases are not necessarily settled by these individuals. The Lega are very democratic in legal matters; almost anyone who is familiar with a case and feels he has the necessary wisdom to solve it may act as spokesman, adviser, or arbiter *(musunguzi, mulongeki)*.

There is no established authority beyond that of the *nenekisi* in Legaland. There are no clan chiefs. When ingroup conflicts create opposition to the *nenekisi* and his *sakania*, or when disputes arise between primary lineages, several *nenekisi* get together and summon representatives of lineages within the clan and of other lineages to a *musumbililo* meeting. Such action is possible because of kinship links between primary lineages and their leaders, and also because the bwami association creates bonds that foster constant social interaction between autonomous lineages.

It must be stressed that power and authority are diffused over a large number of individuals within any single group because of the interlocking of kinship principles with bwami hierarchies and special ritual privileges, such as ownership of the right of the pangolin knife and control over circumcision ceremonies. The Lega are a peaceful and peace-loving people. According to Delhaise (1909a, p. 349), the Lega live in harmony with their neighbors. Internal peace has been achieved through a variety of cross-cutting institutions (segmentary lineage structure and diffusion of power and authority within it; circumcision communities; extended fields of kinship going beyond agnatic and alliance relationships; bwami association) and through the moral philosophy of bwami, which stands for moderation. A Legaland tradition asserts that in earlier times the Lega were torn apart by inter- and intragroup conflict and by internecine feuding and warring until the bwami association, "the fruit that has come from above," was introduced. Yet, as in any human society, there are disputes and conflicts that are not settled by the normal institutional machinery; in other words, there are situations that lead to violence.

The Lega distinguish three kinds of violence. *Muntute* is a simple brawl that does not lead to killing, for sticks are the preferred weapon of attack. Individuals who engage in such brawls automatically exclude themselves from access to, or advancement in, the bwami association. *Kasili* is violence perpetrated by one individual against another which results in death. The Lega insist that as a rule such individuals are not of the same clan. The wronged party threatens retaliation but the offender's people look for a settlement, since in this kind of individualized incident the entire group cannot be held liable. The two parties to the dispute meet at a neutral place between the two clan territories *(geibamba)*. Reconciliation usually takes the form of payment of a woman who is a close agnatic relative of the killer *(kimonano)*; she is given as a wife to a close agnate of the victim. The treatment of the killer varies: sometimes he is chased from his group, but he can find asylum in one of his male mothers' groups; sometimes he carries a message, whose purport is unknown to him, inviting another group to get rid of him. The Lega make a strict distinction between *bita bya ngabo* (traditional warfare among Lega and between Lega and neighboring groups) and *elungwano* (the disastrous fights between Lega and the Arab and Arabized slave raiders in the nineteenth century). The latter period (the years of *elungwano*, as the Lega put it) was characterized by the random killing of elders and old people; it was a time of anarchy, for "the one who kills the old ones destroys the land." *Izombo*, a regular war party, stems from the ambush killing of members of one clan by members of another. The offended party then invites the attackers to fight a regular battle at a place in the forest where two hills face each other *(geisambe)* across a deep glen. Only *mapuka* (nonmembers of bwami) engage in the actual fighting; their weapons are shields, spears, bows and arrows, and sharp sticks. The *mapuka*, led by a protagonist, are magically protected by a strong medicine carried to the battlefield by a medicine man *(mugila wa mulende)*. Reconciliation is sought after the first killing.

The Rites of Circumcision. Circumcision *(bwali)* rites, as a preliminary to bwami initiations, are extremely important to the Lega. A male who has not gone through circumcision rites cannot aspire even to the lowest bwami grades. The rites also provide systematic training in activities, behavior patterns, and values. The Lega sometimes assert that in very ancient times circumcision rites were unknown to them, but that clitoridectomy was practiced on women. According to the folk explanation, circumcision replaced the female ceremonies because an excessively high death rate accompanied clitoridectomy.

Females are rigidly excluded from participation in circumcision rites. The wife of the holder of the *musimbi* right, however, may remain in the village while the actual operations take place, but she is blindfolded and carried around in a dance. As compensation, the Lega say, the secrets of childbirth are known only to women. They are thought to be the equivalent of the secrets of circumcision, since the experience of bearing a child ushers a woman into full-fledged adulthood, as circumcision does for a man.

The organization of circumcision ceremonies, held every five or ten years for large groups of young men whose ages range from twelve or fourteen to twenty and more, follows a cyclic pattern. In other words, clans and lineages spread over wide distances are traditionally linked together as circumcision communities. For example, a cycle may begin in the Beigala clan and spread in a fixed order to the Babongolo, to the Banamuningi, to the Banamusiga, to the Banamunyaga, to the Banamugulu, and so to the Beiamisisi. The privilege of initiating such a cycle is vested in the holder of the *musimbi* right.

Lega Culture

Only a few lineages can claim the *musimbi* right. Some hold it by virtue of tradition, which means simply that nobody knows how or where they got it. Other lineages have purchased the right. In both instances, however, it is transmitted to a very close agnate either when the incumbent in the position dies or when he moves up to the lutumbo lwa kindi grade. The recipient must be a member of the ngandu, yananio, or musagi wa kindi grade in the bwami association. No one can hold the *musimbi* right unless he has previously held the other special rights of *musutwa* (the basket of initiation objects linked with the kongabulumbu grade in bwami), and *lutala* (the right to build a separate circumcision lodge) and has transmitted them to appropriate kinsmen. Moreover, a *musimbi* can initiate a circumcision cycle only twice in his lifetime. Ownership of *musutwa* and *lutala* may lead to nothing at all or to the *musimbi* right, or to the right of the pangolin knife. These four rights are not necessarily inherited from the same agnate, but once acquired by a given lineage, they are transmitted within it in a line of very close agnates.

Lega society may be thought of as being composed of a number of circumcision communities, formed by groups of more or less geographically contiguous clans that recognize a special ritual interdependence with one another. Each clan is made up of a number of lineages that are institutionalized at three different genealogical levels. Each clan has a relatively small number of *musimbi* and a larger number of *lutala* holders. The Beiamunsange clan, for example, which is numerically very strong, comprises seven primary lineages and an incorporated segment (Kilimono, or riverain peoples). In only four of the primary lineages is there a *musimbi* holder. Wherever *musimbi* occurs, the rule is that a primary lineage may have only one incumbent. Primary lineages that do not have these rights are numerically weak; territorially they are always linked with lineages that do hold the rights. Each of the seven primary lineages of the Beiamunsange has a number of *lutala* holders. There may be one or more *lutala* rights in a secondary lineage, but never more than one in a tertiary lineage. All told, there are twenty-four incumbents of *lutala* among the Beiamunsange, as opposed to four *musimbi* in the same clan. In the cyclic organization of circumcision rites, a *lutala* has to obtain permission from a *musimbi* to build his own lodge and circumcise the boys of his group. A *musimbi* must obtain the permission from another holder of the right in a primary lineage (in his clan or in another clan) to which his own group is traditionally linked.

A fixed pattern is followed. When a *musimbi* who has the right to initiate a cycle begins the circumcision ceremonies in his village, it is the duty of another *musimbi* (of another clan), who is next in line, to send one boy of his group to these rites to be circumcised and bring back to his own group the *nkola za bwali* (a piece of *ibesebese* wood which symbolizes the transfer) and the ritual musical instruments, mirliton (made of reed and phrynium leaves) and bull-roarer. The second *musimbi* then has the right to set up his own lodge *(lutende)* in the forest, to build his own circumcision fence *(mulu)* in the village, and to proceed to circumcise the boys of his own group. The boys in a *lutala* lineage are circumcised in the village of the *musimbi* on whom they depend; afterward they are sent back to their own lodge to receive further instruction and training.

The period of instruction and training, briefly described by Burk (1956a), lasts for varying lengths of time, sometimes as much as a year. Systematic instruction in the interpretation of proverbs that synthesize moral and legal principles is pursued afterward, almost throughout a man's lifetime. Lega elders use the *mukunga* or the *mutanga* method to instruct the youth in their villages. They hang a variety of miniature objects, representing hundreds of items derived from the natural environment or produced by Lega technology, from a liana to help the boys to conceptualize and identify principles of moral conduct and general wisdom. All the principles are explained in proverbs, or rather in what the Lega call *bitondo bya kisi*, the words of the land. A similar type of instruction, with visual aids, is used in a majority of the subsequent bwami initiations, from the lowest grade to the highest.

Religion

The essential features of Lega religion have recently been analyzed by a young scholar of Lega origin (Mulyumba, 1968). The basic data provided in his work are correct, although some of them pertain more to the eastern than to the western Lega.

My own brief synthesis touches on the features of Lega religion which are particularly relevant to this study. The Lega have no elaborate myths or cosmology. In contrast with other populations in the eastern Congo which own to a large pantheon of divinities, like the Nyanga and the Hunde, or live by a complex system of religious beliefs and practices, like the Luba, the Lega have a rather simple religion. I have always been impressed by the lack of cultual activity among the Lega as opposed to what I found among the related Bembe. The difference is understandable in the light of the bwami association, which is, among other things, comparable to ancient mysteries and to a form of secularized religion. Among groups of Lega who have been subject to strong influences from their neighbors (Bembe, Bangubangu, Shi groups) the cult activity is more pronounced. In fact, it increased throughout the area as bwami declined under the joint attack of missions and colonial administration.

A trinity of beings ultimately rules over the world and men's affairs: Kinkunga, Kalaga, and Kaginga. Kinkunga, the Joiner, is thought of in two ways: as the father of the primordial human couple, Ntu and Ikulu; and as *mubumbi*, a fashioner. He is an incomplete fashioner, however, because

Lega Culture

he is deprived of *lukese,* the shell that potters use to smooth out earthenware. It is therefore the task of Kalaga, who could be characterized as the divine culture hero, to do the smoothing out, that is, to complete the unfinished work of Kinkunga. The folk etymology for Kalaga is adviser-instructor, comparing him with the person who instructs and advises his kinsmen before they set out on a trip or begin a new activity. It is said of Kalaga that "whatsoever he knew to advise me, he has given me advice of." It is certain that, in Lega thinking, Kinkunga represents the male element, the phallus, and that Kalaga represents the female element, the vulva, but these identifications are made without emphasis. In other words, behind the creator and the culture hero the Lega perceive the symbols of fertility, creativity, order, and continuity. Kinkunga and Kalaga are thus the forces that maintain the life of the group and represent *bunene* (good fortune) for the living. Both are opposed to Kaginga, the spirit with the implacable heart who cannot be counseled by the dead and who epitomizes the principles of evil and of evil fortune *(bwanya).* Folk etymology sees a link between Kaginga and *luginga* (a potsherd the Lega say cannot contain the water that was contained in the pot). The Lega, though frequently mentioning Kalaga in prayers, formulas, and daily utterances, address no cult to him.

The ancestors *(basumbu,* or sometimes simply *bakwa,* the dead, or *bakule,* those who have died) are the center of the religious system. They possess a mediating power that can influence, for better or worse, the conflict between good and evil. As intercessors whose effectiveness depends on human action, the ancestors activate *bunene,* whereas sorcerers and witches (thought to be females) activate *bwanya.* Divination, a male technique for locating the sources of evil, tends to reestablish the trend to *bunene* by neutralizing them. The ancestral cult itself is simple. When the oracles attribute misfortune to the displeasure of the dead, simple invocations are made in which Kinkunga and Kalaga may be mentioned in order to implore and induce the ancestors to relent. The soil or the drums are beaten, and small offerings of food are placed on the ground or on a table. For example, if the collective hunting parties that are organized before bwami initiations are unsuccessful, the candidate and his helpers clear a patch in the forest, construct a small offering table, and place a small termite nest on it. Offerings of bananas and peanuts are deposited, and the dead are invoked for hunting success.

Although no theory is woven around the concept, many Lega actions reveal the existence of a strong belief in *magala* (force). This force is undefined and diffuse. Although its nature is unspecified, it is present in everything. The force of the hunting nets, for example, is increased by blowing smoke into them *(kupupa makila).* The ivory statues used by the bwami association contain a force of their own, and their owners consume some of the dirt rubbed from the surface as the ultimate means of warding off disease. The concept of force is clearly manifested in the *manzoko* rites, designed to neutralize the detrimental effects that follow cursing and anger.

The Lega have a number of magical beliefs and practices, including divination, sorcery, magico-therapeutic actions, and the poison ordeal; these are more elaborate among the eastern Lega than in other parts of Legaland. Such beliefs and practices are of little importance for the understanding of bwami and art. It is necessary to realize from them only that the Lega conceive of all females as potential sorcerers, whereas only a few men are guilty of sorcery *(buganga)*. Of the multiplicity of devices used to detect, fight, and punish sorcerers, the ultimate, and conceptually the most efficient, is the bwami initiation, which pretends to have found the techniques that can make people good and render them immune to evil.

The Arts

Since plastic art and various aspects of oral, theatrical, choreographic, and musical arts are discussed in detail in the section on the bwami association, only a general survey is presented here.

The rich oral literature of the Lega comprises riddles, proverbs, aphorisms, songs, paraphrases for the slit-drum, prayers, tales, eulogies, and epics. Only the proverbs, aphorisms, and paraphrases are vital to the understanding of bwami. The same proverbs occur with only minor variations and dialectal differences throughout Legaland. Loanwords from Zimba, Songola, Swahili, or French are extremely rare in these texts. Metaphors, similitudes, and imagery that occur in proverbs are borrowed from the animal and plant world, and then from the geographical environment, technology, and the social system. References to celestial bodies, mythical events, divinities, and ancestors are negligible, but when they do occur they apply strictly to human social situations, as in the following example: "Nyanasana star and moon to separate, [it means] kinship is dead." (The two symbols stand for a high-ranking member of bwami and his initiated wife, who are united until death.) Folk stories and epics frequently contain references to social groups, fictive as well as real, and subtle allusions to peripeties. Proverbs and aphorisms, which are used by the thousands during bwami initiations, are sung and almost always are accompanied by action: music, dance, gesture, display and manipulation of objects (ranging from natural objects to carvings). Many proverbs are self-explanatory, particularly when illustrated by action. Their symbolism is succinct, precise, and clear. Some proverbs are intricate and esoteric. Invariably, proverbs and aphorisms are explained and interpreted by their users, so that the concrete principles to which they refer are elucidated. Most proverbs are self-contained and are used singly to convey a total idea; some are coupled, as in a short imaginary dialogue. Some are linked

Lega Culture

together in sets of ten or more, complementing one another in the course of a dramatic representation.

Different structural types of proverbs can be recognized. Most of them, however, consist of two parts of a short verse.[19] There are various ways in which the two parts of the text complete and extend an idea. In one type the first part establishes an identity between two entities, and the second part applies the concept or draws a conclusion from it:

> The senior [is] a turtle.
> He was born [for] long distances.

This proverb is interpreted to mean that a senior, no matter how far he travels, finds kinsmen and congeners everywhere. In another type the first part introduces two personages (perhaps well known through a tale), and the second part synthesizes an event that happened to them or a pattern of behavior that characterizes them:

> The blue pheasant and the turtle.
> Animals that challenge each other over territory.

In a third type the first part acknowledges a principle, an action, or a situation which the second verse refines or rebukes:

> You may refuse the senior the meat
> [But] you shall give him the liver.

In still another type the first part makes a statement, or a concession, which is contrastively completed in the second part:

> It [*ibulungu* tree] may be somewhat on the side
> But every distance between two rivers has its *ibulungu* tree.

In bwami initiations, the basic themes in the proverbs and aphorisms are death, sorcery, solidarity of the kinship group, continuity, respect for seniors, the idea of power, women, relationships between kinsmen, character traits, grandeur of the bwami association, the moral qualities of initiates and seniors, and relationships between man and his environment. Motifs of fighting, quarreling, arguing, and verbosity are always dealt with pejoratively: they are ridiculed and criticized as wrongdoing.

The praising of people and animals and the transmission of messages on wooden trapezoid slit-drums are of signal importance in bwami rites. All clans and lineages, all full-fledged adult males, and many ritually and economically important animals have a drum name (*lukumbu*), a short, proverb-like, symbolic statement. These hundreds of drum names form a rich poetic repertoire. For example, the drum name of one initiate whom I knew was "Crescent of the moon, those far away look up at him in awe"; of the hornbill, "Loud-Wingbeat, Eater-of-Centipedes, counts the villages, [but] does not count what sticks out above his beak"; of a clan, "The

---

[19] For a similar proverb structure in another Bantu group see Biebuyck (1970). Examples of Lega oral literature are recorded in Biebuyck (1953*d*), Burk (1956*a*, *b*), Delhaise (1909*a*, *passim*), Liétard (1924), and Meeussen (1959, 1961, 1962).

branch of the *mutondo* tree [*Alstonia* sp.], the parrot-folk are in pursuit of it." A man may receive his drum name from any one of a large group of kinsmen, and he keeps it all his life. Since many individuals have the same, or a similar, drum name, it is customary to cite one's father's or even one's grandfather's drum name in conjunction with one's own drum name. Thus, to the drum name "Crescent of the moon, those far away look up at him in awe," is added "Him who left [i.e., son of], Heart of Elephant does not enclose words [arguments]." The initiates, who are called together by means of slit-drums, are also praised by the drummers during the initiations.

Most of the songs and dances in the initiations are accompanied by percussive musical instruments, principally the funnel-shaped membranophone drums, *kimbili* and *mulingati*. The *kimbili* is beaten by two drummers, one using two drumsticks *(mikoko)* on the membrane, the other using two drumsticks on the top part of the wooden frame. The *mulingati* is beaten with the bare hands. In numerous ritual communities the slit-drum is used along with the membranophones. It is beaten on the left side with the bare hand and on the right side with a beater. None of the drums are carried while being used; they are simply placed on the ground and held between the legs of the seated drummers. In a few rites, however, one or two drums may be suspended from a pole near the initiation hut. In message drumming, the slit-drum is suspended from the shoulder by means of a rope and is held perpendicular to and against the belly.

The *mulingati* is the main drum; it beats the basic rhythm and, in addition, makes improvisations to blame, praise, or encourage the dancers. Rattles *(mizegele)* made of wickerwork or other material are the only instruments used in accompaniment with the drums. Three or four drummers and a couple of rattle shakers make up the orchestra. With them sit a few male singers. Invariably, the choir includes one initiated woman, called *nyagwamana*, who excels because of her strident voice. All initiates participating in the dance sing with the choir. Specialized musical instruments, derived from circumcision ceremonies and used in some bwami rites, include mirlitons, signal sticks (carried under the armpit), a tube of parasol wood which is held in an empty pot and blown, iron axes and drumsticks, bone scepters, and bull-roarers.

The dances are theatrical but not spectacular. Usually the initiates move in a wide circle following one another in a fixed sequence: the preceptors come first, then the males in descending order of grade, and finally the initiated females. Frequently a preceptor with his aides moves to the circle to perform solos. The dance begins as the dancers move slowly away from the orchestra, in the form of a circle, constantly making half-turns and working up to a fast and nervous rhythm. Much of the beauty of the dance is determined by hip movements, which cause the paraphernalia (feathers, hides, and leaves worn around the waist) to shiver and tremble,

Lega Culture

and by gracious movements and gestures of arms and hands. Almost without exception, initiatory objects are carried in the hands of the leaders of the circle of dancers. To express their joy, the dancers frequently caress (with a milking movement) the animal hides they wear around their waists. Kinsmen and other dancers honor them by symbolically wiping the sweat from their faces. The dances and the gestures often underscore and make explicit the meanings contained in the sung proverbs. For example, a proverb like "Nyaluluba brings together Mamba" becomes clear only in a dance context. The circle of dancers splits into two rows, the leaders of the rows carrying, respectively, a piece of raffia cloth and a piece of bark cloth. First the two rows dance away from each other; then they dance back and join, thereby bringing together the raffia and the bark cloth. The meaning of the proverb is thus made clear: people first disperse and then later come back together in the village of the great initiate who calls them for the ceremonies.

Values

Large groups of Lega elders sometimes hold reunions in the evening, gathering to smoke and chat. At these meetings, which usually turn into political sessions where old and new patterns of living are compared and evaluated, it is consistently stated that three things outrank all else in importance: *ibuta* (fertility and kinship), *bwali* (circumcision), bwami (association). Lega men want to have many children, and for that reason they like to be linked with many wives in stable unions. Without children, a real marriage bond does not exist; barrenness is the chief cause of divorce or contempt. Children offer economic and moral support and help to broaden the field of kinship relations, but there cannot be many children, the Lega contend, unless the marriage bond is a stable one. In one of their supreme bwami rituals, the Lega have created a lasting bond between husband and wife. Kinship relations ramify in all directions: "As are the hairs on the body, so are the kinship relations." Solidarity and cooperation within a wide field of kinship relations must continually be activated and consolidated through visiting, gifts, exchanges, restraint, and respect.

Circumcision is not merely a physical operation or a short-lived ritual; it is a systematic education and training in values, techniques, and behavior patterns. It is the initial stage that leads to the moral perfection achieved at the highest levels of bwami. No uncircumcised male can ever hope to enter the association; he would be regarded as an idiot if he tried to do so. Bwami, as the perpetual search for moral excellence, beauty, prestige, wealth, authority, and power, is the goal of Lega life. In theory, it is open to everyone in the society. In practice, most males and a considerable number of their wives achieve one level or another in bwami.

As explained later in the discussion of bwami and art, the Lega place a high value on generosity, equity, moderation, dignity, loyalty, good faith, and cooperation, virtues that are thoroughly cultivated in bwami. Because no one must show weakness in the exercise of such qualities, fame, lavishness in giving, perseverance, individual effort, wealth, joy, and relaxation are also highly rated.

FOREIGN ATTITUDES TOWARD THE LEGA AND BWAMI

In their restless struggles against slave raiders and ivory traders, the Lega acquired the reputation of fierceness. David Livingstone's journal entry on October 20, 1870 (1875, p. 337), reflects their pugnacity: "The Balégga were very unfriendly [toward Hassani and his party], and collected in thousands. 'We come to buy ivory,' said Hassani, 'and, if there is none, we go away.' 'Nay,' shouted they, 'You come to die here!' and then they shot with arrows; when musket balls were returned they fled, and would not come to receive the captives." In August 1874, Verney Cameron, having reached Nyangwe on the southwestern outskirts of Legaland, wrote in similar terms (1877, pp. 268–269): "One party who had been a long way to north-northeast, and reached Ulegga, had especially suffered, having lost over two hundred out of their total strength of three hundred. They described the natives as being very fierce and warlike, and using poisoned arrows, a mere scratch from which proved fatal in four or five minutes, unless an antidote, known only to the natives, was immediately applied."

What impressed the members of such parties was not so much the fierceness of the people as the vastness and inhospitality of the forest habitat. Writing on December 10, 1870, Livingstone complained about the hardships (1875, p. 348): "I am sorely let and hindered in this Manyuema [forest]. Rain every day, and often at night. I could not travel now, even if I had men, but I could make some progress. This is the sorest delay I ever had. I look above for help and mercy." And Cameron added a word about the difficulties of traveling (1877, pp. 268–269): "Ulegga was, they said, a country of large mountains wooded to the summits, and valleys filled with such dense forest that they traveled four and five days in succession without seeing the sun." Lieutenant Glorie (1898–99), who was the first to cross Legaland from west to east, said little about the people but much about the hostile environment. Cordella (1906) has a sympathetic comment on the Lega: "Il carattere dei Warega è dolce; credo che siano i migliori tra le razzeche to visitato." The fear in which the Lega were held by the Arabs and their aides gave rise to what Delhaise (1909a, p. 85) has called "de nombreuses histoires fantaisistes," particularly with reference to cannibalism (of which Cordella [1906, p. 976] said, referring to the Lega, "sono degli antropofaghi convinti"). Ritual cannibalism was in fact practiced after war expeditions, probably on a larger scale during the

Lega Culture

decades of suffering than at other times. By the time Delhaise was working among the Lega, however, all such practices had disappeared (1909a, p. 85).

Delhaise was the first to live among the Lega for a considerable period of time. He was a member of the Dhanis expeditions against the mutineers in 1896, and from 1905 to 1906 he was in charge of the Kabambare section, then in the Maniema district. Finally, he was in command of the territoire Warega. He speaks in the most favorable terms and sometimes with great precision about the Lega. From his reports it would seem that the Lega owed their reputation of fierceness largely to hearsay and to the ferocious battles they fought against raiders and traders (*ibid.*, p. 355): "Les Warega ont toujours vécu le plus loin possible des postes arabes. L'occupation du pays par les Mahométans n'a d'ailleurs pas été facile. Les guerres qu'ils eurent à soutenir pour s'installer d'abord, pour affermir leur autorité ensuite, ont été des plus sanglantes."

On the contrary, Belgian troops encountered no special difficulties in occupying Legaland (*ibid.*, p. 355). According to Delhaise (*ibid.*, p. 359), the Lega were grateful people whenever they were well treated: "J'aurais pu me rendre dans n'importe quelle partie du pays, seul et sans armes, en parfaite sécurité." No wonder then that he (*ibid.*, pp. 49–50) spoke about them in terms that were, at the time of writing, remarkably conciliatory: "Le caractère est plutot mélancolique. Leur sourire parait triste; on ne voit pas chez eux de manifestation de franche gaîté. Leur extérieur dénote la franchise et la sincérité. Souvent ils ont un air bon enfant qui prévient en leur faveur. . . . Les Warega sont plutot calmes et ne deviennent violents et emportés que quand ils subissent l'action du chanvre qu'ils fument rarement."

Many of Delhaise's remarks about the Lega, their culture, and their character are highly pertinent. He shows them to be extremely attached to their culture (*ibid.*, pp. 54, 95), to be critical of European action against their customs (p. 54), to be peaceful (p. 54), to be fond of hunting (p. 54) and of tobacco (p. 81), to be sober in drinking (p. 83), to appreciate aged and putrefied meat (p. 85). They are so bound up in the bwami initiations (p. 95) that individuals who have worked for Europeans use their savings to become members of the association: "le désir d'obtenir des grades dans la hiérarchie sociale tient une place énorme dans la vie des Warega." The Lega are extremely concerned with sorcery (p. 149 n. 1); they severely punish liars (p. 161). Theft and swindling are rare (p. 221). Women are highly respected (p. 169), as also old and sick people (p. 189). The Lega are sincere and frank (p. 221); they keep their word in dealings among themselves but are not faithful in their relationships with Europeans (pp. 221–222). They are charitable and hospitable (p. 222). They are intelligent (p. 293); they make good observers (p. 295). Their philosophy is fatalistic (p. 225).

All in all, these observations are strikingly unbiased. As a Belgian administrator, Delhaise lived close to the Lega and learned to understand and appreciate them in depth, as no official after him ever succeeded in doing. Regardless of their many prejudices, the Europeans who lived among the Lega in later years generally appreciated their qualities of gentleness, poise, and wisdom.

The real confrontation between the European authorities and the Lega centered on the bwami association.[20] In a segmentary lineage system, this association was the only well-organized body of elders, and it was drawn together from many lineages, villages, and clans. Bwami was the real political force in Lega society, the only force that could organize people for counteraction or for passive resistance. Moreover, the initiations and the preparations for them were so time- and energy-consuming that eventually they kept the people from meeting the new demands made by the colonial government.

The *Recueil à l'usage des fonctionnaires et des agents du service territorial au Congo Belge* (Ministère des Colonies, 1925, p. 65; hereafter cited as *Rufast*, 1925), which outlined for colonial administrators the basic principles of *politique indigène*, stated that respect for custom was a legal obligation and a principle of native policy and warned that nonrecognition of native custom would produce disequilibrium and create animosity. The legal force of customs could be denied only "lorsqu'elles sont contraires à la législation écrite ou à l'ordre public" (*Rufast*, 1925, p. 65). It was recognized that certain customs, depending on the manner in which they were applied, could be contrary to law and public order, but that the principles on which they were based could still be sound. Such customs could be accepted only after undergoing modifications that stripped them of their censurable character. Of all customs, the widespread, esoteric, and closed initiations leading to membership in voluntary associations were the most vulnerable. The attitude to adopt vis-à-vis the "secret sects" was one of caution (*ibid.*, pp. 351–352; Piron, 1954, I, 875–877). Administrators were to make an effort to discover the aims, the practices, the membership, the location, and the distribution of these associations by external means, but definitely not by personal initiation. Administrative and judicial measures were called for only when the associations favored infractions or immoral acts, or when they exhibited a political attitude that was hostile toward the new authority. The ordinance of August 25, 1937 (no. 92/AIMO, 6 bis), stipulated that a provincial governor could dissolve any hierarchically organized, native association or sect whose existence threatened tranquillity and the public order. The ordinance of January 14, 1941, went a step further in providing that, if

---

[20] Biebuyck (1954b, 1967) examines the disastrous effects of the suppression of the bwami association on the artistic patrimony of the Lega.

such action was urgently needed, the district commissioner could order the dissolution of a sect, and that a chief territorial administrator could, in the same emergency, order a temporary suspension of all activities of the association or sect.

It is well to keep these principles in mind when examining the various ways in which the all-pervading bwami association was judged and handled. Delhaise (1909a, pp. 228–239, 241, 337–338, 343) made several pertinent judgments about bwami: it is not a secret religious sect but an aristocracy or, better yet, a social hierarchy (p. 241); it is accessible to all and is based on the distribution of wealth (p. 338). But there is some confusion in Delhaise's interpretation. He qualifies the higher grades of bwami as a secret society whose aim is political. He also reports, without further comment, that he has often heard the kindi (members of the highest grade) being accused of criminal behavior.

Little is known about the fate of bwami during the dramatic period of slave raiding and the early rule of the Congo Free State. The documents that would provide the information are nonexistent; it seems that many of the early travelers in the eastern Congo did not really visit the heart of Legaland, but were moving along its rim and frequently reporting from hearsay. The Lega oral tradition makes little mention of this somber period. According to an early Belgian source, Arabs and Arabisés fought bwami by destroying the insignia of the association and threatening to take the life of all those who persisted in exhibiting them. Information provided by the Lega themselves, although scanty, confirms this conclusion. Judging from the enormous number of old insignia left in Legaland in the 1950's, however, the Arabisés, and later the Westerners who fought bwami, although definitely causing much human misery and pain, were not at all successful in destroying the artistic treasures of the Lega or in undermining the relevance of bwami.

The earliest administrative report, written in 1916 by an official working in what was then called Elila territory, is unfavorable. Maintaining that bwami annihilates the authority of the chiefs, the writer of the report expresses regret that many chiefs are bwami members. Bwami's most serious offense, vis-à-vis the government, is that it hampers all efforts at regrouping people and propagating Western ideas. Other adverse reports were written in 1917 and 1918 by administrators working among the Lega, the Bembe, and neighboring groups. One of them, although conceding that "only those were admitted whose wisdom and probity were recognized," concludes that "this social and moral institution is, in reality, only a vulgar exploitation of the native. Its power must be destroyed."

Another report of that time criticizes the spirit of domination that animates the initiates. They want to be regarded as absolute masters; they demand a real cult; they admit no discussion. Later accounts (1920) accuse bwami members of having poisoned certain people and of resisting the payment of taxes. In 1922 an administrator, asked what he thought about bwami, replied: "Every mwami who is encountered in the territory of upper Ulindi will be brought before a police court." A year later the same official deemed the bwami influence "detrimental, first, for our occupation, and second, for the evolution of the population toward a better state." Another document of 1923 says that "chiefs and notables" complain about bwami because it undermines their authority by "living from theft and rapine at the expense of the collectivity." It concludes that "bwami hampers progress because its procedures are opposed to the leading principles of colonial policy." Refreshingly, a 1923 report written by the administrator of the Elila territory gives a different point of view. It asserts that bwami is not a secret society but a social organization; that it is characterized by a broad democratic spirit; that it is a guardian of moral austerity; that it is "the cement, the cohesive force of the Warega texture." In contrast, a higher official in the province reported in 1927 that "according to my instructions this sect has been fought without respite since 1923. This action must be continued." In 1929, however, another document says that the good results of suppressing bwami are "only apparent," and that there has been an attempt to reestablish it. Yet in 1930 another administrator pompously claims that bwami is "consciously hierarchized theft, based on the credulity and self-conceit of the new rich," and that "Lega society is complete without bwami." The same report indicates that the means of action then used by bwami were passive resistance, the "one mouth" [verbal solidarity] policy, and poison.

An outside observer, Major Clarke (1929, p. 67), briefly discusses the "once powerful sect or society known as mwami" which appears "to have fallen into much disrepute of late." Two factors, he maintains, have caused the decline. First, more and more Lega are "able to find work and, after a year or so away, to return and buy positions in the mwami which before were only granted for ability." Second, the bwami association has opposed the whites and "endeavoured to stir up sedition," but "the rising was put down, and the Mwami had to content themselves by passing a rule that no Mwami would work for a white man or pay the white man's taxes." A report of 1931 summarizes the prevailing grievances of the administration against bwami: (1) certain aspects of the female initiations are immoral (because women appear naked before initiates during the bulonda and bunyamwa rites); (2) members of the highest grade appropriate the property of others; (3) bwami applies the poison ordeal; (4) bwami encourages polygyny; (5) it hinders, by means of terror, the real authority of the customary chiefs invested with power by the administration; (6) it opposes the introduction of new crops and of new methods of agriculture; (7) from a certain grade on, the members of bwami do not work.

In sharp contrast, a report by Governor Moeller in 1932 is moderate in tone, suggesting that it is vain to attribute certain wrongs merely to

Lega Culture

bwami. In 1934 an administrator noted that "this elite used to possess wealth, political authority, and, in the eyes of the noninitiates, an occult power. In its recent evolution, this aristocratic cast has no longer rigidly respected the traditional rules, and therefore the number of adepts has considerably increased." In his well-known work, *Les grandes lignes des migrations des Bantous,* Moeller (1936, pp. 39, 135, 295, 316, 405–411, 463), abstaining from interpretations and evaluations, restricts his analysis to a fair description of the grade structure, based on data provided by two administrators in Legaland.

From 1936 to 1948 there was almost no mention in the administrative documents of bwami activities among the Lega. Indeed, there was a lull in such activities before World War II. For a while, inspired perhaps by Moeller's reports, the administration seems to have gotten along with the association. A 1940 report on bwami among the Bembe of Fizi noted the increasing activity of bwami, particularly in the northwestern parts of Bembeland which are in contact with the Lega. Within a year, the document states, about a hundred initiation ceremonies were held in the Lulenge sector alone.

Then suddenly, in 1948, a rapid series of events led to the dissolution of bwami. The action apparently originated with a school report emanating from the vicariate in Baudouinville, which was sent to the governor-general of the Congo without the knowledge of the administrative authorities of Kivu Province. As quoted in a letter from the secretary-general of the government-general to the governor of Kivu Province (June 22, 1948), the school report observed that during an inspection of schools in western Legaland, the monsignor had found schools without children or with only limited attendance. The teachers or *moniteurs,* as they were called, invariably attributed the truancy to preoccupation with circumcision rites and traditional initiations being held at the time. The monsignor was vehement in condemning the circumcision rites as having a "detrimental effect on civilization and on education," thus giving a "deadly blow to discipline." The lack of discipline in turn led to the moral perversion of the children who, "during their sojourn in the bush, are entirely under the influence of the bwami initiates." The letter concluded with a summary of remarks made by the superior at one of the mission stations. In his opinion, all sensible Lega, chiefs and simple subjects alike, wanted the bwami sect to be suppressed. They all regretted that the interdictions imposed upon bwami fifteen years earlier had been lifted: "The day that will see the final interdiction of bwami, with sanctions against any wearer of insignia, against any festivity, against every chief still allowing bwami within his region, will be a relief for the entire country."

A reaction from the local administration soon followed. In a letter to the governor-general, one of the highest authorities in Kivu Province formulated the objections against bwami: (1) The hierarchical bwami sect is a secret organization whose political activities cannot be controlled. Killings by means of poison and strangulation are secretly perpetuated by the sect. (2) Lega and Bembe societies would be complete without the bwami organization. (3) The association is antisocial. (4) The secret character of bwami prevents the European authorities from acting directly against the organization, which therefore becomes an obstacle to civilizing action. The result was almost immediate. Arrêté no. 21,427 of August 6, 1948 (*Bulletin Administratif du Congo Belge*, Sept. 25, 1948, p. 2660), dissolved bwami: "Attendu que la secte hiérarchisée des bami, notamment dans les territoires de Fizi, Shabunda, Pangi, et Kindu, constitue une menace pour la tranquillité et 'ordre publics: arrête: la secte hiérarchisée des Bami est dissoute."

In 1949 an official in southwestern Legaland reported that, in general, the decree had been very effective. The few reunions that were still going on had been tacitly allowed to continue by the local administration because their apparent purpose was to liquidate the payment of debts for past initiations, and so on. Ironically, about this time one member of the association was condemned by a local police court "for having prohibited his wife from following the catechism lessons" on the ground that it was against the principle of freedom of cult! Bwami was not destroyed, however, by the severe sanctions that were imposed on the organization of initiations and on the exercise of bwami power and authority. There were too many initiates in Legaland; bwami was too tightly interwoven with the kinship structure; bwami was too essential to Lega society for colonial opposition to be really effective. Although many of its members were insulted, degraded, fined, imprisoned, or banished from their villages, and although its rituals could not be held publicly, bwami, as an organizing principle, continued to remain the central force in Legaland.

Shortly before my arrival in Legaland in 1951, administrators were again reporting on bwami, some objectively describing certain aspects of its organization, others repeating the old slogans. When I undertook the systematic study of bwami in 1952 and 1953, the administration was most understanding; there was no opposition to the project and I was able to organize the cycles of initiation without interference. Many officials had gradually convinced themselves that it was a mistake to fight bwami because, as one of them put it to me in 1952, in the context of the new social, political, and economic forces that were reshaping the country, bwami was destined to lose many of its original functions and to become more of a folkloristic group. By 1957 many officials were convinced that the ban against bwami was to be lifted, but Catholic missionaries continued to make strong objections. The rapid development of nationalism and the drive for independence in the Congo halted any further colonial action in favor of bwami. When I revisited the Lega in 1958, I found most of the high-ranking initiates showing considerable concern about the number of false accusations leveled against them. To defend their position, they pointed out that none of the cases of theft, sedition, passive resistance, or quarrels with appointed chiefs handled by district tribunals had involved members of the association. They also referred to one of their frequently stated ethical principles: "A member of bwami may fall back in poverty, but poverty is no shame; it is no reason to become a thief." An initiate always remains an initiate: "He who has given you a parrot has also given you its feathers." Poverty and destitution are bearable according to Lega aphorisms: "Even though you are poor, even though you remain with poverty until death, it is all right," and "Even though you lack [things] in the forest, provided you are not beaten by rain, it is all right!" To be persecuted and haunted in addition to such ills, however, causes unbearable suffering.

Leaving aside prejudice, ignorance, and the lack of method and perspicacity which underlie the misconception about bwami, it is possible to find other reasons for the misunderstanding and the ostracism of the bwami association. No government official in Legaland was able to penetrate the complexities of its structure and its ideology. Many of them witnessed "staged" dances and other activities, but nobody was admitted into the arcana to gain full knowledge of the organization and its rites. In a society without chiefs, bwami members hold political power. They are accustomed to acting together as one body according to the principle, "An initiate [is] a beggar for mercy; he is not used to speaking alone." Bwami members are deeply attached to their local values, their patterns of living, and their ideologies. Therefore they became weary of the constant manipulation of their lives and customs by outside forces. Deep melancholy and disappointment were constantly being expressed in such proverbial statements as "Chicken is beaten by rain; the feathers are hanging" (Since bwami was banned, we are cold), and "Each forest shed is supported by poles; ours is broken!" Bwami initiates could not comprehend that change had to be so radical: "In taking the ripe banana away from the small child, it is befitting to leave the snot in its nose" (The sweet taste of snot will be a replacement for the loss of the sweetness of the ripe banana). In Lega thinking, deprivation is bearable, but not destitution: "The small child of the elephant hunter is deprived of the elephant [meat]; it is not deprived of the *yanga* trap."

Part 3 The Bwami Association

Introduction

   Bwami represents, in Lega thinking, the essence and the ultimate goal of life. To have solid kinship relationships, to go through the intensive training and educational process of the circumcision rites, and to rear many children are primary endeavors that lead to bwami, particularly to advancement in bwami. Bwami permeates everything. It is everywhere, like "roasting packages that are spread all over the lowland, that are spread all over the highland." Like the banana trees that grow all over Legaland, bwami is perpetual. It stretches out through a person's life and through the social organization like "a row of villages in a giant stretch of forest between two rivers [*mutandi mulazi*]." Bwami is "something that sticks, that leaves a trace [*kyandanda*]."
   Bwami is many things in one. It has the structure and some of the functions of a voluntary association, but it also maintains and reinforces kinship, lineage, and clan bonds. Access to and advancement in bwami are conditioned by a number of factors: character, kinship support, wealth, initiation. The initiations aim at moral perfection, the principles of which are elaborately explained in proverbs, dances, and objects. Bwami is therefore a moral philosophy. It is also an arts club, for it enjoys and patronizes the fine arts. It is a school of art because it creates, produces, uses, and explains thousands of pieces of sculpture. Bwami has developed its own literary arts, its dances and musical styles, dramatic performances,

The Bwami Association

choreographies, and architectural styles. It is like a big corporation that produces wealth, distributes and redistributes it, invests and reinvests it, and provides economic incentive. Bwami is a religion, a religion without gods, pretending to have a power of its own and to master the secrets of making life good. Bwami is a tremendous and exclusive social force: "Bwami, spots of leopard, they frighten the sheep," and "Leopard, the noiseless one, does not mix up with goats."

In the segmentary society with which it is deeply interwoven, bwami represents the effective system of power and authority. It fosters a sense of unity; it is the basis for group action. Sometimes the initiates refer to themselves as "the ones who assemble, we are gathered together [*bakonge twakongana*]." This point of view is revealed both in theory and in practice. The Lega say, "He who gives you the little spear with the sharp point gives you war; he who gives you the walking stick from the raffia [symbol of bwami] gives you *kisi*." (*Kisi* is a word that simultaneously means land, power, authority, wealth, and wisdom, or everything that is relevant for a Lega.) The Lega also say, "The *nkamba* [fish] folks do not carry those who are not of their group."

In practice, bwami can act effectively against slave raiding, colonial administration, and missionary activity, and can prevent the introduction and spread of new institutions and ideas, indigenous or foreign. Among ethnic groups in neighboring territories like Kindu, Kibombo, Kasongo, Kabambare, Fizi, Lubutu, and Walikale, Islam had managed to establish itself to a certain extent, but bwami kept Islam out of Legaland.[1] In areas near Legaland, such as Lubutu, Masisi, Lubero, Walikale, northern Shabunda, and northern Kindu, the Kitawala prophetic movement had successfully infiltrated, but bwami kept it out of Legaland.[2] Scores of old and new associations, sometimes with xenophobic overtones, developed in areas bordering on Legaland. New movements, such as Toni Toni of the Boyo and Sawasawa of the northern Binja, were unable to get started among the Lega in the late 1940's and early 1950's. The earlier spread of associations like Kabangila among the Boyo and the Bangubangu (to fight sorcery), Mambila among the Komo, and Punga among the Luba and the Bembe (to fight the destructive influences of death and sorcery and to provide members with wealth and make them invulnerable) did not affect Legaland simply because bwami, in a much more refined style, pretended to have the solution for all such troubles.[3]

---

[1] On Islam's spread and impact in the eastern Congo, see Anciaux (1949) and Ceulemans (1959).

[2] There are several interesting studies on the organization and activities of Kitawala in the eastern Congo (cf. Kaufmann, 1964). Biebuyck (1957) discusses the impact of Kitawala on Komo society.

[3] De Jonghe (1923, 1936) and Comhaire (1955) discuss the origin and spread of secret societies and associations.

Varieties of Bwami

The terms "mwami" and "bami" (members or initiates) and bwami (the institution) are widely used among several Bantu-speaking populations living on both sides of Lakes Kivu and Tanganyika, in the eastern Congo, southern Uganda, Rwanda, Burundi, and northern Tanzania. On the Congo side "mwami" designates certain officeholders and incumbents of social positions among Lega, Bembe, Shi, Havu, Vira, Furiiru, Nyindu, Kanu, Tembo, Hunde, Nyanga, Konjo, Kwame, Komo, Pere, Nande, and others. The term "bwami" had to do with a variety of social positions, customs, and institutions. Despite wide differences in form and content, the underlying philosophy of these institutions, as reflected in the procedures, the texts, and to some extent the materials of the initiations, is basically the same. In fact, such populations as Lega, Bembe, Nyindu, Vira, Furiiru, Kanu, and Konjo, with whom I discussed these matters at length, trace the origin of the bwami institution, as each of them knows it, back to the Itombwe region (a mountainous area on the border between Mwenga and Fizi territories, where Lega, Bembe, and Nyindu converge). In the historical development of bwami, Pygmies (Mbuti or Mbote), local aboriginal groups of unknown origin, such as the people of Mwenembumbano and the Baenda, and groups of recorded origin, such as Basim'minje, Banyindu, Balenge, and Lega, played a role.

In the eastern Congo the term "bwami" relates to two different but mutually nonexclusive institutions: exercise of power and authority on the one hand; initiation (meaning paideia) and the resulting knowledge and moral behavior on the other. In general terms one can conceive of bwami as a set of institutions whereby officeholding and the exercise of power and authority are achieved through a process of intensive learning condensed in initiation ceremonies to which one is admitted by consensus on the ground of moral aptitude. The fusion of both concepts is illustrated by the folk etymologies. The Lega perceive a semantic relationship between bwami and the verbs *kwima*, to be able to, and *kwimana*, to help one to stand up, to erect, to make straight. In this manner they emphasize the educational aspect of initiation and the value of moral and intellectual excellence. It is worthy of note that in recent years the Lega have used the verb *kwima* to translate the Swahili term *kusoma* which, according to Sacleux (1941), means to read, to learn by reading or reciting, to study. The Nyanga see the connection between bwami and the verb *iima*, to be strong, to be famous, to rule.[4]

In common parlance "bwami" designates two things among the Lega: (1) the complex voluntary association with its elaborate system of initia-

---

[4] The context in which the abstract concept *wami* is used in Nyanga oral literature clearly indicates that it is equivalent to the French *pouvoir*, which carries the double connotation of ability and authority.

The Bwami Association

tions; and (2) a small hat or skullcap, the most important emblem of membership in the association. Members in all grades and positions must always wear the skullcap, which is made of fibers heavily imbued with camwood powder and is adorned with a wild banana tree seed (*kizombo*) for the lower grades and with four cowries for the higher levels. Affixed to a tuft of hair on the back of the skull, it is worn underneath the larger hats of wickerwork or hide which mark the different grade levels. In Lega thinking the verb *kwima* (to be able to, to be capable of) stands for the ritual placing of the skullcap on the head. The semantic connections are clear. The mwami is not simply allowed to wear the bwami skullcap, but is capable, through appropriate initiatory experience, of supporting the mystic burden of the skullcap.

The groups that live in the zone where Lega, Bembe, and Nyindu meet recognize three varieties of bwami:

1. *Bwami bwa ishungwe*: *Ishungwe*, the central symbol of this form of bwami, is either a piece of wickerwork that contains vegetal and animal ingredients used as medicine or a bundle of iguana skin adorned with a leopard tooth and small horseshoe-shaped copper plates. *Ishungwe* is sometimes identified with red parrot feathers.

2. *Bwami bwa lusembe*: *Lusembe*, the central symbol, is a large cowrie shell protruding from a hat or diadem.

3. *Bwami bwa kikumbu*: *Kikumbu* (*'e'umbu* or *mukuba* in some Lega dialects) is the generic term for all hats that are made of hide or wickerwork and are adorned with different configurations of beads, shells, and other natural objects. A member's position in the hierarchy of the bwami association can be read from the material of which his hat is made and the types of objects used to decorate it. This form of bwami is sometimes referred to as *bwami bwa isengo*, *isengo* being the generic term for all the initiation objects manipulated and explained in the rites.

The Lega, Bembe, and Nyindu groups that are aware of the three types of bwami attempt to account for the differences among them. The story begins in 'Angele, a place in the Itombwe Mountains thought to be the cradle of the pre-Lega and pre-Bembe groups now identified as Basim'minje, Balenge, Basi'asumba, and Banyindu. A group of people led by Kingonya Sunguti and Kaluku left 'Angele to settle in Kitumba, where they met with a certain Mwenembumbano, identified simply as "a man of the bush." Mwenembumbano knew *bwami bwa ishungwe*. Somehow, bwami power in this group came to be identified with the possession of a stool. When Mwenembumbano stood up to help the visitors get dry around a fire, Kaluku sat down on his stool and subsequently refused to leave it. Thus Kaluku seized upon a new form of bwami-ship and was recognized as a mwami by his followers. 'Alenga, a relative of Kalungu's and early head of the Basimwenda clan among the Lega, was also established in the Itombwe area. He had his own form of bwami called *bwami bwa lusembe*. The third variety of bwami is considered to have originated with the southern and western Lega groups.

The true meaning of the distinction among the types of bwami lies in the differentiation of the forms of political organization found among adjoining and/or related populations in Kivu Province. Among such peoples as Vira, Furiiru, Nyindu, Tembo, Havu, Shi, Hunde, and Nyanga, the society is subdivided into a number of autonomous states, varying in size and membership. The king, or paramount, of a state is called mwami, regardless of the number of people or the extent of the land under his rule. Kabare, one of the mwami of the Shi, has 100,000 subjects scattered in thousands of homesteads across his state. Among the Tembo or the Nyanga a mwami has control over only a few villages and their dependent hamlets, jointly inhabited by a few hundred people.

Nevertheless, the character of bwami-ship in these societies is essentially the same. The successor to kingship is a descendant (in the jural more than the biological sense) of the ruling king by his ritual wife (*mumbo, nyangoma*). She is thought to be a close relative of the king's; in some systems she is classified as the king's half sister or as his uterine brother's daughter whereas in others she is his matrilateral cross-cousin. After the enthronement ceremonies, and usually before she has her first child, the ritual wife is sent away from the king's village to live in seclusion in a hamlet of her own, under the supervision and guardianship of one of the highest-ranking titleholders in the state (*shemwami* among the Nyanga; *nabaganda* among the Vira). The successor is "unknown" and unannounced for about a year after the death of the ruler.

The king is surrounded by a number of ritual and political officeholders. Some are counselors who are directly connected with the exercise of political office (*bakungu* among the Nyanga; *bagingi* or *banyambala* among the Vira); others are concerned with the education, enthronement, and spiritual welfare of the king (*bandirabitambo* among the Nyanga; *bazyoga* among the Vira). These societies have one or more royal clans. Excluding the king, few members of a royal clan are entrusted with special political or ritual functions. The most important political and ritual positions are occupied by members of the clans of the exodus (frequently there are seven).

In all these societies the king is regarded as divine in nature. He is allegedly born of an incestuous union between close relatives. Because the king's wife lives a secret life away from the capital village, the origin of her son, who becomes king later on, is always unknown and somewhat mysterious. Among some groups like the Vira the enthronement rites included, in earlier times, a human sacrifice; the king-elect was to walk in

The Bwami Association

human blood at the public announcement of his selection. The state's well-being and survival are linked with the strength of the king. Among the Furiiru the king is increaser of the land (*muruta*), unifier of the people (*kirunga*), and peacemaker in the land (*lenge*). When the king is too sick or too old to embody these ideals, he is ritually and secretly disposed of (usually by strangulation) by the very ritual experts who enthroned him. These men are also in charge of the most important royal symbols: drums, stool, and *ishungwe*. The king's power, or the power of kingship, is thought to reside ultimately in *ishungwe*. In ethnic groups where this centralized type of bwami occurs, the original symbols of *ishungwe* have been merged with those of *lusembe*. In general, *ishungwe* consists of a diadem with a giant cowrie-like shell attached to it (as among the Vira) or of a hat made from a flying squirrel or a potto (as among the Nyanga) to which certain material objects like teeth, shells, and the like are attached.

The *bwami bwa lusembe* tradition is connected with the existence of clan chiefs among the eastern Lega and the Bembe. It is particularly striking in large clan groups like the Basimwenda among the Lega and the Basim'minje among the Bembe. Both groups trace an ancient origin in the Itombwe Mountains. In the course of time it seemed apparent that the character of these clan chiefs was substantially altered by the influences of *bwami bwa kikumbu*, which was brought into the Itombwe region and into Bembeland by the Babongolo (a Lega clan). Originally, the clan chief seems to have been more than a primus inter pares among the heads of lineages that made up the clan. Like a king in the state system, the clan chief was installed by ritual experts from the Basango clan. These experts, who guarded the skulls of deceased clan chiefs, were in charge of the skull cult which symbolized clan unity.

Bwami bwa kikumbu is the central concern of this study. A hierarchically organized voluntary association based on a sophisticated system of initiations and achievements, it admits both male and female members from all existing social groupings in Legaland. In this book the terms bwami and mwami, used without further specification, refer to the *bwa kikumbu* variety of bwami.

Grades, Levels, and Ritual Cycles

Bwami, like other voluntary associations in Africa, is built on an intricate hierarchical system of grades and subdivisions. The bwami association is found throughout Legaland as well as among a number of more or less intimately related neighbors of the Lega. Legaland is inhabited by many different groups of people who have had different experiences; some of them, although largely Lega in culture, are not of Lega origin. There are also substantial variations in the degree to which Lega elements are present among neighboring groups, and in the extent and depth to which these groups are influenced by Lega culture or have influence over it. The bwami organization operates within the framework of kinship groups and of territorially based, autonomous ritual communities.

These groupings, to some extent, have a life of their own. They can modify the organization of bwami by borrowing, inventing, synthesizing, eliminating, reducing, or expanding some of its local elements. Part of this process is an adaptive response to local experiences and problems; part of it is owing to the fact that bwami encourages diversity and inventiveness. The Lega, keenly conscious of these local variations, cultivate them: "Let us put together bwami; each clan puts together its own" (i.e., its bwami). Ethnohistorical accounts are filled with instances of the acquisition of new rites, new cycles of rites, new levels in grades, and even new grades. The rights to set up new initiations are bought and sold between clans and ritual communities, often through the intermediary of in-law and cognatic relationships. These modifications affect the ways of doing things (e.g., the content and number of rites, cycles, and levels; the types of initiation objects and their interpretation) rather than the structural principles that underlie the organization. For example, some ritual communities do not have the higher grades of bwami; some have more of the intermediate levels and steps than others. Invariably, however, the actual hierarchic order of the grades remains the same, and local variations have little effect on the ideology of bwami, which remains constant throughout Legaland.

There are four basic types of grade hierarchies in bwami. Among the northern Banyindu the hierarchy extends from the lowest grade, kalemba ('alemba), through hengwe (hingwi) and mukwendekwende to kidasi, the highest grade. In some southern Nyindu groups that are connected with the Basimwenda, this hierarchy is supplemented by grades borrowed via the Basimwenda from the rest of the Lega. The hierarchy would then include bwami (or isengo), bombwa (or bumbwa), bubake (or buba'e), and ngandu. In the Banyindu system it is true, as in all others, that the higher the grade the fewer the incumbents. The initiations are simple. Access to each grade presupposes passage through a limited number of rites, say six or seven. The ideology and the aims are basically the same as in other systems, and so are the initiation objects which include a small number of ivory figurines ('a'inga) and spoons (lukiri) in the two highest grades.

Among all the Bembe, and some eastern Lega, such as the Basimwenda and the Bamuzimu, the basic hierarchy includes these grades: bukila, the lowest grade, bukabo, pinji, itembu, and biciba, the highest grade. This sequence is universal among the Bembe. Some eastern Lega groups which are in contact with the bwami of western and southern Lega have eliminated certain grades or added others. For example, among the Basimwenda of Miculo the succession includes bukila, bukabo, pinji, itembu, bumbwa,

The Bwami Association

buba'e, and ngandu. The range of initiation objects is limited, but human and animal figurines in wood, ivory, bone, and clay are used.

The third variant, found among the Bakuti and related eastern Lega, is based on this hierarchy: bwami, bumbwa, bubake, mpunzu, and ngandu. Some groups, like the Basimwabi of Isambia, have added the two higher grades of yano and kindi, both brought in via their maternal uncles from the Babongolo.

The fourth variant, the most elaborate and most widely distributed form of bwami in all core areas of western and southern Legaland, serves as the reference point for my discussion. It is found, with only minor nuances, in the following clan communities: Babongolo, Banagabo, Banangoma, Beigala, Baziri, Banakeigo, Banalyuba, Beianangi, Banisanga, Batoba, Beiamunsange, Banisanga, Banamunwa, and Bagilanzelu. Some of the sharper deviations from this pattern are found among the Bakyunga and the Bamuguba. The hierarchic order in this fourth variant runs as follows: kongabulumbu (or bwami), the lowest grade; kansilembo; bombwa; ngandu; bulonda; yananio (yano), with the subdivisions musagi wa yananio and lutumbo lwa yananio; kindi, with the sublevels kyogo kya kindi, musagi wa kindi, and lutumbo lwa kindi, the highest grade; and bunyamwa, the female grade complementary to the highest male grade. In some instances mpunzu is recognized as a separate grade between bombwa and ngandu; in other instances it is absorbed into ngandu. In a few groups, such as Babongolo, Baziri, Banakeigo, Banamunwa, and Banisanga, the highest possible level, called lwanza, is achieved by a member of lutumbo lwa kindi through a massive exchange of valuables. This level, however, has not been recognized by any group in the twentieth century.

The hierarchy merges male and female grades into an indivisible whole. The bombwa initiation, although serving both males and females, addresses itself primarily to females and is an inseparable complement to the male-oriented ngandu rites. A male incumbent of the ngandu grade is supposed to go through bulonda with at least one of his wives to open the path to yananio. A kindi, to complete fully his grade level, is expected to have at least one of his wives initiated to bunyamwa. The two highest grades, yananio and kindi, are usually subdivided into two levels. These two levels, musagi and lutumbo, are distinguished by different rites, exchanges, paraphernalia, duties, and privileges. Sometimes there is a third and lowest level in kindi called kyogo. Initiation to each grade and, when appropriate, to each level in a grade consists of a number of ritual cycles in addition to the preliminary dances (kamondo).

Ideally, a candidate goes through the entire set of ritual cycles pertaining to one grade or one level within a single initiation period (from one to seven days). Each cycle is named after a dominant object, activity, or idea on which the rite centers. The number and the complexity of the cycles increase as the candidate moves higher in the hierarchy of grades. Despite regional variations in number, sequence, duration, and content, the ritual cycles are structured around aphorisms that are sung, interpreted, danced, and acted out, while certain objects (natural artifacts, art objects) are displayed, manipulated, carried, and moved around in dramatic performances by groups of initiates. The candidate, assisted by his tutors and sponsors, watches and learns the procedure, undergoes certain experiences, and indemnifies participants with food, fees, and gifts. The preceptor (*nsingia*) or thinker (*kasimba*) is responsible for and supervises the initiates' participation; the chief sponsor (*kakusa* and other names), the candidate's activities.

The following outline provides an apercu of the succession of initiatory cycles within the grades. It offers only one example out of several possible sequences and combinations I have studied in the field. Only some of the most frequently used initiation objects are briefly mentioned.

I. Kongabulumbu

Kongabulumbu is the lowest grade or, as the Lega call it, "the heart of bwami." The rites, held in a man's village of residence, are organized by the initiated members of a small lineage (a tertiary or secondary lineage group, depending on numerical strength and degree of territorial compactness), provided they hold the right and possess the correlated symbols to ensure autonomous kongabulumbu initiations. The candidate for initiation is tutored by a *kilego*, a close (mostly agnatic) kinsman who is a member (frequently a high-ranking one) of the association. Incumbents of all grades are permitted to take part in the rites, but generally the group of participants is small. A woman, called *kigogo*, who is either the wife of the candidate or his close female agnate, is introduced into some of the ritual. The rites usually begin in the evening and last into the middle of the following morning. They are celebrated inside the men's house, but some dances are performed in the open on the village dance floor. Drumming occurs only in the *kaminankya* rite. Musical accompaniment is provided by anklet bells and percussion with small sticks on iron axes or on pieces of elephant bone. The secret circumcision instruments are used only in the *moza* rite.

A. *Kamondo*: Preliminary songs and dances (28 proverbs sung).
B. Ceremonial entrance of the candidate and his tutor (*kilego*) into the initiation house.
C. *Ziko*: Interpretation of the objects contained in a basket or shoulder bag which is held by any lineage that is allowed autonomously to organize its kongabulumbu rites. The interpretations center on such objects as warthog tusk, pangolin scales,

The Bwami Association

hides of the genet and the duiker antelope, tibia of the *Cercopithecus* monkey, seed from a wild banana tree, pod of an *ibulungu* tree, ivory or bone scepters, ivory or bone spoons, a pipe bowl, and a needle and raffia thread (65 proverbs).

D. *Malimu*: Interpretation of a small empty basket (*kiluba*) and an assortment of items: razor and razor sheath, torch, ax, feather tufts, and a stick representing a house beam (28 proverbs).

E. *Katanda*: Interpretations centering on a man's young wife and/or a close female agnate, who is present at the rite (27 proverbs).

G. *Kagoli*: Interpretations centering on a feather rope, two forked sticks, the *kabubi* liana (a major material in Lega technology), and a stick adorned with feather tufts (53 proverbs).

H. *Myabi*: Enactment of the administration of the poison ordeal (12 proverbs).

I. *Moza*: Blowing on a horn or a piece of bamboo held in an empty pot, and interpretation of the secret musical instrument of the circumcision rites (mirliton, percussion sticks, horn, bull-roarer).

J. *Isengo*: Presentation and interpretation of the small woven bwami hat, and confirmation of the new initiate by placing it on his head.

K. *Kaminankya*: Beating of two drums suspended from a pole while gifts are presented to the new initiate. Force is imparted to him by pulling and rubbing his limbs and by blowing on his head through cupped hands.

L. *Kisakulo*: This rite, used only in some areas, is held sometime after the kongabulumbu initiations to confirm the initiate in his new position and to symbolize that he is destined for higher achievements.

II. Kansilembo

Although kansilembo, properly speaking, is not a distinctive grade, it is always enumerated as such because it represents a higher level of initiatory experience than does the kongabulumbu initiation. The ritual is performed in an isolated hamlet inhabited by the owner of the *lutala* right. A lineage possessing such a titleholder is permitted to erect its own circumcision lodge. Relatively few initiates of higher rank own this right, but all initiates are privileged to learn the meaning of the symbols that go with it. Because women and children are excluded from the kansilembo initiation, they are kept away from the hamlet where the ceremonies are held. Kansilembo is a short rite usually performed in the early morning. Musical accompaniment is limited to the secret circumcision instruments, augmented by a small gong. There are no named cycles. The contents of the *lutala* basket or shoulder bag are shown to the candidate and explained. The objects may include a stone, a feather rope, a little calabash, a wooden trident, a small knife, a razor and sheath, four hollow pieces of wood tied together in a bundle, a small copper plate adorned with oblong beads, and an ivory spoon (11 formulas).

III. Bombwa

This initiation is closely connected with the ngandu grade; it is thought to be complementary to ngandu in that it provides the initiate with an initiated wife. The rites, held in a man's village of residence, are performed partly in the open air and partly in the men's house. The initiation takes place in daytime and extends over a full day. Both men and women of the ngandu and bombwa grades and occupants of higher grades participate. The final part of the ritual (*kampumba*), however, is held only in the presence of initiated women and kindi of the highest level. Apart from *kampumba*, few of the rites have specific names. The interpretations center on such objects as a large shoulder bag, a pad made from dry banana leaves (with which to carry headloads), a forked *nkeka* chair, two crossed sticks tied together with a feather rope and adorned with feather tufts, and a genet hide. Some ritual communities use wood figurines (*keitula*). Wooden masks, in some areas generically referred to as *kingungungu*, are also used. Dramatic performances are particularly well developed in this initiation. In one scene the preceptor, carrying a huge bundle of leaves under his loincloth between his legs and dancing with great difficulty, incarnates a man suffering from scrotal hernia or scrotal elephantiasis (Mr. Isingindu). Another initiate, carrying a smaller bunch of leaves, represents a woman suffering from venereal disease (Mrs. Nitulu). In another performance the preceptor, wearing a feather hat and two wooden masks (one on the cheeks and the other on the back of the head), mimics a poor old man begging for food. In general, sexual symbolism and evocative dances and movements—otherwise very rare or totally absent from the initiations—abound in bombwa. The initiation culminates in the *kampumba* ritual, when five initiated women drum on a slit-drum and two membranophones inside the initiation house (36 proverbs).

IV. Ngandu

In some ritual communities ngandu is the highest grade of bwami, as it was for a long time in the majority of Lega communities until supplanted as the supreme grade by yananio or kindi. Consequently the ngandu initiations are elaborate among some eastern Lega groups, but are reduced in scope elsewhere. In certain communities ngandu is regarded as a crossroads whence the candidate can pursue the normal path to yananio and then to kindi or can be permitted to go directly to kindi. Sometimes a community speaks of the kyogo, musagi, and lutumbo levels within ngandu, like the levels within kindi, but this subdivision is simply a way of speaking and has no influence on the organization itself.

    A. *Kamondo*: Preliminary dances without objects (10 proverbs).
    B. *Bituzi*: Dances with small, roughly carved pieces of parasol wood which are attached to raffia strings and worn like earrings (13 proverbs).
    C. *Kabobela*: Dances with dried banana leaves. In this rite a house door made of planks of parasol wood, feather tufts, woven mats, and little stools are also used (50 proverbs).
    D. *Bilumya*: This rite requires the use of a small pot made from the rotula of an elephant, a miniature ivory knife, a miniature ax made of elephant bone, and two wooden figurines representing Mr. Phallus and Mrs. Buttocks (26 proverbs).
    E. *Yango*: Interpretations of Yango, a human character and also the symbol for penis. *Yango* is represented by a roughly carved piece of wood or by a piece of banana stipe. Sometimes an ivory bark-beater serves the purpose (41 proverbs).

V. Bulonda

This initiation transforms the wife of an initiate into a kalonda woman with whom he can enter the advanced yananio initiations. The rites, which last for one day, center on women, but initiated husbands of the women participate in all but the final climactic *kumoko*, or purification ceremony. The ceremonies are held in the village of the candidate's husband, partly in the initiation hut and partly on the village dance ground. The final ablution takes place outside the village, near the river where the villagers usually draw their water. The initiation consists of numerous short, dramatic representations which are centered on a pile of shoulder bags and small stools. The initiates use a handful of bananas, a young banana tree, a walking cane, a feather tuft, a *nkumbi* nut, and a pot. The rites end with the "enthronement" of the new initiate and her husband—he stands straight on a little stool while holding a walking cane; she is seated on a stool in front of him—and with an ablution (50 proverbs).

VI. Yananio

Yananio comprises two separate levels. Initiations to the first level take from one to two days; those to the second level last two to three days. The length of time depends on whether the initiation is well done (*yananio lyabonga*) or whether it is done in a hurry (*yananio lyasili*). Several of the rites are held in the middle of the village; some take place in the initiation hut; a few, like *kasisi*, are ultrasecret.

A. Musagi wa yananio
 1. *Kamondo*: Preliminary dances.
 2. *Lukenye*: Ceremonial entrance of the initiates into the candidate's village. While marching slowly in a long row they wave flyswatters made of fine reeds and beat them against the genet hides they are wearing. Two drums, suspended at the entrance to the initiation hut, are beaten to provide the musical background. There is no singing or dancing, but as the file of initiates approaches the hut, the leader engages in a dialogue with one of the candidate's tutors before circling the hut.
 3. *Lukugo*: Interpretations centered on the *masandi* flyswatters made of fine reeds (14 proverbs).
 4. *Makumbi*: Interpretations centered on a small basket, its bark cover, a piece of firewood, and a *lububi* liana (20 proverbs).
 5. *Bisukusuku*: Interpretations of a *lukumbula* leaf and a genet skin (9 proverbs).
 6. *Kasuku*: This rite comes a few weeks after the initiations, when the new initiate invites his colleagues to a lavish dinner party and an evening of enjoyment.

B. Lutumbo lwa yananio
 1. *Lukenye*: Ceremonial entrance of the invited initiates into the candidate's village. The participants carry small stools and shoulder bags; a few of them carry baskets containing collectively held initiation objects. The baskets, of which there are two or three, are called *kaluba, mutulwa,* and *kasisi*.
 2. *Isabukilo*: Interpretations about phrynium leaves (11 proverbs).
 3. *Kabobela*: Explanations about bark cloth and raffia fibers (10 proverbs).
 4. *Kimazenze*: Dances with *yango* stick (see description of *yango* rite in the ngandu initiations) and feather rope.
 5. *Lukwakongo*: Dances with wooden maskettes (11 proverbs).
 6. *Mukumbi*: The degree of complexity in this central rite and the number and diversity of objects used in it differ considerably from place to place. The interpretations concern

The Bwami Association

a configuration of objects—wooden masks, chimpanzee skulls, giant snail shells, porcupine quills, small knives, parrot feathers, many types of leaves—covering two pits. One pit is empty; the other may hold a *yango* stick, a stuffed skin of the golden mole or a wooden animal carving, and a raffia ball (69 proverbs).

7. *Nkunda*: A rare rite in which the leaders of the dance are more or less disguised by wearing small face masks, genet and other hides, feathers, and snakeskin trimmed with feathers. This rite is a reenactment of a poison ordeal. An ivory spoon, a wooden animal figurine, and straps of banana leaves are used (72 proverbs and formulas).

8. *Mutulwa*: Display and elucidation of the contents of the *mulama* and *kaluba* baskets. The contents may include one or more specimens of chimpanzee skulls, turtle carapaces, fish skulls, samples of certain woods, bird beaks, pods, wooden animal figures, carved wooden hands and lower arms, and, occasionally, wooden human figurines. The objects are interpreted singly or in combinations (41 proverbs).

9. *Tulimu*: Dances with wooden masks, all having long beards, held in the hands (9 proverbs).

10. *Kisumbi*: Interpretations concerning small carved stools (7 proverbs).

11. *Mulombe*: Dances with flyswatters and genet skins (14 proverbs).

12. *Tulimbangoma*: Display and explanation of small wooden carvings, sometimes in human shape, sometimes in animal form (4 proverbs).

13. *Kasisi kampunzu*: In this ultrasecret rite the candidate for initiation is exposed to four initiates who are completely disguised with bark cloth spotted like leopard skin. He then learns about the *kasisi* configuration, which may include one or more specimens of boar tusks, porcupine quills, monkey skulls, pieces of wood, *ngimbi* snakeskin, and perhaps some rudimentarily sculptured objects in wood and *ntutu* and quartz stones. There is no music, song, or dance in this rite.

VII. Kindi

The kindi grade usually comprises three levels referred to as kyogo kya kindi, musagi wa kindi, and lutumbo lwa kindi. The initiations for kyogo last one day; for musagi, two days; and for lutumbo, four to seven days. The organization of the rites, which are held in the candidate's village, presupposes construction of a large initiation hut with two to four doors, resembling in general shape the carapace of a turtle. The lutumbo initiations also require the building of guesthouses. In the old tradition, therefore, the lutumbo rites included the construction of a completely new village where the new initiate and his kinsmen would reside.

A. Kyogo kya kindi
   1. *Munsembele*: Dances centering on wickerwork rattles, one large and one small basket, and a wooden spear (11 proverbs).
   2. *Lukenye*: Ceremonial entrance into the village, as described under yananio. The initiates shake wickerwork rattles.
   3. *Makumbi*: Dance with basket (4 proverbs).
   4. *Keibi*: Dance with door made of parasol planks and with a bundle of scalelike orchid leaves (11 proverbs).

B. Musagi wa kindi
   1. *Lukenye*: Ceremonial procession after which participants climb up to and down from the roof of the initiation hut (8 proverbs).
   2. *Mulima*: Dances with *mbale* liana, covered by the hide of a potto (7 proverbs).
   3. *Keibi*: Interpretations about a door made of parasol planks (15 proverbs).
   4. *Byambila*: Dances without special objects (7 proverbs).
   5. *Kinsamba*: Display and interpretation of small ivory figurines in human form (17 proverbs).

C. Lutumbo lwa kindi
   1. *Lukenye*: Ceremonial procession not used by all ritual communities.
   2. *Mizegele*: Dances with wicker rattles and with *mizombolo*, a small woven disk in the center of which stands a short piece of wood adorned with a feather tuft (9 proverbs).
   3. *Lusaga*: Dances in which the performers wear collarets of raffia strings (5 proverbs).
   4. *Kilinkumbi*: Display of ivory masks on a small fence. A larger wooden mask may hang in the middle of the smaller ivory maskettes, and an animal figurine, representing a pangolin, may stand on top of the fence (12 proverbs).
   5. *Keibi*: Dances with a small door made of parasol planks (6 proverbs).
   6. *Kabubi*: Interpretations of a *lububi* liana from which hangs a feather tuft (6 proverbs).
   7. *Itutu*: This rite, with both the initiate and his wife partici-

The Bwami Association

pating, takes place on the rooftop of the initiation hut; the main objects used include a fire drill, phrynium leaves, a *lububi* liana, and a polished mussel shell (28 proverbs).

8. *Ibago lya nzogu*: "Ritual killing" of the initiation hut, identified with an elephant, by means of an ivory spoon and ivory knives (8 proverbs).
9. *Kankunde ka kindi*: Interpretations of a masked dancer and a turtle carapace; other objects include an ivory spoon, wicker rattles, phrynium leaves, a *lububi* liana, and two claws of an aardvark (8 proverbs).
10. *Ibugebuge*: Explanations about a large fence from which hang ivory masks. The preceptors dance around the fence, their heads covered with a multitude of masks (4 proverbs).
11. *Mutulwa*: Interpretation of the contents of a collectively held initiation basket, which may include wooden human figurines, one or more wooden animal figurines, a small elephant tusk, and leopard and chimpanzee skulls (9 proverbs).
12. *Kasumba*: Interpretation and display of a fence of belts and feather tufts worn by women of the highest initiatory experience and of hats adorned with elephant tails worn by the highest-ranking male initiates (no proverbs).
13. *Kinsamba*: Massive display of human figurines in ivory (no proverbs).
14. *Bele muno*: Interpretations of a configuration of kindi hats, wicker rattles, and one or more ivory figurines (no proverbs).

VIII. Bunyamwa

This initiation confirms a woman as the initiated wife of a kindi. Sometimes a distinction is made between kanyamwa ka lwemba, the initiated wife of a musagi wa kindi, and kanyamwa ka idulu, the initiated wife of a lutumbo lwa kindi with whom he went through the rite (*itutu*) on the rooftop. It is impossible, however, technically to distinguish these two levels within bunyamwa because the female rites are so intimately interwoven with the male rites. The close relationship is evidenced by the *itutu* rite, which consecrates the perpetual marriage bond between a kindi and his kanyamwa.

The final ceremonies of bunyamwa begin at night in an enclosure built inside the partly demolished initiation hut. Women of bunyamwa dance in front of the kindi. They are naked except for a small piece of dwarf antelope skin, adorned with porcupine quills and red tail feathers of the parrot, which covers the genitalia. One by one, the males dance toward the women trying to touch them, but pulling back as if they had been stung by something. Later in the night, as the dances progress, the initiates shoot with miniature bows and arrows at the genitalia covering. The initiation ends with an ablution ceremony.

ORIGIN AND DISTRIBUTION OF BWAMI AMONG THE LEGA

Associations that are similar in scope to the bwami of the Lega have a wide distribution in the eastern Congo and, indeed, in many other parts of that country. Among the Komo and the Nyanga they are called *mpunju* or *mbuntsu*; among the Lengola and the Mitoko, *bukota*; among the Songola, *nsubi*; and among the Zimba, *luhuna*. Farther away, toward the northwest and the southwest, there are comparable institutions: *lilwa* among the Mbole and the Yela, *nkumu* among the Nkundo, *nkumi* among the Tetela.[5] Bwami not only is distributed among all sections of the Lega, but is also found outside Legaland among the Bembe and among some subgroups of Kwame, Kanu, Zimba, Bangubangu, and Nyindu. In addition, individuals from such ethnic units as Songola, who are permanently established in Lega villages because of cognatic and affinal ties, may have acceded to bwami.

In some texts of the rites, the initiates affirm that "bwami is a fruit that came from above; it has no inventor [lit., it has not the one who first saw it]." This assertion surely holds for the lower grades up to ngandu, which are universally recognized by and known to the Lega and the Bembe. Individual clans and lineages have no theory about the origin of the lower grades and no way of explaining from which groups they might have learned about those grades. In reviewing the ethnohistorical traditions about the upper grades, yananio and kindi, which are irregularly distributed in Legaland and absent from Bembeland, the records of many clans contain references to groups and individuals with whom these initiations originated and mention the individual clan members who introduced them. The Banasalu clan pretends that it derived its kindi from the Basumbu clan; the Beianangi clan claims to owe its kindi to the Babongolo; the Banisanga clan, in turn, derived its kindi from the Beianangi. Sometimes

[5] None of these associations have been researched in depth, but useful general information is available in Moeller (1936, *passim*). Specific data on the *mpunju* initiations among the Komo are given in Galdermans (1934) and Gérard (1956). The *lilwa* association of the Yela has been described by De Rop (1955), and of the Mbole, by Rouvroy (1929). De Heusch (1954*a*, *b*; 1955) and Jacobs (1955) provide valuable data on the *nkumi* of the Tetela. Interesting studies prepared by former territorial administrators—Aurez (1930) on *bukota* of the Mitoko and Bronchart (1931) on *luhuna* of the Zimba—have not been published.

The Bwami Association

different primary lineages within the same clan claim different origins for their kindi initiations.

High-ranking initiates, unanimously agreeing that the kindi initiations are as old as all others in bwami, interpret the derivation as follows. When they were chased at Mingalangala by Kimbimbi's light-skinned followers, the Lega split into two large segments; one formed the basis for the Babongolo and the other gave rise to the rest of the Lega groups. Since at that time only the Babongolo had kindi, all other groups who later wanted it were compelled to obtain it directly or indirectly from them. The Babongolo, thought to be the descendants of Nkulu, one of Lega's sons, are established in the Bakabango chefferies of Shabunda and Pangi and have many ramifications in other parts of Shabunda, such as the Bakisi, Beia, and Babene administrative subdivisions.[6]

The ways in which transfers of kindi were made are clearly recorded in the traditions of several clans. The transfers took place through the channel of in-law and cognatic relationships that bound individuals of non-kindi-owning clans to kindi of other clans. The actual transfer, according to the same traditions, was conditioned and favored either by prolonged coresidence or by an effort to wipe out feuds and violations of taboos between groups. For example, members of the Banamunwa clan state that six known genealogical generations ago a certain Yande settled with his maternal uncles of the Banameya clan, that he was initiated there to kindi, and that he later returned to his own village and introduced kindi there. The story of how the Nangi clan obtained kindi is more complicated. The Beianangi and Banamilunga clans had been feuding for many years when a certain Yango of the Banamilunga, in order to put an end to the hostility, decided to give his own daughter, Naikila, to a certain Misenga of the Beianangi. Then, later on, as the result of a quarrel, the Beianangi killed Yango when he came to visit his daughter. Since Yango was a kindi, the Nangi clan as a whole was threatened by the mystic sanctions (*kitampo*) that followed such a killing. In order to lift the mystic ban, the Nangi decided to induct Misenga into kindi. Later Misenga tutored

---

[6] Administrative reports of 1931 and 1932 deal elaborately with the problem of the origin of bwami. One 1931 source asserts that bwami is posterior to the Lega migration and is only about 150 years old. The same source, claiming that bwami was introduced by a certain Katima from Rwanda, sees in this event an early effort on the part of the Rwanda rulers to establish control over the Lega. A 1932 document concludes that bwami was invented by a certain Muntita from the riverain Luba, and that he introduced it to the descendants of Nkulu (Babongolo) as a lucrative business. Since the Lega have no theory about bwami, "the fruit that came from above," there is no way of unraveling its possible origins. Various Legaland groups are very conscious of the growth of bwami, including the spread of certain grades and rites. The Bakyunga clan of Shabunda believes that bwami was invented by Katinti in order to put an end to the internal wars that divided the Lega, an interesting tradition that underscores the peacemaking function of bwami.

another member of his clan in kindi. No member of Misenga's lineage, however, was ever again initiated into kindi because the ritual pollution continued to weigh heavily upon him and his immediate agnates. Such ethnohistorical interpretations offer a rationale for explaining the ritual links between groups and account for the presence of certain grades and levels in lineages and clans, or for their absence from those groups.

There is no doubt, then, that the bwami association is very old among the Lega. Bwami is so fully integrated with all aspects of Lega thinking and living that it is difficult to conceive of the Lega without bwami. It is also quite clear that the association has been steadily manipulated. New rites, new cycles, and new subgrades have been added; old ones have been abolished. Certain aspects of bwami reveal the internal manipulation. The oral records do not speak only of the introduction of kindi initiations; they also relate the addition or the elimination of certain rites, initiation objects, and paraphernalia. The introduction of a new rite (called *lunkulu*) is always attributed to a certain initiate who learned about it from his maternal uncles or his sororal nephews and then "purchased" it for a certain amount of goods. The generic term for this type of purchase is *mpeneziginga* (lit., the goats of the figurines). The elimination of certain rites or objects is frequently attributed to a breach of rules or to an unfavorable group experience.

The organization and the details of the rites reveal substantial differences from region to region, from ritual community to ritual community, from clan to clan. It is easy to understand the differences in Lega terms. Although bwami functions as an integer of diverse territorial lineage and clan groupings and constitutes a universal frame of reference in Lega society, it has no central organization or central council of high initiates to impose specific laws and regulations upon the people. Even at the highest initiations, which draw together multitudes of individuals from different clans, there is no occasion for representatives of all major divisions in Legaland to come together and interact with one another. On the other hand, the bwami association encourages individual skill, ingenuity, and creativity and is receptive to the testing of new ideas and practices. So, without impairing the structural principles on which bwami operates, it is always acceptable to modify procedures by inventing or borrowing new methods of initiation or by changing or eliminating existing modes. And that is what the Lega have consistently done. Each ritually autonomous community seems to make a deliberate effort to do things a little differently from its neighbors. In going through the records one finds that the basic structural principles of bwami remain constant but that there are hundreds of variations in the ways of doing things: in number and sequence of rites; in number and types of initiatory objects; in number and types of collectively held objects and in the ways of keeping them; in number of goods distributed and in methods and occasions of distributing

The Bwami Association

them; in the formulation of basic moral values in proverbs and in dramatic action, but not in the values themselves; in sequences, groupings, and interpretations of proverbs and assorted objects. For this reason any outline, such as that given above, is precise only as a rough skeleton of grades and levels. The actual rites, their sequence, the dramatic events that take place, and the types of objects that are used show considerable variation within an overall framework of recurring events, actions, and configurations of objects.

Membership

In principle, bwami is open to all Lega, male and female, and to non-Lega with whom specific kinship linkages, based on matrimonial alliance, cognation, and/or friendship, can be traced. The precondition for men is that they be circumcised, which means they have gone through a preliminary system of intensive learning and training. Only a tiny fraction of Lega males are not circumcised. I have met a few of them and, although the circumstances are not fully clear to me, they seemed, invariably, to suffer from some physical or mental abnormality.

For women the process is more complicated. Those who accede to the three basic female grades (bombwa, bulonda, bunyamwa) do so as the wives of men who have previously achieved, or are currently achieving, an equivalent or a higher male grade. Yet there is a process of selection and elimination at work, for not all the wives of a high-ranking initiate are necessarily members of bwami, although they all aspire to it; nor do all those who have become members necessarily achieve equal rank, although several of an initiate's wives may have the same high rank. In some ritual communities a man, married or unmarried, is allowed to enter the lowest grade (kongabulumbu) in the company of a closely related, unmarried, agnatic female relative (e.g., sister, half sister, or patrilateral parallel cousin). This woman, called *kigogo* for the occasion, does not occupy any grade in the female hierarchy, nor is she allowed to be present at all the kongabulumbu rites.[7]

The Lega employ a variety of methods by which they judge an individual to be eligible for access to, or advancement in, the association. The surest and most widespread way of establishing eligibility is predilection (*bungoli*), as when an initiated father invites his beloved son, who excels

---

[7] It would seem that in earlier decades high-ranking initiates sometimes helped their daughters to achieve bombwa, and even bulonda, before they were given in marriage. In some communities high-ranking initiates could also invite a preferred son (*ngoli*) to go through a simple initiation called bubake, which immediately followed kongabulumbu, so that the son could accompany his father to high-level initiations and stay with him in the village during the ceremonies in order to guard his belongings and initiation objects.

in filial piety and in character, to enter the association. The next method is *kuingilila* (lit., to enter on behalf of), whereby the candidate is selected from a certain kinship group to substitute for an agnate who died either during the preparations for initiation or during the initiation rites. Oracle (*bugila*) is a method of accession when oracles ascribe a person's sickness and troubles to his failure to enter the bwami association, as his father had done; initiation is then thought to be the only way for a person to purify himself from his sickness-inducing guilt. A man may also be forced into bwami (*kukandoa*), with or without his agreement (*kwa magala*), when he is found guilty of transgressing bwami regulations by seducing, for example, a high-ranking female initiate. And, of course, the Lega also recognize free initiative as a technique of eligibility; they call it *kutunda* (to love) when a man succeeds because of his personal efforts and will.

Eligibility, however, is not to be equated with automatic membership. To be an acceptable candidate one must satisfy several prerequisites; the higher the grade sought, the more rigid the criteria. For example, larger quantities of goods are necessary for initiation into higher grades because the number of participating initiates increases. As one moves up in grade, one needs more and more kinship support both inside (agnatic) and outside (cognatic, affinal, and friendship relationships) one's group. These kinsmen must make certain that the candidate is qualified. First, they must be sure that his induction into bwami will not lead to tensions within the group; certain principles of seniority and social priority must be respected. Second, the candidate must have the necessary moral prerequisites. Should he be irascible, verbose, quarrelsome, or lacking in piety, the initiates defer the rites, either temporarily or permanently, even though other requirements are fulfilled. The candidate also must solicit help—large quantities of food and valuables—from the widest possible group of kinsmen (agnatic, cognatic, and affinal), for his own labor and enterprise can never produce enough goods. Only when a candidate is sure of sufficient support can he hope to find tutors and sponsors (as many as four are necessary for the highest grades) to counsel and guide him through the initiations. These kinsmen must be incumbents of grades equivalent with, or higher than, the one sought by the candidate. The general principle, therefore, may be formulated as follows: the higher a man wants to move in bwami, the more kinship support and the more wealth he needs, the more virtue he has to display, the more guidance and counseling he needs.

No general rules can be formulated as to the kind of kinship group that autonomously organizes its own initiations and decides the eligibility of candidates. The framework within which this action is taken depends on the grade to which a candidate is to be initiated, the numerical strength and the number of subdivisions in a clan, the number of incorporated groups, the territorial layout of the kinship unit, and the traditional ritual and territorial bonds between groups. The only valid general rules are:

The Bwami Association

the lower the grade, the smaller the autonomously acting kinship unit; the higher the grade, the larger the autonomously acting kinship unit. The highest initiations, to kindi, are the concern of a ritual community, which usually comprises two or more ritually linked clans. To elucidate the point, the situation in the Beiankuku clan may be contrasted with that prevailing in the Beiamunsange clan.

The Beiankuku clan, comprising four primary lineages, Banamugomba, Banamwenda, Banamunyaga, and Banamugulu, is ritually linked with the Banamusiga clan. Members of the Mugomba lineage inhabit five villages; of Mwenda, three villages; of Munyaga, three villages; of Mugulu, one village. Members of the Banamusiga clan have three villages of their own. Each primary lineage in the Beiankuku clan autonomously organizes the initiations from kongabulumbu to yananio. That each group does so is revealed, among other ways, by the fact that it possesses its own *musutwa* and *kasisi* baskets, which contain some of the vital initiatory objects for these two grades. Kindi initiations, however, are organized jointly by the Beiankuku and the Banamusiga. The two clans together own one *mutulwa* basket for initiations into musagi wa kindi and one for initiations into lutumbo lwa kindi. Autonomy in the organization of such rites does not, of course, mean exclusion of other lineages of the clan or of nonclan members. For example, if the Mwenda primary lineage decides to hold yananio rites for one of its members, it has the authority and the power to do so; yet it cannot and does not exclude from participation initiated members from other lineages, either inside or outside the clan.

The large Beiamunsange clan, consisting of eight primary lineages, is heavily fragmented for the kongabulumbu initiations; each primary lineage, depending on the number of its internal subdivisions, possesses from one to seven *musutwa* baskets. In most instances the basket is jointly owned by the initiated members of a secondary lineage. Other times it is jointly owned by the initiated members of a tertiary lineage. The Munsange are aware that every primary lineage originally possessed its own basket, and that in the process of lineage segmentation some baskets were "split" among secondary lineages. The holding of a basket by a tertiary lineage is explained in terms of the numerical strength of sublineages and of their subsequent purchase of the right to own a basket. Thus lineages came to be linked not merely by the agnatic kinship structure, but also through ritual interdependence (one lineage having bought the right to possess its own basket from another lineage).

The distribution of yananio baskets among the Beiamunsange has to do with the size of lineage units. Each of the two largest primary lineages owns two baskets, and each basket is shared by several secondary lineages; each of three other primary lineages has its own basket; a sixth basket is shared by the members of two primary lineages. The unity of the clan is still more strongly affirmed by the possession of the musagi wa kindi baskets. There are only two for the entire clan, one of them shared by two primary lineages and the other by five primary lineages; the incorporated Kilimono group, which forms the eighth primary lineage, has none. The unity of the clan is further consolidated by the ownership of a single large male figurine, kept by the most senior of all living kindi in the clan; a large female figurine which the Lyuba received from the Munsange symbolizes their own unity and their ritual linkage with the Munsange.

The decision-making process, then, operates at many different levels; it is not simply a function of clan structure. The preference for a certain candidate is the affair of an *ibamba* council for initiations up to ngandu, and of a *musanganano* for the higher initiations of yananio and kindi. For the lower initiations the choice of a candidate and the primary decisions are made by a small group of kinsmen and initiates (e.g., for kongabulumbu, by a man, his junior brothers, and his adult sons). For higher initiations the choice and the decisions are made by a large reunion of kinsmen and initiates who represent a broader lineage group, a clan, or several linked clans. In both instances there is much consultation between the immediate agnates of the candidate and their initiated cognates and affines.

As bwami is a goal of life to which, in principle, every Lega can accede, it is understandable that within any lineage a large number of males, and some of their wives, achieve a certain grade. For example, within the Beiankuku clan is the large extended family of Lubumba, who was dead at the time of my research. Lubumba had achieved musagi wa kindi; he had married ten wives; he had eleven sons and a number of daughters. Eight of Lubumba's sons acceded to bwami. Three of them did not make it beyond the first grade (kongabulumbu); one achieved the intermediate grade (ngandu); two (children by different wives) reached lutumbo lwa yananio; one achieved the first level in kindi; and one earned lutumbo lwa kindi. Three sons did not accede to bwami because two of them died fairly young and the third went to work in a European center. In acceding to bwami and advancing to higher grades, this family group had observed the principles of seniority; the son who had reached lutumbo lwa kindi was senior to the son who had reached a lower level in kindi.

Because the entire clan is affected by kindi initiations, it is clear that sequences of such initiations in any group cut across lineage subdivisions. The Banasalu clan, for instance, consists of four primary lineages—Kibondo, Lusumbasumba, Ninda, and Mugila—each subdivided into a cascade of smaller lineages (see App. I). The names of forty-two individuals (four of them still alive at the time of my research) who achieved lutumbo lwa kindi are remembered in this clan (see App. II). Two belong to Kibondo lineage, sixteen each to Mugila and Lusumbasumba, and eight to Ninda. One of the living kindi is a member of Lusumbasumba, one is a member of Ninda, and two are members of Mugila (but of different secondary lineages within it). The sequence in which these forty-two men achieved

The Bwami Association

kindi is precisely known, simply because no living kindi can fail to know the order in which the collectively held *mutulwa* basket is transferred from the most recent initiate to the next candidate. In the Banasalu clan the basket moved in a totally unpredictable line from lineage to lineage and from individual to individual within a lineage (see App. II). A high esprit de corps, and constant interaction between members of various lineages within the clan, are obviously necessary to achieve and to respect such a system of transfers and interdependencies.

STRUCTURE AND ORGANIZATION

Bwami as a Multipurpose Voluntary Association. Bwami has the structure and the organization of a voluntary association. One is not born into bwami, nor is membership reserved for certain privileged classes of individuals. In principle, membership in bwami is open to all physically and mentally normal males; in practice, the majority of males achieve it. Many of them achieve only the lower grades. As one moves up in the hierarchy, the number of initiates steadily declines. In other words, a process of elimination and selection is at work. To become a kindi, one must systematically go through all the lower initiations. Only a few communities allow an initiate to skip yananio and pass directly from ngandu to kindi. An initiate who has taken this shortcut *(lutabe lumozi)* lacks certain privileges and is, to some extent, thought of as an incomplete kindi.

To become a member of the bwami association and move up in the hierarchy implies acceptance of the candidate by the individuals in his ritual community who are already members. Acceptability is based on moral qualities. It is also conditioned by kinship structure, for if two individuals in a given group are equally acceptable, the senior or father receives privileged consideration. The junior or son, however, is not altogether excluded. Membership and advancement in bwami are also dependent on wealth; the amounts and categories of goods specified for each initiation must be available. At the higher levels the necessary goods can be accumulated only with the cooperation of numerous kinsmen (agnatic, cognatic, affinal).

Because the distribution of goods and the arrangements for initiations are complex and arduous, the candidate for initiation needs the constant advice and assistance of one or more seasoned and well-informed tutors and counselors. The latter must literally be won for the cause. They do not like to embark on so delicate a task unless they are sure that their protégé has the proper attitude and the ability to pass the tests he will have to take. The series of initiations prerequisite to achieving a certain grade or level forms the cornerstone of the entire structure. To be valid, initiations must be held in the appropriate place at the appropriate time by the appropriate people in the presence of a group of initiates. The customary songs and dances must be performed, and the relevant initiatory objects must be displayed and interpreted. The symbols of the position must be transferred to the new initiate, who must then exchange and distribute the required amounts and types of goods. During the initiations the candidate must at all times exhibit humility, restraint, detachment, and willingness to cooperate. He must show the necessary intellectual and moral readiness.

Transgression of bwami prescriptions must be avoided at all costs by the participants. Mistakes may cause delays in the initiatory procedures or indefinite postponement of the rites, so that additional distributions of goods may be required later. Most initiations imply, among other things, the transfer of collectively held initiation objects from the most recent initiate to the candidate. To that end, agreements are necessary between the groups concerned. There are also restrictions. For example, a man cannot receive the collectively held objects from his own father or senior brother. Either he must wait until at least one other person in his ritual community receives the objects through initiation, or he must obtain them from his maternal uncles. Frequently the initiate in charge of such objects aspires to a higher initiation either following or coinciding with the initiation of the kinsman to whom he is to transfer them. The ensuing series of chain reactions within the ritual communities makes the problem of consensus particularly complex and delicate.

Bwami has all major characteristics of a voluntary association.[8] It is a specific body of persons who have achieved a variety of statuses or initiatory states. Membership is not specifically based on kinship, age, contract, wealth, or political allegiance. Although all these factors are of some significance in achieving membership, none of them is determining. Ultimately all are overshadowed by the intellectual and moral qualifications of the candidate, by his personal efforts, and consequently by the support he can muster. The privileges of membership range from the exclusive ownership of many kinds of art objects to the possession of distinctive insignia and dance paraphernalia. Initiates possess a special knowledge, condensed in thousands of proverbs and aphorisms which are sung, clarified, and interpreted by means of specialized music, dances, dramatic performances, and displays of objects. Bwami members share common purposes that underlie the political, economic, religious, artistic, and social life of the people. They are expressly organized to achieve these purposes and to satisfy common interests. Therefore they pretend to have the material, moral, and spiritual means to prevent infringements of their rules or impairment of their existence.

[8] For a definition and discussion of voluntary association, see Biebuyck (1955), Bohannan (1963, pp. 154–163), Lowie (1921, pp. 245–323; 1950, pp. 294–316), Mair (1965, pp. 59–60 and *passim*).

The Bwami Association

It would be improper to call bwami a secret society, for its membership is publicly known. A great show is made of the insignia pertaining to the initiatory level; many of the distinctive paraphernalia, particularly hats and belts, are constantly worn. Initiations are not held secretly. Everybody knows when and where they will take place and who the participants will be. And, in one way or another, every adult member of the community participates directly or indirectly in the ceremonies. It is true, of course, that the core proceedings during initiations are not known to outsiders; therefore they are held in closed initiation huts or in a village from which noninitiates are excluded. The purposes of bwami, as well as the basic principles of its teachings, are known to all Lega. A veil of secrecy hides the types of objects used in displays, the configurations that are made of them, and the ways in which they are handled and interpreted.

On the other hand, the association is not fully voluntary. Occasionally certain individuals, particularly those who have violated bwami taboos, are forced into the organization. Since membership in bwami is the highest-ranking value in Lega society, however, it is always difficult to grasp the extent to which an individual minds being forcibly inducted. His main difficulties would be the rapid accumulation af goods necessary for a compulsory initiation and, subsequently, the postponement of other plans, such as an additional marriage. Furthermore, the bad reputation of such an individual might make it difficult for his offspring and other close agnates to be initiated or to move up in rank.

Bwami is a multipurpose association. Its secondary purposes include political, economic, social, artistic, religious, and recreational functions. All these derive from its primary purpose, which is the pursuit of wisdom and moral excellence, a leitmotiv that runs through all the initiations. Even those who have reached the highest grade find many avenues remaining open for enhancing these values and asserting personal achievement, mainly by tutoring the incumbents of junior positions. The acquisition and distribution of wealth play an enormous role before, during, and after the initiations. Yet it must be emphasized, again and again, that the wealthy do not have a disproportionate share of influence and do not achieve the higher grades more easily than others. The principle is aptly summarized in the Lega statements, "Bwami is bought; greatness in bwami is not bought," and "Those who suffer from dizziness never get to the top [of the tree]; they turn back at the intersections of the branches." In other words, moral excellence and wisdom, with everything that follows from them, like support from kinsmen and initiates, are the conditioning factors for levels of achievement.

The Lega are divided into a cascade of ritual communities, small or large, depending on the level of initiations. Whereas autonomous initiations at the kongabulumbu level are frequently organized by a tertiary lineage or by two or three of them linked together (by territorial and uterine links), kindi initiations involve an entire clan or even two or three linked clans. The number of initiates at different levels varies from one ritual community to another. Obviously, the social influence of individuals in a community is determined largely by grade: kindi has social priority over yananio; yananio, over ngandu; lutumbo lwa kindi has social priority over musagi wa kindi which, in turn, has priority over lutumbo lwa yananio.

Because there are no set restrictions as to the number of members in any grade of bwami, several individuals in a ritual community may have acieved the same level. Let us assume that in a specific community the highest grade, lutumbo lwa kindi, is occupied by more than one person. In theory, the kindi emphasize during their initiations that they are all equal; by wearing similar masks, they compare themselves to *tumbukutu* insects, all of which look alike. Practice reveals, however, that differences do in fact exist (but these must not be verbally stressed). Such differences arise from a variety of sources. There are definitely no young men among the kindi, yet not all kindi in the group are of the same chronological age. Those who are older deserve special respect and must be treated with consideration. If they are very old they rarely, or never, participate in dances and ceremonies, but they honor the gathering by their very presence. They share in the distributions equally with the active participants. In addition, they receive select portions of the meat (e.g., the liver and other pieces that are considered delicacies). Special attention is drawn to them in such songs as "The old one of kindi has come for the dances from far away."

Age, as well as kinship seniority, carries privilege and merits consideration, but has no special power or authority. A kindi who occupies a father or senior brother position is entitled to respect from a kindi in the son or junior brother position. The criteria that entitle a man to superior power or authority are seniority in the kindi grade, specialized skill and knowledge, extra- or supra-kindi achievements, tutorship, wisdom. The most senior living incumbent of kindi, unless he is very old or very sick, is usually the one who holds in trust a large ivory figurine or mask that is the ultimate symbol of the unity and autonomy of the ritual community. He must bring this integrative symbol to some of the highest kindi rituals. Since ritual resistance is built into the position he occupies, it is no easy task to persuade him to participate. He has the power to activate and speed up the initiations, or to defer and slow them down.

The most junior in the kindi grade temporarily holds in trust the *mutulwa* basket, containing vital initiation objects and expressing the ritual autonomy and unity of the community. He too has power over the proceedings; since he must transfer the basket to the initiate, the ceremonies cannot be held in his absence.

All kindi are familiar with the initiation objects and their meanings, but only a few, perhaps not more than one or two in a community, possess the necessary skill to organize a rite and lead the songs, dances, and dramatic events. Few know how to construct the configurations of objects and interpret them. These specialists (called *nsingia*, preceptor; *kalinganya*, thinker; or *kantangantanga*, leader) serve as executive organizers of initiations. They ensure the proper sequences, displays, and interpretations of the rites. Some of them have wide fame in Legaland. All are invested with prestige, and all are esteemed.

The Lega believe that a kindi is complete or perfect only if he has performed other duties, such as tutoring new kindi candidates and guiding them through the initiations. In some areas there are as many as two to three levels of tutorship which make the kindi complete. Individuals who have gone through various forms of tutorship understandably have more prestige and authority than those who have just become kindi themselves. For any single kindi initiation, two or more high-ranking initiates fulfill special functions or tutorship. Their specific ad hoc privileges and duties are mainly to supervise the accumulation and distribution of goods, to check the attitudes of the candidate so that he makes no mistakes, and to keep in check the sometimes playfully extravagant demands of other initiates. Some kindi achieve immense prestige and widespread fame from their proven skills as orators, spokesmen, and arbiters. If altercations arise before or during initiations, their intervention usually has a conciliatory effect.

The striking characteristic of the system, then, is that no single person has superior or ultimate control over decisions and procedures. A complex machinery of checks and balances is at work; kinship and friendship relationships between initiates complement and cut across the criteria of differentiation. Bwami, the Lega say, brings together people who otherwise might hate one another. Emulation and social ambition are cultivated, but extravagance and abuse of power among initiates, or between initiates and candidate, are effectively kept in check. A kindi is not a ruler, a chief, or an autocrat. He is, as the Lega put it, "The great one who is known among the good ones."

Bwami as a Hierarchy of Titles. The outline of grades, levels, and ritual cycles presented in an earlier section is but one example of a bwami hierarchy. It does not, nor was it intended to, reveal substantial differences in nomenclature and number of grades and subdivisions between the western and southern Lega, on the one hand, and the eastern Lega and the Bembe on the other. The important fact to remember is that the grades are invariably structured into a fixed, irreversible hierarchy. Privileges, duties, status, prestige, authority, and power are linked with the different grades. In particular, deeper and deeper knowledge is acquired by the initiate as he moves up in the hierarchy. Recognition of seniority in grade, personal achievement, and personal skill create a separate system of titles which do not conflict with the hierarchy of grades, for acquisition of a certain title always presupposes prior advancement to a certain level. An individual does not achieve the utmost position in bwami merely by being initiated into lutumbo lwa kindi. The idea that the path of initiation is endless is frequently stated: "I thought that the water was dried up; lo! under the fallen leaves is more water." Consequently, a kindi covets the temporary titles of tutor, guardian, and so forth, which are available to him, for they will make him into a perfect kindi.

1. *Skipping a grade.*—Normally, in any ritual community an individual systematically passes through the long, fixed chain of initiations from kongabulumbu through ngandu to yananio and kindi, in a procedure referred to as *kutongania*. Throughout Legaland, however, one encounters individuals who have skipped the yananio grade *(lutabi lumozi, kipopolo, or kilolo)*, owing to special circumstances. Most often, when yananio is omitted, it is because an individual already initiated at the ngandu level has been hastily inducted into kindi. In Legaland the ngandu grade is known as *mpala za makano*, the initiation of the crossroads. The situation arises when an initiate dies during the final preparations for the kindi initiations or during the actual initiations. Custom requires that an agnate who can take the place of the dead kinsman be quickly found in the ritual community. The substitute must be acceptable to high-ranking initiates on moral grounds and may therefore have to be someone of lower than yananio rank. The Lega tend to select the substitute from among ngandu initiates. The oral will of the dying kindi may also be decisive in the process of skipping a grade. When Kigumbo, a kindi, was dying he left a will stating that his senior son, Kampanga (then a musagi wa yananio), was to finish lutumbo lwa yananio and that his junior son, Matumba (then a ngandu), was to replace the father in kindi.

The Lega do not consider the skipping of a grade to be a privilege; rather, it is encumbered with disadvantages. A kindi who is not initiated into yananio cannot participate in the vital *mukumbi* and *kasisi* rites of that grade or share in the distributions of goods attendant upon those rites. In some areas it is impossible for a kindi without yananio ever to supervise the yananio initiations. Furthermore, the induction of a ngandu into kindi does not necessarily imply that he will have a complete kindi initiation. If the dead kinsman for whom he is substituting has already achieved musagi wa kindi, the new initiate will briefly be shown some of the basic initiation objects (a procedure called *kukambula*) and then be led directly into lutumbo lwa kindi. In other words, much of the grandeur and prestige associated with the prolonged initiations and the dramatic events, and some of the privileges of kindi, are lost in the abbreviated procedure.

2. *Doubling a grade.*—This procedure, allowed only in some Lega communities, is burdened with numerous restrictions. Under no circumstances can kindi be doubled. If yananio is doubled, the individual con-

cerned is automatically denied access to kindi. In fact, very few individuals have gone through yananio initiations twice, and the immediate reasons for doing so are kept obscure. There can be no doubt, however, that yananio is doubled whenever a yananio initiate, even though he has sufficient goods available for the highest initiations, is unable to reach kindi because he is unacceptable to existing kindi or because he is guilty of transgressing taboos. There is, in short, no special prestige attached to doubling yananio. The only advantage is economic: a yananio who has doubled the grade is entitled to two shares in all distributions of goods.

3. *Lwanza.*—Properly speaking, *lwanza* is not a grade. Rather it is a title conferred upon an individual who, having gone through kindi, has made himself famous by organizing a lavish feast at which large quantities of food and other valuables are distributed among many people, initiates and noninitiates, kinsmen and nonkinsmen, men and women, elders and youths. (*Lwanza* is derived from the verb *kwanza,* meaning to spread out.) In this potlatch-like ceremony, prestige seeking, which is always cultivated in bwami, reaches its most extravagant form.

Special Statuses in Bwami. Special statuses pertain to temporary possession of collectively held initiation objects (kept in shoulder bags, baskets, or singly); circumcision rights; distribution of sacred animals; various forms of tutorship; special skills as preceptor, dancer, or singer; and special functions assumed before, during, and after the death of high-ranking initiates.

1. *Ownership of musutwa, lutala, musimbi, mwene we ikaga, and kibabulilo rights.*—The acquisition, ownership, and transmission of these rights are intimately interconnected with one another and with the system of initiations and grades in bwami. *Musutwa* is a shoulder bag or basket containing collectively held objects of the kongabulumbu initiation. The actual contents differ from area to area; usually the bag contains natural objects like pieces of liana, raffia fibers, jaws of fish and genets, mollusk shells, nutshells, fruit shells, warthog tusks, tibias of monkeys, and pieces of resin.

Lutala is a shoulder bag or basket containing collectively held objects displayed during kansilembo initiations. These objects symbolize the right of a certain group to erect its own circumcision lodge (but not to initiate the circumcision). The bag contains natural objects such as pangolin scales, the end portion of a pangolin tail, giant snail shells, and fish jaws, and manufactured objects like a small pot, a small knife, a miniature dugout canoe, and a sharp scepter-like piece of ivory or elephant bone.

Musimbi, symbolized by a simple piece of *ibesebese* wood, bears on the right "to show the circumcision," as the Lega put it, which means the privilege of initiating a cycle of circumcision ceremonies.

In most areas *mwene we ikaga,* the right of the pangolin knife, is not distinguished from *kibabulilo*, the right to receive and distribute sacred animals in one's village and to hold kansilembo initiations. The sacred animals are: *ikaga*, giant pangolin or *Manis gigantea*; *zuzumba*, the largest species of the smaller pangolin or *Manis tricuspis*; the *izezekumbe* turtle or *Kinyxis belliana*; the *kamitende* snake or *Dendroaspis angusticeps*; *nkenge*, the bongo antelope or *Taurotragus oryx*; *ndio* or crowned eagle. In some areas *mukondekonde*, the small crocodile or *Osteolaemus*, the leopard, and the *nkamba* fish or *Chrysichthys cranchii* are also included. The claws, the tail, and the liver of the aardvark (*ntumba* or *Orycteropus*) also fall into this category. There are regional variations. Sometimes only some of the animals listed are to be handled by the owners of *mwene we ikaga* and *kibabulilo*, while others may be distributed by any kindi or yananio initiate. The pangolin, the *izezekumbe* turtle, and the *kamitende* snake are always handled by the incumbents of special positions. In areas where the two rights are not distinguished, the sacred animals are taken directly to the village of the master of the pangolin knife, who leads in cutting and distributing the animals. In areas where the rights are distinguished, the animals are taken to the village of *kibabulilo*; for their actual distribution the master of the pangolin knife is called in.

The rights discussed here are all held exclusively by members of the bwami association, but not everyone in bwami can hold them. Frequently the acquisition of one right presupposes the prior holding and transfer of another right. Certain basic principles govern the holding and transfer of these rights: (1) One cannot obtain *lutala* without first holding *musutwa*. (2) One cannot get either *musimbi* or *mwene we ikaga* without first holding *lutala*. (3) Before obtaining *lutala*, one must first confer the kongabulumbu grade, with which *musutwa* is connected, upon a kinsman. (4) Possession of *musutwa* does not necessarily imply ulterior acquisition of any of the other rights. (5) Before being initiated into lutumbo lwa yananio in some areas, or into lutumbo lwa kindi in other areas, an owner of *lutala* or *musutwa* must first transfer the right to a kinsman of appropriate grade and social position. (6) Before being initiated into lutumbo lwa kindi, an owner of *musimbi* or *mwene* must first transmit the right to a kinsman of appropriate grade and social position.

Any of the four rights (counting *mwene* and *kibabulilo* as one) is acquired by (1) inheritance at the death of an agnate who held the right; (2) legacy from an agnate who is moving up to a grade that does not permit the holding of the right; or (3) purchase from another group (generally by virtue of a cognatic or affinal link). An individual can acquire these rights successively from different kinsmen by inheritance or legacy; he does not necessarily obtain them from the same person.

In some communities the transfer of *musutwa* follows the cycle of kongabulumbu initiations within the ritually autonomous group. That is, it is transferred by the most recently initiated kongabulumbu to the candi-

The Bwami Association

date for initiation. Elsewhere the transfer is made within a family group or a small lineage when the owner of *musutwa* dies or accedes to lutumbo lwa yananio.

No general rules prescribe the number of *musutwa* baskets or shoulder bags that may exist in a given clan. Nor is the structural level of the group that can have a basket and can act as an autonomous unit in kongabulumbu initiations specified. The level seems to be related to the numerical size of the cooperating groups, to the number of subdivisions in the clan, to uterine linkages that are recognized between lineages, to territorial compactness or dispersal of the group, and to the number of baskets purchased from outside the group by powerful initiates, past or present.

The large Beiamunsange clan illustrates this point very clearly. It consists of seven primary lineages (Kimpiri, Itebo, Nzibu, Ngozi, Nyama, Muzunzu, and Koudo) and includes an eighth incorporated primary lineage (Kilimono) which groups the descendants of riverain populations with whom the Beiamunsange trace an ancient, common history. Kilimono has none of the rights discussed. Kimpiri and Itebo are paired as descendants of the same wife of the clan founder, as also are Muzunzu and Koudo. Nyama is paired with the incorporated Kilimono group, while Nzibu and Ngozi are thought of as the sons of different wives of the clan founder. Only one basket is found in each of the primary lineages Muzunzu and Koudo; there are from three to seven each in the other primary lineages. If several *musutwa* exist within a primary lineage, they are distributed by secondary lineages. In other words, each secondary lineage has its own *musutwa*. If a secondary lineage is numerically strong and genealogically complex, the *musutwa* are held within tertiary lineages, but not every such lineage has its own basket. The individuals who actually hold the *musutwa* in the lineages are all incumbents of lutumbo lwa yananio or musagi wa kindi. In the Beiamunsange clan the *musutwa* is transferred either when its holder dies or when he moves up to lutumbo lwa kindi. For example, when the holder dies, the basket is given in trust to a *musutwa* owner of another lineage in the clan "to hide it away" until a duly recognized claimant asks for it. The claimant is preferably selected from the extended family of the dead owner. The basket then passes from a father or little father to a son or from a senior to a junior agnate or vice versa. Frequently, however, the claimant is selected from another family or lineage within the group associated with the *musutwa*. In this event the basket must ultimately return to a person in the original owner's direct agnatic line of descent.

Lutala and *musutwa* are closely connected. Acquisition of the latter is a precondition to possession of the former. Frequently both rights are held simultaneously by the same initiate. The Beiamunsange clan has exactly as many *lutala* as *musutwa*, and in every instance the two rights are simultaneously held by the same person. The transfer of *lutala* is similar to the transfer of *musutwa;* it occurs during the kansilembo initiations. The owner of the *lutala* right usually lives in a small hamlet, known under the special designation *kankenda,* situated at some distance from the main village where all kansilembo initiations are held. As noted above, possession of *lutala* gives the owner the right to erect a separate circumcision lodge near his hamlet, but not to initiate circumcision rites. This right belongs to *musimbi.* When the owner of *musimbi* initiates the cycle, each *lutala* owner who has a ritual relationship with him sends a young man to the *musimbi's* village for circumcision. The operation takes place in the village behind a fence after a masked mwami (called *mundala*) has chased away all the women. The boy is then returned to his own village, where the circumcision and instruction of other boys can proceed.

The possession of *musimbi* is linked with the right to initiate a circumcision cycle. The number of lineages and individuals holding this right is sharply limited. Not every primary lineage holds it, and no primary lineage ever has more than one *musimbi.* In the Beiamunsange clan I knew of only nine initiates who held this right. All were below the lutumbo lwa kindi level and all belonged to lineages that also had the three other rights. *Musimbi* is transferred in a close agnatic line from father to son or from brother to brother. Sometimes the right is "traditionally" held by a lineage, which means that nobody can explain how it originated there. Sometimes it is bought, and then the details of the transactions (including payments of shell money, a goat, a knife, and food supplies) are well known. A *musimbi* owner has the right to hold the preliminary circumcision dances, to erect the circumcision stockade in his village, and to set up the fence of prohibition (no war or dispute is allowed while circumcision is in progress). The owner has the privilege of proceeding with the first operations on Aluta, the son of the village headman, and on Mukuli, the son of the *musimbi* holder, and to confer upon *lutala* owners the right to organize their local lodges. The senior wife of a *musimbi* is the only female allowed in the village where the operations take place, and she is blindfolded. Permanent ritual linkages connecting *musimbi*-holding lineages of different clans entail fixed sequences in which the initiations can be undertaken. Although each *musimbi* is autonomous in his own sphere, he is dependent on the sequences set by the ritual cycle for the actual initiation of circumcision ceremonies.

Mwene we ikaga, or right of the pangolin knife, is found in fairly substantial numbers in a clan. Acquisition of the knife is preconditioned by earlier or simultaneous possession of *musutwa* and *lutala.* Within any clan, a number of secondary and tertiary lineages have the right of the pangolin knife, which belongs to them by virtue of tradition or through purchase. When the owner of the knife dies or moves to lutumbo lwa kindi, the right is temporarily transferred to another owner in the clan or in a cognatically related group. The knife is transmitted to the rightful claimant when a pangolin is killed and is to be distributed in his group.[9] The owner of the knife lives in a hamlet especially designated as *kibembelo*. Most sacred animals must be brought to, and distributed in, this hamlet.

As noted above, in some communities the *mwene* right is distinguished from the *kibabulilo* right. The former bestows the privilege of cutting up and distributing the sacred game; the latter allows one to make the distributions in one's own village. Where the two rights are separated, there are always more *kibabulilo*-holding lineages than *mwene* owners. The distribution of knives is at the level of the primary lineage; *kibabulilo* is at the level of the secondary lineage. The situation is further complicated when a lineage that holds neither of the two rights is recognized as *mwizamulemba*, that is, when such a lineage has a claim to all the trimmings when the pangolin and other sacred animals are cut.

2. *Tutorship in kindi.*—A ritually autonomous community symbolizes its unity, among other things, by its collective possession of the *mutulwa* basket destined for the kindi initiations. The initiation objects in the basket differ from community to community. They may be natural objects, such as chimpanzee skulls, hornbill beaks, a huge dried mushroom (from the *limbalu* tree), and turtle carapaces, or manufactured items, such as a small, red-dyed, bark cloth apron adorned with porcupine quills, a miniature door of parasol wood with white and red dots, a miniature shield made of open wickerwork, a miniature ceremonial spear, and a few wooden figurines. The baskets fall in the category of objects designated by the aphorism, "Great owl that passes and passes" (*kisulukutu*), because they are transferred with each new initiation.

When a candidate is initiated into lutumbo lwa kindi as a new junior member in the grade, he is classified by the other kindi of his rank as *mutende* (a general term applied to all candidates and newly initiated members). During the initiations the *mutulwa* basket is handed over to him by the most recently initiated kindi within the autonomous ritual community; in fact, the goal of each new initiate is to transfer the basket to a new member. When such a candidate is found, the *mutulwa* holder is given the title of *mukomi*. His presence is vital for the initiations because he has to bring the basket, the significant symbol that asserts the unity of the group and its right to hold the ceremonies. He receives a special share of shell money, a goat with young, a cloth, a basket, and resin torches in the distributions that precede the actual initiations. He also participates in the distributions of gifts and food made during the initiations and receives a special share of game meat in the distributions at the end of the ceremonies.

The *mukomi* belongs to the same clan as the candidate for initiation,

---

[9] The social and ritual aspects of the accidental killing and ceremonial distribution of the pangolin are discussed by Biebuyck (1953d).

and to his primary lineage, but their relationship is usually based on a distant agnatic tie. After performing his functions as *mukomi*, a kindi has one more prescribed duty. He must serve as *kilezi* (or *kyinamizi*) for the second most recent initiate in his group. For example, if A was *mukomi* for B, then B is *mukomi* for C, and A is *kilezi* for C. The *kilezi* brings a basket filled with *ntolo* leaves to the initiation and participates in a special distribution of goods. His share consists of shell money, a basket, axes, torches, and of meat distributed at the end of the initiations.

After a kindi has served as *kilezi*, the way is open for him to sponsor persons who are particularly close to him and whose initiations he wants, as a point of honor, to bring to a fruitful end. He may first serve as *kakusa*, in which capacity he supervises the preparation and accumulation of goods necessary for the kindi initiations and presides over their distribution. Before the initiations he supervises the threading of the shell money, the collection of firewood and leaves (to wrap the meat), and the transmission of drum messages to call the initiates together. During the initiations he has ultimate control over the distribution of victuals and other goods, which he must have available in the required quantities at the right moment (including such things as water which cannot be stored in advance). The *kakusa* fulfills the role of "guardian of the tomb" should the individual whose initiations he tutored die. If that individual did not transfer the collectively held basket before his death, the *kakusa* keeps it in trust, temporarily, until a new initiate is inducted. This delicate task must be performed honestly and impartially, with superior skill and wisdom, so as to avoid tension and friction before, during, and after the initiations.

Every kindi is pretty sure to serve as *mukomi* and *kilezi*, but it is not so certain that he will become a *kakusa*. The competition for this form of tutorship, which carries high prestige, is keen. Some individuals achieve exceptional fame by serving several times as *kakusa*. The *kakusa* is not necessarily an agnatic relative of the candidate; he may be one of the latter's maternal uncles. Frequently, however, to consolidate his position, he is both an agnatic and a cognatic relative; that is, he is a member of the candidate's clan who is also linked through marriage relationships with the candidate's father or paternal grandfather. The *kakusa* gets a more or less fixed share (shell money, cloth, two iron armlets, oil, salt, and one antelope) in the distributions that precede the initiations, but he receives his share secretly. He participates also in the distributions at the end of the initiations, receiving oil, salt, and an antelope. In some areas he is assisted by a *kilego*, an initiate of appropriate rank who is often a rather old man and may be a very close relative (father or little father) to the candidate. When available, the *kilego* is the actual distributor of the goods. Obviously so close a relative receives an important share of the goods: shell money, a freshly killed animal, a bag of salt, a pot of oil, and a pot.

another clan who was the classificatory sororal nephew of Kandolo's father. For many months Kandolo studied the craft with Kintoko. Kizabuti, another preceptor, learned the skill from his senior half brother, who had learned it from his patrilateral cross-cousin. The latter had learned it from his mother's brother (Kizabuti's father), who had learned it from his own father. There is at least one preceptor in most ritually autonomous communities. A preceptor gets special recognition during and at the end of the ceremonies; he receives the hearts of all animals distributed and a large amount of shell money in addition to sharing in regular distributions as incumbent of a certain grade. Some art objects—for example, wooden animal figurines sometimes adorned with pangolin scales—are owned exclusively by preceptors.

5. *Mukondi we idumba.*—This guardian of the tomb supervises the funerary ceremonies when an initiate of high rank dies. He cares for the tomb for several months after the burial and also guards some of the paraphernalia and insignia of the dead. The guardian must be of the same rank as the deceased, and, if possible, he is the person who acted as the dead man's *kakusa*. He may be selected from distant agnatic, or from affinal and cognatic, relatives; he is often a sororal nephew or brother-in-law.

An initiate of yananio or kindi rank is interred in the hut of his senior initiated wife (kalonda for a yananio; kanyamwa for a kindi). The burial proceedings begin with the designation of the guardian of the tomb who, from that point on, takes charge of the ceremonies.[12]

The first phase (*kwangia mwino*), designed to strengthen or to communicate force to the village, consists of a number of ordeals and purification rites to which members of the community are exposed. There exists a variety of procedures. Most deaths are attributed to sorcery, and women, in particular, are held responsible for sorcery practices. They are subjected to several possible tests to find out who among them might have caused the death. They must undergo the *kiloba* ordeal: mashed bananas are placed in the mouth of the deceased and then the women are invited to eat some of this food; or, the body and the clothes of the deceased are cleansed with water, from which the women are invited to drink. The implication of such tests is, of course, that whoever refuses to participate in the tests will be found guilty, or that the participating guilty, though not confessing, will cause their own destruction. Women may also be subjected to *kusuluka kitumba*, to step over the corpse. In this test they are required to jump over the corpse, placed in the middle of the village, while initiates, beating the soil with the petioles of banana leaves, shout, "If you have killed him, you will die." When there is denial of guilt, or uncertainty

---

[12] The burial procedures mentioned here were among the first customs to disappear in Legaland, partly because of the ban on bwami and partly because of strict local legislation on burials.

about it, the initiates have recourse to divination and eventually to the administration of the *kabi* poison ordeal. The drinking of poison does not automatically mean death. One who is already shaking from the effects of the poison may be "pulled out" from *kabi* through a ceremonial procedure and the administration of a counterpoison by a sororal nephew or by the master of the land. If no such help is offered, the person found guilty is beaten to death on the outskirts of the village near a tree that grows big aerial roots, and the body is abandoned there.

The second phase, presided over by the guardian of the tomb, is *kulaga mwino*, to say good-bye to the village. After the grave is dug in the hut of the senior initiated wife, initiates carry the corpse in ceremonial procession to the middle of the village, while three drums are beaten and the *kimbilikiti* mirliton of the circumcision rites sings. The procession walks on *nkumbula* and phrynium leaves that are scattered on the ground.

The third phase is *kwanga idumba*, to arrange the tomb. *Kwanga* also implies to bring in harmony, to arrange something so that it has no dissonance or bad smell. The naked corpse is buried in a squatting position with the head protruding above the mound, which is fenced off with a feather rope fastened to small poles, each holding a *ntolo* fruit (symbol of fertility). Burning torches also surround the mound. A hook placed in the mouth of the deceased against the upper jaw is attached with a liana to a bent stick firmly planted in the soil. The mourning period may last as long as two months, during which most of the participating initiates remain in the village. At this time they may proceed with *bwami wanginga*, induction into kongabulumbu of a young agnate of the deceased. Part of the wealth left by the dead kindi is used for this purpose. In many areas, however, this initiation is deferred until after the final stages of the funerary arrangements.

The fourth phase consists of cleaning and preparation of the skull (*lukungu*). After the head of the buried kindi is completely detached from the body, it is washed in water, rubbed with oil and camwood powder, and then slowly dried above a fire. In some areas the head is placed in the basket of collective initiation objects; in others it is buried separately; in still others it is kept in a small shrine *(bisinga)* constructed on the roof of the hut belonging to the head of the lineage.[13]

The next phase is the "cleansing of the grave." Water is poured over the grave and several of the insignia of the dead kindi are placed on the tomb: an ivory mask, the ivory figurines, the wickerwork rattle, and, if he held it, the pangolin knife.

---

[13] Delhaise observed some of the shrines in which human skulls were preserved. According to some informants, human skulls were also preserved in collectively held baskets. This point is unclear to me because large masks and chimpanzee skulls take the place of human skulls in initiations.

The final stage is *kuigula idumba*, to open the grave. The central rite is an ordeal called *musile*. One or more antelopes are suspended above the tomb for one or two days. The animals are then cooked with bananas, and all participants in the ceremonies, both male and female, are invited to eat the food. Refusal to do so is an indication that one has wronged the dead kindi, either through a curse *(kabamba)*, through sorcery *(buganga)*, or through ritual pollution resulting from adultery in pregnancy *(mpita)*.

In many areas the *musile* rite is followed by the induction of a young agnate into kongabulumbu. The funerary proceedings always end with a council which decides who is the appropriate candidate for initiation to the grade held by the deceased. If the deceased had completely finished his initiations, there is no special urgency for inducting his substitute. If, however, the initiate dies during the initiations or while preparing for them, a real emergency exists, for it is strictly prescribed that the goods accumulated by the deceased in order to satisfy his initiation requirements can, under no circumstances, be divided or inherited. They are to be invested in the initiation of a kinsman.

The *mukondi* takes charge of the insignia and paraphernalia (ivory mask, ivory figurines, necklace of leopard teeth, wickerwork rattle, hats, dance paraphernalia) of the late kindi until a kinsman of the dead man is initiated into the appropriate grade. Under no conditions whatsoever can the initiated wives of the dead kindi hold these objects in trust. Some of the insignia—the *nkumbu* hat, the *bisaba* aprons made from hide, the *mizigi* belts, the *nsago* shoulder bags, the *nkeka* chair, and the *mukulu* walking stick—are displayed several months after the *musile* rite, in the dead kindi's village. This ritual display is called *kakenge*. The objects remain in the abandoned village as a "sign" unless a properly initiated sororal nephew of the deceased appropriates some of them. Also, on the occasion of *kakenge*, it is decided how the widows of the deceased (except for his wives initiated to bunyamwa) will be distributed among the kinsmen. The *kakenge* rite ends with a big dinner party. The remaining objects are brought by the *mukondi*, usually during the initiations, and handed over to the successor in a rite called *mbisulile byasigile tata*, "unfold for me the things that my father has left." For his services as guardian of the paraphernalia, the *mukondi* receives at least a goat. He may also inherit one of the widows of the deceased if her kinship position permits.

6. *Kazombolo*.—Described as "a man of good heart who does not easily refuse to execute tasks, a trustworthy person," the *kazombolo* acts as messenger and *homme de confiance* for the kindi.[14] In a few areas there is only one *kazombolo* per ritual community; he acts as messenger for all

---

[14] Use of the title *kazombolo* was on the decline by the time of my fieldwork. Most kindi no longer had a personal messenger; some had never had one, while others had not selected a replacement when the incumbent *kazombolo* died.

the kindi in that group. Usually, however, each kindi has his own personal messenger, to whom he is linked, in one way or another, by a kinship bond. In actual relationships I have studied, the *kazombolo* is junior half brother, junior agnate, matrilateral cross-cousin, maternal uncle, or sororal nephew to the kindi, but the general tendency is for both to belong to the same clan. The messenger is usually of the ngandu grade but is definitely not higher than lutumbo lwa yananio. He lives in the same village as the kindi to whom he is attached. The form of mild joking that exists between the two men is reflected in various situations. The *kazombolo* is permitted to dance in the row of kanyamwa women. In some kindi and bunyamwa rites he cooks the meat. In some communities a man's *kazombolo* preferably acts as that man's guardian of the tomb. He inherits from the dead kindi the walking cane with genet skin, a small copper knife, and one necklace of oblong beads. In some parts of Legaland he may also claim the matrimonial goods that were disbursed for one of the dead kindi's female agnates. Among titleholders, the *kazombolo* is the only person to wear a special hat; it is either woven from raffia fibers and adorned with rows of cowries or made of goatskin and covered with feathers on the top and decorated with cowries at the bottom rim.

7. *Other special positions.*—Some male and female initiates are designated by special titles because of certain skills they have, certain duties they assume, and certain privileges they have acquired. The title *nyakabundi* is held by a male initiate whose father or grandfather introduced a new cycle of rites or a new grade to the community. Whenever initiations that incorporate these rites are held, special recognition must be given to the *nyakabundi*. Early in the preparations for initiation he is given a goat. Sometimes the title *nyakambunda* is given to a very old kindi who speaks in a weak little voice. The initiates await his arrival before beginning the rites. During some of the rites he sits near the initiation hut and hands to the dancers, in turn, such initiation objects as a collaret of dried banana leaves, a liana with a pangolin claw wrapped in wickerwork, or an iron bracelet.

Initiates at all levels may be drummers, singers, or dancers of fame. They are held in high esteem because they add joy and decorum to the ceremonies. They receive gifts and rewards in recognition of their art, but they derive no special power and authority because of it. The same holds true for the carvers of art objects (*mubazi wa nkondo*, the carver of the adze). Carvers are not always members of bwami. If they are, they may be incumbents of the highest or of the lowest grade. Often they are blacksmiths. From the commissioner they receive the ivory or bone in which to work, and they are paid in shell money after the work is completed. Their social position, however, depends on the titles and special statuses achieved in bwami. Few, if any, individuals are specifically remembered for their outstanding skill in carving. In instances where carvers' names are recalled, it is because the individuals who are celebrated also happen to be high-ranking initiates. If the origin of a particular carving is traced through a list of its actual owners, the names recalled represent a line of inheritance of the object and of succession to grades; the line ends with the name of the real or alleged first owner of the object, not with that of its creator.

Female initiates with special titles include *nyagwamana*, an initiated woman who has learned the special technique of *kanganza*, singing in a high-pitched voice almost to the point of shrieking. One or more of these women join the small group of male drummers, rattlers, and singers who form the orchestra and choir for higher initiations. The *nyagwamana* has the privileged share of the tongue and the diaphragm of all animals distributed. In some areas the *nyamalembo*, an initiate of the bulonda level similar to the *kazombolo* among the kindi, acts as a *femme de confiance* for the highest-ranking female initiates (kanyamwa). She guards all objects related to bwami instead of leaving them in the care of the wife who is a high-ranking initiate.

ACCUMULATION AND DISTRIBUTION OF FOOD AND COMMODITIES

The Importance of Exchange in Bwami. Every initiation is preceded by a period of preparation, whose duration varies with the importance of the grade sought and with the success of the candidate in eliciting support from kinsmen and initiates. During this period the candidate must make a tremendous effort to bring together all resources needed and to prove himself acceptable to the initiates. In other words, he must accumulate the goods necessary for feasts, initiation fees, and gifts. In addition, if he is seeking initiation into a higher grade, he must construct houses and other buildings for accommodation of participants and for holding the rites. The candidate must gain the confidence of and win favors from the members of his own agnatic group, of groups that are ritually linked to his own, and of groups with which he has affinal and cognatic ties. Every cycle and every rite demands the distribution of varied quantities of goods, sometimes strictly specified as to type, amount, and combinations, sometimes more loosely defined.

The many types of distributions cover a wide range of goods. All valuables distributed in bwami initiations may be classified in two broad categories.[15] Some goods are consumed on the spot. They form the basis for the lavish dinner parties that are held throughout the initiations. Each participant has the right to put aside a small provision *(bulungila)* which is sent or taken home to relatives. The general principles prevailing in the

---

[15] Different aspects of the distribution of goods linked with marriage, death, and bwami are discussed by Biebuyck (1953b, d, e; 1954d, e).

distributions of food derive from sexual considerations. Sometimes women have their own share as opposed to that of their husbands, but in a few instances only the women receive a share. The second category includes goods that are taken home by the initiates, principally shell money, salt, and oil. Depending on the rites, such commodities are transferred from the candidate to the initiates, on either an individual or a collective basis. In the latter case a specified quantity is set aside for the participants of a certain grade, each of whom is obligated to further distribute his share.

In the distributions of food and other commodities, different categories of participants must be recognized. First, a distinction is made between initiates who have been formally invited to participate and those who have not. It is a strict rule of bwami that no initiates who have the rank appropriate to the particular initiation can be excluded from the ceremonies. Initiates from remote villages who happen to be visiting kinsmen near the areas where bwami rites are being held thus can spontaneously partake in them, but their shares of distributed goods are smaller. A distinction is also made between male and female initiates. Although women are excluded from some rites, it is unthinkable to hold initiations without the participants' initiated wives being present. Another distinction is based on grade differences. In all initiations there are participants of different grades; obviously the hierarchic organization of the association receives explicit recognition. Kinship principles also play a role: agnation versus cognation and affinity; respective kinship positions occupied by the candidate and by each of the initiates present; chronological age; structural relationships between the lineages of the participants and the candidate. Finally, among the initiates there are some who perform special functions: preceptors, drummers, singers, tutors and sponsors, those who act as witnesses, and those who are in possession of collectively held initiation objects.

All these distinctions receive formal recognition and transform even the simplest distribution into a long and complicated process, as illustrated by the actual distribution of a *mpombi* (Grant's gazelle) during lutumbo lwa kindi initiations. When the animal is cut up, certain parts are given to specific persons or to small groups of individuals: tongue, esophagus, and diaphragm to the *nyagwamana* woman; a piece from the back to the drummers; a piece from the back and the two front legs to the percussionists; heart and lungs to the preceptors; the head to the *kakusa* tutor; liver and intestines to the oldest kindi present. A shoulder and a portion of the trimmings are set aside for the musagi wa kindi who, though not directly participating in the rites, happen to be in the village. The neck, one hind leg, and one shoulder are reserved for the women of kanyamwa rank. The remaining meat (one hind leg, chest and ribs, a portion of the back, and one portion of trimmings) belongs to the lutumbo lwa kindi. In a distribution I witnessed among the Beiankuku, eight kindi of this highest level

The Bwami Association

participated in the sharing. Five were members of the candidate's clan and three belonged to the Banamusiga, a clan ritually linked to the Beiankuku clan. Each of the four parts of the meat reserved for the eight kindi was cut in half so that the two participating groups got equal shares. It was the responsibility of the kindi in each group to make an even distribution among themselves.

A large number of take-home commodities are given during or at the end of the initiations. Some others are promised but their actual transfer may not take place until a long time afterward.

Types of Goods and Commodities Used in Bwami.

I. Edible goods
   A. *Game.* Antelopes and, to a lesser extent, monkeys are the preferred animals. Most other kinds of game meat are excluded, though elephant, buffalo, and wild pig are sometimes used. Among the many varieties of antelope, *kaseti* or duiker is the most favored; next in line are such species as *mpombi, lungaga, kakula,* and the chevrotain *kilebe.* Certain rites require a designated species of antelope, but on most occasions any of the favored antelopes is acceptable. As the Lega are fond of food and are heavy eaters, hundreds of antelopes may be required in some of the larger initiations, for which many high-ranking titleholders convene. The antelopes are used in three possible ways, and a certain rite may strictly specify a particular way: in *kilimungenda,* an entire antelope is smoked after removal of head, hide, and organs; in *kibindi,* a whole, freshly killed antelope is used; in *bungulu,* after removal of head, hide, and organs, the antelope is cut into an upper and a lower part and then smoked.
   B. *Domestic animals.* These animals are presented alive, but some rites require sacrificial killing (suffocation, strangulation, breaking of the neck, hanging), a task assigned to the preceptors and their aides. In general, goats and sheep are ritually equivalent, but some rites and procedures allow for the exchange of goats only. For certain rites the following types of goat are specified: a she-goat *(kibuti),* a he-goat *(kilimba),* a goat with young *(kikundu),* a very fat goat *(kalunga ka mpene),* or a very old he-goat *(kutu).* The categories of kinsmen to whom chickens may be given are sharply restricted: they may be given to one's wives' agnates and to one's maternal uncles, but not to one's sororal nephews or to one's sisters' husbands and their agnates.
   C. *Other foods.* Other foods used in bwami include bananas (most-

ly roasted to be eaten), pounded peanuts *(kinda)*, palm oil, salt, manioc, and rice (introduced in the late nineteenth century).

II. Shell money

The distribution of shell money is required for all rites at all levels and grades; very large quantities are needed for the highest initiations. As I elsewhere describe different aspects of shell money, here the discussion is limited to essentials.[16] Money is made from the shells of two kinds of giant snails: a terrestrial *(nkola)* and an aquatic *(nkese)* variety. The unpolished shells are fragmented into small polygons of roughly equal size, which usually are perforated and threaded *(musanga)* on raffia fibers in the manner of a necklace (pl. 109). Some shell money, however, is not perforated or threaded *(bulula)*. The unthreaded form is used in three different ways, but always in connection with particular exchanges and circumstances. First, it is distributed in small handfuls in the *nkindo* gift giving, when individual gifts are presented during the dances to drummers, singers, and dancers. Second, it is presented in small packages wrapped in phrynium leaves to the candidate when he unexpectedly runs short of money during the initiations and needs quick assistance from a relative. Third, loose shell fragments are placed in oil pots *(izumbi)* and used in matrimonial exchanges outside bwami.

There are three standard units of threaded shell money: *munkinki*, double row; *kako*, four double rows tied together; *ikumi*, a bunch of ten times four double rows tied together. The length of a row is based on body measurements. When an initiate says that he gave *ikumi lya kilunga* (ten of the *kilunga* size), for example, he means he gave ten times four double rows, each double row corresponding to the length between the tip of the middle finger and the fold of the arm. The most important sizes and their usage are as follows:

1. *Kanue:* Double row from tip of middle finger to its base (about 4 inches). Used in matrimonial exchanges and in lower initiations; occasionally used in higher initiations as gifts to visitors with whom there is no close kinship tie and who do not hold high rank in the association.
2. *Ibungakwanga:* Double row from tip of middle finger to base of palm (about 7.5 or 8 inches). Essentially used in ngandu initiations, but also in higher initiations as gifts to unrelated or distantly related participants.

[16] For a comprehensive discussion of *musanga* money and its usages, see Biebuyck (1953*b*), and, for comparative data, see Dartevelle (1953, pp. 36–49).

3. *Magombelo:* Double row from tip of middle finger to base of wrist. Most frequently used in fixed payments to specific participants in the highest initiation.
4. *Mbusa:* Double row, measured on exterior part of foot, from tip of little toe to end of heel. Used in matrimonial exchanges and in *musigo* distributions of two highest grades.
5. *Ndume:* Double row, measured on interior part of foot, from tip of big toes to end of heel. Used for the same purposes as *mbusa*, but value considered equal to one *mbusa* and one *ibungakwanga*.
6. *Kilunga:* Double row from tip of middle finger to fold of arm. Used in matrimonial exchanges and in all initiations at the higher levels. It is the most basic measure of all.
7. *Lyakazigi:* Double row from tip of middle finger to upper part of biceps. It has a value equal to one and a half *kilunga*. Infrequently used in bwami; wealthy Lega use it to a limited extent in matrimonial exchanges and in musagi wa kindi.
8. *Lyakituli:* Double row from tip of middle finger to socket of arm and shoulder. It has a value of two *kilunga*. Used in lutumbo lwa kindi and, in limited quantities, in matrimonial exchanges.

Other, more recently introduced measures—from foot to hip, from foot to nipple, from foot to top of head—have no significance for bwami.

The system of threaded shell money just described is the most widely used in Legaland. Some Babongolo, however, employ a different method of threading and measuring. Instead of working with necklace-like strings, they use small loops onto which two shell fragments are placed facing each other. Fewer shells are needed, but the work of arranging them on loops takes more time. Elsewhere, in the eastern parts of Legaland, shell money either disappeared long ago or is available only in small quantities.

According to Lega custom, everybody is free to collect shells and make his own money. Some individuals, families, and village groups are rich in shell money; other have very little. Various factors account for this inequality. Making shell money requires labor; making large quantities of it is an arduous task. Some families and individuals are industrious and others are not. In some areas the shells are found in vast quantities; in others, they are relatively rare. As a result of earlier warfare, some groups lost a part of their accumulated shell money. Other groups, whose land is rich in natural products, like salt and oil, can easily acquire shells through trade and barter. Such specialists as elephant hunters, carvers, and blacksmiths acquire shell money by selling their products. Congolese currency, earned by Lega laborers in European centers, can also buy shell money, but under no circumstances can it entirely replace shell money in the bwami context.

III. Utilities and implements

Initiations require large quantities of water for washing, drinking, and for the preparation of food. Firewood is needed for cooking and heating. Leaves (especially phrynium) are in heavy demand for wrapping food and other gifts. Resin torches (frequently presented in packages) are needed for lighting the houses. Certain payments and gifts given to specific initiates and relatives comprise iron tools (including axes, knives, billhooks, and machetes) and useful objects (needles, razors, baskets, mats, wickerwork plates, fishing nets, and pots).

IV. Clothing and adornments

Certain participants in bwami initiations receive pieces of cloth made from bark or raffia; European-made cloth is sometimes accepted. Belts made of bongo antelope hide or elephant skin, or woven and studded with cowries, are exchanged. Aprons made from genet and wildcat hides, bracelets, anklets, and beaded necklaces circulate during the initiations. Especially coveted are necklaces made of small, round, delicately polished achatina shells, which are destined for sororal nephews and sons-in-law (pl. 109, inner row).

V. Other commodities

The single most important article in this group is tobacco, which is distributed in leaves. Tobacco gardens are specially planted for the initiations. Beer and fish are excluded from the distributions. In the Bembe and Nyindu variants of bwami, and among some eastern Lega who are in contact with them, beer plays a significant role in initiations, probably because of the influence or the proximity of pastoral groups like the Shi, among whom beer drinking is extremely important in diet and ceremonialism.

Categories of Goods and Exchanges. The procurement, accumulation, and allocation of food and commodities form an intrinsic part of all cycles of initiation. Each cycle begins and ends with collection and distribution; each rite is performed against a background of consumption of food and distribution of valuables. The outline of grades, levels, and rites must be filled in with the different types of exchanges. The Lega distinguish many categories of goods, depending on the ways in which they are acquired, the manner in which they are distributed, the exact point of time when they are needed during the initiations, and so on. According to their source, goods are classified as (1) personally acquired (*ikunza lyane*);

(2) received from close agnates (*kaninkwa*); and (3) obtained from in-laws and cognates (*mululo*).

The third category is by far the most complicated. First, small gifts are deposited by unspecified individuals anonymously, as it were (if such a concept may be applied to Lega human relationships!), on the mats (*mukatanda*) the candidate has placed in the villages of in-laws and cognates when he visits during the period preparatory to the initiations. Second, large contributions are made individually by well-identified persons, such as maternal uncles, brothers-in-law, and so on, before the initiations. Basically, four types of goods are recognized according to the kinship category of the donor: *biga* or *mubigo* are goods given by the wife's agnates and maternal uncles to the husband; *igambia* are goods given by the husband's group to his wife's people; *mitumwa* are goods supplied to the candidate by his maternal uncles and sororal nephews; *ikaso* are the items he returns to them. In addition to these well-planned donations, special emergency gifts may be presented during the initiations, if it suddenly appears that certain goods are not available or are in short supply, as when goats are found to be lacking at the secret *kasisi* rite of lutumbo lwa ya-nanio. Such a situation elicits an immediate sharp reaction, opposition or even threats, from the initiators; usually the sororal nephew provides last-minute support. It is publicly known before the initiations begin, through regular visits by "inspectors" (*tutendela*), what goods have been accumulated by the candidate. Nevertheless, it is the custom for powerful candidates to hide some goods, which can then be more freely used during and after the initiations; such distributions bring desired fame to the candidate. A distinction is made between *kasenga*, declared goods, and *mbiso*, hidden ones.

The next classification has to do with the manner in which goods are distributed; they may be more or less fixed amounts given for specific rites or to specific individuals, or they may have a more casual character. Several categories may be identified. *Biziki* (or *mukano*) comprises goods that are distributed prior to the initiations, when inspectors and other initiates visit the candidate's village. *Kilisio* is all the foods that go into the preparation of the dinners. *Nkindo* includes the small amounts, usually handfuls, of shell money that are continually, but casually, given to dancers, singers, and drummers for almost every dance in every rite. *Mwikio* is a concept embracing both fixed payments given for certain rites and donations to the initiates of one's agnatic and/or ritual group. *Musigo* includes the fixed amounts of goods given to the holder of the collective basket and to the tutors. *Musekelo we isengo* denotes prescribed gifts placed on top of the collectively held baskets containing initiation objects. *Kyako* or *musungu* includes gifts to initiates who unexpectedly participate in the rites.

Distributions of goods are also differentiated according to whether they are made before, during, or after the initiations. The first category, *kukana* (to close, to tie), refers to all distributions of food and goods before the initiations. Gifts to the holder of the basket and to the tutors are prescribed; gifts to inspectors, helpers, and visiting initiates are more casually given. Preinitiation distributions include payments to tutors and payments to induce the holder of the basket to come to the village of the initiations; dinners and gift giving, which may take place long before the initiations, to create a festive atmosphere and impress the initiates; payments for building the initiation hut and making the *byanda* trails; payments for organizing the ceremonial procession of *masandi* (somewhat like a blessing of the village) and for the rooftop rite; gifts distributed during the preliminary *kamondo* dances, held by the initiates while they wait for the holder of the basket to arrive; and, finally, the payment of the *bikulo bya kitampo* (by a person who achieves a high level of bwami without his father being an initiate). The payments and gifts made during the initiations include the distributions already mentioned: *musigo, nkindo, kilisio* (or *kililo*), *mwikio, musekelo*, and *kyako*. The third category (*kukukula*) comprises distributions made after the initiations, when the *kyombi* stick is removed and the village is cleansed. Some are casual; others are prescribed to the holder of the basket and to the tutors.

After his initiations and before settling in his new village, the new initiate hands out a number of return gifts, called *minganangana*, individually to very close relatives of high rank who gave him special help in the preparations and to other close relatives whose rank in bwami is low. The latter, given collectively, are called the gifts of "[not] making the children of my father flee." The initiate also handles the *kasabalala* allocations in the *kasuku* ceremony to most young men and women who contributed to the hunt, to the supply of water and firewood, and to the construction of houses. When the initiate establishes himself in his new village he receives the *muyolelo* gifts from the people there; later he receives additional *muyolelo* gifts when he visits the villages of kinsmen.

Accumulating and Distributing Goods for Lutumbo lwa kindi. This process is long and involved, for it requires cooperation from and interaction with the widest possible field of kinsmen. To suggest the large number of possibilities, I examine here two kindi examples.

The acquisition of commodities.—The candidate for the highest grade is already an influential individual who has many wives and children (a lot of them married), many close male agnates in his villages, and many close female agnates married and living elsewhere. Like any other Lega, he has a number of maternal uncles and sororal nephews. His lineage is an intimate part of a web of other larger and smaller lineages within the clan. Since he is a high-ranking initiate, the candidate has already participated in many initiations. As the head of a large extended family, and/or as the senior of a lineage group, he is, in Lega terms, a wealthy person.

To begin with, the candidate has a number of goods of his own which

The Bwami Association

he reserves for his initiation. Some are the product of his own labor and of the labor of his wives and children (especially shell money, oil, and salt). Other goods have been saved from previous initiations or were acquired as gifts and payments in the rites. Still others are part of matrimonial goods received for his daughters and sisters, or winnings from playing the *mbale* dice game. These personal goods constitute the candidate's credit.

Close agnates individually provide the candidate with commodities (mostly shell money). For example, when Mindo became a candidate for kindi, his father was dead. Mindo had three senior half brothers (each representing a different house), of whom the eldest had two sons, almost of Mindo's age. These five persons made individual gifts of shell money ranging from 10 to 30 *kilunga* sizes, amounting to a total of 115 *kilunga*. Mindo's father's full senior brother had one son who provided 20 *kilunga*. The other males of Mindo's tertiary, secondary, and primary lineages contributed labor in the construction of houses to accommodate the initiates, in the big hunt, and in the provision of water and firewood. They also collectively contributed shoulder bags filled with money during the initiations. Members of the other primary lineages in Mindo's clan contributed nothing.

Mindo sent messengers and his wives to other groups of kinsmen to ask for help. A man can expect assistance particularly from agnates of the wives with whom he plans to go into kindi. Mindo obtained goods (shell money, cloth, resin torches, salt, copper bracelets) through three of his four wives. Nzogu received goods through five of his wives. One's sisters' husbands also make contributions, at least if their wives are alive. Mindo had only one sister but since she was dead at the time of the initiations, nothing was received from her husband. Nzogu received goods through one of his consanguine sisters. A man occasionally acquires goods from his daughters' husbands, from his wives' sisters' husbands, and from his sons' wives' people. Goods were presented to Nzogu by the fathers-in-law of two of his married daughters and by the husband of a third daughter. The next important category of contributors comprises maternal uncles. As noted earlier, the Lega give social recognition to seven categories of maternal uncles. Some may be members of one's own clan; others are not. It is unlikely that representatives of all seven groups will contribute, but any one of the maternal uncles is potentially a provider of goods, advice, or other assistance. If any of them are high-ranking kindi, their very presence before and during the initiations is a moral boost. From his mother's, his mother's mother's, and his father's mother's agnates, Mindo received shell money, bracelets, oil, dried antelopes, and torches. Sororal nephews, in the widest possible sense, are generous contributors. Mindo had no close sororal nephews—his one sister had not married and his father had no sister—but three classificatory sororal nephews made significant contributions: Lukuzi, grandson of his grandfather's sister; Kyabusi, great-grandson of his grandfather's sister; and Ikangamina, great-grandson of his great-grandfather's sister. The goods provided by any of these categories of affinal and cognatic kinsmen are not necessarily the property of the person through whom they are given. Rather, the individual who promises assistance to the candidate solicits contributions from members of his local group.

The allocation of goods.—Distributions take place before, during, and after initiations. In some of them the amounts and/or types of goods are fixed; in others the candidate takes the initiative. I studied several cases in detail. Nzogu, a well-known kindi, distributed shell money, game animals, and oil as food and gifts to a variety of visitors before the initiations began; the distributions were so informal and so spaced out that Nzogu saw no point in trying to recount them. The initiation comprised thirteen rites. Each rite demands the distribution of more or less prescribed quantities and categories of goods, sometimes given individually to each participating kindi and to each participating kanyamwa, sometimes given collectively in groups to all kindi or to all kanyamwa present. Differences in the actual amounts distributed to individuals are based on kinship distance or on "love," that is, on the degree of respect two individuals hold for each other. Several rites require the additional payment of prescribed goods to specific status holders and performers. In the *musombo* rite, for example, the candidate gives to the kindi and the nonperforming kanyamwa as a group ten *magombelo* sizes of shell money, one antelope, a jar of oil, a pack of salt, and a quantity of bananas. Each of the masked kanyamwa women, with her unmasked companion, receives two *tuko* of the *kilunga* size of shell money. On this occasion women engage in a rare performance on drums, for which each receives one *kako* of the *kilunga* size of money. The total amount of goods disbursed during each rite varies widely, from a few handfuls of unthreaded money to large quantities of shell money in addition to victuals (several antelopes and goats, oil, salt, and bananas).

The day following the last rite (which itself ends with a big dinner party) is reserved for *musigo*. *Musigo* means public payment to four status holders for services rendered: *mukomi*, who brings the collectively held initiation basket; *kilezi*, one of the tutors who sits close to the candidate during the initiations and physically supports him; *kakusa*, the head tutor, who acts as adviser and master of ceremonies; and *mwikalizi*, a close cognatic relative who exercises personal supervision. The types and the quantity of goods given to these individuals differ rather markedly from region to region in Legaland. Nzogu's payments were high, as the following enumeration illustrates. *Mukomi* received thirty *kilunga* measures of shell money, one goat, one whole antelope, four iron objects, one basket, one mat, one piece of cloth, five large resin torches, and five packs of salt.

Kilezi was given twenty *kilunga* measures of shell money, three iron objects, one basket, one mat, one piece of cloth, three large resin torches, and three packs of salt. *Kakusa* obtained ten measures of shell money, one dried antelope, one pot of oil, and five large resin torches. *Mwikalizi* was rewarded for his services with twenty *kilunga*, one dried antelope, one pot of oil, five resin torches, and two packs of salt. The *musigo* payments are made in the presence of designated witnesses (*basula*), who receive small amounts of shell money from each of the four status holders, but nothing from the candidate himself.

The rite *ibago lya nzogu* (lit., skinning of the elephant), marking the symbolic dismantling of the initiation hut, is held sometime after the initiations into lutumbo lwa kindi, that is, before the new kindi leaves his old village (*bukindu*) to settle in a new one (*bukumbu, igu*). On this occasion the new kindi makes the *minganangana* distributions to very close relatives who have assisted him. The number of individuals may be large (nineteen in Nzogu's case); their social identity varies greatly, but they are all members of the two highest grades in bwami. Some are in-laws (wife's father, wife's brother, wife's senior sister's husband, sister's husband, daughter's husband, daughter's husband's father, daughter's husband's mother); others are cognates (sororal nephew and maternal uncle, real or classificatory). The amount of goods, as well as the type, given to each relative differs considerably. The criteria for determining amount and type are less the nature of the kinship tie or the bwami rank of the receiver than the patterns of friendship and respect and the nature of previously contracted, mutual economic obligations.

Two additional distributions are made to close agnates before the kindi settles in his new village. The first one, *kasabalala* (an allotment of food including antelopes, oil, and salt), is for all the young men and women who have contributed labor and services, such as hunting and collecting supplies of water and firewood. The second one, *kukinduzia bana ba tata* (lit., [not] making the children of my father flee), includes shell money and food (antelopes, salt, and oil) and is for close agnates who helped to make the ceremonies successful but who could not participate in the kindi celebrations and distributions because of their low bwami rank.

Donation of goods after initiations.—Before the new kindi integrates his new village, those who plan to settle with him (children, married sons, brothers, and some affinal or cognatic relatives) have already taken up residence. The kindi and his initiated wives receive a number of *muyolelo* offerings from them. This close family affair provides an opportunity for a married son to show piety and gratitude toward his father and his initiated mother; for sons' wives to show their allegiance to and pride in their new family; for uninitiated wives to show loyalty and openness toward their husband and his initiated wives; for a junior to show respect for his senior.

The items, given in small quantities on this occasion, range from shell money to iron tools, chickens, and cloth. In the next phase the new kindi visits many villages where he traces agnatic, cognatic, or affinal ties; in each he receives *muyolelo* offerings made collectively (i.e., placed "anonymously" on a mat that is spread out in the village) by a variety of individuals.

Use of remaining goods.—The intelligent and cautious candidate accumulates a quantity of goods before his initiations which he need not divulge to the inspectors who evaluate his readiness for the ceremonies. This reserve *mbiso* (lit., what is hidden), known only to the candidate and his sons and juniors, is designed primarily to cope with unexpected demands and emergencies, such as visits of and participation by unexpected guests, payments of fines for transgressing taboos, and free gift giving. If all goes well, however, there is a good chance that a substantial portion of *mbiso* goods will remain after the initiations, when they are augmented by gifts received by the new kindi. With his accumulations Nzogu, for example, was able to realize the following projects shortly after his initiations: to marry an additional wife, to provide one of his sons with a first wife, to help provide an additional wife for each of two other sons, and to give a classificatory maternal uncle a substantial amount of goods so that he could finish his lutumbo lwa kindi.

Obligations of the grantee.—The variety of goods a candidate receives from many categories of people for his initiations are not all treated as gifts, and none may be considered as pure gifts. All donations entail the idea of counterprestation, immediate or deferred. First, all goods, except chickens and game animals received from one's wives' fathers or brothers, are connected with matrimonial negotiations: they are considered as returns on, or partial reimbursements of, the marriage payments received by the woman's people. If there is a divorce, the husband gets in return from his wife's people the marriage payments he made for her less the counterprestations (*mubigo*) he received from her people. Vice versa, all goods received from sisters' or daughters' husbands are regarded as supplements to the marriage payments (*igambia*) and must be returned if the marriage is dissolved. All contributions from maternal uncles or sororal nephews, however, are prestations that may be classified as gifts, since they entail the idea of counterprestation but not of reimbursement. The same holds true for donations made by agnates. Second, there exists among the Lega the concept of pure loan (*kusomba*). When a relative provides certain goods during the initiations to save the candidate and his tutors from an embarrassing situation, these improvised donations are regarded as a loan and must be compensated for at the earliest possible moment.

Accumulating and Distributing Goods for Lutumbo lwa yananio. To illustrate the operation of the system, I briefly examine the ways in which Lukuku brought together the goods needed for his initiations into lutumbo

The Bwami Association

lwa yananio and the manner in which he allocated them. Early in the preparations he called together a number of closely related initiates of lutumbo lwa yananio rank for a preliminary count of the goods. Lukuku had amassed 110 *kilunga* sizes of shell money, four pots of oil, seven packs of salt, and three antelopes (including a chevrotain). The antelopes had been hunted by his sons and junior brothers. He had acquired the oil at a Songola market by selling three antelopes, and the salt through mediation by his paternal aunt in her husband's group. He had won thirty *kilunga* in the *mbale* game and inherited the other eighty from a sororal nephew. One pot of oil, two packs of salt, and the three available antelopes went into the dinner. Thirty *kilunga* measures were individually distributed among the initiates present at the inspection. A *kakusa* tutor was chosen on this occasion.

When the group of initiates decided that Lukuku needed more valuables for his initiation, he set out on a first fund-raising tour. From his father's maternal uncles he received three sets of goods: the direct patrilineal descendant of his father's mother's brother gave him five *kilunga* sizes and a pack of resin torches; two classificatory junior brothers of this man supplied three pots of oil, ten *ndume* sizes, a pack of torches, and ten *kituli* sizes. Lukuku then contacted his father's father's maternal uncles. Kikuni, the direct descendant of Lukuku's father's father's mother's brother, who also happened to be a real maternal uncle of Lukuku's only wife, provided him with thirty *kilunga* sizes. Twenty of them were given in Kikuni's capacity as maternal uncle of Lukuku's wife and were therefore reimbursable as part of the matrimonial exchanges. Three other members of Lukuku's father's father's mother's lineage gave twenty *kilunga* and ten *tuko* of *kilunga*. Lukuku's wife, finding the goods received by her husband from her maternal uncle, Kikuni, to be insufficient, returned to the uncle and was given a pot of oil, an ax, two jars, three pots, and a long row of oblong beads. Lukuku next went to his mother's mother's people. Kaongania, the direct descendant of Lukuku's mother's mother's brother, offered him two pots of oil and thirty *ndume* sizes, while Kaongania's senior brother's son provided him with a pot of oil and ten *kilunga*.

Lukuku then called closely related initiates for a second inspection. Three antelopes, hunted for the occasion, were distributed along with a pot of oil, two packs of salt, and twenty *kilunga* sizes. The *kakusa* tutor received a special payment of one blue antelope, a pack of salt, and one *kako* bunch of the *kilunga* size. At this second meeting the initiation hut was constructed, but it was decided that the goods available were still insufficient to proceed further with the preparations. So Lukuku went on a second tour. From Katumbi, the son of Lukuku's father's father's sister's daughter, he got an unusually large quantity of goods: a billy goat, thirty *ndume* and ten *kilunga* sizes, a pot of oil, a knife, and a piece of cloth. In addition, Lukuku collected two pots of oil, fifty *ndume* from his real maternal uncle, and five packs of torches from members of his lineage. A collective hunt organized by his maternal uncle brought in three antelopes and four duikers.

After Lukuku had organized his own hunting party, which realized three antelopes and one duiker, he invited the initiates back for a third inspection. On this occasion several important steps were taken. The initiates held the *kimpilinda* ceremony, in which the bunches of bulrush (*masandi*) carried by initiates in the ceremonial processions are tied together. Because his father had not been initiated, Lukuku was now invited to settle a taboo by paying ten *ndume* sizes to the initiates present. At this time the *kilezi* tutor was selected. The *kakusa* tutor established himself in Lukuku's village, not to leave it until all initiations had been finished. A big dinner, including eleven antelopes, two pots of oil, and three packs of salt, was provided, and *kako* bunches of the *kilunga* size were allotted to all participants.

Properly speaking, the initiations could now proceed, but the affair was not so simple. Several things remained to be done. A larger number of initiates, representing diverse lineages and clans, had to be invited and persuaded to come; large-scale collective hunting parties, involving all the young men of Lukuku's village and of several related villages, had to be organized under the supervision of the *kakusa* tutor. The meat had to be transported from the hunting camp to the village, sometimes a long distance. Most important, the *mukomi*, or temporary holder of the collectively owned initiation objects, had to be induced to come to the village of initiation. For this part of the proceedings the bwami association has introduced its ideology of circumspection into a tricky game of hide-and-seek. For days and days the *mukomi* lingers in nearby villages. Meanwhile, all invited participants have arrived. They spend the waiting hours in preliminary dances (*kamondo*) for which they receive handfuls of money. They are also given lavish food supplies. Messengers are continually sent out with substantial presents to persuade the *mukomi* to bring the initiation objects to the candidate's village. When the *mukomi* finally arrives, a small allotment of goods is made to the basket. The *musigo* distributions begin. They consist of fairly large, individualized payments to the various people who tutor the candidate and to the keeper of the basket. This distribution is accompanied by a dinner for which a collective hunt brought in one antelope, one chevrotain, and one *mbezi* monkey. At Lukuku's initiation, four people were rewarded with these special payments. The *mukomi* received twenty *kilunga*, a pot of oil, five torches, three packs of salt, a fresh antelope, a large goat, a hen with six chicks, four neck-to-nipple lengths of oblong beads, a razor, a needle, a knife, a piece of cloth, a fishing net, a spear, and an ax. The *kilezi* tutor was given twenty *kilunga*, a piece of cloth, a rooster, an ax, an iron tool, the lower part of an antelope, two packs of salt, and three torches. The *kakusa* tutor got a large goat, two pots

The Bwami Association

of oil, four torches, ten *kilunga,* and two packs of salt. The *mwikalizi* received an antelope and ten *kituli* sizes.

The actual initiations, which consist of a sequence of rites, each comprising a cycle of dances, songs, and displays of objects, demand several kinds of distributions: a *mwikio* payment of goods for each rite, *nkindo* gifts to individual performers, *mwikio* gifts to specific groups of kinsmen, and distributions of food. Ten representatives of tertiary lineages in Lukuku's clan received sizable shares of shell money, and so did a classificatory sororal nephew.

At the beginning of the initiations Lukuku secured additional goods from two sources. His hunters brought back more than a hundred antelopes from a one-month hunting expedition. Several closely related individuals brought *mululo* gifts: four members of lineages closely related to Lukuku each brought ten *kilunga;* two members of two more distantly related lineages presented ten and twenty *kilunga,* respectively. Lukuku's paternal aunt provided a billy goat, twenty *kilunga,* and twelve packs of salt. A relative through his mother's sister gave ten *kilunga* and a pot of oil; two classificatory grandsons brought loose shell money and two antelopes. The final payments *(kukukula)* were made during the removal of the *kyombi* stick from the pit in which it had been planted during the *mukumbi* rite. The participants received thirty *kilunga,* two packs of salt, one wild pig, and two halves of two other pigs. Soon after this initiation, Lukuku began preparing for the first level of kindi.

Conclusions. The distribution and redistribution of shell money and of scarce commodities (game, goats, oil, salt, torches) which accompany bwami initiations have many meanings and functions. These exchanges of commodities reach a climax at the lutumbo lwa kindi level; initiations into the lower grades (kongabulumbu, kansilembo, bombwa, and, at least in some areas, ngandu) are lineage affairs that affect only small groups of kinsmen and require limited amounts of goods, few of which are obtained outside the agnatic unit through cognatic and affinal relationships. As one moves from musagi wa yananio to lutumbo lwa kindi, increasingly large groups of initiates representing many lineages and clans participate both in the rites and in the exchange process. Lukuku, for example, gave fifty *ndume* sizes, two pots of oil, two torches, three packs of salt, and five antelopes for his ngandu initiations, all of which had been accumulated mainly with the help of members of his secondary lineage. For the musagi wa yananio initiations he asked the cooperation of a limited group of cognates and affines. The distributions included eighty *kilunga* and ten *ibungakwanga* sizes, three pots of oil, two packs of salt, one billy goat, and seven antelopes. For the lutumbo lwa yananio initiations he had to call upon a wide variety of agnatic, cognatic, and affinal kinsmen; his solicitations resulted in the massive accumulation of 285 *kilunga* and 120 *ndume* sizes of shell money, 128 antelopes, one monkey, fifteen pots of oil, nineteen packs of salt, seven packs of torches, and two billy goats, besides small quantities of other items (ax, knife, cloth, pot and jars, beads). If Lukuku had been entering kindi, the amounts would have been still more impressive.

Whereas game, oil, salt, and torches are distributed in all the initiations, goats are reserved for yananio and kindi. Shell money, threaded in lengths ranging from 2.5 to 16 inches or more, is standard in all initiations, but the longer sizes are used in initiations to the higher grades. It is typical that Lukuku, for example, used the *ndume* size (foot length) for ngandu and the *kilunga* size (hand-forearm length) for yananio. The type of goods given at all levels is also determined in part by kinship categories. Goats, game, oil, salt, torches, and shell money may be given to any category of kinsmen. The critical goods are chickens, *myambalo* (beaded necklaces), and *kigela* (necklaces made from small polished disks of giant snail shells). Chickens cannot be given to sororal nephews or to other members of the families into which one's sisters or daughters married. *Myambalo* necklaces cannot be given to members of the families into which one's sisters or daughters married. *Kigela* necklaces can be given only in affinal relationships to members of one's wives' families or members of the families into which one's daughters and sisters married. In recent decades, when Congolese money and European-made cloth became available to the Lega, certain types of exchanges included these commodities as substitutes for the traditional ones, but others did not.

Although an undefined minimum of goods is required for any initiation, it is clear that there are no set price tags. The Lega concept of *kasaganwa*—initiations in which an individual with few relatives (and therefore a limited supply of goods) is inducted as a high-ranking member of bwami—suggests that the criterion of acceptability on moral grounds is ultimately the decisive one. At the highest levels, the candidates for initiation rival one another in generosity and find added prestige in lavish giving. Lega ideology places heavy emphasis on the candidate's obligation to give and to give generously. Some of the rules expressed in song during the initiations specify that the candidate must invite as many relatives as possible from his own ritual community and from the wider field of kinship relationships. Failure to invite the proper initiates is equated in Lega thinking with "war," that is, with strained relationships that may result in retaliation. Also, the obligation to admit and to share with unexpected arrivals at the ceremonies is made clear.

The tendency to give generously is enhanced by the basic philosophy of the initiates, which is told in many proverbs: to "destroy" and to "eat" as many goods as possible. Coming to the village of the candidate to take all his goods, the initiates compare themselves to *kisanda kya mbili* (poison that kills off all the fish). The members of the candidate's immediate lineage unconvincingly object to this tendency, because another philosophical principle holds that in initiations and distributions there should be no special treatment of a son, a junior, or any other close relative. In the minds of those who give there is the idea of vindication: "I give much; others will give me; I will be merciless in asking." The tutors who assist the candidate are mediators between these conflicting tendencies. It would, of course, be totally wrong to think that high-ranking initiates turn both initiations and distributions into a personal businesslike enterprise from which to derive the lion's share of benefits. It must be remembered that participating initiates share the commodities they receive with absentee members of family and lineage. During the initiations they regularly send food supplies known as *bulungila* to nonparticipating members of their group. Most significantly, however, the exchanges emphasize dependencies, obligations, and liabilities between individuals and groups.

Some goods received for the initiations are a straightforward loan; others are simply part of the matrimonial cycle and may be considered as extended credit. Almost always, however, the acceptance of goods implies immediate, or deferred, reciprocity. In at least one instance the reciprocity is total: the candidate must, as a minimum requirement, return to the *mukomi* whatever goods the latter has given in order to acquire the basket. Some services rendered by close kinsmen require compensation. Hunters, though receiving neither shell money nor animals in return for their labor, are entitled to share in the bountiful meals prepared during the initiations and also to be given a special dinner toward the end of the ceremonies. Some goods are given in compensation for the loss of rights and do not call for reciprocity. For example, the kindi whose wife accedes to bunyamwa is obligated to give goods to her father or brother to compensate him for his inability to claim death payments *(idigo)*, since a kanyamwa woman is fully integrated in her husband's group. There is also the factor of social recognition in the goods given to a senior whom one happens to surpass in initiatory rank.

Bwami Ideology

Introduction. No Lega philosopher has constructed a synthesis of the ideas and the values that the bwami association stands for. These ideas and values are conveyed during initiation ceremonies in thousands of proverbs and aphorisms which, directly or indirectly, and more or less symbolically, express basic Lega principles. Yet the texts, and the interpretations of them, deal with realities. Some concern the bwami association and its significance in Lega society, the initiate and his characteristics, or the candidate and his status and obligations. Others recite the duties, privileges, and qualifications of the master of the land, the headman of the village, the head of the lineage, tutors, and preceptors. The texts speak about the initiations, the difficulties of participating in them, and the glory that results. They contain warnings for noninitiates. They condense information about the environment, technology, and social organization; they elucidate prescriptions, taboos, and principles of law. Yet they have very little to say about change in general, or about the changes that occurred with the advent of foreigners, particularly the moves against bwami. At times, however, the proverbs sound like statements of self-defense against critics.[17]

Above all, the proverbs and aphorisms affirm moral principles. Together they form a complete outline of the moral philosophy that underlies bwami. The practicality and the viability of the bwami philosophy may be assessed by observing individual and group action and by studying prevailing customs. Man, not the universe or a group of divinities, is the center of the bwami world. Members of the association are concerned mainly with harmonious and peaceful human relationships. Bwami is a technique to ensure harmony by making people better, by helping them to achieve the supreme value of *kalokagathia,* as the Greeks called it; the Lega use the word *busoga* for this value, and we would have to define it as "goodness-beauty." It is explicitly stated in some initiations that "we initiates prepare the heart for *bunenekisi,*" that is, mastery of the land, greatness, fame, wealth, happiness.

Sequence of Ideas in Kongabulumbu Initiations. From one to three hundred proverbs are sung during the initiations to kongabulumbu, the lowest and simplest grade of bwami. Accompanied by dances, gestures, and displays of objects, they express ideas bearing on the moral code of bwami, on Lega social relations, and on the association itself. The ideas, however, are not systematically grouped together in sets. Each proverb or aphorism enunciates a self-contained idea that may or may not be directly linked to the preceding or the following one. The link between proverbs sung in a dance sequence is not necessarily in their content, but in the fact that they relate to the same initiation object or configuration of objects in the same rite. Thus, one proverb warns against arrogance, and the next one attributes the bad behavior of a child to sorcery.

[17] Self-defensiveness is particularly apparent in the exegesis of some aphorisms. For example, the aphorism, "There the land is in good order where the old ones dance with the dried banana leaves," is frequently quoted to say that joy and order had gone with the advent of the colonial system because it undermined bwami. The proverb, "You kill the old animals, but you have old guardians of the village," expresses a reaction against Europeans who said that old men were without value or promise. The proverb, "At the crossroads a short man may be encountered, but there may not be encountered a newborn baby," inculcates the idea that the Lega, since they had been found on their land by the whites, necessarily possessed rights and prerogatives. The aphorism, "The river dries up; the Lualaba sees the sandbanks," complains that the Lega, after the loss of bwami, felt like a giant river that had dried up.

The Bwami Association

It is almost impossible for an alien like myself to detect any internal coherence in the sequences the Lega choose to follow. That they tend to emphasize and visualize the totality of events in a sequence, the totality of sequences in a rite, and the totality of rites in an initiation, rather than each individual happening or component, is unquestionable. It is the total impact that matters. One must also bear in mind that the individual style, preference, and taste of each preceptor are cultivated and highly respected, and that improvisation and new ways of doing things are constantly sought. In the kongabulumbu initiations I witnessed, there was no standard pattern of sequences. Each preceptor performed his duties very much as he preferred to and was used to. The internal logic lies in the coherence of the themes that are expressed, in the recurrence of proverbs and associated objects, and in their interpretation.

In regrouping the proverbs sung and interpreted in kongabulumbu, one discovers that certain coherent themes are discussed. Some of the main ethical values for which bwami stands are stated both positively and negatively, as in all other initiations. In some instances stress is directly placed on the values of filial piety, hospitality, and so on. In other instances the disastrous consequences resulting from morally unacceptable behavior, such as boasting, arrogance, disobedience, and covetousness, are emphasized. Positively stated in kongabulumbu are such values as circumspection, filial piety, hospitality, love of the good and the beautiful, and "heart" (i.e., good disposition and intelligence). Negatively stated are those of moderation and temperance (don't overreach yourself; boasting, arrogance, and cursing lead to serious difficulties), of restraint in words (the big mouth of an important person may disperse the village; the bad talk of one's brother scares one's wife away; the master of the land is not a man of rancor).

Social relations are illustrated in many ways: if a beloved child acts badly, sorcery is at work; the orphan is destitute; fear the adulterous young man (a bad heart in a beautiful body); love your wife and children if they act well; one's enemies rival in building up evil talk; without a wife one is lonely; yours are all the people whom your father left in your care; yours also are all people who do good to you; your father's problems and affairs remain with you after his death; a village without an old man cannot operate; sharing with kinsmen and village people is necessary; one can expect help and protection from maternal uncles; one always returns to one's village; the village headman must be respected; all children are to be treated equally; every lineage has its own master; one does not retaliate against a sororal nephew.

Some proverbs deal specifically with bwami, its nature, and its pattern of organization. The following principles are expressed: one can always expect help from one's tutors; bwami brings people together; kongabulumbu is the beginning of everything, for however far one may go in bwami, one cannot despise kongabulumbu just as one cannot despise one's first child; bwami initiations demand cooperation; bwami brings together people who are scattered in many places; members of bwami, who flock together for initiations even if not called for, are like flies attracted by the smell of meat; the candidate must not cultivate pride; initiates are at one during initiations, even though hatred may cloud their relationships in other spheres of life. A few proverbs reflect the general philosophy of bwami: all new patterns of behavior introduced from the outside are bad; bad persons can be turned into better ones; there is danger in playing games or in throwing things around; one does not go to places where one is not known.

What the Lega Say about Bwami. Since the Lega refuse to acknowledge that bwami is their own creation, they do not regard it as a human invention. But neither do they attribute its origin to a god or to a culture hero. "Bwami has not the one who first saw it; it is a fruit that came from above." Bwami, like death (about which the same aphorism is often quoted), has no beginning and no end; it is universal. The implication of the Lega attitude toward bwami is that it is not to be argued about: "What has been encountered [like the Pygmies, bwami, etc.] cannot and does not need to be explained." Precisely because nobody in Legaland can claim to have invented bwami or can pretend to be the first to have discovered it, nobody holds a monopoly of it. No single group in Legaland is excluded from it: "Bwami, the crescent of the moon, every clan has seen from it." Bwami is spread throughout the land: "The roasting packages are spread all over the lowland, are spread all over the highland," and "Bwami: the *lukundu* tree [*Piptadenia africana*] has made its buttresses and aerial roots reach far." Bwami is not the exclusive property of the elders, the seniors, and the wealthy; rather, it holds attraction for all, like the *ibulungu* tree (*Autranella congolensis*), "A big place of much food which has many animal trails." Bwami belongs to the many, not simply because it allows all social groups to have initiated members, but because its initiations and the preparations for them require the cooperation of many people: "Come here, for one man [alone] cannot bring harmony to the initiates," and "One finger cannot pick up a clod, even if one possesses [every possible kind of] shrewdness."

Bwami brings people together; it unites them "even though they are scattered and may hate one another." Bwami is not discriminatory, yet it is closed and exclusive in the sense that no one can participate in its rites or benefit from its advantages without being initiated into it: "The Banankamba [fictive group named for the *nkamba* fish, *Clarias lazera*] do not carry him who is not of their group." The initiations have secret aspects: "The porcupine does not eat fallen bananas in the clearing." Bwami is *kitindi* (the long thing) because its initiations, its requirements, and its possibilities are without end. Bwami is *kayamba*, an inextricable forest

The Bwami Association

difficult to traverse, where trees, shrubs, epiphytes, and grasses intertwine. The achievement of bwami is therefore an arduous task: "Bwami: spots of the leopard frighten and chase the sheep." Only those who cultivate excellence can hope to move ahead in bwami: "Those who suffer from dizziness do not get to the top [of the tree]; they turn back at the intersections of the branches." Bwami is a source of fame and prestige for individuals and groups. Members of the association pursue honor, not profit: "They do not merely take goods; they give greatness." Bwami leads to great honor, very much like the parasol tree which has so many uses that it is called the "great one of honor, not of size [*munene we idimba*]." Bwami brings immortality: "Lububi [personification of the most useful liana, *Eremospatha* sp.] died below [on earth], but above [on top of the tree] it has placed its grave." Bwami has a purifying effect on Legaland: "There alone is the land in good order where bami dance with dried banana leaves."

Bwami is the strength of Lega society; it sustains the social structure as the "middle pole sustains the forest hut; when the pole is removed the hut collapses." Nothing surpasses or excels bwami: "Kalububi [Lububi], the great one, has no work that surpasses him." Strife, violence, disruption, and warfare can never be reconciled with bwami. Initiations must never lead to inter- or intragroup tensions. Bwami presents a powerful threat to those who create conflict: "Bwami, the stampeding of elephants; the place where it [i.e., the stampeding] has passed cannot be forgotten," and "Bwami, the little spear with the sharp blade, with the well-polished shaft." In bwami there is no discrimination, only a basic search for congeniality and equality. Initiates perceive a close similarity between their ways of operating and the nesting habits of wild pigs; males, females, young, and old all stay together. That bwami members are fundamentally all alike is emphasized by masks that are similar in appearance; they are like the "*tumbukutu* insects that resemble the *ndoku* insects."

What the Lega Say about the Initiate. The noninitiate in Lega society is compared to a shoulder bag: "it has a mouth, it has no heart"; to a *zogozogo* monkey that goes places where it does not belong; or to a walking stick made of raffia wood which, "even though you are strong, does not kill a snake" (because it breaks too easily). The initiate is a person with a heart, a person of deep sentiment and of wisdom (*bwenge*). The basic wisdom (*kizio*) a man builds up early in life, when he sits and listens to seniors and high-ranking initiates while others are already in bed, is gradually enhanced through bwami initiations. The summit of insight (*izu*) is reached when one achieves kindi. The candidate caught between two worlds must show modesty: "The one without fear, banana tree, the tough one, is waiting for the stampeding of the elephants."

The mwami is a negotiator, a mediator. The initiate of the highest grade is identified with a big tree that, having fallen across the river, helps travelers get to the other side. He is a man of clear and honest talk, "a seducer with words." He is not a liar, nor does he like to listen to lies: "Mwami is not a man of lies; what you have not seen, do not tell him." He is a man of character and strength who dares speak up against his own people, in contrast with the weakling, the yes-man, who is "a cut tree that still shakes its leaves while the roots are rotten." He is a well-motivated person who finds salvation in his work and effort: "Bami are guinea fowls; it is in their nest that they find their things." The mwami is an *isingu* fruit (symbol of heaviness) which "does not lean against bulrushes." This aphorism means that the fame and reputation of the initiate are solid and lasting, and that it is dangerous to displease him or to rebel against him: "He who falls from the hill may cure; he who falls on the eyebrow of Zumbi cannot last." He is a man of circumspection and prudence, who well informs himself before embarking on a project: "Bami, a smithing stone, I call them, but they cannot come." Above all, the mwami is a *musoga*, a good and beautiful person.

Understandably, the loftiest and most meaningful sentiments are addressed to kindi initiates. Kindi, like the pangolin, is *kinkutu*, something that brings people together. Kindi is a *kimini*, a great dancer, a man who likes and knows how to make the ceremonies successful. He is *mukota wa kabilundu*; that is, he is like the *kabilundu* tree whose branches, stretching wide in many directions, generously offer food resources and shelter to many kinds of animals. He is *mulumbilwa*, "famed and great one known among the good ones" (*mungu mumenywa wa basoga*). He is *mutondo*, the beam without which the house would collapse.[18]

Initiates frequently refer to themselves as *bakulu*, the great old ones; *balubungu*, those of the initiation house; and *banamombo*, the anointed ones. The most significant identifications, however, relate initiates to certain animals and to the *lububi* liana (*Eremospatha* sp.). In the animal world identifications are made with elephants (*bananzogu*), "who do not shake off the little bloodsuckers," to emphasize magnanimity; with white *binyangi* (*Bubulcus ibis*), birds "that float around in the air," to stress beauty and lightness; with *nkamba* fish (*Chrysichthys cranchii*) to point out exclusivity; with *nsamba* fish (*Clarias lazera*) to stress endurance and fame; with the turtle to accentuate wisdom; with the *ngimbi* snake (*Boulengerina annulata*) to emphasize destructive power; with the *kinsuluka* centipede, which "does not return blank from the trip," to stress skill in acquiring things; and with *tumbukutu* insects to emphasize similarity.

Synthesis of Bwami Ideology. Bwami has no theory about the universe, its origins and organization, or about the place of divinities, animals, and men in the universe. Bwami has no myths. It does not practice a specialized cult. Its ideology is essentially oriented toward men, toward

---

[18] On the position of the kindi see Biebuyck (1972).

the moral improvement of the individual and toward harmonious relationships between men. Bwami is a search for the mastery of the good and for moral and spiritual excellence. The intent is both theoretical and practical. The Lega are convinced that moral improvement, moral and spiritual excellence, and absolute good can be achieved only through initiation into and membership in bwami.

The supreme value for which members of bwami stand is attainment of the state of *busoga*. I see no better equivalent for *busoga* than the Aristotelian concept of *kalokagathia*, which expresses a combination of social, moral, and physical distinction.[19] This state is fully reached at the summit of all bwami initiations. *Busoga* is a promise and a goal for all members of bwami. It is the quality of the highest-ranking initiate. The question is: How is *busoga* defined? Definitions must be distilled from the proverbs and their interpretations sung or recited during initiations to enhance or to stigmatize certain aspects of the human personality. All teachings in bwami center on a system of opposites, characterized as *bunene* (virtue) versus *bwanya* (nonvirtue). Bwami teachings are both positive and negative; they illustrate what a mwami should be and what he should not be, what he is and what he is not. *Busoga* means beauty and goodness, but other concepts as well stress good and beautiful activities: *kukonga*, to produce harmony and unison in singing together; *kwengia*, to be shiny like a well-polished chair or statue; *kwanga*, to be in good order like a country that thrives; *kuswaga*, to be at peace; *kubonga*, to be in harmony, in unison. The suffix *nyange* bears on splendor and shine; *-koma*, on a flawless body that is beautiful because it has no scabies; and *-limbo*, on something pleasing like a bunch of feathers.

Clearly *busoga* is much more complicated than these concepts suggest, for it has both physical and moral implications. It is first defined as *izu*, deep insight and wisdom, as opposed to *kizio*, simple knowledge. Wisdom itself is measured in action. In all his dealings the wise man practices the virtues of temperance, moderation, restraint, poise, and equity: "Cautiously goes the trip of the great ones," and "Kingili [Proud Walker] was the first to join the trip, [but] he now remains behind." The *izu* concept of the Lega comes very close to the Greek sophrosyne. As the Greeks contrast sophrosyne and pathos, so the Lega contrast *izu* and *nduma* (lit., bad heart). An individual proves he has *izu* by not being quarrelsome, adulterous, violent, ostentatious, or meddlesome. A man of *izu* brings *ibonga*, smoothness in social relationships at all levels and in all circumstances. Lega proverbs vehemently criticize individuals who indulge in verbal quarrels (*myanga*), in vanity (*bigulugulu*), in slander (*kibazonga*), in

---

[19] The brief references to Greek moral philosophy in this section are based on Cresson (1962, *passim*), Demos (1939, *passim*), and Gould (1955, *passim*). I am presently working on a small book that will analyze the moral philosophy of the Lega, and its implications, in great detail.

vagabondage (*kitandala*). They chastise those who show stupidity (*kisapupa*), crudity and thoughtlessness (*bunumbu*), rawness of heart, clumsiness (*temeteme*), boasting (*kitumbilwa*). They castigate personages like Isawabulambula, who takes people's things; Isakabitabita, Mr. War-Maker; Isabumania, Mr. Sexomane; Sawakisuka, Mr. Big-Penis; Isabuku, Mr. Hatred; Salagana, Mr. Temerity; Nyamalendelo, Mrs. Unfaithful; Nyabeidilwa, a woman overcome by night because of many visits elsewhere; Kyengengwa, a woman who refuses to sleep with her husband; Salugi, Lazybones; Kitumbilwa, Braggart; Ikili, Smarty; Mukobania, Divider.

Second, *busoga* is conceived in terms of *bunyemu*, piety and respect, oriented not toward divinities but toward men and toward the customs and mores of the country. The good man respects other members of bwami, officeholders and little men, old and young, kinsmen and strangers. Humility opens the path for great achievements; conceit (*ngana*), envy (*kisyenge*), pride (*kinkwankondo*), slander and seduction (*kisesa*), evil feeling (*lugono*), and lying (*buza*) lead to self-destruction.[20]

Third, *busoga* is defined in terms of *bukota*. In some non-Lega groups this concept stands for chief or headman; among the Balega-Mitoko it is the name of a voluntary association. Among the Lega, whose concept of *bukota* is more far-reaching, the only precise equivalent is leadership through generosity. The wise mwami of high rank is frequently identified with the *ibulundu* (*kabilundu, kabilungu*) tree (*Autranella congolensis*), which is the king of trees because its branches stretch and ramify widely and because it offers shelter and food to many species of animals. Bami, in contradistinction to noninitiates, are men of heart, a concept expressed particularly through generous rendering of gifts, services, and justice. The initiate is a man, not merely of physical power (*kamangu*), but of moral strength. He has a deep sense of responsibility (*katati*). He is a man of reconciliation, compromise (*malonga*), love (*malebo*), and friendship (*busikila*). The competition for the highest initiations and achievements in bwami is not simply a search for personal prestige or a way of satisfying material interests. It is a technique whereby the well-being of the entire group is ensured and enhanced. As among the ancient Greeks, true virtue is realized only through the counterbalancing of opposites.

The wise initiate is neither materially nor morally weak (*bulema*). He must build up a strong kinship group; he must marry many wives, have many children, attract many other kinsmen, and keep the group together. He must be able to demand respect, to enforce the moral code and the law. He must have a strong character: *bwami kasumo kansongo kabutege*, "Bwami, the little spear with the sharp blade, with the well-polished shaft."

---

[20] Delhaise (1909a, pp. 161, 221) shows how lying, theft, and swindling bring severe punishment to the wrongdoer.

The Bwami Association

He must be just and altruistic, yet he must also cultivate a keen sense of rivalry in striving for honor and power. He must pursue his goals with tenacity; he must compete with others for honor and generosity. He must not be easygoing. Whenever invited for initiations, therefore, he must wait and ponder, considering the desirability of his actions. He must let those who invite him overcome his reluctance and soften his apparent hardheartedness. The moderation for which he stands must not lead to asceticism or to self-punishment. In other words, the mwami must enjoy life and cultivate pleasure (*mbogimbogi*). He must delight in the dances, the music and songs, the displays of objects, the ceremonial gatherings of people, the lavish distributions of food. Celebrations, prestige, participations in gift distributions, however, are only apparent pleasures. The real pleasure is spiritual: it is the acquisition of *bwenge bwatinga*—wisdom that surpasses —which leads to *busoga*.

An individual who has all these qualities is a *wabume*, a full-fledged adult male. The suffix *-bume*, however, does not merely signify manliness or virility; it is a concept that can be opposed to *kamangu*, sheer physical power, to mean strength. Strength is measured by the number of followers one attracts, by one's initiatory level in bwami, and by simple economic success. In Lega society, however, these achievements and advantages are available only to those who practice the virtues that converge in *busoga*. Ultimately, *-bume* comes close in meaning to the Greek *anthropismos*, humaneness or humanism.[21]

The interesting fact, then, is that theory and practice are intimately merged in bwami philosophy. On the one hand, *busoga* is the ultimate value cultivated by bwami, the supreme goal to which one can aspire. On the other hand, nobody can hope to accede to bwami, to move up in it, and to get to the summit without manifesting a predisposition for *busoga*, for practicing *busoga*, and finally for cultivating and increasing it. Those who reach the summit in bwami do not merely learn the principles of the moral code; they live by the code. If they had not done so, they would never have attained their goal. Once a man is initiated to the highest level, he must continue to live by the principles of the moral code. As Aristotle said, there is no virtue if those who claim to be virtuous do not enjoy being virtuous. An initiate must constantly give proof of virtue. It permits the highest-ranking members of bwami to discharge the functions of tutorship, the exercise of which is not only prestigious, but essential to the completion of total man. Only by discharging these functions does the kindi become *lwanza* or *nenekisi*. One might elaborate upon this extremely complex term, which I have translated as "master of the land," because the word *kisi* encompasses in Lega thinking everything that has relevance, everything that is good of its kind and has utility: the country, the land, the

---

[21] See under *anthropismos* in Bailly (1929) and Pring (1965).

people, the animals, children, wives, relatives, wealth, wisdom, initiatory experience. From many points of view, *kisi* seems to mean plenitude. Since *busoga* is not inherited or ascribed, those who are unable to achieve it lack *wabume*, that is, humaneness.

Social Functions of Bwami

It is difficult to characterize bwami. Obviously it has the structure of a large-scale voluntary association whose members are organized into groups at various levels for the pursuit of a number of common interests, both material and spiritual. These interests, oriented toward bringing about the good life in the broadest possible sense, concern all dimensions of culture, technological, sociological, and ideational. The orientations of bwami are creative and exploitative, political and economic, religious and philosophical, social and legal, educational and recreational, practical and theoretical. Ultimately, bwami is the integrating and consolidating force in Lega society, and, because of its vast and unlimited membership, it is to a large extent Lega society itself. To qualify bwami simply as a voluntary association is, therefore, misleading. Bwami is a paideia, a system of instruction in a unique moral philosophy and social ethic; it is not merely a religion, but a mystery; it is an academy whose members practice and honor the fine arts. Its functions encompass all these fields.

Bwami integrates and consolidates existing kinship relationships and kin groups: "Where the arm cannot reach, gaffle of his mother can arrive at." From some points of view bwami emphasizes the autonomy of such groups, their differences and oppositions. From other points of view, however, it underscores their unity and solidarity; it reaffirms the existing segmentary lineage structure and solidifies it by lending it additional ritual sanctions. By widening the field of kinship relationships at the highest level of initiations, bwami creates a new unit of social interaction, the ritual community, which encompasses a vast network of relationships comprising more than one local clan. Here bwami may be conceived of as an incipient system of centralization. Through its entire organization and ideology, bwami compels people to interact, and to show hospitality, generosity in sharing, and solidarity in planning and carrying out the initiations: "One finger cannot pick up a clod of dirt, not even if you are [self-]sufficient." Through tutorships and exchanges bwami creates many personal interdependencies between individuals of different lineages and clans, and of different villages and ritual communities. Bwami helps produce smooth and ready communication across the boundaries of kinship groups. At all levels it enhances the personal status and prestige of the individual, regardless of his position in the kinship structure. The organization of the initiations is such that the individual senses the value of personal achievement at all levels, in the planning of initiations, in the accum-

The Bwami Association

ulation of wealth, in the expenditure of wealth, in generosity in giving, in kinship cooperation, and in tutorship.

Bwami does more than consolidate and reinforce existing categories of kinship relationships; from some points of view it transcends such relationships by building distinctive fields in which a particular individual selectively establishes close and lasting linkages with certain kinsmen. Several examples will illustrate the point. At the higher levels of bwami the accumulation of initiation goods involves many categories of persons. These categories of agnatic, affinal, and cognatic relationships are prescribed by the kinship structure. But the individuals whose help is actually solicited are not designated by any scheme. Their selection depends on several criteria, among which personal compatibility and friendship are prominent. A well-established initiate aspiring to higher levels has an enormous field of kinship relationships on which he can draw for support: the stable innercircle of close agnates, more distant agnates, members of the seven socially recognized lineages of "male" mothers, sororal nephews, the sisters' daughters' and matrilateral cross-cousins' husbands' groups, the mothers' sisters' husbands' groups, his own wives' groups. Spatially and psychologically, however, an individual is closer to some of these kinsmen than to others, and it is in these terms that he selects his helpers and advisers and builds a field of intensive relations. Special marriage strategies extending over several generations also help to narrow the vast field of relationships and to make them more intensive and productive. Many Lega trace relationships with several lineages of "male mothers" (that is, lineages to which some of the nonconnecting parents, grandparents and great-grandparents belong) within their own clan. Because such individuals have particularly strong fields of cognatic relationships, they can expect help not merely from representatives of the tertiary lineages to which these females belong but from many collateral lines as well.

The emergence and the self-assertion of the individual, and his quest for status in bwami, are, however, not determined by kinship positions but by intelligence, moral quality, leadership, wealth, and other imponderables. It is common for individual members of junior houses and lineages to achieve a bwami rank higher than that of their seniors. Yet the quest for bwami must never be disruptive of normal ingroup relationships. Since the Lega conceive of such disruption as the mild transgression of a taboo, the transgressor must give public cognizance of his offense in a ceremony marking the transfer of specified goods to his immediate senior kinsmen, "in order not to make the children of my father flee."

The manner in which kinship and bwami complement each other is well illustrated by the custom of tutorship. An individual aspiring to the highest initiations needs advice and active sponsorship from a mwami of highest rank with whom he has a strong, close kinship connection. By building large kinship-based communities bwami emphasizes the unity of such groups rather than the segmental opposition of lineages within them. The component sections of these large communities, which own common initiation objects, may or may not be territorially contiguous with one another or historically related. When they are not close, either territorially or historically, the ritual linkage is interpreted in terms of fictive cognation or agnation. The examples of ownership of collectively held initiation baskets and carvings given above, however, aptly illustrate the other side of the connections between bwami and kinship. The hierarchy of grades is completely interwoven with the lineages and clan structure, although the size of the group, the number and size of the lineages, and the actual relationships among lineages determine the way in which these correspondences are brought about.

The Beianangi clan, for example, has a single kindi basket and three yananio baskets, precisely illustrating the unity of the clan and its segmentation into three primary lineages. The Banasalu clan has a single kindi basket and two yananio baskets. The clan is subdivided into four primary lineages, but these are coupled because their founders are thought to be the descendants of two different wives of Salu. The numerically strong Beiamunsange clan has two kindi baskets distributed according to the double alignment of primary lineages in the clan (two series of linked lineages descending from the ancestor's two wives) and eight yananio baskets for seven primary lineages. The situation is complicated: three primary lineages have one basket each, two linked lineages share one basket, and two other primary lineages have two baskets each (reflecting a degree of internal dissension).

Another aspect of cross-clan interaction in bwami is provided by looking, not at kinship positions, but at the clan and lineage origins of individuals who are invited to, and participate in, one of the higher initiations. Lukuku of the Banalyuba clan remembers having called together seventy-nine initiates of lutumbo lwa yananio or musagi wa kindi rank for his lutumbo lwa yananio initiation. Fifty-four of them represented twelve different lineages of the Banalyuba clan. Eight belonged to the Banangumbu clan, which has close historical, territorial, and ritual connections with the Banalyuba. Seven initiates came from the Banameya clan, which also has close connections (reinforced by fictive agnation) with both Banalyuba and Banangumbu. The other ten initiates represented five other clans, all located in the same general area as the Banalyuba.

In the absence of a centralized political system, bwami counts all influential leaders of the community among its members. There is no male in Legaland who does not aspire to become a member, indeed, a high-ranking member, of bwami. Authority in both lineages and villages is largely a function of seniority patterns in the kinship structure and of skills as orator, judge, and arbiter. Access to bwami and progression to the highest levels, however, are not restricted to seniors, but are privileges open

The Bwami Association

to all who are so disposed. Bwami is an aristocracy of the mind and of the heart, not a monopoly of the firstborn or seniors; it is neither a gerontocracy nor an oligarchy. The village or lineage head is usually not the most senior or the highest-ranking mwami in his group, but mwami he is. The interaction of seniority patterns, leadership, and bwami rank constitutes a delicate system of checks and balances. The village headman who holds his position by virtue of unalterable and unquestionable principles of kinship structure is just as eager to acquire bwami rank as is any one of his subjects. To achieve his goal he must do nothing that is contrary to bwami; he must also show respect toward his kinsmen and dependents (or subjects) who hold bwami, possibly at a level higher than his own. Political power and authority and bwami are not coterminous, yet they are inseparable and, to a large extent, convergent. From many points of view it is justifiable to say that there is little politics in Lega society. Warfare and physical violence are incompatible with bwami, whose aim it is to eliminate those evils from society rather than make decisions about them. In the politico-judicial sphere the role of bwami is overwhelming, but informal and discreet. Disagreement, for example, is expressed "by being terribly taciturn" or by tacit refusal to participate in the proceedings. The bami are spokesmen for order and peace, arbiters and counselors, men of conciliation who look for informal negotiations and settlement. Individuals who are unwilling to accept their counsel can never hope to get anywhere in bwami because of the extreme solidarity that marks relationships among initiates. There are, of course, more positive ways in which justice is rendered, ranging from expulsion and social ostracism to the administration of the *kabi* ordeal, from forced induction into bwami to death by poison. But the general trend is toward social and moral pressure rather than toward formal procedures. In general, then, bwami upholds a moral code of unusual depth and unusual elevation, and the Lega attitude is that nobody must be found in opposition to, or guilty of offenses against, the code of bwami.

The elaborate, ongoing initiations that span a human lifetime form a strong economic incentive for individuals and groups and stimulate them to hard manual labor. The initiations presuppose much strategy in planning. They ensure the flow of goods from group to group and from area to area, thus leading to a continual redistribution of wealth. Bwami is not destined to produce a class of the very wealthy. A kindi may have great wealth and may use it generously, but his affluence results from what the Lega would call his good luck (e.g., he has many sons and daughters, brothers and sisters, and other kinsmen who get along well together and who use their resources wisely rather than dissipating them), not from his social position as kindi. In other words, bwami cannot be used to build up personal power and wealth. On the other hand, membership is a security, a safeguard, an insurance. Whether or not one is old, sick, or decrepit, whether or not one actively participates in ceremonies, one is guaranteed a share. The initiate evokes the image of "a fisherman in the Kalumange River who may fail to kill catfish but cannot fail to kill crabs."

There is an element of potlatch in bwami because many goods are required for lavish distributions. No megalomaniac spending or destruction of goods, however, mars the scene. The candidate must not exhibit his wealth or bring it together in a spectacular way. Fundamentally, there is only a slight difference in the quantity or the quality of goods spent by various kindi. Yet those who come to the initiations pretend to come there to "eat" (destroy) as many of the candidate's goods as possible. The entire procedure is a carefully calculated and well-balanced game. The initiates desire to receive as much as possible, even before the initiations begin. Although the candidate is eager to give and to show generosity, he must be certain to have sufficient goods to ensure his initiation, while reserving some for his own future rites and for those of his kinsmen. This subtle game of giving and not giving, of displaying and hiding, is played on behalf of the candidate by his *kakusa*, a well-established and well-informed incumbent of the highest grade of bwami. The distribution of goods demands of the donor and his advisers both brilliance and moderation. At one time a superceremony called lwanza developed in a number of ritual communities; it was considered by some individuals as a grade superior to lutumbo lwa kindi. The rite consisted essentially of an enormous display, distribution, and consumption of food. Many communities never accepted lwanza, and it disappeared rapidly from those groups into which it had been introduced.

Formalized cults, pantheons, cosmologies, and dogmas are unknown among the Lega. Bwami does not adhere to any special cult. Dead kinsmen and members of the bwami association, though casually referred to in proverbs sung during initiations, are not made the object of special worship or veneration. The very notion of a cult for the dead is misleading. The conception cultivated in bwami is that dead kinsmen-congeners are amidst the living (a fact symbolized by the ivory anthropomorphic carvings). It is believed that bwami provides eternal life for its dead members and, for its living members, the capacity to be in direct contact with them. This subtle religious concept has many implications for Lega ideas about the scope of bwami.

As a form of secular religion without gods which brings the initiates into direct confrontation with the supranatural, bwami has an expiatory, cleansing, and soterial power. It is a means by which guilt can be extinguished without suffering or penalty, by which the individual can be ritually and socially purified, by which salvation can be found without the intervention of divinities. Although material and secular sanctions (such as expulsion from the group or poison) are always applicable for serious misdemeanors, induction into bwami is the preferred and normal solution. For

The Bwami Association

seducing a woman of kanyamwa level or killing a kindi in a feud, both extremely grave transgressions (*kitampo*) of the bwami code, compulsory initiation into bwami is usually prescribed. Other culpable actions, some voluntary, some involuntary, are expiated through initiation into bwami; an example is the "accidental" burning of a hut containing figurines used in bwami, either by the owner or by the keeper of the objects.

Ultimately, then, bwami is thought to be a soteriological or free religion in that it offers salvation and immunity to its members and cannot be qualified as a cult system, a clique, or an association of medicine men. Bwami is an open, secular religion. It is the channel through which, and the framework within which, all good can be achieved. Sometimes bwami is directly alluded to as a countersorcery institution: "Bami come together as come together the sorcerers." Bwami neutralizes the agents and the effects of sorcery and witchcraft. Through induction, it transforms the sorcerer into a noble and gentle being. It accomplishes neutralization by using as initiatory objects all the items (horns, hair, nails, shells, etc.) most frequently employed by sorcerers and witches. Bwami frees from sickness, from the contingencies and imponderables of life, and from the taboos of impurity (cursing, adultery, etc.).

Bwami has a transcendant force of its own. Whenever bami attend initiations, this force precedes them; thus, just by being there and going about their business, they ensure the strength and well-being of the country without resorting to cult action. Moreover, the objects used by the bami in initiations contain a force of their own. The ashes of the leaves used in initiations and burned afterward have healing power; so does the dust removed from ivory statues. In general, the bami have the power to cleanse the village and its inhabitants (as a group or as individuals) from impurity and misfortune. This service is accomplished through *mubiko*. A dinner of reconciliation is held in which all members of the village participate. A senior mwami pronounces the solemn and compelling words: "You woman, if this child was bewitched by you because it had difficulties with a mwami, today we are eating the meat of reconciliation. Let this child be cured."

The communication of force to members of the association is dramatized at the end of certain rites. In some areas, for example, the kongabulumbu initiations finish with the *kaminankya* rite: while two suspended drums are beaten, the initiates present small gifts to the candidate, pulling at and rubbing his limbs and blowing in their cupped hands over his head. Both activities, respectively described as *kunanula* and *kibunga*, are explicitly intended by the Lega to communicate force. Finally, bwami gives its members a sense of continuity. The endless repetition of initiations, the continual substitution of one person for another as individuals die or move up in the hierarchy, the never ending transfer of initiation objects, particularly precious art objects kept as *kasina* (pleasant memories of good men), and many other features of the initiations give the Lega strong assurances of self-perpetuation.

The initiation process itself constitutes a significant portion of the total activity of bwami. The most important part of the initiations consists of proverb-songs, dances, music, displays of objects, and dramatic performances, all slightly recreational and explicitly educational.

Any ceremonial event of bwami, whether related to initiations, funerary ceremonies, or distribution of the pangolin, is characterized by the singing, dancing, and acting out of a large number of recurring proverbs. Every ceremony gives initiates an opportunity to reaffirm among themselves the principles of the bwami moral and social code and the ways in which these principles can be implemented. The educational aspect is never deliberately placed in the foreground; yet, clad in a delicately balanced symbolism, it is present in every utterance. The same basic ideas, principles, and prescriptions are repeated over and over again in an extraordinary variety of proverbs, with never a pedantic overtone. The value of filial piety finds hundreds of ways of indirect expression: for example, "A child: a dugout canoe; you carve it, it takes you across," or "The young child that knocks at the door is your companion in the village."

The *bitondo bya kisi*, or words of the land, are sung by groups of dancing, drumming, and gesturing initiates in a choreographic and musical context. The dramatic setting is enhanced by the manipulation, rarely the mere display, of large numbers of objects varying from natural items to carvings. The full meaning of the proverbs, or of the sculptures and other items, can be understood only if they are analyzed in the total context. Such analysis presupposes a thorough familiarity with a broad range of action and thought patterns in Lega society.

In a typical example, the Beiamunsange, at one stage of their initiations, sing and dance out the following proverb: "To bring together the unsuccessful hunting nets, Isasamuna will come to cut [the tongue]." The initiates first dance in a row in the middle of the village. One by one they receive an *isasamuna* (*Fagara melanorachis*) leaf from an initiate who is sitting near the entrance to the initiation hut. As the initiates continue the dance, each one rubs his leaf against the tip of his tongue. To anyone familiar with the Lega world, or with the African world in general, the context suggests that reference is being made to hunting and to the ritual pertaining to it ("bringing together" the nets and cutting the tongue with a leaf). At this point the meaning of the proverb and of the accompanying action is perfectly clear to the Lega, because they are familiar with the ways in which things are done in their society.

A vast range of activities is condensed in this simple dance. The scenery to be visualized is the hunting camp where a group of young men are settled for a month or longer. They organize daily hunting expeditions. After a few successful rounds, luck turns against them and no animals are killed. The explanation is readily found: among the participants there must be a "bad" person, one who has infringed upon hunting taboos either by seducing the wife of another hunter, or by mating with his own wife during the hunt, or possibly by participating in the hunt though having a pregnant wife. To restore balance and optimum ritual conditions, the hunters proceed with the *isasamuna* ceremony. Each hunter receives a freshly cut *isasamuna* leaf. Then, while agitating dog bells, the hunters sing: "May everyone who has eaten from the meat *kikikiki!* [onomatopoeia for saying "cut the tongue with a leaf"]." Thereupon each hunter cuts the tip of his tongue with the leaf and collects a drop of blood on a piece of bark cloth torn from his own loincloth. The hunters place the pieces of bark cloth in a funnel made of *muntolontolo* (*Fagara macrophylla*) leaves. This ritual explains the second part of the proverb and the ceremonial action that takes place during initiations.

The first part of the proverb, which is not accompanied by explanatory action, is accounted for by the *nkinda* rite that follows the preceding ritual. Again the setting is the hunting camp. All leaves on which animals have previously been skinned, and which are therefore imbued with dried blood, are burned, and the ashes are distributed among the hunters. All participants, each with his hunting net slung over his left shoulder, then pass under an arch constructed of two branches, while a celebrant (*mulondosa*) blows smoke from a burning funnel over the nets. Each hunter repeats the following formula as he passes beneath the arch: "If the possessors of small pregnancies go to sleep with women, and if this affects the nets, all sorcery [= evil] is finished [because] we have cut ourselves on the tongues." The hunters then go into the forest to the *makia* (place where the hunting nets are set up) and fasten what remains of the leaf funnel to one of the poles where two nets are joined together. Performance of this rite explains the first part of the proverb, "To bring together the unsuccessful hunting nets." The entire proverb means that initiates do not indulge in acts that are ritually degrading (second part) and that they are unifiers (first part).

Bwami provides its members, and Lega society as a whole, with a coherent system of ethics. It is a pragmatic philosophy built on the commonsense notions that virtue is enjoyable and that virtue is revealed, not merely by what one says, but by what one does. Aiming at the achievement of *kalokagathia*, it is rational and is clearly understood by both members and nonmembers. Bwami may be thought of as an academy of knowledge and learning oriented, not toward the accumulation of data about the universe, but toward the improvement of man. Because of the rich symbolisms that illustrate and underscore ideal behavior, the initiations offer a vast survey of everything that is known in the Lega environment, whether relevant or irrelevant. Something is said about hundreds of animals, from the lowest creatures to the highest primates, and about hundreds of plants, even about distinctive parts of the animals or plants which sometimes stand for the whole. Interpretations are made, not only about a certain species of tree, but about its roots, leaves, bark, and fruits; not only about a certain species of animal, but about its hide or scales, its teeth, claws, tail, skull, spine, or carapace. Other references and interpretations have to do with techniques (trapping, hunting, and fishing, preferably) and with the results of using them. In other words, the knowledge communicated during initiations is encyclopedic from the Lega point of view.

Characteristically for the Lega, nothing in the philosophy of bwami is speculative, hypothetical, heuristic, or epideictic. There are no speculations about the divine or the sacred, about the universe, or about non-Lega. The philosophy is anthropocentric, pragmatic, rationalist. Consider, for example, the three most frequently quoted aphorisms about death: "Death has no possessor; [it is] a fruit that came from above" (everybody is affected by it); "Death is the back of a snake; wherever you eat [bite] there are bones" (death is always bad); and "Who died does not come back; on ivory mushrooms do not grow." Consider also the rational viewpoint expressed about the sky (*igulu*): "Where there are no beings, there is no noise; in the sky there are no [beings]," which means that those who think there are beings in the sky because of thunder, and so forth, are like noninitiates who have only empty thoughts. Bwami philosophy has no room for skepticism or pessimism, as it has no room for metaphysics. The ethics of bwami are both high and deep; and initiated Lega who have been exposed to Bible teaching or have heard about the Bible believe their moral philosophy to be on a par with Christian principles.

The Lega conceive of their universe as a simple construct governed by antithetical forces. At the supranatural level, Kinkunga (creator-god) and Kalaga (culture hero), who are both good, oppose Kaginga (evil). At the human level, the children of Idega and Kakinga (Pygmy girl) are set against the Barimi (people not of Lega culture). Conceptually the idea is expressed by the terms *bunene* and *bwanya*, plenitude versus calamity. The antitheses are not rigidly or strictly formulated. For example, Barimi may be initiated into bwami and thus become Idega. The separation between good and evil is easily bridged by the mediating and reconciling force of the ancestors, which is guided by the propitiatory rites of the living.

Much of the so-called recreational activity of the bami (dances, dramatic movements, music, sung aphorisms) has an aesthetic quality which is also visible in the care and adornment of the body, the intricate architectural forms, and the verbal arts (speeches, proverbs, praise names). During initiations special attention is given to sound and lighting effects for musical and dramatic performances. Musical instruments include membranophones, slit-drums, and rattles; occasionally there is percussion on ax blades with wooden sticks or scepters made of elephant bone. In rites with

The Bwami Association

no music at all, or with only intermittent music, the candidate's entrance into the initiation house may be preceded or followed by beating or scratching the ground with dried skins, leaves, or sticks. Sometimes a dead silence during a ceremony is interrupted by the imitation of animal noises or the shouting of praise names, or complete darkness is dispelled by the sudden lighting of torches. The swift change from silence to noise, from darkness to light, may be accompanied by a dramatic event such as the unexpected killing of a goat by strangulation or trampling.

A special relationship exists between bwami and the sculptural arts. The Lega, who are prolific, original, and masterful artists, make small-size sculptures of elephant ivory and bone, wood, mud, resin, soapstone, hide, and leopard teeth to be used and owned by the members of the association and to be interpreted by the bami. Enormous quantities of these objects are needed for the large number of individuals who can own them and for the variety and multiplicity of ritual contexts in which they must be used.

Those who have been initiated to kindi enjoy a kind of personal immunity. It is not permissible to insult them or beat them, or to request them to carry loads. Aged kindi are never asked or permitted to perform physical labor. Elderly initiates who take part in initiations usually do nothing but sit, sleep, observe, and enjoy themselves. Special privileges are reserved for initiates. They have exclusive rights in distributing and sharing certain sacred animals. They alone can claim ownership of a wide variety of natural objects, artifacts, and objets d'art. Their control of circumcision cycles is, among all rights and privileges, the one that carries the most social weight (or so the bami say, indirectly). Finally, high-ranking initiates alone possess the secret of certain ritual actions which bring harmony and peace to the communities.

For the Lega, bwami is *bigagazi,* a thing that cannot be measured. And so it is for me. For the Lega, the "initiation that father has done is a tall *katondo* tree [in which the crowned eagle likes to nest]." And that is the way I see the immensity and the endlessness of bwami initiations. For the Lega, the mwami is Mpimbi, the "Strong-One who is not overcome by things that climb [difficulties]." And I look at the initiate in the same way. For the Lega, the "words of the land are things that tie together, things that transform [like the clouds], things that are high [like the sky]." And so I regard the unfathomable depth of the teachings and principles of bwami.

Part 4 The Art of Bwami

Range of Initiation Objects Used in Bwami

The initiations (*mpala*) through which membership in a given grade or level of bwami is conferred upon men and women comprise three interconnected categories of activities. At the center of the proceedings are dramatic performances, including music, dancing, singing (in proverb form), gestures, light and sound effects, and, occasionally, formal message drumming, praise name shouting, and recitation of formulas and orations. Specialized paraphernalia and limited body painting add to the dramatic effect of the dance. Performances are accompanied by the revelation, display, manipulation, and interpretation of artworks, used jointly with manufactured and natural objects. These initiation objects usually occur in specific associations and configurations, rather than serially. Initiations are the setting for the transfer of some of these objects from initiates to the candidate for initiation. Finally, the initiations are preceded, accompanied, and followed by he exchange of commodities and food to entertain, to reward, and to pay participating initiates, kinsmen, and guests. These three predominant categories of activities are closely linked. Initiation objects almost always find a place in a sequence of dance, song, and music; almost every song and dance demands the use of initiation objects; each rite

The Art of Bwami

requires the donation of many goods. Initiation objects may conveniently be classified as natural objects, manufactured items, and artworks.

Natural Objects. The wide range of natural objects includes items derived from the vegetal, animal, and mineral worlds. Initiates use many different kinds of leaves, some freshly cut, some dried; in one rite alone I recorded the display of more than thirty-five varieties of leaves. Among those most frequently used are banana leaves, phrynium (*Sarcophrynium arnoldianum*), raffia palm leaves, and leaves from *Gilbertiodendron dewevrei* (*limbalu*), *Alstonia* sp. (*muntonko*), *Musanga smithii* (*musagi*), *Macaranga* sp. (*mabilabondo*), *Tylostemon* sp. (*munsongensonge*), *Pancovia harmsiana* De Wild (*kagolomba*), *Ferdinandia* A. F. (*muntuluntulu*), *Scaphopetalum thonneri* (*lubeketa?*), *Bosquiaea angolensis* (*kikagu*), *Staudtia gabonensis* (*bugubi*), *Pentaclethra macrophylla* (*mbala*), *Schotia* aff. *Bergeri* (*nkumbi*), *Macaranga monandra* (*kantengentenge*), *Albizzia zygia* (*nkungu*), *Pithecelobium duinklagei* (*lusele*), *Fagara* sp. (*kimpangampanga*), *Pachypodanthicum* sp. (*kyombi*), *Xylopia* sp. (*lusangi*), *Autranella congolensis* (*ibulungu*), *Homalium* sp. (*kakolokolo*), and *Carapa procera* (*mugulugulu*).[1]

In selecting these species of trees, Lega symbolic thinking seems primarily to be guided by such factors as speedy growth, tallness, and straightness of the tree, the span of its crown, the massiveness of its buttresses or aerial roots, its location in the forest or its relative predominance in forest formations, and its material usefulness to humans and animals. And, of course, the component parts of these trees may help to convey general ideas, regardless of their specific meanings. In the kyogo kya kindi initiations among the Babongolo, I witnessed a rite in which various species of leaves were carefully placed, in layers, in a small basket. Inside were hidden the scaly leaves of an orchid. The layers of leaves were identified with levels of knowledge one has to attain in order to discover supreme wisdom (symbolized by the scaly orchid leaves). At the end of the rite the leaves were hidden inside the bunch of scaly leaves and attached with a liana to the roof of the initiation hut. This bundle symbolizes the "strong heart" of the kindi who stands above the imponderabilia of daily life.

Nutshells, pods, seeds, dried fruits, pieces of bark, twisted roots, forked sticks, beams, and gaffles from the trees mentioned above, and from many others as well, are employed in select rites. Of these, the first four are most frequently used. Among the more important items are the seeds (*kizombo*) of the wild banana, the seeds (*kituta*) of *Tridesmostemon*

---

[1] Thorough botanical surveys of the Lega forests have not been undertaken. For assistance in my endeavor to identify some of the species, I am indebted to De Wildeman (1909), Vermoesen (1923), Lebrun (1935), Michelson (n.d.), and Troupin (1956), and to initiates to whom I submitted photographs of tentatively identified species for verification.

claessensii, the fruits (*ntolo*) of *Costus lucanusianus*, the fruits (*kitugu*) of *Pachyelasma tessmanii* (*mbili*), the fruits (*atampoa*) of *Gossweilerodendron balsamiferum* (*ngale*), the nuts (*ikili*) of *Autranella congolensis* (*ibulungu*), the nuts of *Annonidium mannii* (*busingu*), the nutshells (*bunkaga*) of *Syncepalum longaecuminatum* and of the unidentified *mugandwe*, and the pods of *Pentaclethra macrophylla* (*bubala*), *Antrocaryon* sp. (*bukongo*), *Entada abyssinica* (*mputi*), and the unidentified *nkebe*. Bulrushes, the petioles of banana leaves, the rachises of raffia and oil palm, and several kinds of resin (*kiwagavwaga* from *Copaifera demeusii* [*ngale*], *kasuku* from *Gossweilerodendron balsamiferum*) are also of service. Redwood and red powder obtained from *Pterocarpus tinctorius* (*nkula*) are used only occasionally. *Bulago*, with which the initiates perfume their bodies and their ivory carvings, is derived from the *lungo* and *makoma* trees. Cosmetic oils are obtained from the fruits of *Lebrunia bushaie* and other trees. Black sap for coloring and dyeing is extracted from certain lianas. Charcoal obtained from the parasol tree is also applied in coloring. The hard core of fallen and decayed trees (*ntutu*) is utilized in its natural form or as a rare medium for carvings. The initiates also find a need for dried mushroom growths (*kyagogo*). Flowers, to which the aphorisms rarely make reference, are of no use whatsoever in the rites. Calabash, despite its value in Lega technology, has no special significance in bwami. Several kinds of lianas, such as the rubber-producing *Landolphia* varieties, are used, but of more importance are the *Eremospatha* liana (*lububi*), such varieties as *lukusa* (*Polycephalium poggei?*) and *lwamba*, and pieces of twisted lianas (*lubugu*).

Items derived from the animal world also cover a wide range. Skulls are used in many rites, especially those of chimpanzee, leopard, forest crocodile (*Osteolaemus*), warthog, and *kagelia* monkey (*Erythrocebus patas*).[2] The large beaks of hornbills (*Bucerotidae*), particularly species (*mutu, magasa, kazombolo*) whose bill is surmounted by a large casque, are of extreme ritual importance. Except for the bills of *kakulikuli* (an ibis species) and *kwangwakwa* (an unidentified species of extremely talkative bird), few other beaks are used. The Lega, though finding little use for feathers, prefer russet and white chicken feathers and the red tail feathers of the parrot. Teeth of leopard, buffalo, dendrohyrax, crocodile, lion (occasionally), and the *Hydrocyon goliath* fish, molars of elephants, and fangs of the *Bitis lachesis* viper are turned into initiation objects and paraphernalia. The patrimony of the initiates includes tusks of elephants, wild boar, and warthogs; elephant tail, bone, rotula, and foot; tibia and hands

---

[2] In the identification of animal species I have been helped by the monumental publications of Schouteden 1947; by Sanderson (n.d.), Pilsbry (1919), Burton (1962), and Bequaert (1950); and by initiates who brought me animals that had been killed in the hunt.

The Art of Bwami

of the *Cercopithecus* monkey, crab pincers, hoofs of the duiker antelope, beards of goats, claws of the aardvark (*Orycteropus*) and eagle (*Polemaëtus bellicosus*), and scales, claws, and scaly tail of the pangolin. Hides or skins of genet, golden mole, wildcat, duiker, bongo antelope, otter, leopard, *Colobus* and *Cercopithecus* monkeys, snakes, goats, and, less frequently, of iguana, crocodile, elephant, and hyena are made into many kinds of initiation objects or put to use in their natural state. Horns of rams, billy goats, and antelopes (duiker; *Oreotragus*), porcupine quills, and carapaces of turtle (*Kinyxis erosa*; *Kinyxis belliana belliana*; *Pelusios subniger*) play a significant role in initiations. Insects are of little importance in initiations, although reference is made to termites, red ants, centipedes, and bees, and beeswax, honeycombs, and certain ingeniously made insect nests are used as initiation objects. Cowries, shells of large *Mutelidae* found in local rivers, several varieties of achatina shells (the giant *nkola* snail), some *Pila dewulfi* shells (the giant *kikoku* snail), *Limicolaria*, oyster shells, and occasionally *Neothauma* shells imported from the Lake Tanganyika area have initiatory value in a natural or modified form.

Minerals have little significance in bwami rites, except for quartz stone, pebbles, soil from termite nests, red earth, and white clay.

All these objects—vegetable, animal, mineral—can be and are used in their natural state. Many of them occur in combinations, or with more or less significant modifications, as a few examples will illustrate. Porcupine quills are sometimes adorned with red parrot feathers. A hornbill beak may be decorated with beads and cloth; a pangolin claw may be wrapped in wickerwork; mussel shells are sometimes polished. A snake skin is often trimmed with chicken feathers or porcupine quills. A wildcat hide may be embellished with cowries; a goat skin, with nutshells. Some natural objects are impregnated with oil or painted with white or red colors, but this practice is not customary. Most of the natural objects are preserved in baskets or bags by all initiates of a certain grade or by specific officeholders and ritual experts. Like all other objects, they are transferred and inherited, owned and kept in trusteeship. Leaves are usually burned after the ritual and their ashes are preserved for medicinal use.

Almost all the natural objects have several possible uses. They may be part of the insignia and dancing paraphernalia. Some have special purposes: the goatskin may be used to display various objects; the wildcat hide, to display figurines or to receive the corpse of a dead initiate. Used singly, or in a configuration including other natural objects, manufactured objects, and artworks, all natural objects serve as initiatory items that help to evoke and convey deep sentiments about the moral code of bwami. The seeds that scatter when the *mbala* pod falls from the tree are a reminder that the clan disintegrates when it is torn by disputes. The sharpness of porcupine quills reminds an initiate that his heart should not be so "sharp" (quick-tempered) as they are. The skull of *Erythrocebus patas*, to which its tail is fixed, symbolizes a master of the land who behaves badly. The giant snail shell of *kikoku* symbolizes slow but straightforward progress toward a goal. A warthog tusk, held in the mouth of an initiate, evokes Kisibula, the destroyer, the sorcerer who causes the village to collapse.

Any natural object that serves as an initiatory device may convey several different messages which are not necessarily related. As an example, let us take the hide of a genet (*musimba*). In kongabulumbu initiations I heard the following aphorisms and interpretations, with symbolisms mainly inspired by the animal's habits and the spots on its hide. In "Genet, turning and sneaking behind the house," the *kakusa* tutor is identified with a genet because he lingers near the house of the initiate looking for goods to distribute. In another aphorism, a low-ranking initiate is identified with the genet, whereas the hawk symbolizes a high-ranking initiate: "Genet, the clever catcher, cannot arrive where Hawk arrives." In other words, a high-level initiate can get more than a person of low rank. Since the spots on the genet's hide remind initiates of the leopard, the two animals are symbolically identified. The aphorisms, "Spots of the leopard frighten the goats," and "Spots of the leopard, you have said to the grazing sheep that what kills them is good," are meant to emphasize the exclusive character of the bwami association. The color contrast of the spots evokes a different concept: "Bad kinship, here light-colored and there dark-colored." The spots are also referred to as stains to stress the idea that a person is affected by the deeds and the reputation of his parents: "Stain that stains his mother stains the mother of your companion." Some metaphors go much further, retaining only the idea of the leopard: "To die without giving birth, the leopard rots with the claws." The fact that the genet is a carnivore and hunts around village and houses to steal chickens and that the *mpoma* viper (*Bitis lachesis*) hunts for rats in the same vicinity leads to the following proverb: "In the new field where *mpoma* lays its eggs, there is no rat." This text means that it is the purpose of the association to "eat" all the goods available.

This shifting of the center of symbolic focus from a physical trait to a behavioral characteristic, and from one animal to another with similar physical or behavioral traits, runs as a constant theme through bwami initiations. (It is clarified later, in the discussion of artworks.) To completely understand the Lega initiation scheme, the objects used must not be taken at face value. Form is not necessarily a sign; form alone does not necessarily convey meaning. Rather, the activities and the realities that underlie the form, the content and the configurations of objects and actions in which the form is used, the form and its details—these are the focal centers of the symbolism. An example will illustrate the point. In many rites chimpanzee skulls are used and interpreted as such. In some rites, however, the initiates dance with chimpanzee skulls but talk about the *kagelia* monkey, and in others the interpretations center on Mulinga

The Art of Bwami

(Chaser-of-Animals). Obviously the initiates see a skull in the abstract, not the skull of a particular animal. Both Kagelia and Mulinga are personified. In both instances one eye socket of the skull is covered with beads or with a simple leaf, and the emphasis in the symbolism is directed toward this fact. The first proverb, "Kagelia grumbles at people; he does not grumble at his [own ones]," is critical of the person who always sees the wrong in others but does not see it in his own children. In contrast, the second text, "Mulinga, the Great-One, has hunted a *mpombi* antelope with one eye," criticizes the man who takes care of other people but not of his own.

Manufactured Goods. Manufactured goods include articles and assemblages of articles made of basketry, rope, wood and bark, pottery, iron and copper, leather, bone, ivory, resin, stone, and *ntutu*, and also woven objects. As noted earlier, many natural objects receive minimal modification before being used in initiations. Several holes may be drilled into a pangolin scale; the end portion of a pangolin tail may be wrapped in wickerwork; a piece of forest crocodile skin may be sewn onto a stick; a snake or otter skin may be stuffed with leaves, grasses, or moss. The following categories of manufactured goods can be recognized:

1. Assemblages of articles may be simple or complex. Examples of simple combinations are the fangs of the *Bitis lachesis* viper inserted into a ball of glue, a piece of parasol wood decorated with glue and cowries, or a ball of wax studded with little seeds and attached to the end of a porcupine quill. More sophisticated assemblages include human-like figures made of a piece of banana stipe covered with genet skins, beads, and sticks.
2. Bags, baskets, mats, wickerwork rattles, small round mats, hat frames, belts, girdles, diadems, and ceremonial shields are all made of slit lianas, among which *lububi* and *lukusa* are by far the preferred ones.
3. Brooms and flyswatters are made from grasses and bulrushes.
4. Plank doors, ladders, fire drills, gaffles, walking staffs, stools, chairs, figurines, masks, axes, hornbill knives, double-edged knives, bark beaters, miniature mancala game boards, slit-drums, dog bells, dugout canoes, beaters, phallus-like sticks (*kizingio*), and the *yango* stick are all made of wood. Although parasol and *Allstonia* woods are preferred for many of these articles, a wide variety of woods is available. For certain objects the material is specified: the *yango* stick is made of *kyombi* (*Pachypodanthicum*); the slit-drum, from the camwood tree (*Pterocarpus tinctorius*); and the *nkeka* chair, from the aerial roots of the *mutondo* tree.
5. Knives, spears, razors, needles, bracelets, anklets, and armlets are made of iron. Some knife blades (*bubenga*) and horseshoe-shaped

or crescentic pieces of adornment for hats are made of copper (post-European).
6. Belts, girdles, hats, chest and arm straps, certain types of rattles, and small disk-shaped mats are made from select hides. Usually the type of hide for belts and hats is strictly prescribed because they are linked as paraphernalia with the hierarchy of grades in bwami. Belts are made of bongo antelope hide or elephant skin. Hats are made from the hide of black- or reddish-haired goats, antelope, leopard, and *Colobus* monkey. Some very rare hats are made of elephant ear, crocodile skin, pangolin scales, or the mane of an old sheep. A few extremely rare hats are covered with nutshells. These hats have many adornments, most of them made of materials other than hide.
7. Except for cooking pots and jars for storing water, oil, and red and white paints, few pottery items play a role in bwami initiations. The only ones I have seen in use are pipe bowls and the *moza* pot (in which the preceptor blows on a bamboo pipe during kongabulumbu initiations), but there are also some artworks in clay.
8. Other objects used in bwami include necklaces of beads and teeth (mostly leopard teeth), small bows and arrows made from *lububi* lianas, pieces of elephant bone, feather ropes (*munana*), feather tufts (worn on hips, arms, and head), strips of bark cloth, aprons, loincloths and costumes made of bark, and balls (*lwenze*) of raffia fibers or rubber. Much decorative use is made of nutshells, beads, buttons, cowrie shells, polished mussel shells, and disks derived from polished achatina shells. These attractive adornments are placed on belts, straps, aprons, girdles, diadems, hats, and round mats. Many of these objects are manipulated, owned, and transmitted by all individuals who have achieved a certain grade and a certain level in the association; others are collectively held initiation objects. Although hats, belts, girdles, necklaces, and feather tufts are used mainly as paraphernalia and insignia, they are also interpreted and explained during initiations, as are other types of natural objects, artifacts, and artworks.

Ideas about the moral philosophy of bwami are conveyed by these manufactured objects. A broom of bulrush, which helps to keep everything clean, is identified with bwami which cleanses the heart of men. A wickerwork rattle is "the call of kindi" because it transmits secret messages to other kindi; it is a symbol of wealth, for only the highest-ranking initiates may have it; it lends beauty and harmony to music and dances; finally, it symbolizes the meaningfulness of everything in bwami because every seed in it adds to the sound. A small hunting net hung over the bodies of two initiates is the symbol of harmony and unity between them. The

The Art of Bwami

walking stick, like the transverse beam of a house on which all the other beams rest, is like the headman or the master of the land on whom all others rely.

Artworks. On the basis of shape and material, artworks may be classified in many categories.

1. Masks and maskettes of wood, elephant ivory, elephant bone, and occasionally elephant leather, with or without fiber beards. Wooden masks may be painted white or red.
2. Anthropomorphic figurines, mostly in wood, elephant ivory, and elephant bone, but occasionally in clay, resin, soapstone, and the inner marrow of decayed trees. Red and white coloring is sometimes used on wooden figurines.
3. Zoomorphic figures in wood, ivory, elephant bone, and very rarely in clay. Usually these highly stylized figurines represent the animal in general rather than a particular species. Some, however, are fairly naturalistic representations of such animals as crocodiles, turtles, snakes, centipedes, frogs, lizards, and antelopes. Other rudimentary animal carvings become specific representations when scales or other exuviae are added to make identification easy.
4. Occasionally small human-shaped heads (with or without a neck), resting on a socle or a small stool, are carved in ivory. A few examples in pottery are also known.
5. Spoon-shaped objects with shallow, oval bowls and stylized handles are sometimes carved in the shape of a human body or fashioned in *ajouré* work.
6. Small carvings in ivory, with or without a human-shaped head, are sometimes in spiral shape; sometimes they are oblong pieces in the round which resemble phalli.
7. Miniature spear-shaped knives, hornbill knives, spearheads, ax blades, hammers, scepters, pin-shaped objects, dice, and stools in ivory or bone. On rare occasions these objects are made of wood, but then they are so rudimentary that they could hardly be called artworks. The Lega also carve imitation leopard teeth, and oblong and rectangular pieces to be worn as armlets or bracelets, from ivory and bone.
8. Although many of the *nkeka* stools (made from the aerial roots of the *mutondo* tree) and the *kaongama* chairs (heavy and long, with shallow, bowl-shaped seats on four short legs) have a fine patina and are well carved, they cannot be classed as artworks. The smaller, round stools, however, with four short supports on a base (*kisumbi*) are finely carved, well polished and patinated, sometimes embellished with copper nails, and artistically appealing. They play an extremely important role in initiations.

9. Some infrequently used objects possess great artistic merit. In some of the assemblages prepared for certain rites I have observed well-carved wooden hands and upper-arm pieces. I have also seen in use in bwami ceremonies elegantly patinated bark beaters made of wood or ivory and identified with *yango* sticks; beautifully patinated roots or other woody excrescences equated with human figures; and expertly made forks or gaffles, some shaped in the form of an ibis neck. Some of the disk-shaped mats in wickerwork or hide, trimmed with porcupine quills or feathers and decorated with cowrie shells and nutshells, are genuine art pieces. Sometimes the handles of the large *kabemba* knives are made of well-patinated ivory. The sheaths for these knives are masterfully fashioned from planks of parasol wood, fastened together with antelope leather and straps of metal. I have also seen an extraordinary staff made entirely of wickerwork with several swellings, as if *mizegele* rattles in wicker had been placed one on top of the other.

The setting up of a separate category of artworks is not meant to detract from the quality of artifacts and natural objects. Some of them, especially the hats, are outstanding examples of artistic excellence. Some hats are made of fibers, dyed black to resemble women's hair. Others are colorfully studded with cowries, nutshells, buttons, and beads, and are further adorned with dendrohyrax teeth, elephant tail, or polished mussel shells. Very few objects of European origin are used in bwami initiations. Those that are have recently been substituted for traditional objects that have been lost, destroyed, or confiscated and, because of general insecurity, have not been replaced. Foreign replacements are limited to such things as well-shaped perfume bottles, bulbs, madonnas, and china plates.

The foregoing outline presents the categories of objects used in bwami as they appear to outsiders. In ensuing sections I discuss initiatory items, paraphernalia, and insignia from the Lega point of view. I want to stress again that the entire range of natural objects, whether or not they carry the mark of man-made modifications, and of manufactured items forms a closely interrelated whole. The unity and the complementary character of all initiation objects are well demonstrated by the contents of the collectively held baskets.

Despite variation from ritual community to ritual community, the basic nature of the contents remains constant. In one community a collectively held basket for lutumbo lwa yananio contains a hornbill beak, two chimpanzee skulls, a skull of a forest crocodile, a giant snail shell, a pangolin scale, one *mbili* fruit, one *kitugu* mushroom, a wooden animal figurine, a horned mask, one male and one female wooden figurine, and a wooden triple-gaff hook. The basket is covered with bark cloth, to which a wickerwork shield and spear are attached. In another community the lutumbo

The Art of Bwami

lwa yananio basket contains a wooden animal figurine, a wooden horned mask, three larger wooden masks, three forest crocodile skulls, a turtle carapace (*Kinyxis erosa*), one end of the tail part of the pangolin, a molar section of elephant teeth, one *mbili* fruit, two hornbill beaks, one *kyagogo* mushroom, and the hide of a golden mole stuffed with moss. Closely related ritual communities that ritually interact with one another choose different items for their baskets, but invariably natural and manufactured objects and artworks are intermingled. This mixture of objects is typical for all rites at all levels and grades. Each individual object conveys several levels of meanings, but the totality of ideas pertaining to a certain rite can be communicated only by the total configuration of assorted objects.

An outline of the *mulama* rite as held in the Banamunwa and Bagilanzelu communities will clarify the point. During the *mulama* rite, the ninth of twelve initiatory phases through which an initiate of musagi wa yananio passes before achieving lutumbo lwa yananio, the collectively held basket of initiation objects is opened and the objects are displayed on the ground. The preceptors who lead the row of dancers pick up the objects, sometimes one by one, sometimes two or more at a time. They dance with them, holding them in their hands, moving them up and down, and showing them to the seated candidate who, supported by his tutors, silently watches the proceedings. One or more aphorisms are sung about each object by the preceptors, the row of dancing initiates, and the members of the orchestra, which includes drummers and rattlers. In one instance the contents of three baskets were displayed and interpreted. Two of them were held by the yananio members of two different primary lineages in the Banamunwa clan, and one belonged to the yananio of the Bagilanzelu clan. Several of the objects that have been discussed here turned up in all three baskets, but each basket also contained several objects peculiar to itself. The following outline lists the seventeen different types of objects illustrated in the rite.

1. A large wooden animal figurine identified as *mumbilumbilu* (aquatic animal) expresses three ideas.
   a. "Mumbilumbilu, an aquatic animal, drinks water." That is, an initiate is involved with bwami and cannot prohibit other people from attempting to achieve it.
   b. "I have not trapped for it; the hospitality gifts eat my meat." Here the figurine evokes the idea of the hunt and suggests that the candidate is complaining because so many initiates whom he did not expect to come are now eating his meat.
   c. "A large predator is not caught with the feathers in his mouth." One does not know who slept with one's wife during the day.
2. The skull of *munkondekonde*, a forest crocodile, is associated with the following statements.

    a. "The crocodile does not eat catfish in its hole." A master of the land who is always trying to seduce the wives of his subjects is criticized.

    b. "Mukondekonde, whom I bring forth, makes fun of the scales." Here a son is warned not to laugh at his father's infirmities; and the candidate, not to despise those who helped him through the initiations.

    c. "As is the animal, so is the skinner." A father and a son who are both bad are criticized.

    d. "Mukondekonde remains in the pool; he closes the ears." An old man who remains to take care of young people but is unable to advise them is blamed.

    e. "Iguana is not water, but the animal that resembles a fallen tree." This statement stigmatizes a person whose heart is just as bad as that of his father.

    f. "Splashing in the water is the reason why Kwale [fish] was killed by Mulinde [snake]." A candidate is determined to achieve bwami: others achieved yananio, and so will I.

    g. "Lwindi [large river] is not a river, [but] the little brook that is crowded with crocodiles." Those who finish the initiations before the candidate will receive his goods.

3. A hornbill beak, called *nkoko*, in this instance, as if it were a chicken's beak, is used with a large number of aphorisms.

    a. "The chick: the tender care of both father and mother." Children, even bad ones, cannot be "thrown away" or "abandoned."

    b. "The male chicken: the bird that has seen early morning." The headman of the village is identified with a rooster.

    c. "Hornbill feeds; the hunters see your spoor." A man runs with other women, whose husbands have heard about it.

    d. "Hornbill, the miserable one, has tried to say [to imitate] the call of animals." Here the person who pretended to prepare for the initiations but does not have the necessary goods is criticized.

    e. "It is not a call; the bird has come with a sad message." It is extremely bad to get from passersby the message about a kinsman's death or about the organization of an initiation, and not to hear it from one's own people.

    f. "Hornbill would not have died; it is because of the crested beak that Hornbill died." The idea is stressed that nobody should ever boast of having received more at an initiation than he really has.

    g. "Hornbill passes me with force, Mrs. Wingbeat." This aphorism refers to a woman who likes to run around with her lovers but neglects her husband.

The Art of Bwami

    h. "Mr. Hardhearted, child of my father, callousness has made his body dry up." For a callous person there is neither fame nor a good fate.

    i. "Chicks of Earthquake, we are dead altogether; we grow tails." If your wife is a sorcerer she will kill all your children.

    j. "Hornbill counts the villages; he does not know what sticks out above his neck." The initiates are full of joy because of the dances but they are ignorant as to what may kill them.

4. A piece of the skull of the *nsamba* fish (*Clarias lazera*) evokes the following thoughts.

    a. "Nsamba [fish], you will eat your things; [but] Mbili [fish poison] tastes your liver." This statement is attributed to a sorcerer who says to himself: "Let the man eat much and enjoy himself; I will kill him."

    b. "Nsamba is being spoken to [honored] by every fish that is in the river." The tutor, on whom the burden of responsibilities rests, is here identified with Nsamba.

    c. "I have not eaten *nsamba* fish; it is from catfish that I have eaten." If one says he stole only a little, he is still a thief. The statement also means that in bwami one begins with simple little things in order to rise to the highest achievements.

    d. "Nsamba astonishes me; he who gave you the belt of bongo hide, he who gives you *mpala* [initiation], gives you greatness." People are encouraged to enter bwami, to progress in it, and to achieve plenitude.

5. A miniature mancala game board (*lusolo*) conveys two thoughts.

    a. "For him who does not count, Lusolo [Game Board] has burned the stakes." An initiate who does not follow the prescriptions and customs of bwami is worth nothing.

    b. "A child [is] a dugout canoe: you carve it, and it will take you across." This oft-quoted proverb underscores the immense material and spiritual help that parents can expect from well-cared-for children.

6. A wooden, stylized animal figurine, called *mugugu* (lit., chameleon), conveys two ideas.

    a. "Mugugu, I sing during the rainy season; I have no hornbill knife." This statement warns that without effort and without goods, one cannot hope to achieve bwami.

    b. "Kakungukia [a variety of chameleon] has covered long distances slowly, slowly." An old man may have no physical strength, but his intelligence has helped him to achieve goals that seemed remote.

7. A piece of liana, shaped into a highly stylized human form, called *muzigi*, has three meanings.

a. "Muzigi, who does not close itself [hold on], will fall down with crown and root." This aphorism refers to a woman who does not listen to the advice of her husband.
  b. "Initiates exterminate one another [only] with the twinkling of the eyes; in the leopard claw is [true] destruction." Initiates should try to acquire goods, not by violence, but by smartness and intelligence.
  c. "I remain behind at the bwami [initiations] of Lwamba [liana], to which I would have gone with a little goat." Here an initiate who was too sick to respond to the call for an initiation registers a complaint.
8. A large *kikoku* shell (*Pila dewulfi*) reminds the candidate of the following principles.
  a. "Kikoku, my maternal uncle, helps me across the rapids of the river." A man cannot succeed in bwami without the help of his maternal uncles.
  b. "The initiate is a giant snail; the solitary monkey does not die a good death." An initiate must go to the ceremonies with his wife; otherwise, if he dies, who will know the cause of his death?
  c. "My Nkola of the newly cut field, Kokola leaves me with slime." This aphorism applies to a bad woman who sleeps even with her husband's sons and destroys the village.
9. A plank of parasol wood (*musagi*) conveys two messages.
  a. "Two parasol trees are in the clearing; the strong one will break his companion." Here is a warning against the lethal effects of quarrels.
  b. "Kyamusagi is light among others; he is heavy in our place." One loses much of one's importance and status when one settles elsewhere than in the home group.
10. About a small gaffle (*igobo*) the initiates sing; "My good and beautiful one, Igobo, has made me reach the intersections of the branches," which means that help may be expected in difficult circumstances from a *musoga*, a good and beautiful person.
11. Three pieces of *kantamba* wood are explained by the aphorism, "Hawk [there is a play of words here] glides low; he glides high," to say that an initiate knows many things, remote and hidden.
12. The initiates sing about a carved arm and hand, with indications of the fingers (called *kuboko* or *weisatu*).
  a. "Weisatu died without finishing lutumbo lwa yananio." A quarrelsome individual will suffer physical damage and will therefore not be able to go further in the initiations.
  b. "The arm of the sick one stretches out to forbid the sorcerer." A sick man beseeches his wife not to bewitch him any more.

The Art of Bwami

13. The initiates sing about a stick: "The walking stick of the cripple or of the leper is what he uses to defend himself." One uses the means he has available; the symbol of bwami is not the spear (violence) but the walking cane (peace).
14. A piece of strangely twisted wood, substituted for what in other communities is a rudimentarily carved wooden figurine with extended belly, is interpreted to mean that "Wayinda has died, and in the belly there was a fetus." This often quoted and complex aphorism speaks of a woman who committed adultery during pregnancy and thus, by an act of ritual pollution, caused her own destruction. The exegesis implies that, when a person who was preparing for an initiation dies, his goods will be used by someone else to achieve the same grade.
15. A phallus-shaped piece of wood is explained as "Katimbitimbi, the little penis that has not seen [undergone] circumcision." It means that women do not want uncircumcised men.
16. The initiates sing about a canoe-shaped piece of wood: "The source of Nalongo [a river; here, a woman], the little stream that destroys the big jars." The obvious reference is to a woman's vulva. In more general terms, the aphorism bears on the inheritance of women; as the initiates say: "One dies, and someone else sleeps with one's widows."
17. A rudimentarily carved animal figurine, explicitly said to represent a dog, is interpreted as: "He who does not stop quarreling will fight with whatever has the mouth widely distended." Usually this aphorism is sung in conjunction with a realistically carved crocodile figure to warn against hot temper.

The *mulama* rite is only one example of the kinds of objects, and of aphorisms and interpretations connected with them, which may be used in one specific ritual community. In *mulama* rites I have observed elsewhere, the configuration of objects may differ from the one I have just analyzed. Some communities use wooden anthropomorphic carvings, horned wooden masks, chimpanzee skulls, elephant molars, and turtle carapaces, and may have no snail shells or animal figurines at all. Others may exclude wooden carvings altogether from the *mulama* rite. Each autonomous ritual community has its own tradition, but the variations are always limited to certain sets of alternatives. When animal skulls are used, they are likely to be those of either the forest crocodile or the chimpanzee. Beaks come from hornbills or ibis. Carvings are in wood, not in ivory or bone. Furthermore the specific aphorisms associated in different ritual communities with any one object used in the *mulama* rite are not necessarily identical in formulation.

Let us take, for example, the hornbill beak, whose meaning is discussed above (item 3, *a–j*). The Banasalu clan sings only three aphorisms, instead of ten, to interpret the beak in the *mulama* rite. First, "What lacks water has protruded [its] beak into the hole [filled with water]" means that one who cannot enter the initiations in his own agnatic group tries to do so among his maternal uncles. Second, "The addition [to the beak] has made the hornbill [look] ugly" criticizes a candidate who wants to have a different tutor or a candidate who, while preparing for his initiation, seduces a woman. Third, "Hornbill, the weakling, has imitated the call of animals" warns the candidate not to call upon initiates to proceed with the ceremonies before he has completed the necessary preparations. Only the third of these aphorisms comes at all close to those formulated by the Banamunwa and the Bagilanzelu, described above; it is almost identical with 3*d*. In other communities the aphorisms would be expressed in still different ways. In most instances, however, the hornbill beak with its giant casque, which looks like a grotesque anomaly, is preferably treated as a symbol of an abnormal social situation (e.g., failure to have the goods necessary for an initiation; failure to accede to the initiation in one's own group; the unexplainable cause and moment of death).

In other words, there seems to be an underlying symbolic meaning for each object. The situation is complicated, however, because an object is not only what it appears to be; it can stand for something else. It can also represent qualities that go beyond its actual form. Sometimes the hornbill beak is no longer conceived of as a specific beak, but as a generalization, an abstraction, of the beak. Its occurrence can therefore suggest other birds and interpretations of them. Further, the hornbill (*mutu*) may become a human personage, called Mutu after the bird or designated by one of the bird's nicknames, drum names, or epithets, such as Nyalugugumo (Mrs. Wingbeat), Nyabeidilwa (Mrs. Overcome-by-Night), Sanzugunzugu (Mr. Hardhearted). Finally, the use of the hornbill beak, as indeed of almost all other categories of objects, is not restricted to a single rite or even to the initiations into a particular grade or a particular level in a grade. Since the beak is found in the lowest as well as in the highest initiations, it occurs in different settings, in different configurations of sequences and of items, and in rites of varied scope and purpose. All these factors exert an influence on the interpretations of the hornbill beak and, for that matter, of any other object.

The guiding and unifying forces behind any rite or any initiation are the moral philosophy of bwami, its organizational and structural principles, and its goals. The interpretation, diversity, and reversibility of objects converge in these principles and goals which, as I point out in Part 3, are universal in Lega culture. Regardless of the choice of objects and related aphorisms, the *mulama* rite is concerned with the inculcation of a sample of the basic ideals of bwami: harmony in social relationships; goodness and beauty; circumspection; filial piety; group spirit; obedience and self-

The Art of Bwami

discipline; tenacity of purpose. Concern is expressed about women, sons, fathers, maternal uncles, husband-wife relationships, elders, tutors, headmen, the master of the land; sorcery, adultery, disrespect, megalomania, boasting, and callousness are also discussed. All these subjects are treated in a highly symbolic way in metaphor, image, allusion and suggestion; almost never is the reference direct.

Even for the Lega, the striking and unexpected interpretations, along with the element of surprise, the festive mood, and the poetic style, transform every dance and song, every display of objects, every rite and initiation, into a fascinating and entertaining experience. Although the basic themes are well known in advance, the atmosphere that is created on each occasion keeps the ceremonies from being tedious or redundant. The total impact of uncommon forms, variegated colors, musical sounds, verbal artistry, and rythmic movements, and the feeling of joy and repose, make each rite seem unique and original.

LEGA CLASSIFICATION OF INITIATION OBJECTS

Students of African art pay little attention to linguistic data. The European's knowledge of African terminologies and conceptual systems of classification of works of art is therefore extremely limited; descriptive accounts sprinkled with African terms, largely unexplained and unrelated, do little to improve the situation. Labels, such as figurine, statue, mask, maskette, nail fetish, and so on, may seem obvious and understandable, but the significant question is: Do equivalent concepts exist in African terminologies? How do African speech communities label and classify the products and activities that we group under the general heading of art? Insight into the various terminological systems will add substantially to the outsider's understanding of exactly what the art objects are, do, and mean for their makers and users.

Among the Lega, all artifacts commonly qualified by Europeans as objets d'art are made exclusively for the bwami association and are used, owned, and interpreted by its members. These objects, and the numerous natural and manufactured items that are associated with them, are essential to the complex ritual of the initiations. These initiations are known to the Lega as *mpala*, a term used by other Kivu populations, such as the Nyanga, to designate a set of ritual practices through which individuals are inducted into particular cults. In Lega thinking, the term evokes the concept *bimpa*, which bears on things that change color. To the Lega, initiation also has the connotation of modification and transformation.

All objects, natural as well as manufactured, which are used in bwami are jointly referred to as *masengo* (sing., *isengo*). The term *isengo* refers to something "heavy" in the double sense of cumbersome, burdensome, serious, dangerous, ominous, and potentially evil on the one hand, and sacred on the other. Dreams, with all their potential implications, are sometimes placed in the category of *isengo*, as is any form of dangerous activity (feud, war) confronting the village. At least one type of figurine depicts "Old Man succumbing under the burden [*isengo*] of the shoulder bag." In one aphorism, *isengo* is used synonymously with initiation (*mpala*): "Kikulu, the drummer, they call him whenever they go to the initiation [*isengo*]." Most frequently, when used in aphorisms, *isengo* occurs in association with *mulama* or *mutulwa*, either of which is an appellation for the collectively held baskets containing natural and manufactured initiation objects. The two most frequently quoted texts are: "I shall not find a place to sleep, for I am carrying *isengo lya mulama*," and "I give what I have [or, I give you my being]; I give *isengo lya mutulwa*." In both aphorisms direct reference is made to possession and transfer of initiation baskets filled with initiation objects.

The context and the Lega interpretation of these aphorisms emphasize that possession of the basket creates a mystic link between holder and object, and that its transfer results in communicating "essence" between initiates. The *isengo* object is equated with a woman whom one ardently desires to possess; the keeper of *isengo* is seen as a father who desires to marry his daughter to the solicitor who owns the necessary amount of marriage goods. The candidate is sometimes reminded of this fact during initiations: "You were wanting to possess the woman; she is here now, ready to receive you, lying down with open legs." The object classified as *isengo* has momentum, sacredness, essence, and status, and is the focus of competitive behavior.

By placing all objects used in bwami in the single category of *isengo*, the Lega stress their unity, uniformity, and homogeneity. Simple leaves are as significant and as essential in communicating the total bwami message as are more elaborate cultural products. Through a simple act of consecration (*kubonga*)—that is, the decision that these objects are to be used within bwami—their status is changed from an ordinary piece of ivory (*mulamba*), piece of wood (*kate*), piece of bone (*ikua*), tusk (*linyo*), or seedpod (*mbuto*) into something that is imbued with intrinsic significance. Possession of such an object without a rightful claim is dangerous; possession is good if the possessor has a privileged right in the object. Even for the rightful possessor, however, the object is "burdensome" in that it demands a correct moral outlook.

The *isengo* object requires special care. The aphorism, "I came from the abandoned village; I am carrying the *isengo* and my old mother," stresses the fact that an *isengo* cannot be thrown away just as an old mother cannot be abandoned. In times of warfare the *isengo* could not be destroyed; it was as inviolable as the drum, the beer pot, the kanyamwa woman, the pregnant woman, the blacksmith, and the individual sitting in the men's house. The *isengo*, carefully kept in the house of a man's initiated first wife, was sometimes guarded by the preferred son initiated to bubake or by the *kazombolo* messenger. It was not to be seen by noninitiates. Should an unqualified woman open the shoulder bag or basket containing initiatory objects, she would be treated as a sorcerer. A complex ritual and the payment of fines by the woman's family would be needed to cleanse her from her guilt and to lift the prohibition against her. On the other hand, initiates do not hesitate to say that the *isengo* has a more pragmatic meaning as a device that permits the acquisition of goods. *Isengo* is compared to the ears of the elephant, "it is the clapping of his ears with which he lures them," and to the trunk, which is "the arm of the elephant to eat banana leaves."

At the next level of classification the Lega differentiate between two complementary sets of *masengo*: the *mitume* and the *binkunankunga*. Under the concept *mitume*, which seems to be related to the broad concept of "hunting for natural things in the environment," are grouped all the items previously described as natural objects, such as beaks, skulls, carapaces, leaves, and the like, and numerous manufactured objects, such as razors, needles, mats, torches, shoulder bags, and so on, which are used in daily life as well as in bwami. The majority of these items are kept in collectively held initiation baskets. Some are burned after the initiation, and their ashes are collected by the initiates. A very few are kept in the shoulder bags of the preceptors. All individual items included in this category are nondistinctive of rank in bwami, but specific groups of them, contained in baskets, are linked with particular initiations. The *mitume* are often referred to as "*kisulukutu*, great owl that passes and passes," to stress that they change hands as the initiation cycles within the ritual community proceed. This category is a fairly simple one because it contains no further subgroupings; classes of objects are simply referred to by their common generic names, such as mat (*katanda*), skull (*lukungu*), shoulder bag (*nsago*), needle (*nsinge*), fruits (*biguma*), roots (*misi*), pods (*mbuto*), or leaves (*lusamba*). When necessary, the generic appellation is made more specific by mentioning the term for a particular species of leaves, skulls, and the like.

The concept *binkungankunga* literally means "things pieced together," "things put together or assembled." This broad category of items includes all objects manufactured specifically for the purposes of bwami. Most of these objects indicate rank and status. They are owned individually or by closely knit groups of agnatically related persons as a function of the particular grade level they have achieved.

This complex category is divided into two subcategories, *bitungwa* and *binumbi*. The *binumbi* (lit., a crowd united for dance and joy) category, including various insignia of rank and all dance paraphernalia, is divided into *bingonzengonze* (things of the ball; things of play) and *bilondo* (things that are being followed, that are coveted). The dance paraphernalia (*bingonzengonze*) include such items as feather tufts worn by men around the hips and arms (*misisimba, milombozi*), feather hats (*idumbi*), feather tufts affixed to the top of a woman's head (*mizombolo*), aprons made of bark cloth (*nsulu*), hides worn as aprons by men (*kikoba*), anklet bells of nutshells (*maseza*).

The insignia of specific rank in bwami (*bilondo*) cover a wide variety of objects: hats for men (*kikumbu, mukuba*), diadems for women (*imenya, binyenye, lukunia*), necklaces with animal teeth for men (*mibanga*), necklaces of shell disks and beads for men and women (*kigela, mwambalo*), hide or bark belts for men (*mukoma*), woven belts, chest straps, and armbands studded with cowries for women (*kibulibuli, bibizi*), hide aprons for men (*kisaba*), and bark aprons for women (*kingungu, kampiki*). (See pls. 1–16 for examples of paraphernalia and insignia.) Flyswatters of split reed (*isandi*) for yananio, wickerwork rattles (*mizegele*) for kindi, and staffs (*mukulu*) for all initiates of higher grade also fall into the *bilondo* category.

The most important of all insignia, indeed the most important of all the objects used in bwami, is a small wickerwork skullcap that is impregnated with red powder and, at the yananio level, adorned with four cowries and a *kizombo* nutshell. The hat, called bwami like the association itself, is received during the kongabulumbu initiation. It is attached to a tuft of hair on the back of the skull and must always be worn except that it can be removed in privacy for shaving purposes. In public the skullcap is always covered by a large hat, which is for this reason sometimes referred to as "what sticks to the body." As the single most important object signifying membership at all levels in bwami, the little skullcap is said to symbolize the power of the association as well as the fame and the intelligence of the initiate.

The *bitungwa* (lit., something that is being tied together; something unifying) encompass sculptures in various materials and the assemblages I have referred to before (e.g., teeth, quills, claws, and seeds glued together, and more complex temporary configurations). The sculptures are stylized human figurines in wood, ivory, and bone, and sometimes in pottery, stone, and *ntutu*. They differ substantially from one another in size, volume, finish, and subject matter. Heads and busts are also in the *bitungwa* group. Despite regional variations in nomenclature, there are three basic and recurring generic terms for this category of carvings: *iginga, kalimbangoma, katimbitimbi*.

By far the largest number of human figurines are identified as *iginga* (pl., *maginga*), the only category of human figurines found throughout Legaland (see pls. 63–78, 81–87). The figurines are also used by the Bembe, the Nyindu, and other transitional groups, under such names as *'a'inga, m'meci, kitumba,* and *nyasompo*. In some areas where ngandu and bombwa initiations remain elaborate and socially significant, and where

The Art of Bwami

yananio and kindi grades are relatively recent, there is a tendency to group the wooden anthropomorphic figurines as *tute* and *keitula*. Since there is no strict morphological categorization, any stylized human figurine may be referred to as *iginga*. For initiates, the term designates "what sustains," "what keeps from falling." It is precisely with this meaning that *iginga* is sometimes used to designate the kanyamwa (the highest-ranking initiated wife of a kindi), without whose participation the initiation of a high-ranking male is thought to be incomplete.

The *maginga*, whether individually or collectively held, are associated with the lutumbo lwa kindi rank and regarded as the "heart" of kindi. They are extensively used in kindi initiations but also make an occasional appearance—always singly or in very small numbers—at the lower levels. There are no specific subgroupings among the *maginga*, but each figurine is associated with at least one aphorism which identifies it and gives it its name. It is possible to recognize several morphological prototypes as separate semantic categories. The most recurrent among them are the following:

1. Multifaced or multiheaded figurines (from two to eight opposing faces in juxtaposition or superposition; two heads in opposition, usually sculptured as part of one body but sometimes as part of two bodies) called Sakimatwematwe, Mr. Many-Heads (pls. 73–74, 86). In some instances these figurines are also referred to as Kimbayu, Dead-Heart.
2. Figurines with one arm, called Kuboko kumozi, One-Arm.
3. Figurines with distended abdomen, called Wayinda, Adulterous-Pregnant-Woman (pls. 67–68).
4. Figurines with one natural cowrie eye glued onto each face of the figurine, sometimes above the carved eye, called Wansonga wa liso limozi, One-Eye.
5. Figurines with one or two raised arms, called Kasungalala, What-Shoots-up-Straight (pl. 66).
6. Figurines with holes in a flat body, called Katanda, Mat, Dispersal-of-Red-Ants, Evil (pl. 63).
7. Figurines with bent back and knees, called Kakulu kamwenne ku masengo keikumbila, Old-One-Who-Has-Seen-the-Initiation-Objects-Is-Bent (pl. 64).
8. Figurines with a fairly heavy circle-dot design, called Nawasakwa nyona ku malanga, the One-with-the-Signs-of-Beauty-Engraved-on-the-Cheeks (pl. 73).
9. Figurines wearing a little cap made of hide, called Kakulu ka Mpito, the Old-One-of-the-Mpito-Hat (pl. 60).

There are, in addition, a large number of semantic prototypes without corresponding prototypical forms: Wankenge, the Good-and-Beautiful-One; Mwelwa, the Glittering-One; Kalonda, the Initiated-One; Kakinga, the Maiden; Nyabeidilwa, the One-Overcome-by-Night; Nyaminia, Mrs. Black; Nyantuli, Mrs. High-Hips; Katindili, the Lazy-Weakling; Nyatwiso, Mrs. Twinkle-Eyes; Mpimbi, Door-Latch; Sawamazembe, Mr. Plaited-Hair; Keitula wa Yimbo, the Strong-One-Son-of-Singer; Nyabilimbio, Mrs. Buttocks; Sakakuliso, Who-Has-Something-in-the-Eye; and many more (some of these, and others of the same type, are illustrated in pls. 66, 70, 72, 75, 76, 78, 81, 84, 87).

The *kalimbangoma* are ivory, bone, and wooden figurines (mostly anthropomorphic, but in a few areas also made in animal form) which are in the possession, respectively, of musagi wa kindi, musagi, and lutumbo lwa yananio (pls. 79, 88). They are smaller, less numerous, not as well finished, and less widespread than the *iginga*. On the basis of form it is almost impossible to draw a dividing line between *kalimbangoma* and *iginga*. Once again, the only sure criterion for differentiation is the actual classification made by the owners of the objects. Some groups classify small assemblages (teeth and quills on resin; pincers on glue; claws on glue; and miniature stools in ivory or bone [pl. 100]) as *kalimbangoma*. The term, which literally means "what guards the drum," is not easy to understand. The aphorism, "Every initiate has his *kalimbangoma*, even though the one of the body has died," is interpreted to mean that everybody has his own wife who takes care of him, and therefore he does not have to bother with other men's wives. The context suggests that *kalimbangoma* can mean as much as protector, guardian, or caretaker (it is to be noted that the little statues were stuck under the belts while the song was being performed). According to one interpretation, *kalimbangoma* signifies a token left by a father to his son; the aphorism then means that everybody continues to have a protector (guardian), even when the real one of the flesh (father in this instance) is dead. In another aphorism the figurines, having been placed on their backs, evoke the *Bisengalingali binamulua byana bya Makamba,* the Ones-Who-Lie-on-the-Back (old men lying in their deck chairs to guard the village), the Ones-of-the-Elephant-Herd (epithet for initiates which stresses their power), the Children-of-Bark-Cloth-Aprons." In this interpretation the *kalimbangoma* are tokens of morality, of greatness and fame, and of continuity.

Depending on the area, there are *kalimbangoma* in human or in animal form, and some are assemblages of natural objects, but the Lega make no semantic distinctions within the category as a whole. A few aphorisms are sung about the *kalimbangoma* as a group. Few of the carvings have individualized names; the only one I have recorded is Nyantuli, "Mrs. High-Hips strives for preferred status without having the buttocks flattened [by work]." The assemblages are more frequently named; for example, crab pincers on glue represent Nyakinkende, Mrs. Pincher (i.e., Troublesome Woman).

The third group of more or less anthropomorphic figurines consists of

The Art of Bwami

the *katimbitimbi* (lit., phallus). It is an undifferentiated category of rare carvings in ivory and bone—very rarely in *munsemunsemu* wood—which sometimes suggest the penis shape; frequently, however, they are simple pieces of bone or ivory, more or less ellipsoid and sometimes helical (pl. 99). In a few instances miniature figurines are placed in this category (pl. 80). *Katimbitimbi* carvings are owned by women of the bunyamwa grade; they are worn on a ring hanging from the belt to indicate virile status and inviolability. The same objects, as a sign of inalienability, may be tied around the neck of a goat or to the leg of a chair. On rare occasions a larger, wooden, rudimentarily carved *katimbitimbi* is part of the initiation basket of kindi. An object in this category is referred to as "the phallus, the little penis that has not witnessed circumcision."

Animal figurines in wood and ivory are found in the grades of yananio and kindi, in a wide variety of carvings and assemblages ranging from realistic, self-evident animal representations to highly stylized abstractions. First, stuffed hides (the stuffing is moss or a piece of banana stipe) are presented as animal characters; examples are the golden mole, the viper, the small *kabanga* anteater, the genet. Second, wooden neck-beak sculptures of birds, rudimentary carvings that are sometimes not very different from a small gaffle (pl. 27), are classified as *kakulikuli* (a kind of ibis). In some areas there is a rare ivory carving of a bird (always from the small tusk [*kikalasa*] of a female elephant).

Larger, rudimentarily carved, generalized wooden animal figurines fall into four categories, each category characterized by a detail added to the figurine: with a few pangolin scales added to the back, it represents *kilinkumbi*, drum name for pangolin; with a wooden dog bell attached to the neck, it stands for *kafyondo*, the well-trained hunting dog; with a few waffle-shaped incisions on the back, it stands for *mukondekonde*, the forest crocodile; with two heads, it represents *mumbilumbilu*, drum name for a variety of otter. These added details, even though lending realism to the identifications, are of secondary significance; Lega symbolism shifts easily from one interpretation of an animal figurine to another.

More realistic miniature carvings, in wood or ivory, represent specific animals, such as pangolins (pl. 91), centipedes, frogs, snakes (pl. 94), powerful bull elephants *(kabukutu)*, crocodiles (pl. 90), and chameleons *(mugugu)*. Snake figurines, usually called *ngimbi*, sometimes have two or more short legs; some crocodile figurines, consisting of a crocodile head with distended jaws and a small part of the body, are referred to as *kyasula kanwa*, "what has a widely distended mouth."

All these types of animal figurines occur in small quantities; frequently they are kept by preceptors, but they are also found in collectively held initiation baskets. As a sharply differentiated group they present a contrast to the large, widespread category of fairly uniform *mugugundu* animal figurines (pls. 25, 88–89, 92) which are the insignia of yananio (if made of wood) or of kindi (if made of ivory or bone). These stylized quadrupeds do not suggest, either to outsiders or to the Lega, precisely defined animals. The term *mugugundu,* when opposed to *lwanzaza,* signifies a dog of high intelligence and skill, but this meaning is misleading. The carvings are not meant to represent specific dogs, but rather the animal par excellence; it may be a hunting dog, a pangolin, an aardvark, a turtle, or some other animal. Some *mugugundu* animals with little horns tend to be identified as the *lungaga* antelope (pl. 89). An example will illustrate the casual and nonchalant attitude taken by the Lega vis-à-vis their artworks. In the *kilinkumbi* rite of the Banagabo-Beigala-Banangoma group, a ceremony that usually requires a large animal carving, the sculpture was replaced by four sticks of parasol wood laid on the ground, roughly in the form of an ✕. Throughout Legaland, animal skulls (especially of the chimpanzee, but also of the forest crocodile, the young boar, and the *kagelia* monkey) and birds' bills (particularly of the *mutu* hornbill and the *kakulikuli* ibis) are widely used as complements to or substitutes for animal carvings.

Masks, after anthropomorphic and zoomorphic figurines, constitute the third significant morphological and semantic category of art objects in Lega culture. The Lega differentiate five categories of masks, based on material, size, and form. The largest category includes wooden maskettes with beards which are called *lukwakongo* or, less frequently, *tulimu* (pls. 34–36, 60–62). The former term literally means "death gathers in"; the latter connotes spirits and ancestors. In songs these masks are sometimes referred to as *malumba,* graves. Associated with the yananio grade, the masks are held individually by the incumbents at the appropriate level. The categories of *kayamba,* large, horned, whitened wooden masks (pl. 37), and of *idimu,* large wooden masks or ivory masks without horns (frontispiece; pl. 38), are extremely rare. *Kayamba* masks are kept in collectively held baskets; *idimu* masks are held in individual trusteeships by kindi. *Muminia* masks (large masks in pls. 39, 42) are large, very rare wooden masks that are used in a variety of initiations from kongabulumbu to kindi. They are linked with a specific lineage group whose tradition of preceptorship is highly developed. Finally, *lukungu* masks, made of ivory or bone, are used in kindi initiations (pls. 38, 39, excluding the large wooden masks, and pls. 56–58). *Lukungu* literally means skull.

Spoons in ivory or bone *(kalukili),* sometimes suggestive of human shape (pls. 95–97), form another fairly common category of artworks. The Lega produce a number of other carvings in wood, ivory, and bone. The wooden objects include chairs *(kisumbi;* pl. 101), carved arms *(mugombo),* shields and wooden spears *(ikomelo;* pl. 13), phalli *(kizingio),* doors *(keibi),* walking canes *(mukulu, mulonge),* and the *matakale* stick to the top of which a figurine may be attached. Rudimentary knives, ax heads, hornbill knives, forked sticks, and dog bells, as well as miniature slit-drums, dugouts, and mancala games, are also carved in wood. Among ivory and bone

The Art of Bwami

objects are knives (*kabemba;* pl. 102), hornbill knives (*mugusu;* pl. 103), ax blades (*isaga;* pl. 105), scepters (*nseti, kituta;* pl. 104), pegs and pins (*kinsamba*), bark beaters (*nkingi;* sometimes identified as *yango*), hammers (*nondo;* pl. 107), dice (*kibukilo*), pieces of elephant bone, small female elephant tusks (*kikalasa*), small pieces of ivory to be worn as bracelets (*bikingi*), miniature chairs (*kisumbi;* pl. 100), and carved imitation leopard teeth.

Finally, the Lega create a vast number of assemblages with modified and unmodified natural objects; most of them are permanent structures, such as *mpoma* snake fangs on glue. The structures the Lega call *kitunda* or *kizumba* are put together in the initiation hut for temporary use during rites of the highest grades (pl. 47). They are often made of one or more pieces of banana stipe which are clothed with paraphernalia and insignia and sometimes adorned with a mask.

None of the Lega categories of initiation objects is subdivided beyond these taxonomic levels. In fact, the Lega system of classification reveals to only a limited extent the Lega cognitive system of artworks and other objects. For further insight one must look to the aphorisms that are sung about the objects, to the actual ways in which the objects are used, and to the interrelationships of the objects in a ritual context. Yet the classification system does reveal the following significant points:

1. There is no fundamental distinction among any of the objects used in bwami. Each object traditionally made for and used in initiations acquires special meaning and weight as a result of this simple form of consecration.
2. Art objects, manufactured products, and natural objects (with or without modification) complement rather than detract from one another.
3. The Lega implicitly recognize a hierarchy of objects because of the semantic refinement and functional diversity of the categories devised for carvings, and because of the complex differentiation of art objects as opposed to paraphernalia, insignia, and natural objects. Art objects appear in large numbers only in the two highest grades and, within those grades, in certain climactic rites. The anthropomorphic figurines form a semantic and morphological category much more complex than the zoomorphic figurines and the masks. Together they rank higher than spoons, axes, knives, and the like. There is also a hierarchy of the raw materials of which objects are carved, but it is only partly discernible from the classification. Ivory and bone are associated with the highest grade; wood has a broader distribution among bwami levels.
4. The terminology applied to the objects clearly demonstrates the emphasis the Lega place on their social functions and social dimensions.

Usage, Functions, and Ownership and Transfer of Art Objects

The essential properties of Lega works of art relate to use, function, meaning, and ownership and transfer patterns[3] of objets d'art in particular and of initiation objects in general. Where are the objects kept, and by whom? How, when, where, and in what context are they used? What social functions are attached to them? What meanings at various levels do they convey? By whom are they owned and how are they transferred? This section is limited to the general aspects of these questions; specifics are dealt with in the next section.

Usage. When not in use, initiation objects are kept in shoulder bags or in baskets, depending on whether they are individually or collectively owned. Ivories may be wrapped in bark cloth before being placed in a shoulder bag. All ivory carvings are kept in shoulder bags, except for an occasional ivory bark beater, pieces of elephant bone, and small ivory tusks that accompany wooden sculptures and natural and manufactured items in the baskets. The bags and baskets are normally kept in the house of the initiate's first wife, who is a high-ranking member of the association.[4] Noninitiates are allowed no contact with these containers, and low-ranking initiates must avoid seeing them. If the house where the objects are preserved should burn, the guilt must be expiated by induction of a kinsman into bwami.

Initiation objects are carried by their owners and keepers in the bags and baskets to the village of the candidate. Bwami prescriptions demand that some objects not be taken directly to the place of initiation. The owner or keeper of important initiation objects is Isamalomingi: "Mr. Many-Halting-Places, Yango, is dancing on his way." He comes to the initiations with caution, and only after he has repeatedly been informed about the good intentions of the gathering and well rewarded in advance. Individually owned objects are simply carried into the village by their owner (pl. 8). Collectively held baskets are brought into the village in a ceremonial procession (*lukenye;* pls. 6, 13–14) which requires the donation of presents, both to the participants and to the basket. Depending on the type of basket, the ceremonial entrance may be made in complete silence; if there is sound, it may be only the clattering of wickerwork rattles, the rustling of reed flyswatters, or the beating of suspended drums in the *kamimankia*

---

[3] Linton (1936, pp. 397 ff., 404, 442) recognizes four mutually interrelated, but not completely interdependent, qualities or properties in culture elements: form, usage, function, and meaning.

[4] In recent decades, to protect their art objects against raids by the police, the military, catechists, and Europeans, the Lega have hidden them in safer places, such as holes in trees. This practice led to irreparable damage of many pieces by rodents, termites, and humidity.

The Art of Bwami

rhythm (pl. 5); sometimes Kingili, the great master of the circumcision, sings (symbolized by a kazoo).

The objects are taken into the initiation hut before the rite in which they are to be used; this action is described as *kisomba,* a special term signifying the transfer of something from outside to inside. Then the initiates of yananio or the *kazombolo* messengers of the kindi, and the preceptors, proceed to the *kubongia masengo* rite (lit., to bring the initiation objects into harmony). The objects are displayed on a mat; parts of wooden objects from the baskets are covered with white paint, and ivory objects are rubbed with a kind of castor oil *(mwambo)* and perfumed with *bulago.* At the same time such songs as "The legs of the orphan do not shine if he does not go in the water," and "Kabongi [Who-Likes-to-Oil] of the Lowlands, Kabongelo [Little-Oiling-Calabash] does not sleep without oiling," are usually sung. The objects are then put back into their containers, and the rite may continue with interpretations performed around the mat on which the objects were displayed.

There are standard methods of presenting the objects to the candidate and interpreting them for him. In one method the initiates dance around their shoulder bags (pl. 46) and then display the objects in front of themselves (pls. 25–26). The preceptors usually pick up the objects in small groups and dance with them while singing interpretative aphorisms (pls. 28–33), but in the highest rites, *kinsamba* and *bele muno,* of lutumbo lwa kindi there is nothing but display and contemplation. In a second type of presentation the objects are brought out singly or in groups from the initiation hut, danced with, and sung about (pls. 44, 54). The third and most complex method requires the items to be displayed on the ground in the initiation hut in either a simple (pl. 49) or an intricately arranged configuration. When the candidate enters the initiation house the configuration called *ziko* (lit., hearth) is covered with hides. He is led around the structure and then seated, but sometimes he is first invited to jump across the *ziko.* The hearth is uncovered and the objects in the configuration and the configuration itself are explained in song, dance, and dramatic action. Another way of viewing and presenting the objects is *kizumba* or *kitunda,* which, as already noted, is an assemblage that may be temporary or permanent; an example is a resin torch covered with shells, scales, claws, and so on. The new insignia of rank are sometimes presented in a *kikuni* structure, banana stipe adorned with hats, belts, necklaces, and the like (pl. 47).

Masks play a part in all forms of presentation. They may be worn on the face, the temples, or the top or the back of the head; they may be fastened to other parts of the body, such as the knees or the arms; they are sometimes dragged over the ground, swirled around by their beards, or attached to a fence (pls. 34–45). In some rites masked dancers emerge from the initiation house; in others they remove the masks from their shoulder bags or baskets during the rite and do with them whatever the ritual prescribes.

Rites differ widely as to the number and variety of objects used and the number of individuals using them. Certain rites may require only one specimen of a certain object. For example, in the *katanda* rite the initiates use only one mat, and in the *nsansaga* rite, only one collaret made of banana bark. Other rites require extensive use by all participants of objects of similar form and of a functional type. For example, in the *lukwakongo* rite all participating yananio must produce and dance with their wooden masks (pls. 34–36); in the *mugugundu* rite they must produce their wooden zoomorphic figurines (pl. 25). Other rites prescribe several objects of similar or different type, but complementary in function, to be used by the preceptor and his aides only. For example, different types of masks are used in the *nkunda* and *ibugebuge* rites (pls. 42–45). Still other rites, particularly the *ziko* configurations or the display of initiation baskets, demand a large number of different objects (pls. 23 and 27 give a limited idea of the range of objects). In the majority of rites natural and manufactured goods appear jointly with artworks; insignia and paraphernalia appear jointly with initiation objects (in the strict sense).

Except for rare rites (such as *kasisi* in yananio, and *kinsamba* or *bele muno* in kindi), the procedure is the same: the objects, singly or in groups, are manipulated, danced with, moved about by singing preceptors who are eventually followed by other participating initiates, while the members of the orchestra beat the drums, shake the rattles, and sing. There are always some initiated onlookers who are too old, too sick, or too tired to take part (pls. 15–18, 28–33, 36–37, 46, 53–54). One aphorism after another is sung to identify and interpret the objects. The dramatic action is enhanced by gestures, mime, and the interactions of performers, orchestra, and onlookers. Sometimes the objects are handed from initiate to initiate or from group to group of initiates. Or an old initiate seated near the initiation hut may present the objects in turn to the rows of dancers.

The candidate, poorly dressed and without ornaments, and frequently supported by one of his tutors (pl. 21), watches silently, without visible emotion. Sometimes he circles around with the preceptor or is invited to jump over a *ziko*. Sometimes he is more roughly treated: the initiates may roll him over on the ground or the preceptor may rub his anus against the candidate's nose.

All Lega initiation objects must be visualized either as part of the dance movements, accompanied by music, song, literary texts, and gestures, or as part of the specific arrangements and relationships within a configuration, or both. The initiatory procedure is enlivened by the continual distribution of gifts, by praise shouting or praise drumming, by honorific gestures (such as the symbolic drying of sweat or the pulling of limbs). At any given moment an incredible succession of happenings un-

The Art of Bwami

rolls before the eyes of the participants. Objects are picked up, deposited, passed from hand to hand, rolled over, or placed against something (a fence, a pole, another object). When the preceptor dances while holding a representation of the *lungaga* antelope, the object moves in his hands as if a real antelope were capering. When he dances with the representation of a pregnant adulteress, his face reflects the contractions of a woman suffering in labor (pl. 31). When singing about the destructive effects of quarreling and fighting, groups of initiates run wildly about making threatening gestures in mock fighting.

Functions. All art objects, like all objects used in bwami, fulfill several of a series of functions.[5] First, they are insignia of rank in bwami, just as specific hats, aprons, and belts are indicative of certain levels and grades. Among the Babongolo, the distinctive insignia of a lutumbo lwa yananio are a hat with dendrohyrax teeth, a necklace of leopard teeth, a reed flyswatter, a large *kikoku* snail shell, a *lubumba* mussel shell, an apron made of wildcat hide, genet hides, a beak of the *ngate* bird fastened to a stick adorned with feathers, a wooden *lukwakongo* mask, and a wooden *kalimbangoma* animal figurine. The vital insignia of a lutumbo lwa kindi include a *mukuba* hat of wickerwork studded with cowries (or buttons, beads, or nutshells) and surmounted with an elephant tail, a necklace of leopard teeth, an apron made of wildcat hide, a wickerwork rattle, a belt of the central part of the bongo antelope hide, a *lukungu* mask in ivory or bone, and several anthropomorphic figurines in ivory, bone, or polished wood (pls. 1–5, 7, and 9–10 show kindi with some of their insignia).

These insignia are all of equal importance, although some are worn openly and others are hidden. Distinctive hats are worn at all levels of bwami, but artworks are insignia for the highest male grades only (yananio and kindi usually, but ngandu in some areas). Women of the kanyamwa grade have the small *katimbitimbi* sculptures (pl. 99), visibly hanging from their belts, and sometimes tiny *kalimbangoma* figurines in ivory or bone. Since most of the artworks are insignia of rank, specific types are mandatorily owned by all incumbents of a certain grade, such as the wooden *lukwakongo* masks by lutumbo lwa yananio and the *lukungu* masks in ivory or bone by lutumbo lwa kindi. At the local level, however, exceptions are made for certain individuals. For example, the yananio who holds the *kasisi* basket has none of the art objects. Some artworks, such as spoons, realistic representations of animals, billhooks, and so on, are insignia of special status holders in the association. Among them, the most important are the preceptors, the holders of circumcision rights, and the kindi with the most seniority.

[5] Some aspects of function, usage, and meaning are inadequately described by Delhaise (1909a, pp. 209–210, 231–239). Merlot (n.d.) gives an interesting enumeration of functions. See also De Kun (1966, *passim*) and Hallet (1963).

Art objects are also tokens that establish evidence and credibility. In rites that demand a huge display of artworks, each initiate present must produce his badges at the order of *Wake wake bukota wa kabilundu*: "Everyone his one, everyone his one, the generosity [leadership] of Kabilundu [name of a tree on which many animal species feed, symbol of generosity, and king of trees]."

Art objects are prestige items. Their ownership is associated with high social rank. At the highest level of initiations there is no limitation on the number of art objects, specifically ivory figurines, which a high-ranking kindi can possess or hold in trust. Kindi may have as many as from ten or twenty ivory or bone figurines, some of them outright possession and some kept in trust for dead colleagues until a successor is initiated or for colleagues who perform special functions. Only kindi with seniority can hope to fulfill special social functions that may bring them additional figurines. Possession of many figurines and display of them at *kinsamba* and *bele muno* rites in lutumbo lwa kindi is clear proof of an individual's outstanding social achievements. Prestige is measured not only by the number of figurines. Certain large rare ivory figurines (pls. 86–87) and masks (frontispiece), and some special wooden figurines (pl. 65), may be kept only by kindi of superior intelligence and moral strength. Again, a person's fame is enhanced by possession of the large figurines and masks that are thought to be the mothers (*nina*) and the masters (*nenekisi*) of the lesser objects.

Sculptures are iconic devices that play an essential role in bwami initiations, singly or in conjunction with hundreds of other natural and manufactured items (see pl. 110 for a small sample). They are an intrinsic part of initiations, as inseparable as dances, songs, music, dramatic performances, and exchanges. Sculptures are completely integrated with all these other features in sustaining and upholding, in positive or negative expression, the principles of the moral code, the ideas about bwami and its social role, and the foundations of the network of social relations.[6] On the one hand, concrete objects help to clarify the intricate, abstract notions of the code. On the other hand, the objects themselves demand interpretation, since their forms do not reveal what they are and what they mean. From one point of view sculptures and other initiation objects are reminders (*kalolesia*) of things to be done or not to be done and mnemonic devices (*kakengelezio*) that facilitate the enormous amount of memorizing, of aphorisms and of actions, required by the initiations.

As initiation devices, masks have the additional function of making possible the transformation of a person into another human character,

---

[6] In some of their properties, Lega carvings do not differ from sculptures that are used in the girls' initiation system of East, Central, and South African populations (see, for example, A. I. Richards, 1945; Cory, 1956; Stayt, 1931; Delachaux, 1936; Shaw, 1948; Roumeguere and Roumeguere-Eberhardt, 1960; Biebuyck, 1968).

The Art of Bwami

into an animal character, or into an undefined spiritual being. Masks are not always worn on the body, but may be used and manipulated like any other initiation object (placed in a configuration, fastened to a fence, held in the hands, swirled around, dragged over the ground, and so on). When worn on the face, however, a mask helps to produce a change in the personality of an actor. The individual masked dancer is Samunyama, Mr. Pride; Sakalangalanga, Mr. Tough; Mutimbu, the Exterminator; Ibugebuge, Danger; Munyugu, Who-Looks-for-Trouble; Zambazamba, Who-Is-Always-Sick; Sawakala mbala, the Cutter-of-the-New-Field. Masked dancers as a group are Bakulu ba Kwalanga, the Great-Old-Ones-of-Where-It-Climbs, or Tumbukutu, insects that have the same head. Sometimes a masked dancer incarnates a legendary personage, such as Kampumba, Nsamba, or Mumpanda, or an animal or insect (turtle or queen bee). On occasion the reference is to unspecified spiritual beings (*balimu, tulimu, basumbu*), as in the aphorism, "They are not ours, those beings that went [i.e., the dead] and that come out of the tangle of trees." In this context the mask is sometimes referred to as *kansusania ka muntu*, semblance or reflection of a man (i.e., a dead man, more particularly a dead grandfather or senior brother); *lukugu lwa tata*, the skull of my father; or *nondo za balimu*, the hammer of the dead.

Since the sculptures pass from hand to hand and are inherited, they are symbols of continuity in families, lineages, and ritual communities, symbols that link the dead to the living members of the group and serve as evidence of the timeless and uninterrupted chain of initiations and interdependencies among individuals and groups. Initiates can generally trace the ownership of the majority of objects they have back through five to seven names. Most of the previous owners are dead, but it is possible that one or more may be alive because of the custom of passing along insignia as initiates move up in rank or acquire special functions. There is, of course, an element of fiction in this way of counting, for the original object that signified the continuities over several generations may have been replaced by a new one. Such a replacement, however, does not rupture the chain of continuities created by successive initiations to a specific grade within a family or a lineage. In this context masks are often referred to as the "hammer of the dead and of the people" or the "hammer that the ones-who-have-gone forged for us." Figurines are sometimes called *kasina*, the pleasant memory of something or somebody) good, as if they were some kind of daimonion upholding the virtues of the great people of the past.

Continuities and interdependencies among groups—lineages and clans—are also symbolized by collectively held masks and figurines and initiation baskets. Lineages and clans trace back with precision and pride the origin of a collective possession by recalling the names of those who introduced the object into the group and the place of origin. Moreover, two clans may own individual figurines which are thought to be complementary. For example, the Beiamunsange clan possesses a large male ivory figurine said to constitute a ritual entity with an analogous female ivory figurine owned by the Banalyuba.

Social cohesion, social solidarity, and ritual autonomy are promoted by some sculptures and other initiation objects. As shown in Part 3, the possession of collectively held initiation baskets is not a random affair; established patterns reflect very closely conflicts and unities in the segmentary lineage and clan structure. Also, the higher the initiatory level, the less numerous the sets of collectively held objects. Every Lega clan has a large number of *musutwa* bags for the lower kongabulumbu initiations and an extremely limited number of baskets for higher initiations, sometimes only one for lutumbo lwa kindi. The bags are connected with small lineage groups; the baskets, with larger, more encompassing lineages or clans. Since the small groups are segments of the larger groups, there are necessarily more of them, thus reflecting the well-known principle of complementary opposition in lineages and clans. The component segments of the clan act as a multitude of autonomous, decision-making, ritual units at one level of the initiations, and as a unified totality at other levels.

Sculptures always form a part of initiatory baskets and help to foster these oppositions and unities. But there are other sculptures that are not part of the baskets; because of their uniqueness, they play an integrative role in the highest rites. Such sculptures, large masks and large anthropomorphic figurines almost always made of old, heavily patinated ivory (frontispiece; pls. 86–87), are held on behalf of the total ritual community (a clan, or even several linked clans) by the kindi with the most seniority. A few wooden sculptures (the large mask on the fence in pl. 38 and the figurine in pl. 65) are kept for the ritual community by a famed kindi of outstanding intelligence and integrity.

These objects must be present at the initiations to be valid. Any attempt to hold a higher initiation without such an object and its keeper would be an act of rebellion that would lead to a serious prohibition (*kitampo*). The misdemeanor must be cleared lest the initiations bring on a calamity. High-ranking initiates never go to initiations at first call: "The mwami is a stone anvil; he does not go on one call." Initiates who keep the collectively owned initiation baskets and sculptures are even slower in accepting a summons. The candidate and his tutors, advisers, and kinsmen must show deep piety and strong allegiance to the power of the symbols in order to be successful in their aspirations. Finally, the group that possesses these supreme symbols of the initiations has wide-ranging autonomy in the entire decision-making process of organizing the rites.

For the initiates, sculptures and other insignia, paraphernalia, and initiation objects are considered as wealth. I have never heard any special emphasis placed on this aspect, except when candidates speak about their

The Art of Bwami

initiation objects as "the clapping of elephant ears," by which insects are caught. The obvious reference is to the fact that the candidate pays large amounts of goods in order to see the objects, to learn about them, and to receive them in temporary trust or permanently. Since the artists who carve the sculptures receive only a token gift plus the raw material in which they work, sculptures are only indirectly an aspect of wealth. Their owners receive them only at the end of laborious initiations for which they pay heavy initiation fees and give generous gifts to many initiates, in and outside their own group. Sculptures and other insignia obtained at the end of initiations for a certain grade symbolize the great display of wealth that was necessary. This aspect is evoked by the aphorism, "In the village of an initiate, the Binankusu [Parrot-Folk] lay their eggs on the ground," which is sung while the initiates lay their prized possessions on the village ground as if they were golden eggs.

Except for the feeling of community and continuity with dead predecessors fostered in the minds of initiates, the religious function of sculptures is subjugated to their social, political, and economic functions. Cultual manifestations in Legaland are reduced to a minimum, except in areas where the Lega have been thoroughly exposed to the religious systems of neighboring groups.[7] Yet religious connotations are not altogether lacking. As explained in Part 2, after the death of a yananio or a kindi his insignia and dance paraphernalia are placed on his tomb, which is taken care of by a high-ranking initiate who acts as guardian of the tomb.[8] The objects thus displayed to the dead include the deceased's ivory mask, ivory figurines, necklaces, wickerwork rattle, hats, aprons, and belts, and possibly his chairs, walking cane, and shoulder bag. Months after the *musile* rite (described in Part 2) these objects, except for sculptures, necklace, and rattle, are arranged in a *kakenge* display at the end of the village. They will be abandoned unless a properly initiated sororal nephew of the deceased appropriates them, although in some areas the *kazombolo* of the dead may take away at least the walking cane. The sculptures, the necklace, and the rattle are kept by the guardian of the tomb until such time as a successor to the dead kindi is initiated. This exposure to the dead adds a mystic dimension to these objects. What remains after death is the permanent objects that were part of the dead man, will be part of his living successor, and will remain after the successor also has died.

All objects used by the members of bwami have a special significance and power; the term *isengo* seems to corroborate this statement, as I have explained earlier. For example, the *lukumbulwa* leaves that are brought in

---

[7] Delhaise (1909a, p. 225) characteristically notes that there is no "manifestation de religion dans les formes diverses de la vie privée et sociale."

[8] Delhaise (1909a, pp. 199, 201–202) has useful information on burial arrangements. He notes that paraphernalia and ornaments were placed on top of the grave, not inside it.

baskets during the *iduli* rite of musagi wa kindi are afterward burned. The ashes (*mbilu*) are kept by the initiates and given to hunters and fishing women to eat and to rub on the shoulder and arm that carry the nets so as to strengthen them and to increase their chances of success.

The ivory sculptures, and in particular the anthropomorphic figurines, have a special power in that they can increase and strengthen a person's *kalamo* (the fact of being alive; life-force; health). When a person is thought to be very sick and the normal pharmacopoeia seem to fail, he is given water to drink in which some of the surface dust from the figurines has been mixed. To obtain the dust, the figurines are lightly sanded with leaves, usually on the back, so that a difference in degree of patination is often noticeable. Thus the patient literally "drinks" the figurines, which are thought to contain a force of their own, though initiates do not explain how the force gets there or where it comes from.

The underlying logic, is fairly easy to understand. As initiation objects the figurines are already powerful, but because of their display on the tomb and their exposure to the dead they have a still greater power. It would be hazardous to qualify the figurines as soul carriers, as are some sculptures of other populations in the Congo. The Lega themselves have no theory about this subject, yet there is some justification to think that the Lega—those of past generations rather than for the ones I encountered—believed that identity between the living and the dead is achieved through the medium of the sculptures. It is said about masks that "I know my father because of the skull [mask]; I do not know where [when] he has died; [or], I have not seen him by the time he has died." In reference to the figurines it is said, "He who died does not come back; on ivory, mushrooms do not grow," and "What remains of him who died is the ossature [structure] of the arms." These profound aphorisms, which are quoted only in some of the highest rites, such as *mukumbi* in yananio, indicate that artworks are equated with the vital and permanent bony parts of the human (skull, limb) and animal (ivory tusk) body, that they are a part of the dead, and therefore that they are either a semblance of the dead or an idea about them.

This interpretation is reinforced by the very name of the climactic rite, *bele muno*, in lutumbo lwa kindi, which requires an extensive display of ivories. The term *bele muno* is a complaint uttered when persons in distress weep for the loss of a relative or a senior: "Oh! were they but here!" (*bele muno!*). The setting of the rite is very special. The naked candidate is brought into the initiation hut lying back down on the back of the naked preceptor. There is no music or song, only the rustling of leaves over the ground of the initiation hut, which is identified on this occasion as *lugumbo lwa kindi*, lair of the kindi. The position of the candidate's body on the back of the preceptor reminds one of a corpse: "Kanya stares upward [in the sky]; all those who stare upward are dead." After being twice carried

The Art of Bwami

around a covered configuration of objects, the candidate is deposited on the ground and invited to jump over the configuration twice, shouting his drum name. When the configuration is revealed it is seen to consist of a number of ivory and bone figurines arranged in a circle and resting on the ground against the hats of the initiates. In the middle of the circle stands a larger anthropomorphic figurine in ivory, which is the mother (*nina*) of them all. The revelation is followed by silent contemplation and communication with the figurines. There is little further action, but explanations of the figurines follow in the subsequent *kinsamba* rite. The symbolism of the rite seems to communicate to the candidate that his dead body will wake up to be perpetuated in the ivory images, and to console him with the assurance that the departed are not really dead but are, in fact, "here among us."

An aphorism frequently sung at the end of important kindi rites and during the burial of kindi also seems to underscore this idea: "Everyone who has come will go home. The Anointed-Ones go to *itima*." *Itima* refers to the initiation hut with the full display of all the most secret objects. The exegesis given for the aphorism clearly alludes to death: "All people die and nobody returns from the tomb, but the kindi go to join the gathering of objects in the initiation hut." Kindi is a promise of glory, immunity, perpetuity. The sculptures, particularly the ivory figurines which are all linked with kindi, help to foster this belief.

Another interesting function of artworks, essentially restricted to the small ivory and bone carvings called *katimbitimbi*, is to confer inalienability and inviolability upon the persons who own and wear them, and by extension upon animals and objects to which they may be attached. These small sculptures are owned by kanyamwa women and worn by them around a ring attached to the belt in the area of the hips or buttocks. The full name of the objects is "*katimbitimbi* [lit., what shivers passionately; phallus], the little penis that has not seen the circumcision." The kanyamwa, as the highest-ranking female initiate and the wife of a kindi, is a socially prominent woman who wields great influence in the polygynous and extended family. She participates actively in councils and deliberations and goes with her husband to initiations at all levels to which he is invited. She usually plays a vital role in the stages preparatory to their joint initiation. The kanyamwa, in short, has virile status, and that is what the *katimbitimbi* figurines clearly say to all. The naked kanyamwa has no shame in coming before the men, and the men should manifest no sensual attitudes toward her.

This nonsexual approach is dramatically depicted during one of the bunyamwa rites. The kanyamwa dances in the initiation hut in the middle of the circle of kindi, wearing only a small tuft made of red tail feathers of the parrot and porcupine quills over the genitalia. One by one the kindi approach her, pretending to touch her genitalia, then pulling back in disarray because of the stings of the porcupine quills. The rite symbolizes the inviolability of the kanyamwa, and the *katimbitimbi* figurines are a reminder of it. Furthermore, the kanyamwa is perpetually married to her husband; in the old Lega tradition she cannot be divorced, remarried, or inherited. When she dies the normally scheduled death payments are not required from her husband. The kanyamwa is the only female who is fully incorporated into the husband's group. She is, so to speak, inalienable.

The indissolubility of the kanyamwa's marriage is symbolized in the elaborate *itutu* or kindi rooftop rite (pl. 19), to which the initiates refer as the true and full marriage. The candidate, his wife, the preceptor, and other kanyamwa climb, by means of specially constructed ladders, onto the roof of the initiation hut. The aphorisms, "We climb the slopes of the big mountain, the mountain that is excessively difficult to climb," and "We sleep on the slopes of the mountain, on the mountaintop that rises high in the sky," stress the greatness of the couple in achieving social visibility in the presence of all the other initiates who remain on the ground as "witnesses and guardians." In the ritual actions that take place on the rooftop, phrynium leaves and *matungulu* stems *(Costus lucanusianus),* the normal roof coverings of all Lega houses, and the fire drill set *(buza)* play the central role in the symbolism. The phrynium leaves covered with *matungulu* stems (female and male element), and the fire drill and the softer piece of wood in which it is turned (male and female element), are inseparable because they are functionally necessary for each other, and so are the kindi and the kanyamwa. The concept of inseparability and inalienability is clearly expressed by the *katimbitimbi* figurines. When an initiate desires to protect an object or an animal from being confiscated by a sororal nephew in a permissible joking move, he attaches a *katimbitimbi* to that object or animal, which thus becomes immune to the capricious exercise of arbitrary claims against it.

No matter how serious the functions of sculptures are in bwami initiations, the dramatic contexts in which artworks appear are characterized by entertainment, play, surprise, a reach for effects, and even playful deception. The combinations of objects, movements, and interpretations astonish the Lega candidate as well as outsiders, but he is not allowed to express amazement or disappointment. The candidate goes into the initiations full of fears and apprehensions, the Lega say, and even thinks he may die in the process, but it all turns out to be less complicated and gentler in tone than expected. The experience is exemplified by a rite in which the preceptor dances with a large fiber collaret around his neck, singing: "I thought Saluzugu [a bird whose calls imitate human sounds] to be a human being, and lo! it is a little bird that fools me with its many feathers." There is much good humor and a general atmosphere of joy and relaxation. Some scenes are incredibly funny, as when the preceptors

The Art of Bwami

mimic a man suffering from scrotal elephantiasis. Art objects, including masks, are never used to inspire fear or terror.[9]

Kasisi is one of the few rites in which there is a deliberately created mood of gloom. It is held in the darkness of night, unaccompanied by song or music. When the candidate is led into the initiation hut he is attacked by men dressed like leopards (pl. 20), a goat is strangled or trampled to death, and suddenly, when the torches are lit, the candidate is faced by a wierd-looking array of unusual objects, such as elephant molars, chimpanzee skulls, quartz stones, and rudimentary figurines of human and animal shape in *ntutu* or resin. The objects are given the usual interpretations of characters and symbols of virtues and nonvirtues, but the atmosphere created by the rite is staggering and forbidding.

The aesthetic function of artworks is the most difficult for Europeans to comprehend. I have very little information to give. At the time of my research, after decades of harassment from Arab raiders and colonial administrators, traditional artists were no longer at work in Legaland. Since several well-known artists in areas where I worked had recently died,[10] I was unable to gain the insight they might have given me as to their aesthetic criteria of quality and excellence. The patrons of the arts, high-ranking initiates who own, use, and interpret the objects, make no evaluations of quality; for them to speak about the relative aesthetic appeal of art objects would be an infraction of the bwami code, which claims that all *isengo* are *busoga,* good-and-beautiful, because they are accepted and consecrated in bwami and are meaningful to initiates.

In the years I spent among the Lega, I never heard aesthetic evaluations of art objects. Any attempt to elicit verbal responses to questions on that subject would have infringed upon bwami principles and would have qualified me as *buzonga* (wild, inconsiderate) and as a noninitiate with "a heart of feathers" rather than "a heart of *kalenganio*" (wisdom acquired by absorbing the teachings). The Lega have produced many beautiful and splendid works of art which appeal to the aesthetic consciousness of men all over the world. Yet they have also created numerous sculptures that look poor or mediocre. To my knowledge, Lega initiates do not make discriminatory statements about their artworks. In the highest rites, outstand-

---

[9] Outside the bwami initiations, a larger whitened mask in wood of the *idimu* type was worn during circumcision ceremonies by an initiate of middle rank, who was completely dressed in bark cloth spotted like a leopard's skin, to chase women and children away from the village.

[10] The rapid decline, or the complete disappearance, of artistic activities was a widespread phenomenon in the Congo, except in certain areas, like Pende and Yaka, where artistic creativity had maintained relative vitality. In other spheres of artistic excellence, such as epic narration, activity was also rapidly diminishing. In a large group of southwestern Lega, Mubila was the only surviving bard who had a complete knowledge of the great Mubila epic, which I was able to write down.

ing and mediocre carvings, artworks, and natural and manufactured works are displayed together as complementary items that all converge in the moral philosophy and social functions of bwami.

Most initiates take a casual, unconcerned attitude toward any single initiation object. An artwork that is broken, lost, abandoned, or taken away by an outsider is easily replaced by something else, not a copy, not necessarily another artwork, but something that is functional and is the semantic equivalent of the original article. When the possessor of a particular carving traces its previous owners it is impossible to know whether he is talking about replacements or about the original; what is important to him is the certitude that what he now has is the true equivalent, or substitute, of what existed before. Moreover, initiates are used to the constant transfer of objects, when they move up in grade, when they perform certain special functions, when they act as sponsors.

Whatever the actual significance of a work of art in bwami, its function is easily transferred to something else.[11] In the extremely important *mukumbi* rite of lutumbo lwa yananio, the delicately carved animal figurine that represents *mukumbi* in one community may be replaced by a stuffed skin or by a piece of banana stipe in other communities. There is no way of finding out whether or not the replacements are substitutions for lost objects. It is possible that, as artworks became scarcer in the twentieth century because of breakage, loss, theft, abandonment, sale, and decline of artistic output, initiates became more and more willing to find easy solutions; the contexts of bwami rites clearly indicate that capricious substitution is a standard procedure. In any event, the characters represented and the meanings conveyed by artworks at the higher levels of initiations are not different from those at lower levels; the meanings are simply more abundant and more diversified.

Occasional hints in Lega attitudes permit me to make a few observations about their aesthetics, though it must be remembered that their ethics and aesthetics are completely blended. One of the two climactic kindi rites that feature a vast display, with interpretation, of ivory figurines is called *kinsamba,* a term that refers to a multitude of white mushrooms. As the initiates imitate a plucking movement above the exposed figurines, they sing: "The *kinsamba* are plentiful; every Great-Old-One culls mushrooms." Among the natural objects the Lega use as symbols for beautiful

---

[11] During a 1952 initiation I discreetly admired an exceptionally large and socially meaningful human figurine in ivory displayed as the central object in a kindi rite. While briefly revisiting Legaland in 1956, after witnessing a most enjoyable series of dances, I was, to my great astonishment, given the figurine as a "departing gift" from a group of high-ranking initiates. They told me that they now had a substitute for the piece and that they had always known how much I had admired it. Unfortunately, in 1958 this precious object was stolen from my home in Kinshasa, and no trace of it has since been found.

The Art of Bwami

and pleasing things are bongo antelopes *(nkenge)*, the white *bubulcus* birds *(binyange)* that follow the herds, and the white *kinsamba* mushrooms. It is significant that all these are light-colored and therefore somewhat shiny or glossy, and that the same qualities make ivory very attractive. Also, the very name of one of the two principal rites has a connotation of beauty.

The ivory figurine that leaves the carver's atelier is unfinished because it lacks the shiny reddish and yellowish patinations that come with usage. The act of consecration through usage, and prolonged and repeated treatments with ointments, give art objects their characteristic finish and rich patination. They are rubbed with a form of castor oil *(mombo)*, plain or mixed with red powder, and then polished to a shine with *lukenga* leaves and perfumed with *bulago* scent. This process is called *kubongia*, meaning to bring in harmony, to produce unison. Again the reference is to beauty. The initiates give the figurines the same treatment with oil, red powder, and scent as they give their own bodies. Many of the praise names and epithets that the initiates reserve for themselves in aphorisms insist on this aspect of beautification; they call themselves Banamombo, the Anointed-Ones, or Binyangi, "white *bulbucus* birds that float around in the air," to place in perspective the impeccable care they give their bodies. The glossiness and the paleness of the reddish and yellowish hues that are the basis of patination are definitely the highest canons of beauty.[12] Ivory and well-polished wood (which is functionally equated with ivory) are the highest-ranking materials used by the Lega; objects made of these materials are socially the most important because they are associated with the highest grades and rites.

The search for constrained diversity—that is, creative originality—of forms underlies all Lega works. One extremely frequent and widespread functional prototype is Sakimatwimatwi, Mr. Many-Heads (pls. 73–74, 86). Figurines of this type are carved of wood, bone, and ivory, but double spoons may also be placed in the same category. The objects are either individually owned or held in initiation baskets. The ways in which individual artists have rendered the idea of multiheadedness or multifacedness are truly diverse. Some pieces have two freestanding heads on one body;

---

[12] Delhaise (1909a, p. 295) mentions two anecdotes that help to clarify the Lega focus of aesthetic reaction. In one instance, Delhaise exhibited a lodestone and used it to pick up steel pens, but the Lega man to whom he was showing it admired only the beautiful red color of the lodestone. Another man, to whom he showed the mechanism of an alarm clock, was intrigued only by the polished metal in which he saw his image reflected. In 1952 I had a similar experience with a car. My research institute had generously provided me with a new Mercury station wagon to replace my old Ford truck. I had specifically asked for a better-looking vehicle in order to enhance my prestige among Lega initiates. To the Lega, however, the only intriguing features of the car were its shiny, honey-colored gloss and the smoothness of its wood trim. They admired the trim because to them it was ivory, not wood.

some consist of two freestanding bodies with separate heads; others suggest two bodies merged together with different faces. Other figurines have from two to eight faces, placed in opposing pairs adorning a stylized body or a simple pole. Or the entire sculpture may consist of the superposition of several opposing faces or of superposed faces, some of them in reverse position. In a few instances small faces adorn the shoulders of the figurine.[13] In addition, there are some double-headed animal figurines and some very rare figurines of two superposed animals. These astonishingly varied forms, all elaborated on one basic idea, fulfill identical social functions and reveal a common meaning. Only encouragement of and appreciation for individual creative ingenuity and local tradition can account for such wide-ranging diversity within a single functional category.

The diversity is even more striking in many other functional categories which include forms that cannot be related so easily as those just discussed. The Lega exegesis of symbols is extremely flexible and can readily accommodate a variety of apparently unconnected or unusual elements. Among the other implicit characteristics of the Lega aesthetic code are smoothness of surface, lightness and smallness of the object, and overall simplicity of the forms, which are usually stripped of excessive ornamentation. Within this general framework some pieces have specific, additional, and sometimes unexpected functions and usages.

Spoons made of ivory or bone (pls. 95–97) are placed in the mouth of a person to whom the *kabi* poison ordeal has been administered so he will not bite his tongue. Masked dancers are sometimes symbolically fed with these spoons, and old initiates use them to eat porridge or other soft foods (Delhaise, 1909a, p. 275). The spoon is used in some rites to replace a knife in symbolically scraping off the bark of the *kabi* tree or skinning the elephant represented by the initiation hut. Little ivory or bone knives (pl. 102), hornbill knives (pl. 103), and axes (pl. 105) are symbols of special statuses in bwami, such as possession of the right to distribute sacred animals or recognition as a preceptor. The little knives may also be used in the symbolic skinning of the elephant.

Other pieces also have special functions. Ivory or bone hammers (pl. 107) and scepters (pl. 104), or simple rudimentarily carved pieces of elephant bone (pl. 106), are used as percussion instruments in a few rites. Scepter-like objects in bone (sometimes replaced by porcupine quills) serve as pegs around which a feather rope is fixed to signify the sacred fence that encloses the display of a configuration of objects. Flat, spherical pieces of bone are thrown like dice in rites that dramatize the rendering of an oracle. An ivory figurine, carefully wrapped with a wickerwork rattle and a number of knotted raffia fibers, may be sent as a secret message to

---

[13] De Kun (1966, pp. 88–89 and *passim*) inventories multifaced and multiheaded figurines, as well as other carvings.

The Art of Bwami

another kindi. In a rare kindi rite among the Lega, ivory figurines are tightly held between the thighs, close to the genitalia, by seated kanyamwa women to signify that a woman who loves does not easily give herself away. Some figurines (pls. 72, 76) are hung with a string from the roof of the initiation house to represent a bat that "hangs with the head downward because of the bad word he was told by Sun."

Ownership and Transfer. Patterns of ownership and transfer are understandably complex because art objects fit into a system of social hierarchies and initiatory experiences as insignia of rank and as symbols of social and ritual solidarities. Several aspects of transfer and ownership of collectively held initiation baskets, which include art objects, are discussed in Part 3.

The first general distinction to be described relates to the raw materials of which objects are made. Ivory and bone sculptures are owned by kindi or by initiates of the ngandu, hingwi, or kidasi grades in the few areas where these are the highest grades. Wooden sculptures are owned by yananio and kindi. The rare sculptures in *ntutu*, resin, and clay from termite nests are owned by the keepers of the *kasisi* baskets of lutumbo lwa yananio.[14]

The most important distinction is between objects held individually and those held in trust by specific persons on behalf of a community of individuals (family, lineage, clan, or ritual community encompassing several clans). Among individually owned sculptures are, first, those that must be owned by all incumbents of a certain grade as a specific badge of rank. Because of well-cultivated regional variations in the ways of doing things, certain categories of individual insignia are mandatory in one ritual community but not in another. Throughout Legaland, regardless of other differences, wooden *lukwakongo* masks (pls. 60–62) are individually owned by lutumbo lwa yananio; ivory and well-polished wooden *lukungu* masks (pls. 56–58) and ivory and bone anthropomorphic figurines of the *iginga* type (pls. 73–78, 81–85) are owned by lutumbo lwa kindi; ivory and bone *katimbitimbi* are owned by women of kanyamwa grade. An initiate may not own more than one mask although he may keep in tempo-

---

[14] Sculptures in ivory and bone, although used in small quantities at the lower levels of initiation, are owned by the highest-ranking initiates. A person who holds the *kansilembo* and *lutala* baskets may occasionally own an ivory piece because he is thought to be "a sororal nephew of the kindi." Wooden anthropomorphic figurines are much rarer than ivory ones; wooden *lukwakongo* masks are much more numerous than ivory *lukungu* masks. Sculptures in *ntutu*, or in soapstone, resin, or clay, are extremely rare. Minor pieces like billhook knives, axes, and hammers are rare; ivory knives are found in somewhat larger numbers. The frequency and the quantity of objects are directly correlated with the functional position of the objects and with the principles of ownership.

rary trust the mask of a dead kinsman. A lutumbo lwa kindi and a kanyamwa may, and generally do, possess several figurines.[15]

Yet there are nuances in the canons of ownership. In most communities the yananio who holds the *kasisi* basket may not have a wooden mask; in some communities the yananio or kindi who is temporary keeper of the basket is not permitted to own a mask; in still other communities there is only one wooden mask in an extended family, even though several living individuals have achieved lutumbo lwa yananio. In some groups one *iginga* figurine in ivory (but smaller in size than the majority) may be owned by a musagi wa kindi (pl. 79) or by a kanyamwa (pl. 80). For some individual kindi, well-polished wooden figurines (pls. 66, 71–72) may replace the ivory ones of the *iginga* type.

In addition to these key art objects, initiates of yananio and kindi grade may individually own other sculptures, depending on the local customs of ritual communities. Zoomorphic figurines in wood called *mugugundu* (pls. 88–89) and anthropomorphic figurines in wood called *kalimbangoma* may be held by a musagi wa yananio or, more frequently, by a lutumbo lwa yananio. Sometimes *kalimbangoma* in ivory (pl. 79) are owned by musagi wa kindi. Zoomorphic figurines in ivory and bone, of the *mugugundu* type (pl. 92) or of more realistic types (pls. 90–91, 93–94), are sometimes owned by musagi wa kindi and lutumbo lwa kindi. Anthropomorphic and zoomorphic figurines are always used interchangeably. Also, initiates in all ranks individually own other distinctive insignia, such as a wooden *kisumbi* chair (pl. 101), a reed flyswatter, a polished mussel shell, and various hats for a lutumbo lwa yananio, and a wickerwork rattle, a giant water snail shell *(kikoku)*, a polished mussel shell, various hats, and a wickerwork staff (pl. 55) for a lutumbo lwa kindi.

Other art objects are held individually only by the incumbents of certain special positions and statuses. The only examples of a specific object in bone or ivory being owned by a non-kindi are in this category. The little ivory knife (pl. 102) connected with the rite of *kibabulilo* (skinning and distribution of sacred animals), and the miniature stools in bone (pl. 100) associated with the ownership of the *kansilembo* bag and with the rights of circumcision, may be held by initiates of a rank below kindi. Other sculptures in wood and ivory, such as hornbill knives (pl. 103), scepters (pl. 104), ax blades (pl. 105), hammers (pl. 107), tesserae, and large animal figurines (e.g., *kilinkumbi* representations of a wooden animal covered with pangolin scales), are frequently owned only by preceptors of

---

[15] Some ownership patterns were disturbed when objects became scarce in the 1950's because there was little new output and many existing pieces had been lost. In one area, of the forty-two lutumbo lwa yananio present at an initiation, only twenty-four possessed a *lukwakongo* mask. Some masks had been lost, thrown away, or given to Europeans; some initiates could no longer possess a mask because of special temporary positions in bwami; others had lost their masks in raids.

The Art of Bwami

yananio or kindi grade. Some of these ivory objects, however, may be substituted for ivory figurines in kindi, and some of them (e.g., hornbill knives) are also in the possession of kindi who have served as tutors. Apart from ivory and bone figurines of the *iginga* and *katimbitimbi* types, which may be owned in fairly large quantities (ten to fifteen) by a single kindi or kanyamwa, only one specimen of any of the other carvings is held by a particular individual. Should he have more than one, he is guarding some on behalf of a dead kinsman or of a kinsman who is temporarily charged with a special function.

There are several kinds of collectively held artworks and other objects and different modes of holding them. The largest number, together with natural items, are kept in the baskets described in Part 3. Usually it is the wooden figurines (pls. 23, 27) that are preserved in these baskets (pls. 6, 13, 14), but horned, wooden *kayamba* masks (pl. 37) and wooden *idimu* masks that are slightly larger than but very similar to *lukwakongo* masks (large whitened mask, pl. 38) may also be kept there. Ivory figurines and masks are not held in the baskets, but ivory bark beaters representing Yango and old tusks sometimes engraved with circle-dot designs may be. The baskets for yananio or kindi are held within the ritual community by the most junior incumbent of the respective grade, and they circulate as the cycle of initiations proceeds. In some areas the *kasisi* baskets are the only ones that contain small rudimentary animal and human sculptures in *ntutu*, resin, and clay from termite nests. Unlike other baskets, *kasisi* baskets are transmitted in an almost direct agnatic line in a closely knit lineage. Some large wooden or ivory anthropomorphic figurines (pls. 24 [two figures on left], 65, 86–87) and large wood or ivory masks (frontispiece; pl. 42) are held in trust for a large community either by the most senior kindi or by a kindi famed for his wisdom.

The patterns of acquisition and transfer of objects are of significance. Except for the *kasisi*, collectively held baskets circulate with the cycles of initiation. Collectively held figurines and masks circulate at the death of their keeper, or, if he has seriously weakened, they pass before his death to the kindi who is next in seniority. Carvings individually held by a lutumbo lwa kindi remain on his tomb for some time; one or two of them may be left there indefinitely, and the others kept by the guardian of the tomb (himself a kindi) until such time as the successor-kinsman of the deceased is being initiated. The objects are then transmitted to the latter during various rites, such as *kilinkumbi* and *kinsamba* for kindi. The situation is suggested by the aphorism, "Let me open for you that you may see the things that remained with father." Ideally, the transfer to the successor-kinsman takes place within a field of closely knit agnatic relationships. The higher the initiations, however, the more difficult it is to observe the pattern, since affinal and cognatic relationships also enter into consideration.

One anthropomorphic ivory carving, for example, had a complicated history of transfers. First it went from the alleged original owner to a man of another clan who had married a close agnatic relative of the first owner's wife. Then it passed to the second owner's son; from this third owner it moved to a maternal uncle in another clan. From this fourth owner it passed to a junior agnatic parallel cousin; and from this fifth owner it went to a junior half brother (same father) who owned the piece at the time of my research. This series of transfers, of course, shows only one of a number of possible patterns for an ivory figurine (for others, see pls. 59–61).

The transfer of objects falls completely within patterns set by the kinship system. The individuals concerned may have a very close relationship, but they are not necessarily inhabitants of the same village or group of villages or members of the same lineage or clan. This fact explains why art objects have traveled so far from their places of origin and are so widely scattered. Speculation about local schools and local substyles is therefore a fruitless exercise, especially when the artists and their schools no longer exist. The dispersal of art objects has also contributed to the neglect and indifference of owners in tracing the names of the artists.

Because the number of yananio or kindi positions that can be occupied at any given time within an autonomous ritual community is not fixed, a candidate for initiation must not wait until another dies to get the distinctive art objects. A minimum number may be commissioned by the *mukomi* tutor, who is in charge of the first acquisition of new insignia of rank. For grades below lutumbo lwa kindi, the transfer of objects takes place when their owner dies, moves up in grade, or occupies a special status. If, for example, a lutumbo lwa yananio desires to ascend to the first step in kindi, he may not keep the *lukwakongo* mask and other art objects and insignia that identify him as a yananio. They must be transmitted to a kinsman who is being initiated into yananio as a substitute for the one who is moving up; if such a person is not immediately available, the objects are temporarily transferred to another incumbent of lutumbo lwa yananio. Moreover, in some areas certain status holders (e.g., the kindi who keeps the collectively held ivory sculptures, or the yananio who has the *kasisi* basket, or the old kindi who has assisted many kinsmen as tutor and adviser in their initiations) are not supposed to have any of the sculptures. These objects are transmitted, according to the previously mentioned rules, within a field of close personal agnatic, affinal, and cognatic relationships. In historical perspective, specific art objects and other initiation items were also introduced into a family, lineage, or clan through "purchase" or fission of existing baskets or existing sets of complementary objects.

MEANING, CONFIGURATION, AND CONTEXT

In preceding sections I have discussed in great detail the vast quantity of objects—natural and manufactured—that enter into the bwami initia-

The Art of Bwami

tions. Whether used as insignia and paraphernalia, or destined primarily to serve as initiatory items, these objects are all named and explained in a context of dance and drama. The explanations are given not merely to indicate what the objects are and what uses they have, but rather to relate them to the social system, the network of social relations, the moral philosophy, and the nature and structure of bwami itself. To achieve this end, hundreds of references to and correspondences with the environmental and behavioral worlds that surround the Lega are pointed out. The references are not merely verbal, but also kinetic and iconic. The initiatory objects form a vast storehouse of symbols that help to translate in metaphorical language the essence of Lega society and thinking. Every object is much more than its total form or its formal components could ever synthesize. Every object is explained in highly succinct and terse formulations of the aphorism. The superb mastery of the Lega language which pervades all these aphorisms, the refined nuances of expression, the choice of words, the shades of meaning, and the many grammatical subtleties further increase the difficulties of interpreting the material symbols.

The aphorisms are sung and danced out: "Dancer and Singer, we were born together as twins." The dance movements, together with the gestures and action patterns that accompany the manipulation of the material symbols, add further shadings and nuances to the meanings expressed in the verbal statements. In a dramatic setting, the objects appear in fixed sequences, in certain sets, in established configurations, as part of a total initiation to a certain grade level. This configurational aspect of the presentations lends a further dimension to the interpretation of meaning.[16]

Each item used in an initiation—not only the figurine, but the mat on which it is oiled, the basket or shoulder bag in which it is contained, the object against which it rests—must be explained in terms of its relevance for the social and moral code. Every object, particularly the natural and manufactured objects and the masks and animal figurines, can therefore support more than one interpretation. For spoons, knives, hornbill knives, and axes, the interpretations are more restricted and stereotyped. The meanings conveyed by any single anthropomorphic figurine in wood or ivory are also strictly limited, but since the category of figurines is sharply differentiated, many different messages are provided by the many different figurines.

Most objects form a cluster of symbols, not simply because whatever the form suggests is enriched by the verbal, choreographic, gestural, and configurational dimensions, but also because the form itself has many components, including details of morphology and surface, material, process,

---

[16] Turner (1962, pp. 125, 172–173; 1965, pp. 79–84; 1967, pp. 19–47) has made admirable analyses of the multivocality of symbols and of the exegetic, operational, and positional levels of meaning in Ndembu rituals.

and so on. The actual manipulation of the object and the correlated gestural behavior help to make clear which aspects of an object are emphasized at a given moment. The change of emphasis from one aspect of the object to another may occur within a single rite in rapid sequence, or in different rites.

The well-polished wooden chair (*kisumbi*; pl. 101) is a good example of symbolic meanings and emphases. It is used in several rites at different levels of initiation, and in some areas a special rite is built around it. The *kisumbi* chair has a specific form and surface: the seat and base are cylindrical (like sections of a cylinder) and slightly concave; the seat is sometimes decorated with copper nails; there are four legs; two declivities in the base suggest that a fifth leg in the center has been removed; the surfaces have a deep brownish black patina and a heavy gloss.

These properties have symbolic meanings for the Lega. Most objects that have four components (legs of the chair) arranged in a circle or a square, with a fifth component in the middle, signify the clan structure: "The clan has four hearths [branches or primary lineages] and the *kidande* [incorporated group]." The reference is to a conventional clan structure of five primary lineages, four having agnatic linkages and the fifth being an incorporated group of cognates. The center of a circle or a square, represented here by the declivities, suggests the enormous significance of the sororal nephew in the social structure: "The sororal nephew is a kidney; deep inside the animal has slept the kidney." The aphorism, "I am astounded: one man [with] four arms," refers to the four legs of the chair to symbolize the strength that comes from the agnatic sides of kinship. The aphorism, "Big-One-Many-Heads has seen an elephant on the other side of the large river," refers to the cylindrical shape of the seat and base. The seat and base are referred to here as two opposing heads, a theme frequently represented on anthropomorphic figurines. Many-Heads is a symbol of the wisdom, perspicacity, and equitableness of the kindi. Everybody can achieve status and self-expression through bwami: "Every chair has an open space; every *mulega* is [a potential] *wabume* [one who has virility and manhood, poise and character, and status; one who is fully human]." The statement, "The chair was very bad; *bukenga* leaves have made me shine around the eyes," bears on the beautiful gloss obtained by sanding the chair with *lubenga* leaves and by oiling it. The reference is to a man whose goodness or whose kanyamwa wife (both represented by the *lubenga* leaf) have brought him fame. An uninitiated person is in darkness; bwami brings light and gives greatness (shine) to people. The typical bend in the legs of the chair is reminiscent of death: "The branch of the *nkungu* tree: the bending is the reason why it dies." The aphorism refers not merely to knees bent by old age, but to the use of a bent branch of the tree to tear off the head of the decomposing corpse. As a specific form the *kisumbi* chair is sometimes contrasted with one of the other chairs known

The Art of Bwami

to the Lega. The opposition then is between the smoothness of *kisumbi* and the unpolished roughness of *nkeka*, a forked chair made of a large aerial root: "He who talks behind my back has given me a *nkeka* chair and other oddities that burn [hurt] me."

The *kisumbi* chair is a useful object on which one can sit comfortably, and as such it is the symbol of hospitality. The aphorism most frequently sung in conjunction with the chair is "Give him a chair; a foreigner does not go with his own." So when many people are carrying their chairs, something bad is happening: "Chair does not go to foreign [to an unknown place] unless the village burns." In this aphorism Kisumbi is personified and means the Good-One. In other contexts the chair personifies the initiate through whose tutorship or advice one achieves one's own initiation.

The symbolic associations go beyond the actual form of an object to the creative process, the materials, and the usages that underlie it. The *kisumbi* chair is usually made of *muntonko* wood (*Alstonia*), and the principal tool used to carve it is the adze (*nkondo*). The aphorism, "Muntonko has no imputrescible heart; the adze is its heart," suggests that as the soft, easily decaying *Alstonia* wood is perpetuated by the carver's art, so a person is perpetuated by the transformation wrought by bwami. The *muntonko* tree is found in most forest formations: "The tree near the village, I hear the sound of axes on it" means that people try the sharpness of their knives and tools on it. The tree is a symbol of the old initiate who remains in the lineage as the supreme possessor of all teachings, from whom everybody is trying to get the best. Since *kagumo* is a strangler vine that grows on the *muntonko* tree, "Kantonko has called Kagumo to sit in its branches; Kagumo dries him out." The reference here is made to any person (son or sororal nephew; guest or protégé in bwami) who would turn against a benefactor and destroy him. In the aphorism, "The piece of wood of the branches has taught your child to climb," the piece of wood is the extremely useful *kagumo* liana, from which one kind of bark cloth is made. Bwami, and the greatness it offers, have made people strive for higher things. Sometimes the creative act that has produced the finished chair is placed in perspective: "Every blacksmith forges his own; Byembo [Penis] has known to forge" means to praise a father who has a virtuous son. There is also the suggestion that the object remains while its maker disappears.

The *kisumbi* chair has specific uses. Male and female initiates sit on it. It plays a role in the enthronement of a new member of the association (pl. 50), and, as an initiatory object, it is used in certain ways in dance movements (pl. 18). The aphorism, "Great Initiate, I harvest fruits and from the chair I do not stand up," means that a new initiate may travel to many places to receive gifts from many people while sitting on his chair, an animal hide spread out before him. An old initiate, just for being present, shares in all the goods without directly participating in the dances. "Kisumbi does not go to [does not have] menstruations; I shall try when I shall be a young mother": women sit on the *kisumbi* chair only rarely, except during enthronement or coming-out ceremonies. To be allowed to sit or stand on such a chair is a mark of status for a woman, achieved first of all through motherhood.

Since chairs are in direct contact with the genitalia, two other ideas are brought to mind. The aphorism, "Chair, I smell something bad; I smell the bad odor of the buttocks," criticizes a child who, when requested to do something, always asks for presents. Reference is also made to the fact that the chair cannot see Nyabungu (genitalia) because the loincloth is in between, but that the fallen tree can see them because the loincloth is hanging low or because it was taken off to bathe or to wade. That is, certain things that are veiled for noninitiates can be known only to old people and high-ranking initiates.

Sometimes during a ritual an initiate sits on a *kisumbi* chair making a gesture with his hand which means refusal, or clenching his fist: "Stupid-One, they prepare for me the *nkeka* chair; they insult my virility," or, "The children of a poor devil can build a village; it will not live." He holds the chair under his armpit: "I go with the red-skinned woman to the dance [where there is only food, but no other valuables]; I go to be ridiculed." The initiate dances while rubbing the seat of the chair: "Nyakabomba [personification for the chair; lit., a woman who continually leaves her husband], you cannot go to a foreign place." The range of references and meanings conveyed by the *kisumbi* chair is truly remarkable, for the Lega as well as for outsiders. These meanings, which are all culturally determined, are based on a number of experiences that are known to the Lega, and to them alone. The full understanding of the *kisumbi* chair can therefore be reached only through analysis of the social context.[17]

A basic referent, or set of referents, seems to underlie the symbolism of most objects used in bwami initiations. The following list is a sample of correspondences I have derived from recurrent meanings attached to certain objects.

> Arm and hand carved in wood (*mugombo*): Dispute leads to destitution. Symbolizes "The arm of the Sick-One stretches out toward the sorcerer who kills him," or Kagolomba, "the destroyer of axes" (i.e., the person who does not listen to advice), or Sabigombo, Mr. Arms, who went elsewhere to die.
>
> Ax made of ivory, bone, or wood (*isaga; kakuma*): Symbol of things that, too often borrowed, get lost or are destroyed. It applies to children who do not listen. It also means that a person has in him, or produces, what will destroy him: "On the parasol tree

---

[17] Lewis (1969, p. 20 and *passim*) presents a helpful interpretation of the social contextual meaning of artworks in New Ireland society.

grows the ax [i.e., the handle of the ax] that will cut the new field."

Bikuwe and *byenze*: Small disks in wickerwork or hide, covered with cowries or beads or trimmed with chicken feathers. They are sometimes referred to as palms of hands (*tukasa*), as "the shield of the initiates," or as the "heart of bwami."

Broom of bulrush (*kikuko*): Symbol of bwami which "cleanses the heart"; symbol of the initiate who cleans the village and makes it good.

Bulrush (*isandi*): Its knots symbolize the country's problems.

Bwami hat: Sometimes called *ikangamina*, the powerful, or *kilembo*, the coveted, it is a symbol of status, widespread fame, and intelligence.

Cane (*mukulu wibondo*): The weapon of the Old-One and the symbol of his wisdom, his power and authority, and his wealth: "He who gives you the cane, gives you mastery of the land." Initiates are masters of the cane, not of the spear.

Carapace of turtle (*kikuku kya nkulu*; *kibengelo*): Symbol of an old man with wisdom and circumspection, who eats only soft things.

Claw of the pangolin: Warning signal (*masasa*).

Costus lucanusianus (*itungulu*): Used to cover the phrynium leaves on top of the roofs, it is the symbol of the lineage whose roots are everywhere.

Door, in miniature, made of parasol planks (*keibi*): The door knows the things from inside and outside the house; it also symbolizes a shield or an elephant.

Dugout in miniature (or miniature slit-drum): Symbol of a child's helpfulness; symbol of the good that is done both on the father's side (agnatic) and on the mother's side (maternal uncles).

Feather rope (*munana*): The *kindanda kya bwami* (what closes everything of bwami), used to make a sacred fence, to close in, and to tie objects during initiations. It is the symbol of the hunting net, particularly of the leading rope, and of something that is very long like the initiations themselves.

Forked stick (*igobo*): Symbol of mutual aid in kinship: "Where the arm cannot reach, Igobo, child of my mother, can reach." It also symbolizes the head of the village without whom the group scatters.

Hornbill beak (*mutu*): Symbol of pride and ambition: "Mutu counts the villages; he does not know what hangs above him." It is also the symbol of a woman who goes places and does not return unless she is called back.

Horns of billy goat (*mega*): Symbol of aggressive strength; symbol of perpetual things that remain, such as skulls.

Idumbi feather tuft: Symbol of the new, strong heart created by initiations.

Kikoku shell (giant aquatic snail): Symbol of the maternal uncle who helps his nephew overcome difficulties; symbol of the old person who is bent, has no teeth, and has many wrinkles; symbol of *lubingo* (lit., something that turns around, what is twisted), that is, of the endlessness of evil.

Lububi liana: Symbol of strength, durability, and productivity.

Lubumba mussel shell: Symbol of status, wealth, respect, and continuity.

Nkola shell (*Achatinae*): Used to make shell money. Symbol of the female, of eggs, and of endlessness.

Mat (*katanda*): Symbol of death and of destruction caused by the dispersal of red ants.

Needle and raffia thread: Father's problems always remain with you; intelligence will help when one goes to unknown places; bwami brings people together; one's relatives are those who were left by father and those who do good to one.

Parasol wood (*musagi*): Used to build doors, shields, and plank wall around initiation hut. Symbol of what is light but durable.

Phrynium leaves (*igungu*): Used to cover roofs; symbol of the female.

Porcupine quills (*mulungi, kinsamba*): Symbol of sharpness (e.g., of the heart).

Resin torch (*kasuku*): The Beloved-One-of-the-Night: symbol of light and fame, which attract others.

Scale of pangolin: Symbol of piety and of respect: Isamukulu, the Great-Old-One.

Seedpod of *lubala* (*Pentaclethra macrophylla*): Symbol of breakup of the lineage because of strife.

Shoulder bag (*nsago*): Symbol of greatness and leadership; symbol of the noninitiate; refers to theft, adultery, and sorcery.

Tibia of *kagelia* monkey used as sheath for an iron needle (*idonge*): Symbol of the unbreakable bond between people.

Warthog tusk (*linyo lya nsyenge*): Symbol of Kisibula, the Destroyer, that is, the village headman with a big mouth or the sorcerer.

Wickerwork rattle (*mizegele*): The "call of the kindi" and the "harmonizer of the dances"; as every seed in it speaks, so everything in bwami has meaning.

Only the action surrounding an object and the formulations of an aphorism can fully clarify what the object means in any given situation. The horns of a billy goat, representing strength and aggressiveness, are sometimes held by a dancing, bucking, capering preceptor who is tightly clasped around the waist by another initiate. The meaning of this action is

The Art of Bwami

that a person, even though he is tough and strong, will find somebody to stop him, and that if he persists he will be killed. A piece of a *nkomo* jaw refers to the voracity of the fish of that name, which makes it vulnerable to baited traps. When a preceptor, holding the jaw in his mouth, dances around wildly, he represents one who talks too much, asks everywhere for advice, and is bound for trouble. When the same jaw is used, wrapped in a genet hide with a *lubumba* shell and a *yango* stick (a piece of banana stipe) and hanging from the roof in the initiation house, the implication is that young men should not ridicule old men who are constantly asking for something. The *lubumba* shell, held in the outstretched hand, is a symbol of fame and status, as is also the polished *lubumba* shell attached to the front of a yananio hat. When the shell is held in the mouth it symbolizes an evil tongue. When it is placed in front of the mouth it advises the initiate not to quarrel with the children of the village; the concave inside of the shell valve reminds them of the flat buttocks of a woman who has had many children.

The situation is still more complicated because objects, and the symbols they represent, are interchangeable. The horns of the billy goat may be replaced by a forked stick; a multiheaded statue, by a *kisumbi* chair. The idea of Nyanjinjinji (Mrs. Black, whose body is unattractive but whose heart is good) is rendered by an ivory carving or by the mud nest of the *kisise* insect. Kakulikuli (a bird that symbolizes a big talker) is represented by a real beak or by a rudimentary carving in wood representing beak and neck. A spoon in bone or ivory can express the symbolism associated with a miniature ivory knife. A distorted piece of wood from the strangler vine may be used as an anthropomorphic figurine. A woman who goes places and does not return unless she is called back is symbolized by a carving or by the hornbill beak.

The number of interchangeable objects is strictly limited. Many objects contain their own contradictions. The *lubumba* mussel shell is a symbol of status, wealth, respect, and continuity, but the emptiness of the shell also suggests a person with a beautiful, but empty, body. The horns of the billy goat signify strife in a group of leaders but they also remind people of the continuity of leadership, for when the old billy goat (*kilimba*) dies the young one with smaller horns (*kankutungwa*) may take over. The shoulder bag, as a receptacle for objects, is a symbol of fulfillment and leadership, but as an object without content it stands for the emptiness of the uninitiated, "who has a mouth but has no heart."

Most objects occur in groups of varying composition, but only a few are paired. Examples of paired objects are the needle and the raffia thread, the razor and its sheath, the hornbill beak and the *nkola* shell, and some figurines representing complementary characters.

Symbolism moves easily within the same rite from one form of interpretation to another. In some areas a rite built around a door (*keibi*) is part of the lutumbo lwa kindi initiations. The dances and interpretations first address themselves to the door as such, to stress the piety of the young man who continually knocks at the door of his senior or his father to present gifts. Next, the interpretations call attention to the dots painted on the door, which suggest the "dots of the leopard which frighten the goats and the animals." This interpretation is meant to glorify the power of the bwami association. A preceptor carrying the door and sitting near the initiation hut is then joined by a group of dancers, who are referred to as the herd of elephants (*idumbu*) joining the little elephant (*kalupepe*). The dancers, who move around the initiation hut, have the power to make the initiations successful and to help the candidate through the initiations, provided they are willing to open their hearts: "Masters of the initiation hut, open the door for me that I may see how it is adorned."

The symbolic interpretations return to the elephant. The aphorism, "Stately goes the elephant when he arrives in the new field," refers to the candidate who possesses goods and strength but has no fear. Another one, "When he hears about the young field with new shoots, the elephant does not know to flee," refers to initiates who do not fail to go to an initiation where there is plenty of oil and meat. "Flat-Buttocks, the elephant does not listen to the things of others," means that initiates when called upon cannot listen to other advice and cannot refuse to do what is asked of them. Kanyamwa women dance up to the door with swirling arm movements: "What has emaciated the mwami is to open and to close" (criticizes one who goes after women too much).

Next, the door becomes a shield. The slightly bent shape of the shield suggests the bent old man who made the shield; the dancers laugh at him because he is bent, but not at his bent shield. Running around with the door-shield, the initiates are invited not to leave the village until everything is finished: "Come to see how we parry with the shields in this village." The preceptor holds the door, under protest from the others, against his ribs and neck—"The shield of the dead one is not held well"—to criticize a wife of one's father whom one has inherited and who constantly says that it was better with the father. The preceptor holds the door against his buttocks and in front of his penis—"Manly was the march of the shield that father left"—to warn somebody who annoys a congener who inherited his father's possessions that he may die the same death as his father. The preceptor stands still, looking at the door-shield, and others come to take it away: "I carved a shield, the well-hollowed-out shield is with others." This complaint is that of a man who did much for his father, but when the father died early all his things went to others because the son was still too young to inherit them.

The initiates now pass the door-shield from hand to hand. The aphorism, "I carved a shield; it turns into something that is being borrowed," is a complaint that one's wife is running around with others. The preceptor

The Art of Bwami

carrying the shield is attacked with sticks: "The small, very light shield is not a shield; I am injured [by a spear] in the wrist." The interpretation is that when one's best wife leaves, one remains with another wife of no quality. The preceptor hides under the door-shield: "The small bat hides under the shield; war is coming." That is, the war of the initiates is coming and one must be prepared. This proverb leads to the concept of coverage, expressed in the saying, "The maiden hides in her mother's house; the seducer is coming," which means that they who come with the initiation objects know how to divide well. Next, "The parasol tree, which I had designated for the shield, becomes a small tree to be trampled by an elephant," meaning that the father wanted his son to succeed him in bwami but the son is gone. "Two trees were designated for the shield" stresses that if the senior fails, the junior will get the shield. The symbolism thereafter is concerned with a bunch of porcupine quills fastened to one end of the door.

Artworks are intimately and inseparably interwoven with the many natural and manufactured objects used in bwami. Except for the preliminary *kamondo* dances, each rite requires and is centered on the display and manipulation of objects. The iconic component is as vital and intrinsic a part of the rite as are the dance and the music, the aphorism and the song, the exchange of goods and the interaction of initiates. Every rite is not only meant to be an essential step in the progress toward a grade of bwami; it also aims at interpreting the moral code, the system of social relations, and the structure and aims of bwami in a more and more detailed way, and always in a new and unexpected manner. In so doing the rites constantly provide new information about things that pertain to Lega culture and environment.

Besides interpreting codes and structures, bwami rites celebrate, and sometimes criticize, actions, events, and things that are known to the Lega. Some rites evoke activities of the hunt, including trapping, skinning, and distribution of animals. Others relate to harvesting, with special emphasis on the gathering of honey, mushrooms, and termites, or reenact divination, administration of the poison ordeal, or gambling. Still others commemorate procedures that were known in times of warfare and feuding. Some rites are meant to reveal certain aspects of secret customs, such as the burial of high-ranking initiates. Very rarely, a little-known story is told and danced out in a sequence of aphorisms. Some rites center on a plant (banana tree or dried banana leaves, raffia), an animal (pangolin, turtle, elephant), or a manufactured object (collaret, door) which is then used as the focus for the symbolism expressed in word and dance. Many rites use a more complex set of objects, either of one type (e.g., *lukwakongo* masks, *mugugundu* figurines, wickerwork rattles) or of different types. In the latter instance different kinds of artworks may be used by themselves, or they may be mixed with manufactured and natural objects.

The total context in which art objects are seen can best be examined by an outline discussion of an actual case I observed in a lutumbo lwa kindi initiation. The total cycle comprises thirteen named rites. Since the initiation is at the highest level, a large number of artworks are used in conjunction with manufactured and natural objects. The objects and the meanings conveyed by them, the action and the context may be described as follows.

1. *Mizegele*
    Objects: Wickerwork rattles and bunches of feathers.
    Action: The initiates shake the wickerwork rattles; they dance holding the bunches of feathers in their hands; sometimes the objects are placed on the ground and then picked up again.
    Interpretations: Nine aphorisms
    Call together the initiates because many are needed for a successful initiation.
    If we die here it will be because of those who called us together.
    The rattles get on nicely; they are in unison.
    We must show the things we have brought.
    Kanyamwa women do not run with young men.
    We are all big men, but we cannot despise those who preceded us in the initiations.
    We came here for dances, not for disputes.
    There is continuity in bwami: one initiation finished, another follows; one initiate dead, another substitutes for him.
    In the village of the initiate, there is much wealth.

2. *Lusaga*
    Object: A collaret made of raffia leaves.
    Action: The preceptors dance holding the collaret; they roll it up and one preceptor dances with it; they place it on the ground; several initiates, in turn, pick it up and dance with it; one preceptor hangs it around his neck and waddles around.
    Interpretations: Five aphorisms
    Call the kanyamwa women together.
    Let us greet Lusaga (collaret; symbol of labor) as a guest.
    Criticizes the yananio who seduces a kindi's wife; his action destroys his chances for initiation.
    Criticizes a kindi's son who does not achieve as much as his father did.

The Art of Bwami

> Before going into the initiations a man thinks he may die there; when he has gone through them, he thinks that it was not so dangerous after all.

3. *Kilinkumbi*

   Objects: Ivory masks are fastened around a large wooden mask on a pala fence (pls. 38–39); a *kilinkumbi* figurine representing a pangolin is placed on top of the fence; a feather rope connects the fence with a *matakale* cane, whose top is adorned with an ivory figurine.

   Action: The initiates dance holding the feather rope and moving toward the fence; they dance around the fence pointing to the feather rope; they dance around the fence pointing to the animal figurine; they place the animal figurine on the ground and then move it slowly up against the fence; they dance around the fence pointing to the masks; they pull the fence up and lay it on the ground.

   Interpretations: Eleven aphorisms

   > Those who go to kindi follow one row; that is, they have one goal in mind.
   > All paths lead to the place where a kindi resides, as animal trails lead to the hunting grounds.
   > Criticizes a man who seduces one of his father's wives.
   > Criticizes a man who seduces somebody's wife thinking that this act will not be discovered.
   > Kindi is a pole of attraction for all.
   > "Bring together the graves [i.e., the skulls; the masks] that I may know the skull [mask] of my father."
   > Criticizes a son who despises his father who is a kindi.
   > Quarrel and competition destroy the group.
   > If one is in good standing within one's group, one may expect help in times of difficulty.
   > Refers to the vain attempts of a kindi to instruct his wives and children, who do not want to listen.
   > "Everyone who has come will go home; the Anointed-Ones go to their meeting place."

4. *Keibi*

   Object: A small house door, made of parasol planks, covered with dots, and held together by a feather rope; feather tufts are placed on the ends of the door.

   Action: The preceptor dances with the door; he sits down with it in the door opening of the initiation house; he dances around with the door, then sits again in the door opening, moving the door to and fro; he moves around with the door in the row of dancing initiates; he places it on the ground, then carries it on both hands as a present.

Interpretations: Six aphorisms

"The small child that knocks at the door is your companion in the village."

The big door of the initiation house is a trap: Who will open it?

"The spots of the leopard fool the sheep and the red-haired goat."

One must keep one's heart low (i.e., keep emotions in low key); a bad person who would succeed in kindi tries to keep others out.

When a little person is in trouble, he calls upon the big ones for advice.

"What emaciates the initiate is to open and to close" (refers to continued giving).

5. *Kabubi*

Objects: A *lububi* liana hanging from the roof of the initiation hut, and a feather tuft attached to it.

Action: The preceptor holds the liana in the hand; he points the feather tuft toward the participants.

Interpretations: Six aphorisms

One goes always to ask the help of affines and maternal uncles.

One house is rich and has many children; another has nothing.

If an initiate dies in a foreign part of the country, his corpse remains there but his bwami returns home.

When the initiations are over, all the dirt remains to be cleaned up by the host.

The initiation becomes useless when one is sick, injured, or infirm.

A sick person has no rest and does not know what he wants (about one who does not get anywhere).

There is, throughout this interpretation, a play on *lububi*, the liana, and Kabubi, Mr. Liana.

6. *Itutu* (pl. 19)

Objects: Phrynium and *matungulu* (*Costus lucanusianus*) leaves; fire drill; *lububi* liana; torches; mussel shell; ladder.

Action: Most of the action takes place on the roof of the initiation hut. The principal actors are the preceptor and his aides, the candidate and his wife, and the wife's tutors;

the rest of the initiates sit on the ground looking on, but the candidate's tutor sits near the door of the initiation hut on the ladder. The preceptor rubs and waves the leaves and the liana; he shows the fire drill; he passes burning torches through a hole in the roof; he hides away the torches and the fire drill in the roof coverings; he shows a *lubumba* shell. After the principal actors climb down from the roof they move toward the drummers, holding one another by the shoulders.

Interpretations: Twenty-six aphorisms

All initiates must stick together and form a solid body (they are "knotters knotting a dense forest").

If one takes good care of an old initiate, the latter will remember him and help him in bwami.

When a man thinks about his initiation he tries to bring together as many people and goods as possible.

"We climb the slope of a big mountain; the mountains are excessively high."

Everybody enjoys fame and prestige.

Sadness afflicts the man who goes through kindi and is observed by the children of others because his own are too stupid to go through the rites.

The death of kinsmen hampers many enterprises.

One boasts of being big, but he has nothing except a big mouth.

Criticizes a person who leaves his group to have children elsewhere.

Criticizes a person who does not want, under any circumstances, to help his kinsmen.

Somebody with a bad heart does not want others to get as far as he did.

A person without a good disposition cannot achieve kindi.

"Initiates are *mbubi* lianas; the joints ramify and ramify."

One with high intelligence and plentiful goods is sure that the initiations will go well.

Kindi cannot be achieved without going through the lower initiations; a father may be poor, but his son may become wealthy. A young man must not despise bwami.

Criticizes a woman who continually returns to her people during her marriage, compelling her husband to travel to get her back.

Wherever one goes one must remember to take the fire

drill (young people often forget it); a kindi goes always with his kanyamwa.

Some children are strong and some are weak, but the strong ones may be very stupid.

Many are unable to achieve what they aspire to because they lack character and wealth.

Praises the candidate who has finished an important part of the rites.

"You leave your companion and bid him farewell; there will be no discussion or fighting and no war."

"The mwami is the crescent of the moon; every clan has seen [from] it."

"Crescent-of-the-Moon, those who are far away look up at him in awe."

There is joy because of the successful progress of the initiation.

"The Banankamba [Fish-Folk] do not carry him who is not of their group."

"The White Birds float around in the air; they will go home" (to signify that the rite is finished; but the aphorism is also sung during the burial ceremony of a kindi).

7. *Ibago lya nzogu*
   Objects: Ivory and bone spoons and knives.
   Action: Kindi and kanyamwa, holding the spoons and knives, dance around the initiation hut; they place the objects in the roof; they dance around, pointing to their heads; they slowly approach the initiation house, holding their hands before their mouths in astonishment; they take the candidate around the hut and then invite him to pull one of the spoons out of the roof and to shout his praise name while stabbing the roof; they shake the initiation hut and dance around it again.
   Interpretations: Twelve aphorisms

   When one is going to undertake an initiation one sends messages to all one's kinsmen.

   When one undertakes an initiation one does not rebuff an old initiate by saying that he asks for too many of the goods being stored away for the rites.

   One does not despise initiates who have already finished the initiations.

   Be prepared, for the achievement of kindi is near at hand.

   Let us share in the right manner, according to "the way in which we were born."

The Art of Bwami

To achieve kindi is difficult; one must concentrate all one's efforts.

When kindi hear about an initiation they all burn with the desire to go, but they go slowly.

One who approaches kindi must do everything with respect and circumspection; dispute is not tolerated.

Let us see how many goods the candidate has left for the initiation.

There is joy, as when an elephant is cut up, because there are many goods.

The name of a person who has many children cannot be forgotten.

"The place where the elephant rots, there are ribs and ribs and chunks and chunks."

8. *Kankunde*

   Objects: A wooden *muminia* mask with a long beard; a piece of bark cloth; a turtle carapace; a log; an ivory spoon; a wickerwork rattle; phrynium leaves; small pieces of firewood; a *lububi* liana to which an aardvark claw is attached.

   Action: A preceptor wearing the *muminia* mask kneels inside the initiation house, near the entrance, which is half closed with a piece of bark cloth, and behind a small log; he holds a turtle carapace. The movements of the carapace and of the mask's beard are visible below the bark cloth; the carapace is moved against the log as if a real turtle were trying to crawl over it. An aide symbolically feeds the mask by means of an ivory spoon; the mask is then moved up to the preceptor's head so that its beard covers the part of his face above the mouth; the masked preceptor shakes the wickerwork rattle, holding it behind the beard, and moves up toward the threshold of the hut while initiates outside try to chase him with symbolic firewood and leaves. The masked preceptor withdraws inside the hut, shivering and shaking the rattle. The initiates then pull a liana fastened to the underside of the mask so that part of the mask is pulled outside the initiation hut; further pulling draws the masked preceptor completely out. The candidate clasps the masked preceptor firmly from the back, placing his legs on the preceptor's thighs, and the candidate's kanyamwa holds her husband in the same manner, as they all move on their buttocks over the ground, dragging some of the dirt with them.

Interpretations: Eight aphorisms
"Old-Turtle pays a formal visit to kindi" (i.e., when one is visited by an old kindi, one rejoices, thinking that one's chances for kindi are good).
"Old-Turtle crosses the fallen tree" (an old kindi coming to the village as tutor will not leave until all the initiations are finished).
"Old-Turtles, I leave them behind eating banana porridge" (i.e., visiting kindi receive only the very best food; it is never raw or poorly prepared).
"I was thinking that it was Golden-Mole, and lo! it is Aardvark" (i.e., I thought him to be a man of great skill and capacity, but he acts badly).
To overcome big problems or to achieve a high-level initiation, one needs many goods.
"Cut *mbubi* lianas, for Aardvark gets stuck in the hole" (a reminder that more goods must be provided).
"Aardvark comes out of the hole" (there are enough goods now, and the initiations can proceed).
"You have seen *mulombe* of kindi" (both *kankunde* and *mulombe* refer to the ritual removal of dirt).

9. *Ibugebuge* (pls. 44–45)
    Objects: A fence; ivory masks; large wooden masks; feather tufts and many feathered dance paraphernalia.
    Action: A fence is built of three poles driven into the ground and surmounted by a transverse beam. Each kindi hangs his ivory mask on the fence. A row of standing kindi space out and face the fence on one side; a row of kanyamwa face it on the other side. Two preceptors, each wearing a large wooden mask on his face and smaller wooden masks on his temples and against the back of his head, holding a feather tuft in his mouth, and wearing an abundance of feathered dance paraphernalia, move around, shivering, circling the fence and zigzagging between the rows of kanyamwa and kindi. Then the two masked preceptors hold each other tightly back to back, then belly to belly and move forward. Then they crawl under each other's legs. Finally, one floors the other and goes to lie on him.
    Interpretations: Three aphorisms
    Two of the aphorisms are sung while the fence is being built and adorned with the masks; the third one is sung during all the rest of the action. Most of the interpretation lies in the dance action.

"Initiates are bats; one by one they build the house."
"One man alone does not finish a latrine; let a second one come."
"I climb the *munkugu* tree: danger is already here."

When they first emerge from the initiation hut, the preceptors run about as if telling the other initiates that they are in trouble because they have committed a wrongful act. When they circle the fence, shivering, they symbolize war coming from all sides, but a kindi holding a wickerwork rattle cannot be killed in war. Circling the women means that even a bad man cannot indulge in seducing a kanyamwa woman. Standing back to back they signify, first, the kindi who when war comes stand back to back, shaking their rattles and trying to convince the opponents to stop the feud. Second, the action signifies that all turn their backs on a quarrelsome person. When the preceptors move along, belly to belly, they symbolize mock fighting and warn the candidate that real or mock fighting is always to be avoided. Passing under each other's legs (lit., "to take away your companion from between the legs") indicates that a kindi forgives those who despise him or fight him. When one preceptor lies on the other, the action means that a kindi should not try to seduce the wife of his colleague; it also reminds one that fighting and flooring someone on his back are bad.

10. *Mutulwa* (pl. 23)
    Objects: The collectively held kindi basket is opened. It contains four anthropomorphic figurines in wood; one bird figurine in wood; one small, well-patinated piece of ivory engraved with circle-dot designs; one chimpanzee and one leopard skull; one elongated animal figurine in bone.
    Action: The preceptors dance around with the figurines, one at a time or two together, holding them in their hands (as in pls. 28–30).
    Interpretations: Nine aphorisms
    "The Old-One of the *mpito* hat dies in the very early morning."
    "[The words] Divider has sliced up have killed Little-Old-One of the *mpito* hat."
    "The Pregnant-Adulteress has killed herself because of mixing the sperm; she has removed herself out of life."
    "Kakulikuli [the Tattler] is a bird that sings for the termites."

"When you administer water [as an enema] to Great-Old-One, you look at the anus which is turned upward."
"Ivory does not get off the shoulder; he will be caught on the track."
"The children of Leopard weep in confusion."
"The chimpanzee is a penis; those who like confusion cause your destruction."
"The small child plays at the wading place in the river; the *ngimbi* water serpent is death."

The first figurine in wood, representing Kakulu ka Mpito, the Great-Old-One of the *mpito* hat, clearly has female indications (pls. 23 [extreme right figure], 69), yet its name suggests that it represents an old male initiate, since only old high-ranking initiates wear the *mpito* hat, made of the hide of an *ambela* monkey.

The second figurine (pl. 23, second from right), which is used in the same dance context as Kakulu, is a rudimentary carving in wood with two heads on a pole; it represents Kamukobania, the Divider. The following story is depicted. Mukobania, the Divider, who slanders and betrays people (cutting up words as if he were slicing bananas for brewing), called people together for a drinking party. Kakulu, who was supposed to be much wiser because of his status in bwami, went to participate without fully assessing the situation. Mukobania deliberately called people together who were at enmity with one another and then served them a drink. Kakulu underwent a sad fate as everyone does who goes to meddle elsewhere.

The third figurine, representing Wayinda, the Pregnant-Adulteress, is a rudimentary carving of a woman with excessively distended belly (pl. 23, fourth from right). It is followed by another rudimentary carving of a bird, representing Kakulikuli, the Tattler (pl. 23, extreme left). The woman who commits adultery during pregnancy is the prototype of ugliness, since she potentially causes the abnormality of her child and death in her family; in this instance she commits suicide out of shame, although her life-force is still very strong. Kakulikuli represents an old man of the lineage who is supposed to give advice and orders in the village, but who alienates his people because of excessive talking.

The fifth figurine in wood, though at first glance resembling a stylized animal, is in fact a stylized human body with a funnel in the anus (pl. 23, second from left). It represents a personage receiving an enema, but the symbolism refers to an evil person who would try to seduce his father's wife. The wordplay is interesting; looking at the anus would cause dizziness as if one were looking down from a cliff into the abyss. Dizziness is equated with incapacity and failure. The person who seduces his father's wife will fail in his attempts to move up in bwami.

The piece of ivory (pl. 23, forefront on left) traveling on the shoulder calls to mind a young man who runs everywhere and gets into trouble. The leopard and chimpanzee skulls are used jointly (pl. 23). When a kindi dies and only young people remain in the village, the inhabitants scatter and weep in vain over their loss. The chimpanzee skull suggests an old initiate who is in charge of and guards many young people, but who acts badly toward them and causes their destruction.

The animal figurine in bone, representing the deadly *ngimbi* snake, symbolizes the destructive effects of evil persons in the group (pl. 23, forefront on right).

11. *(a) Kasumba and (b) byanda*

These two closely interwoven rites signify the transfer of vital paraphernalia, respectively, to the kanyamwa and to the kindi.

a) *Kasumba*

Objects: A fence of five poles is covered with dance paraphernalia and insignia of kanyamwa. Around it lie the women's diadems and among them stand little ivory figurines of the *katimbitimbi* type.

Action: The dance action is limited. The display is made outside the village on the rim of the forest. The purpose is to "show" the objects that are the hallmarks of the kanyamwa.

Interpretations: Five aphorisms

"Kanembwe [symbolizing a very great mwami] carries burdens."

"The Great-Old-One is not a sorcerer; relieve me of this apron."

"The miserable News-Dispatchers, they bring me lies, and I will refuse [to recognize what they said]."

"Ibulungu is not a tree; it is a place that is rich in animal trails."

"You borrow, you return [what you borrowed]."

The transfer of the essential insignia to the kanyamwa is an occasion to bring up again the problem of lying and false accusation against a background of sorcery and witchcraft, which are characteristically associated with women. Kanyamwa women stand above such human weaknesses.

b) *Byanda*
   Objects: Wickerwork rattles; giant *kikoku* snail shells.
   Action: The rattles are so placed as to form a circle, and the shells are put in the middle of the circle. The preceptor draws circles on the ground within the circle formed by the rattles.
   Interpretations: Five aphorisms
   "Lubingo [state of spiraling or circling; talking back] of kindi."
   "The Snail-Folk will die; the Iguana-Folk will break one another."
   "What do the initiated women show to the Snails?"
   "Wickerwork-Rattle, I will die here; it is because of the one who has called me."
   "The Little-Child of the Master-of-the-Land, in deep water it is that Nkamba [fish] swims."

   The transfer to the kindi of the extremely important *mizegele* rattle, used to dispatch secret messages between colleagues, is an occasion to reemphasize the power of the "old man," that is, the kindi.

12. *Bele muno*
    Objects: Display of figurines in ivory, some in polished wood, resting against kindi hats on the ground around a very large ivory figurine and covered with wildcat hides.
    Action: The naked candidate is carried, lying with his back on the back of the naked preceptor, around the covered *ziko* (lit., hearth) which contains the figurines. The initiates rub dried leaves over the ground. The preceptor, the candidate, and other initiates jump over the *ziko*, shouting their drum names. The *ziko* is then uncovered. Each initiate has placed one of his anthropomorphic figurines against his hat.
    Interpretations:
    No aphorisms are sung, but the scene I have already described is filled with meanings (see preceding section). The initiation hut is identified as the lair of wild pigs (*lugumbo*), where none of any other breed than kindi can be found. The figurines rest against the hats as a kindi rests against his kanyamwa; the large ivory

The Art of Bwami

figurine (called Nyantuli in this instance) is the mother of all the figurines and the symbol of the unity and autonomy of the ritual community. Every other figurine has an identifying aphorism. Among the figurines displayed are Kimbayu (Bad-Heart), Nawasakwa nyona (the One-with-the-Signs-of-Beauty ...), Kabunkenge kagunza (The respected woman with fallen breasts), Wansongo (the One-with-One-Eye), Kagalama (Lazybones), and so on. Figurines of this type are illustrated in pls. 74–78, 81–85).

13. *Kinsamba* (pl. 26)
   Objects: Figurines in ivory, some in polished wood; spoons, hammers, and ax blades in ivory or bone.
   Action: Kindi and kanyamwa seated on little chairs form a large circle; the kindi hold their shoulder bags beside them while the preceptors dance with their shoulder bags in the middle of the group. After several preliminary songs and dances, the initiates are instructed to display their objects; all kindi and kanyamwa place in front of themselves most of the anthropomorphic figurines, *katimbitimbi*, spoons, and hammers they own individually (pl. 26 shows the variety of objects displayed; note the presence of non-Lega figurines, like the equestrian statue in the foreground).
   Interpretations: Ten aphorisms
   "The very large shoulder bag: a woman with fallen breasts dies for me because of the shoulder bag."
   "The noninitiate is a shoulder bag; he has a mouth, he has no heart."
   "Give me my shoulder bag; far away there is the joyful call."
   "The great distance is destroyer of traps."
   "Give me my large shoulder bag that I may enter the forest."
   "Mubinga [dendrohyrax] dies because of the shoulder bag, and lo! it is only the dog bells and little nets."
   "I am going to inspect the traps; the barricade of thorns falls on me."
   "Everyone his own one, everyone his own one, the generosity of the *ibilundu* tree."
   "Every Great-Old-One culls mushrooms; the multitude of white mushrooms is glittering."
   "Porcupine does not eat fallen bananas in the clearing."

Despite differences in the number of rites and in the quantity of objects used, the foregoing condensed example of a lutumbo lwa kindi initiation reflects a pattern in the tone and content of the moral precepts, in the mixture and manipulation of objects, and in the massive use of artworks. It is important to remember that fewer artworks appear in the initiations leading to lower grades and levels, except for several lutumbo lwa yananio rites in which wooden masks and wooden animal figurines are used abundantly. The complex system of payments, gift giving, and food distribution, which marks every one of the thirteen rites discussed, adds much action and interaction to the occasion. The distributions of goods, in themselves, express many of the key principles of the bwami moral code because they emphasize generosity, total sharing, honesty, respect for seniority and kinship patterns, and reciprocity.

There is also a great deal of variety in the individual dancing and gestural behavior of participating initiates. The rhythm, slow (*nsombi*) at the beginning of the dance, shifts to a nervous trembling and twirling (*luzanzia*) as the initiates are taken up by the dance and the songs. The gestural expression of the hands (*kwandizia*) is rich and refined. Each dancer, particularly the preceptors, knows how to execute his own little fantasies (*tungeningeni*). As an expression of pleasure and enjoyment, some initiates caress in a milking movement the tailed hide aprons they wear (*kupola kisaba*); others honor the drummers by symbolically drying their sweat *(kunyonyona kumeiso)*. Still others offer, in dance movements, a handful of shell money to relatives. Groups of preceptors break away from the row of dancers and perform *apartés* or solos with objects on which the dance focuses.

Many things happen during the kindi rites outlined in the preceding pages. A well-known person goes through the highest initiation rite in the presence of high-ranking male and female initiates coming from many different places. The event brings pride to the candidate; it is a festive occasion that provides joy and entertainment. The candidate sees and receives the paraphernalia and insignia of his dignity, which remind him of his dead predecessors. He also gains knowledge of certain secret procedures. His marriage to a kanyamwa wife is sealed as an indissoluble union. He learns more about the moral precepts and the greatness of bwami. The kindi rites give initiates an opportunity to emphasize their power, authority, fame, and, in particular, their oneness with nature. As shown in the preceding outline, the initiates identify and characterize themselves as Bambubi, Folk-of-the-Mbubi-Liana, and Banamulua, Folk-of-the-Elephant-Herd, to emphasize their power; as Bankulu, Turtle-Folk, to stress their wisdom and circumspection; as Binyange, Folk-of-the-White-Bubulcus-Bird, and Banamombo, Folk-of-the-Oil, to point to their beauty and glory; as Banankamba, Folk-of-the-Nkamba-Fish, to emphasize the depth of their knowledge. Above all, a large part of the initiation ceremony resem-

The Art of Bwami

bles a play in which evil and good characters are criticized and praised: Kishabukali, Mr. Violence; Sabigombo, Mr. Big-Arms (or Mr. Clumsy); Kabubi, Sick-Person; Kalububi, Preceptor; Kakwabubi, Genitor; Lusaga, Barricade (or Tutor); Segele, Mr. Unproductive; Kakulu ka nkulu, Old-Turtle; Kamukobania, Divider; Wayinda, Pregnant-Adulteress; Kakulikuli Tattler.

Some rites of lutumbo lwa kindi are infinitely more complicated than those mentioned in the outline. The complexity derives both from the diversity of objects used and from the special configurational bond that links the objects together. One of the most complicated rites, *mukumbi*, occurs in all lutumbo lwa yananio initiations with different degrees of elaboration, but basically within the same ideological scope.[18] Mukumbi is the name of a kind of golden mole, but it is also a name used for a high-ranking kindi who is deceased. Mukumbi is represented in the rite by an object whose nature differs considerably from ritual community to ritual community. It may be a stylized animal carving in ivory, wrapped in the hide of the *nsongi* rodent, or a *mukumbi* or *nsongi* skin stuffed with moss, grasses, raffia, or a stick. When there is a fusion between the characters of Yango, "the one who sleeps in many places," and Mukumbi, the representation is an ivory bark beater or a wooden phallic-shaped *kyombi* stick. Rarely, the representation is an assemblage consisting of a genet hide containing an aardvark claw, wrapped in a feather rope and adorned with a porcupine quill.

The mukumbi rite is secret; initiates who have not gone through it themselves cannot participate in it. Initiated women are always excluded. All actions take place within the initiation house. There is no normal drumming, but only percussion with drumsticks on the wooden frame of the membranophone. The candidate is led into the initiation house and around a large covered *ziko*. The participating initiates imitate various animal noises, an impressive procedure that has a special meaning. The noises symbolize the backbiting of young men when they see an important person entering the village and remind the candidate that he ought not to call his colleagues names when he quarrels with them (such as, you swell like an aardvark; you talk like an elephant; you act like a chimpanzee). The candidate is seated. Four objects that stand in front of the *ziko* and are not covered by the hides are meant to impress the candidate with the seriousness of the occasion:

1. A ball of leaves is "the signal of war." A person without respect will die because of it. The candidate, however, is a respectful person who is now following the path of his father.

---

[18] A brief discussion of a *mukumbi* rite is given in Biebuyck (1968, pp. 40–42). The configurational bond between two figurines is analyzed in Biebuyck (1953e).

2. A porcupine quill means: "The young porcupine goes to inspect the lairs." The candidate goes to witness the different rites; the initiate constantly looks out for candidates to succeed him.
3. Three sticks symbolizing a fire drill mean: "The abandoned village is empty. Who emptied it? The one who supports the candidate emptied it." Thus the candidate is warned that big things are involved in this rite.
4. Two flyswatters made of bulrushes say: "The knots of bulrush are identical with the words of the land." Every day brings its problems; the understanding of these problems is a laborious task.

The hides (genet or goat) are then removed. A complex configuration of objects, all heavily coated with white clay, confronts the candidate. I have observed from eleven to sixteen groups of objects arranged on the ground in a particular manner. Each group may comprise a small number of identical objects or a large number of different ones, including works of art and many natural and manufactured objects. Except for the different types of leaves cut especially for the occasion, most objects displayed in the *ziko* are part of one or more collectively held yananio baskets, though there are also a few individually held items. Each category of objects, singly or in contrast with or in opposition to other objects, is interpreted in aphorisms. In clockwise order, the sequence of objects and ideas is as follows:

1. A row of pangolin scales: the path of initiation is long.
2. A giant *kikoku* shell of a water snail: the person who goes through all the initiations has nothing to bar his way; he overcomes difficulties (like *kikoku* crossing rapids) because he is intelligent.
3. A hornbill beak: on earth, everybody achieves what he is able to; nobody knows when death will strike.
4. A twisted piece of liana: well-spoken words produce good things.
5. A row of chimpanzee skulls and, parallel with it, a row of wooden *lukwakongo* masks: the stupidity of the person who wanted the initiation but lacked the force to achieve it is contrasted with the sense of fulfillment of the strong person who achieved what he wanted.
6. A group of little knives planted in the soil, interspersed with porcupine quills adorned with the red tail feathers of parrots: many dangers and evils threaten the existence of the weakling and the noninitiate (the arrangement is referred to as Thorny-Village); bwami (represented by the tail feathers of parrots) is a rock shelter (*kalemba*) that offers safety.
7. A wooden animal figurine of the *mugugundu* type and a row of giant snail shells: by following the path of wisdom the candidate will emulate his father's wisdom and achievements.

The Art of Bwami

8. Two pits, some distance apart, form the focus of the symbolism. One is covered with phrynium leaves only; the other is covered with phrynium leaves on top of which there is a pile of dirt supporting a wooden *lukwakongo* mask and an ivory spoon. Both objects reflect high status and are intended to say that good dispositions lead far. As so often in Lega symbolism, the message is conveyed in an indirect and negative way. The mask is placed high up against the pole of the initiation hut to signify a bat flying about in a tree, unable to finds its own hole from which it was chased because of trouble with other animals: "The bad heart of Bat is an endless war." The ivory spoon is used by the preceptor as a knife in a mock attack on the seated initiates to say: "Father-Knife destroys the forest because of violence."

The preceptor rubs his hand over the pile of dirt covering one of the pits to establish the true meaning of the pit. It represents the grave (*idumba*) of "him who has brought forth," which never disappears because it is taken care of by his descendants: "The grave of him who has brought forth does not disappear; whenever it is encountered, it is swollen." The preceptors next scratch away the dirt from the pit and place it in several heaps: "The initiates are guinea fowls; by scraping [fumbling] they find their things." The initiates take the opportunity to praise themselves as well-prepared organizers: "The guinea fowls, animals that make the forest lovable." They also remind the candidate that they lived in peace with his father within one row of villages. The pit is covered with phrynium leaves, but when these are removed several layers of different species of leaves are revealed. More than thirty samples of leaves may be superposed on one another. Each leaf is interpreted in an aphorism. All references celebrate the greatness of the high-ranking initiate and master of the land, who keeps his people together by settling their affairs in the right manner. The trees, vines, and shrubs from which the leaves come, and the leaves themselves, have special qualities for the Lega. In some instances the wood is used for making ax handles, or for construction; in others the vines are used for making hunting nets. Some leaves are used for covering and wrapping or for medicine. Sometimes the fruits are eaten when one is lost and hungry in the forest. The second pit is covered with phrynium leaves only.

When all the leaves have been removed from the first pit, there remain in it a ball of raffia fibers and Mukumbi himself, represented by a carving or by a stuffed hide. The raffia ball means that everybody has his own heart and ideas, which he simply cannot reveal to an ordinary person: "Know this other little thing: a man does not know whom he has not talked to." The representation of

Mukumbi has several meanings. It stands for the animal itself, in which a man's father has a preferential claim. It is a symbol of high achievement in bwami. Moreover, Mukumbi is the corpse of a high-ranking initiate whose grave and memory are well cared for: "The tomb [but also the skull and corpse] of him who brought forth does not rot; it remains swollen." This saying points out the contrast with the grave of the noninitiate (the empty pit), which, like the tomb of a man without progeniture, is forgotten.

The *mukumbi* rite, in addition to being one of the principal steps toward the achievement of lutumbo lwa yananio, serves other purposes. It is an occasion to illustrate and display the objects contained in the collectively held baskets. In other words, the rite is an assertion of group cohesion and solidarity. It is a method of teaching, at different levels of complexity, the principles of bwami, the code of ethics, the system of social relationships, and the hidden properties of natural objects. Many of the aphorisms are concerned with death (real and symbolic) and with the factors that cause it: fighting, arrogance, backbiting, pride, and so on. Most important, it is the dramatic reenactment of the secret burial procedures reserved for high-ranking initiates. Mukumbi is the dead initiate; the pit is his grave; the layers of leaves are the layers of wisdom the dead initiate possessed, for which his son is now striving; the objects on the grave are some of the essential belongings of the yananio which are to be transferrred to his son; the preceptor is the "guardian of the tomb"; the other participants are those who have come to weep because of the death of a great man. The sequence of groups of objects arranged in a circle means that bwami is "a long distance" (*mutandi mulazi*) and an endless sequence of abandoned villages (*bukindu nu bukindu*); that is, there are always new rites to go through. But greatness achieved through bwami is something that sticks (*kyandanda*), something that leaves a trace even after death.

In this section and in earlier ones I have discussed the functional and morphological types of artworks, the ways in which they are classified, used, held, and transferred, and the relationships between them and other objects in a configuration of dance action and aphorisms. I want now to synthesize the general meanings that are conveyed through each of the four principal categories of artworks, regardless of specific details.

Masks. Masks play an important role in bwami initiations, in large quantities at the yananio and kindi levels and in smaller quantities at lower levels. Although owned exclusively by initiated men, masks are used in some rites by their initiated wives. Occasionally a mask is used singly, but usually several masks (from a few to a multitude) are used simultaneously in the same rite.

Masks are used in an astonishing variety of ways. They are worn on

The Art of Bwami

the face, on the skull, on the back of the head, on the temples, near the shoulder on the upper arm, and on the knee; they are attached to a pole, fastened onto a fence, or placed on the ground; they are swung around or dragged by their beards; they are part of an assemblage; they are displayed in the *bele muno* rite of kindi. They are placed in a pile, in a circle, or in a row. They are pointed to, attacked in mock fighting, shot at with mock bow and arrow. They are reversed on the ground, on the fence, on the face. The emphasis may shift from the mask per se to the beard, to the mouth, to the eyes, to the nose, to the baldness of the mask, to the gathering of similarly masked persons, or to the collection of similar masks.

In ceremonies with masks, gestures and dance movements are significant. Initiates point to the masks, rub them on the forehead, turn them upside down, place leaves in one of the eye openings or a stick in the mouth, and so on. In some rites masks are worn by preceptors only; in others, by all participants of relevant grade. There are no special costumes that are worn with masks. Most often initiates are dressed in their regular dance paraphernalia, but in a few instances white bark cloth is worn. Masked initiates engage in dancing, or move around in a squatting position, or crawl around, or run and chase and take part in mock fighting, or sit on chairs while moving their heads and bodies. As noted earlier, there are no named subcategories within each category of functionally different masks. All wooden *lukwakongo* masks are supposed to be the same and to have identical usages and meanings. The same is true of the ivory *lukungu* masks of kindi. Moreover, despite the strict functional distinction between these two major categories of masks, there is no basic difference in meaning between them.

A mask is *kansusania ka muntu*, a semblance of a man, or, more precisely, *lukungu lwa wakule*, the skull of a dead one, or, still more narrowly, *lukungu lwa tata*, the skull of my father. Basically, therefore, the mask serves as a symbol that intimately links a living human being to a dead agnatic relative who was very close. Indeed, through this relative it links the living man with an unspecified group of dead kinsmen and initiates who have been associated with a specific mask (or its tradition), for the mask is *nondo za balimu na beinda*, the hammer of the dead ones and of those who have gone, or *nondo zasigile balimu*, the hammer that the dead have left or "the hammer that was forged by the dead and by the people." The mask that A now calls "skull of my father" was called "skull of my father" by B and C, and so on, who owned it before. The mask is a symbol of continuity and perpetuity. It is "the limb that remains of the dead one," and it is also a "hammer," which is the symbol of procreation and creativity.

The *lukwakongo* and *lukungu* masks symbolize the perpetuity of a line of initiated kinsmen; at a higher level, the *idimu* mask celebrates the perpetuity of the entire kinship unit. *Idimu* or *kilimu* seems to mean one "who is full of intelligence and cunning." Masks in a group are sometimes referred to as *malumba* (graves): "Bring together the graves, that I may know the skull of my father." When the true grave of the dead is no longer visible, the mask remains as a memento that keeps the dead alive. Any mask, however, singly or as one of a group, may symbolize many beings and ideas, depending on the dance context and the rest of the configuration. Below is a brief summary of some of the principal meanings conveyed by the *lukwakongo* mask.

1. Masked initiates represent the Great-Old-Organizers (or Smoothers) who "agitate the beards because they have eaten nothing," that is, old men who like to eat, who beg for food, and who should not be ridiculed or rejected.
2. Masked initiates enact the Great-Old-Ones-of-the-Turtle who came from afar, yet others listened to them because what they said was good.
3. Masked initiates incarnate the Bearded-Folk, all of whom have similar beards so that nobody can distinguish the senior from the junior. The reference is to a group of people in which everybody has his say because there is no leadership.
4. Masked initiates are referred to as *tumbukutu* or *ndoku*, insects that all look alike, to emphasize the spirit of oneness and solidarity which guides them.
5. Masked initiates may symbolize the gatherings of all, including clever and intelligent beings as well as persons of evil wit and purpose.
6. In rare instances, masked initiates evoke strangers, unknown persons coming from unidentified places.
7. Masked preceptors may personify creatures like the pangolin, the turtle, the queen bee, an old chimpanzee, a *kagelia* monkey, the *moko* bush baby, or generalized characters like the diviner, the tracker, the harvester, the guardian, and the old beggar, or specific characters like Kiliabundu, the Glutton; Samulangalanga, Mr. Well-Shaped-Nose; Munyungu, Who-Looks-for-Trouble; Zambazamba, Who-Is-Always-Sick; Samunyama, Mr. Pride; Sawakala, the Cutter-of-the-New-Field; and Sulukutu, Owl (Bad Person).
8. Masks hung on a fence or placed on the ground may be a reminder of war and destruction. In this context masks are often referred to as the skulls of the Banamuningi, a legendary group wiped out by its enemies.
9. Special emphasis may be placed on the rigid and silent mouth of the mask (sign of dissatisfaction), on the nose (Well-Shaped-Nose, the Seducer), on the skull without hair (a candidate without goods), on the dotted design (transience of youth and phys-

ical beauty). Emphasis is placed on the blindness of the eyes: "The Great-Old-One who has carried me does not see any more," but blindness is no reason not to ask his help and advice; and "Eyes-That-Do-Not-See does not see the *nkumbi* fruits," which means that people know the things that go into bwami, but not the way they are used and interpreted. The interpretation may focus on the mouth in which a little stick is placed: "You eat with a Great-Old-One; the toothpick is between the teeth," which says that verbal restraint is necessary when the senior is angry.

10. Other ideas are expressed when the objects are handled in unfamiliar ways. A mask hanging downward by its beard reminds one of a *mulima* bat that is angry with the sun, of a person who prefers stupidity to bwami. A mask attached to the knee illustrates the aphorism, "The long well-shaped nose becomes a licker of honey," which stigmatizes interference in other people's business. A mask hanging on the back of the head recalls the battle of Tubala: "When we were beaten at Tubala, on our backs we carried the shields." Masks are mentioned as fallen leaves or leaves that are impregnated with white. Hanging a mask against the pole of the initiation hut suggests that "The bad heart of Mulala [Bat] is destruction without end." Rubbing the eyes of a mask with a leaf implies sorcery: "The Pygmy, Son of Honey and Wax, bewitches him with an eye disease." Showing the beard of a hand-carried mask, the dancers sing: "The billy goat does not grow a beard, which has no breeder," and, catching a masked dancer by the beard, "The billy goat that escaped my father, I hold it by this beard." Masks placed closely against one another symbolize a herd of elephants. Holding a mask by the forehead and swinging its beard in the air and over the ground means: "I have arrived at the place where elephants slept; every leaf has a stain of soil" (all come to the initiations, kinsmen and nonkinsmen). Picking a mask up from the ground with his teeth, the preceptor symbolizes the strength of a person who, lacking a father or a senior brother, achieves bwami by his own power. Holding two masks together as if they formed a double-faced mask means: "Sawabuzumbu [Raffia] disperses the top of the *Raphia* trees" (one finished the initiation, and it is up to somebody else now to do his initiation.

Any one of these meanings can be expressed by the wooden *lukwakongo* masks. The bone and ivory *lukungu* masks condense a much more limited set of meanings. A *lukungu* mask is never worn on the face or elsewhere on the body, a limitation that in actual usage seems to reflect on the range of meanings. In general, the masks bring to mind death and sorcery, which is at the root of death. Ivory masks on a fence remind one of a multitude of skulls of people who died in a war, or who perished in a village where there was much cursing and accusation of killing. They recall the death of the kindi, which leads to reflections about death itself. For example, a mask attached to a high pole suggests the universality of death: "Death is the rising moon; every clan has seen it." The rare, horned *kayamba* mask with whitened face has a very narrow range of meaning. It represents a clever and shrewd person: "Kayamba, who has come from afar, cannot be bad." When used in pairs (pl. 37), however, *kayamba* masks may portray a confrontation of Kabimbi, the Clever-One, and Kalulungula, the Liar.

Anthropomorphic Figurines. In earlier sections I have repeatedly mentioned the wide diversity of anthropomorphic sculptures made exclusively by Lega artists for the purposes of the bwami association. These figurines, usually carved in wood, ivory, or elephant bone, are infrequently made of *ntutu* (core of a decayed tree), resin, clay (derived from a termite nest), or stone. They are all small; the range of wooden figurines is from three inches to almost seventeen inches in height. The largest ivory figurine is about ten inches tall; the smallest, about two and a half inches. The range into which most ivory figurines fall is three to eight inches. The figurines differ in volume, form, finish, quality of craftsmanship, and degree of patination. They fall into different functional categories, and they are owned and transferred in different ways.

Except for the *katimbitimbi* figurines owned by kanyamwa women as symbols of virile status, all categories of figurines express very much the same types of meanings. The range of meanings expressed by figurines is narrower, more rigid, and more sharply defined than the range of meanings expressed by manufactured or natural objects. Most figurines have only one meaning, condensed in an associated aphorism. The actual use of the figurines, which is also restricted and stereotyped, does, however, add substance to the meaning of the piece. And the configuration or assemblage of objects in which the figurines appear throws considerable light on the interpretations expressed in proverbs. What gives unexpected flexibility and complexity to the symbolism is that any specific meaning condensed in an aphorism may be illustrated by a number of figurines and other objects that are morphologically quite dissimilar. Only a few morphological prototypes are linked with specific meanings. For the rest, the association between a figurine and a specific meaning expressed in an aphorism is purely arbitrary, conventional, and traditional (in the sense that one inherits a piece with a certain meaning attached to it). For a vast number of Lega figurines, therefore, the exact meaning can never be inferred by looking at the formal characteristics. The exegesis must be understood in the context of initiation and transfer of objects.

Lega figurines represent a vast constellation of characters and person-

The Art of Bwami

ages who illustrate and uphold for their owners virtues and nonvirtues.[19] Indeed, many characters and personages are represented only by figurines, but the values and nonvalues the figurines depict can be illustrated in initiatory contexts by natural and manufactured objects as well. Very little is said about figurines as an undifferentiated group. The interpretations are specific; they focus on a single piece (sometimes represented in the dance by several specimens) or on sets of two pieces with different, but complementary, meanings. Occasionally the totality of figurines contributes to illustrating a coherent set of values.

I want to illustrate the *mutulwa* rite from the point of view of the totality of figurines. In this rite a varying number of wooden figurines and possibly of other objects, all contained in the collectively held baskets, are displayed and danced with (pls. 23, 27–33). All the figurines represent characters—some good, some bad—who are thought of as kinsmen or as the subjects of one master of the land. In one instance the row is led by Kagelia, the master of the land, represented by a monkey skull, and he is followed by a number of characters (his kinsmen, such as Sakimatwematwe, Mwelwa, Kwangwakwa, Wayinda, Nsamba, and so on). These kinsmen are represented by anthropomorphic figurines and also by zoomorphic carvings and natural objects (pls. 23, 27). Usually the master of the land, represented by the skull, is said to have died because of some inappropriate action. In one instance, for example, the skull represents a master of the land whose name is Kabamba: "Kabamba, the Protagonist, died very early." The reference is to a pugnacious leader who was the first to engage in violence (a master of the land is never a protagonist in times of trouble) and died. Whatever the reason for his untimely death, the master of the land is revenged by his kinsmen, who are represented by the other objects. Violence leads to more violence. The crowd of characters who follow him is a mixed one. Most of them represent nonvalues, that is, they are nonvirtuous and morally ugly, according to the bwami code. Here and there, among them, is a noble character who falls victim to the internal strife in the group.

Let us further examine the case of Kabamba. He, as the dead master of the land, is followed by a wooden carving representing Mwelwa. Mwel-

---

[19] Delhaise (1909a, pp. 209–210, 231–239) unfortunately categorizes Lega figurines as fetishes, a term misused by so many people that it has come to sound derogatory. He realizes that the objects are used in bwami initiations and that they are preserved by kindi and their initiated wives. Although he fails to cite the precise aphorisms, he does provide some adequate information; yet he does not grasp the full significance of the objects. Merlot (n.d.) is the only unpublished administrative source to provide valuable nomenclature without adequately interpreting the figurines. He lists such characters as Kakulu ka mpinda, Kasungalala, Muzumbi, Mwelwa, Wayinda, and Kimatwemate (Sakimatwematwe). More recently, De Kun (1966) has supplied names and explanations for figurines.

wa is the Glittering-One, successor to Kabamba, who sets out with a crowd of kinsmen to revenge the leader's death. They sing about him: "Who kills is being retaliated; behind Mwelwa there is a large crowd." In this instance, however, because the figurine has only one arm, Mwelwa already carries the stigma of violence. Violence has degraded him from "goodness and beauty," the hallmark of Mwelwa, the Glittering-One, to something laughable: "Mwelwa has one arm; do not laugh."

The crowd of kinsmen is represented in the following way. (Pl. 27 illustrates the figurines that follow Kabamba and Mwelwa; pls. 28–33 show how the preceptors dance with these sculptures.) The first character to come up is Katanda (pls. 27–28, 63), a symbol of ugliness: "I used to like you; fondling kills the good and beautiful ones; it killed Katanda." Basically, the text refers to an adulterous woman, but the term for "fondling" also implies the broader concept of inconstancy. Katanda is, therefore, the person whose bad habits will prevent him from achieving kindi.

The next character is Sakimatwematwe (pls. 27 [third and fifth figurines from left], 30). A multifaced figurine of this type generally represents the aphorism, "Mr. Many-Heads has seen an elephant on the other side of the large river," to illustrate the wisdom, fairness, and quasi omniscience of the kindi. Here additional verbal exegesis and the context indicate that the reference is to backbiting against and gossiping about a high-ranking initiate.

The third character to follow is represented by an ugly-looking pregnant woman figurine (pls. 27 [sixth, seventh, and eighth figurines from left], 29, 31). This character is Wayinda: "Wayinda died because of ritual pollution; the enema is between the buttocks." (Note in pls. 29, 31, and 32 that the preceptors hold a little stick against the genitalia of the figurine; this little stick represents an enema or a penis.) Wayinda symbolizes the Ugly-Woman who commits adultery during pregnancy and brings destruction upon herself, her child, and her husband.

The next character to appear is portrayed by four rudimentarily carved bird's beaks and necks (pl. 27, ninth to twelfth from left): "Kwangwaka, the bird that sings for the termites" (the Lega say that this bird is heard singing about the time that the termites swarm). Kwangwakwa represents a leader remaining alone in his group after his people have dispersed or died. Here the character brings a premonitory message about the fate of the group leader whose people are wiped out by violence and dispersed because of immorality.

The fifth character is represented by two figurines (one large and one small) with no particular identifiable characteristic in form. The figurines are explained as, "The Old-One-of-the-Buttress wakes up [to go] in the very early morning." Buttress here means the giant base of the forest tree which cannot be cut by axes. The Old-One-of-the-Buttress is a man with an implacable heart, a callous man who achieved the initiations but does not want to help others when they are to be initiated. He goes to persuade

The Art of Bwami

other initiates not to participate in the ceremonies. (The expressions "to wake up to go in the very early morning" and "to die in the very early morning" refer to an activity with evil intentions.)

The next character is portrayed by a simple gaffle-shaped stick whose top is slit so as to suggest an open mouth (pl. 27, in foreground on right). The object illustrates the saying: "He who does not put off his quarrelsomeness will quarrel with something that has the mouth widely distended" (in other rites this idea may be rendered by a crocodile figurine with widely distended jaws). The aphorism alludes to the disastrous effects of quarrelsomeness and meddlesomeness.

In initiations the Lega occasionally use figurines recently made by foreign carvers working near mining centers in Legaland. In this rite three such figurines occur (pl. 27, last three on right). One of them, holding a spear, represents Isakasumo, Mr. Spear: "Isakasumo is ready to hurl [the spear]; when he enters into the fight, he no longer knows how the land will perish." That is to say, bad examples and precedents set by leaders must not be followed, and a bad person must never be allowed to start anything of importance. The bust figure of foreign manufacture (pl. 27, third from right) is interpreted by the aphorism, "The Unnamed-Ones are not gnawed [lit., eaten] by hunger; they are the first to call 'Oh! give to eat,'" which stresses the necessity for generosity in giving; foreigners and uninvited persons must receive donations. Lack of generosity in giving is another reason that a group falls apart. The third figure of foreign manufacture (pl. 27, extreme right), representing a standing man, illustrates a similar idea: "I go begging to Ngeze [lit., a rat]; I will not eat [one] ripe banana." Without the accumulation of quantities of food by preliminary work in the hunting grounds and the fields, one cannot satisfy the requirements of generosity.

In the same rite the initiates dance with two more wooden figurines which are displayed in the initiation hut and are, therefore, not illustrated in plate 27. One of them, a large wooden figurine with whitened face (pls. 33, 70), is explained by the aphorism, "Mutu [lit., Hornbill], the One-Who-Is-Overcome-by-Night, wherever she goes I am calling her back." Again the emphasis is on a woman who likes to run away from home and who, in so doing, destroys the unity of the home. The second rudimentary carving represents Kimbayu: "May he not come back [from the journey] he is making, Kimbayu, the One-of-the-Bad-Heart." Kimbayu symbolizes the individual who does not want to listen to the teachings of or advice from others. In a dance concluding the *mutulwa* rite, the preceptor performs again with one of the Wayinda figurines, pressing the object against his stomach and mimicking the winces of a suffering person: "You will be stuck with [lit., sit with] the One-with-Swollen-Belly; you will come to her [death]" (pls. 31, 32). This proverb sounds like a concluding remark, saying that bad dispositions will be punished sooner or later.

The other kindi rites, *bele muno* and *kinsamba*, are marked by a massive use of figurines in ivory or bone, each figurine symbolizing a character that has no direct relationship with the characters represented by the other figurines, except that they all illustrate formulations of virtue and nonvirtue as defined by bwami. Each of the ivory or bone figurines has an aphorism of its own; each has a concrete and restricted meaning. Only rarely do particular usage, mode of presentation, and context add something to the meaning.

Below is a list of some of the recurring principal characters I have seen condensed in these figurines, with a brief indication of the basic meaning of each.

>Beikalantende (pl. 81): One who ponders in silence about many things.
>Kabongelo: One who hears things said behind his back.
>Kabukenge: One with four eyes who sees hidden things.
>Kagalama: Master of the men's house who is the first to perceive things.
>Kakazi ka mungu: Little wife of a senior or a high-ranking initiate who lets herself be seduced by Tongue.
>Kakinga (pl. 77): Young maiden who was beautiful, but adultery cut her an arm (i.e., caused her destruction).
>Kakulu kengila mumpita: The Great-Old-One who becomes part of the brawl rather than being its arbitrator.
>Kakulu kakumba mulomo: The Great-Old-One who bends the lip (i.e., lets his lip hang) because he was scorned.
>Kakulu ka mulubungu: The Great-Old-One who is guardian of the men's house and of the village, although he is blind.
>Kakulu kamwenne ku masengo (pl. 64): The Great-Old-One who is bent under the weight of initiation objects.
>Kakulu ka mpinda: The Great-Old-One who has an implacable heart.
>Kakulu ka Mpito (pl. 69): The Great-Old-One with the black hat of monkey hide, who died a bad death because of his pregnant adulterous wife or because of his lack of circumspection.
>Kakumi: Maiden who is forbidden certain things because of her youth.
>Kalemba: Junior wife of the high-ranking initiate who carries the initiation objects, or the junior wife who is adulterous.
>Kamukazi wazamba: Woman who is poor and hungry and in whose group others are wealthy.
>Kanya: One who stares at the sky (looks upward) is already dead.
>Kasegasega: Steady asker who begs again and again of those who have already given.
>Kasungalala (pl. 66): One who arbitrates a cause that is important.
>Katanda (pl. 63): Seducer and person given to inconstancy.

The Art of Bwami

Katemene: Lazybones who calls people to work in the fields when the season is already too far advanced.

Katetele: One who remains behind in his work and for whom people cultivate in vain.

Katindili (pl. 75): One who lacks strength to persevere in his work.

Katwe (pl. 85): Little head filled with hatred.

Kaungukana: Junior initiate whose initiated wife was taken away from him during the initiation.

Keida mazi: One who lacks water and places his lips near the puddle.

Keitula wa Yimbo (pl. 81): Strong one (lit., one who forges himself), the son of the good singer.

Kilinga: Kilinga (lit., a bird) who inflates his chest; one who interferes too much in other people's business and who will soon find death.

Kimbayu: One with the dead heart.

Kitende (lit., frog): Frog (initiate) who does not play with children and juniors.

Kuboko kumozi: One who lost an arm because of meddlesomeness.

Mpelempele: Arrogant person who attempts to throw the child of his mother into poverty.

Mpimbi (lit., the latch): One who reveals to those on the outside the things from the inside.

Mukobania (pl. 23, second from right): Divider who brings together people who hate each other.

Mulima (pls. 72, 76): Bat who is hanging with his head downward because of the bad word the sun told him.

Mungu: The Great-One who has an evil tongue and who is, therefore, being accused of sorcery.

Mutu Nyabeidilwa (pl. 70): One who is overcome by night because she spends too much time elsewhere.

Muzumbi (lit., the dead one): One who has seen the depth of the initiations.

Mwami ntanagamboe: Initiate who knows about all the gossip behind his back.

Mwami we idungu: Initiate who comes from far away and who is as well received as those from nearby.

Mwelwa: The Glittering-One who has many kinsmen behind him.

Nawasakwa nyona (pls. 73, 82): One with signs of beauty engraved on his/her back is no longer as he/she used to be.

Ndumbe (pl. 71): Older initiate who remains with younger men has no force left in him and thinks that the others will kill him ("May I die today; may the little neck be cut by a claw").

Nkumba (pl. 72): "The one of the *nkumba* headdress," that is, the woman of kanyamwa grade.

Nyababa: The Old-One who keeps his ears open and does not sleep even if he seems to.

Nyabilamba: Woman who cooks well.

Nyabilimbio: Mrs. Thighs, whom father married; father died because of her running around; she also died "in the place where she had gone."

Nyabisabusabu: One who wears many beaded necklaces around his neck.

Nyabwindibwindi: One who died in the river.

Nyakabumba: A bent (or stupid) woman.

Nyanjinjinji: Mrs. Black, the Old-One who is black but is not a sorcerer.

Nyantuli: Mrs. High-Buttocks, who craves for preferred status, saying to the senior wife that her buttocks are flat because of work.

Nyatwiso: Mrs. Twinkle-Eyes, who destroys herself in joy and interference.

Sakakuliso: One who has gotten something in his eye; the person of bad intentions.

Sakimatwematwe (pls. 74, 86): Mr. Many-Heads, who has seen an elephant on the other side of the large river.

Sawamazembe: One with plaited hair (as women have) who does not listen well.

Walemba: One who was killed, but a crowd follows in his tracks.

Wankenge (pl. 87): The Beautiful-One who has many kinsmen following him.

Wansongo wa liso limozi: Mr. One-Eye who does not see well, or "I thought that my father was asleep, and lo! he looked at me with one eye."

Wayinda (pls. 67, 68): Pregnant adulteress who destroys herself and others because of ritual pollution.

Of all these meanings only a few, as I have earlier indicated, are associated with forms that can easily be recognized. The forms are particularly well defined and stereotyped for example, in Sakimatwematwe, a multifaced or multiheaded figurine (worked out in many ways), or Wayinda, an ugly-looking female figurine with distended belly. Most frequently, however, the linkage between figurine and meaning is based on a purely conventional, traditional, and arbitrary association, permitting no speculation about meaning. Only the knowledge gathered from owners of the object gives a clue to understanding it. Even when there is a clear correspondence between form and meaning, unexpected elaborations of meaning are possible.

Let us take as an example the multifaced or multiheaded figurine generally known as Sakimatwematwe, Mr. Many-Heads, who "has seen an elephant on the other side of the large river." This aphorism is brought

The Art of Bwami

to bear on the wisdom, fairness, and omniscience of the initiate. But the Sakimatwematwe figurine may also mean that one should not contradict a kindi or talk behind his back. I have seen, moreover, the classic multifaced or multiheaded figurine being used with five additional meanings usually associated with other figurines. In one instance, the double-headed figurine was a symbol of Mukobania, the Divider. In another, a four-faced figurine represented Kimbayu with the dead heart. In a third, a two-faced figurine represented Kyegelela: "He Who-Descends-with-the-River died; he has not seen the man to save him." This aphorism refers to the necessity for a candidate to find a tutor, because without a tutor there can be no initiation. The object seems to underscore the bond between candidate and tutor. In one instance a figurine representing a male and a female body joined together back to back symbolized Kabukenge, the one with four eyes who has seen hidden things. Here there is a direct reference to the close bond between the kindi and the kanyamwa. Emphasis may also be placed on another aspect of the figurine, such as the dotted motif around the faces (pl. 73). On the other hand, the idea of Sakimatwematwe is almost never expressed by any object other than the multifaced or multiheaded figurine. In only one instance did I hear of this idea being conveyed by two wooden masks held together.

Some non-Lega carvings are used in bwami initiations. I have seen them in almost all areas when a kindi rite demanded a massive display of sculptures. The objects were mostly human figurines, but sometimes animal representations (e.g., an elephant or bird figure) were also used. These carvings, made of mahogany, were imported from the northeastern Congo or from areas near the Kisangani-Banalia-Buta-Paulis axis, or were locally made by carvers from the same areas. They had nothing to do with traditional carvings from the Zande, Mangbetu, and Bwa regions, but had been produced for the European market.

The Lega, identifying these sculptures as the work of the Bausa, are attracted by their smoothness and gloss and by such standard subjects as a woman carrying a bowl, a spear holder, a drummer, a bust, a person sitting on a chair. Because of their flexible and easygoing symbolism, the Lega have no difficulty in adapting these objects to interpretations of their moral code. For example, the drummer figure, which is unknown in the traditional Lega patrimony, is interpreted in three different ways: "Drummer, I will not teach you the drum; in the way you love it, you will drum," is addressed to the *kakusa* tutor who knows what to do; "The fool, the beater of the drum, drums for me the way I want it," expresses joy because no mistakes were made during the initiations; "The Great-Old-One, who beats the drum for me, covers the arms," criticizes the person who used to give to his tutor but fails to do so now that he is up for kindi.

Animal Figurines. Animal figurines made of wood, ivory, or bone fall into two basic categories: generalized animal forms (pls. 25, 88, 92) which are known as *mugugundu,* and the more realistic-looking animal forms (pls. 90, 91, 93, 94) which do not come under a single designation. The generalized animal forms with horns (pl. 89) or with animal exuviae sufficient to make them recognizable, or with carved beaks (pl. 27, ninth to twelfth figures from left), are also in the latter category.

During the lutumbo lwa yananio initiations the wooden *mugugundu* animals always occur in groups; I have seen the ivory *mugugundu* in isolated usage only. *Mugugundu* figurines are found in a very few ritual communities as a substitute for, or in addition to, *kalimbangoma* figurines. As a group, *mugugundu* animals have no specific name. In areas where they are substitutes for small wooden figurines, the rite does not even refer to animals. Rather, the focus is on the initiation object as a legacy of the wisdom of one's father and as a symbol of continuity. Any *mugugundu* animal, however, may also be used separately with a specific meaning. Movements made with animal figurines, aphorisms, the context of the rites, and on occasion some other identifying object become the decisive factors.

When a generalized animal figurine stands for a dog, the generic name *mugugundu* under which the figurine is classified may become the name of the dog: "My dog Mugugundu, chasing animals has exhausted [lit., finished] our legs" (no initiation is possible without good understanding with the tutor). Sometimes the transition to dog is facilitated by hanging a large wooden dog bell around the neck of the figurine or by opposing the figurine to a horned *lungaga* antelope figurine. In one rite the preceptor runs about with the *mugugundu* figurine, shaking a dog bell and singing: "Mugugundu, rattle your bell; the chaser [hunter] is always chasing" (it is impossible to surpass someone who is bigger than you are). In another rite, similar action is accompanied by the aphorism, "Little white dog, spotted dog, circles the tail around me," which refers to the genuine youth who follows the council of seniors.

In still another rite the action concentrates on an animal figurine identified as *kafyondo* (a very good hunting dog) and a porcupine quill. The quill, representing a porcupine, is placed against the roof of the initiation house, while the animal figurine is moved around on the ground: "Porcupine climbs up with shrewdness," and "Call the dog; porcupine climbs up with shrewdness." In this scene the porcupine represents an initiate with bad intentions who wants to refuse induction to a kinsman; the dog symbolizes the maternal uncles who circumvent the initiate and insist that their nephew be initiated. The animal figurine is then moved over the legs, the body, and the head of the candidate to the roof where the porcupine is hidden: "Etabinge [Bad Chaser] brings forth Wazanza [Good Chaser]."

Generalized animal figurines sometimes represent a *lungaga* antelope, which is also characterized by a generalized figurine with small horns (pl.

89). I know of four aphorisms that go with this animal figurine. One stresses the fact that one who is a talker and has an evil tongue will be refused initiation even though he is otherwise qualified: "What has horns is being hooked where there is no vine [trap]." Two other texts suggest that one may sometimes succeed in fooling a big person but will finally be trapped by a smaller person: "Lungaga of the meandering river, in the small hunting nets, in them you will die," and "Lungaga of close to the village, it is in the forest between two fields that you will die." A fourth aphorism warns women going to the initiations not to fool around with other men: "Youthful Lungaga does not step on a tree [lying] on the trail."

A generalized animal figurine (*mugugundu*) may also be identified as a chameleon (*mugugu*). In one instance little red seeds were glued onto the back of the figurine. Mugugu symbolizes the powerful word of the old initiate: "Mugugu has no cheeks; [however,] his voice goes far," and "You scorn Chameleon's body; you do not scorn his voice." The *mugugu* figurine also symbolizes the concept of slowness, which is a good quality when it implies circumspection: "Kakungukia [another name for chameleon] has finished the distances slowly, slowly." Slowness is evil when it is a sign of weakness, lack of initiative, and laziness: "Mugugu, I sing during the rainy season; I have no hornbill knife."

The larger, more massive, and rudimentarily carved generalized animal figurine in wood also represents the forest crocodile (*Osteolaemus*) or the giant pangolin (*Manis gigantea*). If the forest crocodile is being depicted, the figurine may have one head on each side of its body, waffle-shaped designs on its back, and white coloring on its heads. It is called *mukondekonde*, the name for the forest crocodile. Frequently it is replaced by the real skull of the animal. Mukondekonde is celebrated and interpreted in many aphorisms. "Mukondekonde does not eat the catfish that are seated in their holes" warns a junior not to seduce the wife of his senior when the senior leaves her in his custody. "Mukondekonde is not a Great-Old-One; the scales have given him greatness" stresses the fact that a youthful person may be able to stand up because of his powerful words. "Mukondekonde, the animal that resembles a fallen tree," criticizes one who has a beautiful body but an evil mind. "Mukondekonde, the child that I bring forth laughs at my scales," castigates a child who lacks respect and piety. "Mukondekonde does not glide forward to where there is no pool" advises the candidate to address himself to a person of status in order to be initiated. Sometimes the symbolism abruptly shifts from *mukondekonde*, the forest crocodile, to *mumbilumbilu*, the giant forest otter, "the animal that drinks water."

A generalized wooden animal figurine representing the giant pangolin may have real pangolin scales attached to it. The figurine may be replaced by the stuffed, scaly body of *kabanga*, the smaller tree-dwelling pangolin (*Manis tricuspis*). The symbolism centered on the pangolin is most often conveyed, however, by the real scales, the claws, or the scaly tail end portion of the animal itself. The pangolin, referred to as *ikaga* (real name for the giant pangolin) or *kilinkumbi* (drum name for the giant pangolin), is associated with a wide variety of aphorisms, a sample of which follows. "Pangolin has taught the people who are beaten by rain" celebrates the pangolin as a culture hero. The initiates pretend that the phrynium leaves covering their roofs are arranged in the same manner as the scales on the pangolin, and that they learned this technique from the pangolin. "Kilinkumbi is full of joy because of the greatness of which he partakes" criticizes a junior initiate who would look down on a kindi. "The tongue of the pangolin surpasses in length the *sanda* snake" stresses the endlessness of the initiations. "Ikaga Kabulubuta [who rolls himself up in anger], the one who finishes the initiations scorns him," places emphasis on the fact that a high-ranking initiate is allowed to demand services from the giant, the strong fellow, who is at a lower grade level. "Pangolin, bad, bad animal that finishes the *milunda* [animals paid as a fine]," explains that anyone who finds a dead pangolin and hides it away for himself or his kinsmen will be heavily fined and punished. The pangolin belongs to bwami and it must be ritually distributed by its members to a large group of participants.

Among the realistically carved animals, those most frequently represented are the snake (pl. 94), the frog, a bird's neck, the centipede, the crocodile (pl. 90), and the elephant. Some of these sculptures are fashioned of wood, ivory, or bone. Others, like the frog and the centipede, seem to occur in wood only. In extremely rare instances, the rudimentary elephant, bird, giant snail, and chameleon figurines are made of *ntutu*. Realistically carved representations of the pangolin (pl. 91) or of the aardvark (pl. 93) are infrequent. In all circumstances the number of explanations given for each type of figurine is limited.

The snake figurine most often represents the deadly *ngimbi* serpent. The aphorism, "The little child plays in the wading place; *ngimbi* is death," warns individuals not to consider initiaton objects as harmless and meaningless playthings. In the 1950's it was often quoted to stigmatize Lega individuals who rejected bwami or thought they could profane it. "I have been bitten by *ngimbi*; therefore I shall not die because of a *mulinde* snake," is the confident exclamation of the initiate who has successfully passed through yananio and is not afraid to seek advancement to kindi. The snake figurine may be an unnamed serpent: "Snake has bitten me at night; I do not know its name." In this aphorism a candidate who is ready with the needed goods expresses astonishment that the initiates do not want to begin the proceedings. Finally, the snake figurine may personify somebody, known under the name of the *igilima* snake, who is lucky enough to go through high-level initiations while his father is still alive: "Igilima, child of Ikuka, in the fallen tree, therein it is that she [the snake] has built

The Art of Bwami

the house." Again it must be stressed that the forms are deceptive. Some figurines that morphologically seem to have a snakelike body are not representations of snakes. They are suspended from the roof of the initiation house by a raffia fiber to illustrate this aphorism: "Bat hangs the head downward, because of the bad word spoken to him by Sun" (pl. 76).

Frog figurines in wood represent Kitende (general name for frog) and Isilia or Nyangulanga (frog species): "Kitende sees the Stupid-One; at the end he goes in the river," informs the new initiate not to go to a kindi initiation unless he is called; "Isilia, Great-Old-One, I shall look at the ones in the river," instructs the new kindi to look carefully and to avoid difficulties; "Nyangulanga does not experience the swelling on account of which Nyangunu has died" says that when an experienced senior tutor in the lineage dies without replacement, there is little hope that one will rise further.

The wooden neck-beak figurines of birds represent Kakulikuli (a species of bird; the Tattler) or Kwangwakwa (a species of bird). Kakulikuli, most often symbolized by his real beak, is "the bird that sings for the termites" and "the bird that likes to talk much." In the former aphorism the bird represents the senior of the lineage; in the latter it symbolizes the candidate who speaks with too much arrogance. As "Kwangwakwa, the bird that sings for the termites," the carving depicts the master of the land, or the most senior kindi in the group. In a rare instance the bird *nyandende* (a kind of heron) is represented in an ivory figurine as a scandalmonger: "Nyandende, the tongue surpasses the lips [the beak]."

The wooden figurine of a centipede (*nyongolo*) is interpreted as, "Centipede, if you want to flee the fire, flee the sound [of iron axes] in the new field," to encourage a person seeking kindi to follow the advice of his colleagues.

The crocodile figurine, which sometimes consists only of an open crocodile mouth and a piece of the body, warns against the dangers of constant arguing: "Who does not stop quarreling will quarrel with one who has the mouth wide open."

A rudimentary elephant figurine made of *ntutu*, in the secret *kasisi* rite, illustrates the principle that the master of the land is not like any other person: "The pregnancy of the elephant is unlike that of any other animal." Some more realistic elephant figurines in ivory represent the strong, solitary elephant *kabukutu*: "Kabukutu, strong elephant, may he flatten the trees." This aphorism illustrates a father asking his son to do work that is worthy of a man.

It is hardly necessary to point out that a very large number of texts deal with personified animal characters. Much of the iconic documentation that accompanies these texts consists of animal exuviae (skulls, hides, beaks, scales, claws, jaws, teeth or fangs, tusks, etc.). Among the most important and the most widely used items in this category are skulls of chimpanzee, *kagelia* monkey, and forest crocodile; hides of genet, wildcat, and some snakes; beaks of the hornbill and *kakulikuli*; scales of pangolin; claws of pangolin and aardvark; teeth of dendrohyrax and leopard; jaws of some species of fish; fangs of some species of snake; tusks of elephant and warthog; quills of porcupine; pincers of crabs; hoofs of dwarf antelope; horns of billy goat and *ntundu* antelope; shells of giant snails and mussels; and carapaces of turtles. Some of these exuviae are made into assemblages by means of glue. In one ritual community all animal figurines were replaced by such assemblages, including claws of leopard, teeth of dendrohyrax, and porcupine quills fixed together with glue, or fangs of the *mpoma* snake put together with glue.

Spoons (pls. 95–97). Spoons in ivory or bone carry a limited number of meanings. In some rites the masked preceptors feed themselves, or are fed symbolically, with the spoons to designate that old initiates like to eat heartily but consume only soft and choice foods: "Old-Turtle eats pounded bananas," and "The person who eats much, you will see how he eats the pounded bananas." In reenactments of the administration of the *kabi* poison ordeal, the spoon is placed in the mouth of the accused: "They place a little stick in the mouth; she was not unjustly charged." In several rites spoons are used as if they were knives or other weapons in an imaginary monkey hunt, or in the symbolic skinning of an elephant, or to scrape away the bark of the *kabi* tree; but mainly they seem to stress the nonviolent activities of initiates. The spoon is also a symbol of continuity and perpetuity: "Everything rots; the limb (bone) of the arms does not rot," and "I came to the place where an elephant rotted; there is nothing else but large ribs and femurs." Striking the back of the spoon, the preceptors identify its flatness with "The flat buttocks of the elephant [which] have no regard for other people's things," to criticize an adulterous son or a thief who does not want to listen. In the most frequently quoted aphorism, the spoon is personified as Kalukili to symbolize a woman who first gave a man joy and friendship but now rejects and despises him: "Kalukili, you used to give me the lap; now you give me the wickerwork [chest] of ribs."

The Artist

My information on Lega artists is tenuous, and understandably so. As I have explained, by the time of my research the bwami association and its members had been misunderstood, harassed, and persecuted for at least two-thirds of a century. The great artists of the Lega tradition—Lusungu, Kalimu, Kayokela, Lukelwa, Kilunga, Itongwa, and many others whose names are not even remembered—were dead long before the period of my research in Legaland, but the sons and grandsons of these men were still alive. Even though these descendants more or less secretly continued the bwami initiations, activities, and ideals, they were unable to maintain

The Art of Bwami

and perpetuate the superb artistry of their fathers and grandfathers. Constant action against bwami by the administration, the judiciary, the police, and the missionaries; strict legislation concerning the ownership and use of ivory; compulsory agricultural activity; widespread suspicion of bwami initiates—these were hardly conducive to continued artistic achievement (Biebuyck, 1967). The minds and the energies of the people were focused on other occupations. The uncertainty of the outcome of initiations, and the long periods of ritual inactivity brought on by foreign pressures, caused the demands for artworks to become more and more intermittent. Of course such demands had never been overwhelming, because artworks are carefully kept and transmitted, they are owned only by the highest-ranking initiates and are massively used only in the highest-level initiations, and there are limitations on the number of objects one person may own. Moreover, although their importance is great, artworks are very easily replaced by other objects in Lega initiations. At any given period of time, therefore, the number of artists at work in Legaland probably was not very large.

In times of insecurity and upheaval the chances for a smooth transfer of technical skills are diminished. Since these skills are learned and transmitted through the personal interaction of two close kinsmen, the slightest disturbance in the family structure causes difficulties so serious that techniques are transmitted only in part, or not at all. For example, the artist or the apprentice may be jailed or exiled; the apprentice may leave the village to seek work in a mining center; evangelization or new labor demands may lead to cleavage in the group. So by the time I arrived in Legaland artistic activity had completely ceased. It was impossible to watch carvers in action, to observe their working methods, or to discuss with them their standards and judgments. Since initiates who use artworks are obviously uninterested in the artists who have created them, there was no living tradition of any significance about the sculptors and no special reference to them in the context of the initiations.

Valid and fascinating information about the artists—his methods of working, his criteria, his traditions, his judgments—about the creative process, and about the actual learning of the craft has been irretrievably lost. Surely the sculptors must have had a range of professional knowledge which is neither reflected in the initiations nor known to the initiates; how extensive or well formulated this knowledge was is a mystery to me.

In this section, therefore, I can only tie together bits and pieces of scattered information. As I have already indicated, there probably were few sculptors among the Lega. The sculptors were, it is said, either members of the bwami association or noninitiates. Because of the enormous attraction of bwami, and because of its large membership, it seems quite likely that most carvers were members of the association, though not necessarily high-ranking members. The few artists of the past whose names I could discover were all incumbents of the higher grades (ngandu, yananio, kindi). It is perfectly possible that these persons were remembered primarily because of their high status in bwami, rather than because of their artistry. Initiates in every lineage show a remarkable knowledge of the respective grade levels occupied by six or more generations of their dead predecessors.

In any event, the artist would not know the precise meaning, usage, and function of his own creations unless he was an initiate at one of the higher levels, where such knowledge is preserved and cultivated. Moreover, the direct relationship between form and meaning is tenuous, except for the few prototypes such as Mr. Many-Heads (or Faces), Pregnant-Adulteress, One-Arm, and so on. The artist worked when an object was commissioned, carving his figures very much in the tradition of his local group. When he was commissioned to produce a specific object it was customary for the patron to provide at least the ivory of which the piece was to be made. The sculptor was rewarded with a *lukambu* gift of shell money and a porcupine.

According to Delhaise (1909a, p. 138), blacksmiths were few in number and produced no artworks. Yet I was told that sculptors were sometimes blacksmiths, but not always. In a seldom used aphorism the blacksmith is referred to as "the maker [lit., who fits together] who has carved the *malimu*." *Malimu* is an infrequently used term for mask. Whether or not blacksmiths carved only masks is totally uncertain.

It has also been pointed out by Delhaise (*ibid.*, p. 275), that the sculptor occupies no special social status. This neglect is not surprising, since his art is no more important than that of the gifted preceptor, dancer, drummer, orator, singer, tutor, or maker of insignia and dance paraphernalia. Bwami and kinship confer status on people. A person is remembered as a kindi; his prestige and fame as a kindi are enhanced if he is also known as a great tutor who, through wisdom and honesty, helped many others to achieve high rank.

The sculptor is known as *mubazi wa nkondo*, the carver of the adze, and as *mulonga*, the craftsman who fits things together. I have also heard him mentioned as *mukulumizi* (an unexplained term that may mean "the Great-One of the figurines"). The sculptor had simple tools: the ax, the adze, the knife, a small rod to drill holes, a *kapiya* (*kabiga*) or a kind of little caliper with which the circle-dot designs (*bitondi*) are made, a needle-like object to do the stippling and dotting (*kyembe*), and *lukenga* leaves for sandpaper.

The materials in which the artist worked were prescribed. Elephant ivory (sometimes it had to be from the small tusk of a female [*kikalasa*]), bone (mostly derived from the rotula, foot, or ribs of the elephant), and wood (*Allstonia* and parasol wood were preferred, but a variety of other species could be used as well) were the primary media. Other materials,

The Art of Bwami

like copal resin, *ntutu*, stone, clay, elephant leather, and hippopotamus tusk, were also used; they were usually prescribed for objects used in secret rites such as *kasisi*. Artists worked in different media, apparently with no difficulty since no major change of technique accompanied a shift from ivory to wood in making masks. Decorative designs were limited to the circle-dot, the dot and stipple, the incised striations, and the chevron.

Limitations on size and volume were dictated partly by the nature of the material (when the artist worked in ivory or bone) and partly by the nature and the destiny of the piece. The work of art is hidden, is kept in baskets and shoulder bags, and is carried over long distances. There were also unformulated conceptions about optimal size. The key measurements in Lega, as revealed by the size of the strings of shell money, are the length of the middle finger (*kanue*), the length from the tip of the middle finger to the middle of the palm (*ibungakwanga*, where snuff is rubbed to be taken in), the length from the tip of the middle finger to the base of the hand (*magombelo*), and the length from the tip of the middle finger to the fold of the arm (*kilunga*), but there are also some intermediary measures (Biebuyck, 1953a). The overwhelming majority of Lega figurines, indeed also of masks, animal figurines, and spoons, fall within the range of these measurements, with only slight variations.

The colors available to the artist were limited: white clay, red camwood powder or red stone, and black made from charcoal of the parasol tree or sap of the *kalisa* and *ikamba* vines. The fine gloss and patination of ivory pieces, and of some wooden pieces as well, was produced by repeated oiling processes which accompanied the rites and extended over generations. These extraordinary patinations, ranging from orange red to pale yellow and honey, and from brownish red to purplish black, give a distinctive and unparalleled quality to Lega works of art. But they are the work of the users, not of the artists. The artwork is unfinished and socially meaningless when it leaves the artist's atelier. Consecration through use makes it into a vitally meaningful object.

Since artworks were to be neither seen nor handled by children and noninitiates, artists worked in semisecrecy. Much of their work was done away from the main village in small hamlets inhabited by certain officeholders in bwami, such as the holders of *lutala* and *kansilembo*. The *kazombolo*, who were servants and messengers of high-ranking initiates, played the role of guardian to keep unqualified persons away. The strict separation of art objects and noninitiates is also marked by the fact that the secret mirliton, called *kingili* in this instance, sings during the oiling of the objects prior to the rite. It is unclear whether Lega carvers worked in isolation or in small groups and to what extent there were schools of artists which left an imprint on the local style and on the iconography.

Within the Lega style of art, which overlaps into neighboring areas, there is much more stylistic variation than is generally thought, particularly in the anthropomorphic figurines. Some have a spherical shape, somewhat reminiscent of Luba work, while others have the flatter and more angular traits that are found in the northeastern Congo. The form of the faces ranges from almost circular to oval, trapezoid, and heart-shaped. The eyes are shown in a wide variety of ways: some are in the form of cowrie shells with narrow slits, occasionally combined with a round hole to indicate the pupil; some are in the shape of coffee beans; some are solid eyes carved in relief, or in a round or square elongated form, with or without a hole; some are simply indicated by a circle-dot design or by a deep notch. Similar variations occur in other morphological details.

Because objects travel in the process of transfers, and also because individuals, families, and lineage groups settle away from their areas of origin with cognates, affines, and very distant affines, it is hazardous, in the absence of active groups of artists, to link any one stylistic or morphological feature to a specific group of people or a specific subarea. It is, however, perfectly legitimate to think that in different ritual communities, all of which cultivate local variations, certain local ways of doing things prevailed.

That the individual artist enjoyed a wide freedom of choice in his sculpturing is evidenced, for example, in the many ways that the basic concept of multiheadedness is rendered in Lega art (see also De Kun, 1966). Moreover, his creative freedom was enhanced by the flexible arrangements and adjustments the initiates make in the interpretation and use of objects. Most of the basic characters mentioned earlier are represented by sculptures that look very different from one another. The initiates appreciate expressions of individuality and originality, and readily accommodate themselves to what is available for use in the bwami rites.

Postscript

In this book I have attempted to put into perspective the use, function, and meaning of the art of a single African people. In order to do so I have placed Lega art in its social, ideological, and ritual context. I have stressed its interrelationship with oral literature, with nonartistic objects, and with patterns of action; I have emphasized the significance of configurations of objects. Because Lega culture is largely undocumented in published sources, I have examined, in some depth, select aspects of it to place the bwami association, the art-using body in Lega society, in its proper context. The immense complexity of the bwami association has made it imperative for me to examine extensively the fundamental aspects of its organization, structure, and ideology.

The social framework within which Lega art objects play so important a role is intricate and difficult to study. An atmosphere of semisecrecy, of closedness, surrounds the use, manipulation, and interpretation of artworks. Delhaise, a sympathetic and apparently well-accepted observer of the Lega scene, makes few comments on bwami and art because he was allowed to witness only superficial and piecemeal dramatic actions of the kindi in the village of Kurulu (1909a, pp. 228, 231–239). Art forms a hidden dimension in Lega society. Carefully concealed, it is almost invisible. Artworks appear only on select occasions as part of an esoteric and closed set of initiations. Lega art is not an art of display and ostentation. Neither is it an art destined to inspire awe and terror, or an art that addresses itself to gods and other hidden forces. It is primarily an art that inspires and underlies a humanistic view of man, an art that is reflective of what Mauss called "la tonalité morale d'une société." As I have tried to show, art performs many functions and has many meanings for Lega initiates. It cannot be understood unless it is examined in a broad and flexible approach from many points of view and at many levels of inquiry.

Many authors have provided lavish illustrations of Lega art (see second section of bibliography). Experts on African art have rightly praised the diversity, simplicity, and compactness of Lega art forms, the quality and variety of the patinations, the inventiveness in the representation of human forms, and the sensitivity of feeling. They have, with varying results, attempted to isolate the essential characteristics of form and style; they have hesitantly tried to situate Lega art on the stylistic map of the Congo as transitional between northeastern styles (Zande, Mangbetu, Bwa, etc.) and the styles of the Katanga and the northeastern Kasai provinces. Many writers have been intrigued by the concave and heart-shaped face styles found in a wide array of art-producing ethnic groups, stretching from the Fang, Kuta, and Kwele through the northern Congo to the Mitoko, Mbole, and Lega.

Most of this pioneering work remains at a low level of sophistication and is far from being insightful. A great deal of serious and detailed work remains to be done in the world's collections on the morphology and the style of eastern Congo sculptures. New insight into stylistic patterns and developments can be gained from careful scrutiny of the lesser-known sculptures of such peoples as Pere, Komo, Yela, Mbole, Lengola, Mitoko, Nyanga, Tembo, Kanu, Songola, Tetela, Boyo, Zimba, Bangubangu, Tumbwe, Holoholo, Nyindu, and Bembe, and of the northern riverains on the western shore of Lake Tanganyika (such as Ciba and Homa). It is with these peoples that the Lega share numerous linguistic, cultural, ideological, and artistic bonds.

The degree to which these different groups possess common cultural elements is, of course, variable. The commonality is not necessarily rooted in common origin; it is also due to gradual overlapping among groups, to the influence of common substrata, to local migration and territorial shifts, to relationships of contact, and to the diffusion of cultural elements. The Boyo and the riverains shade into the Bembe; the Bembe, Zimba, and Bangubangu into the Lega; the Lega into the Songola, Komo, and Nyanga; the Komo and Nyanga into the Pere, and so on. Segments of clans and lineages that are centered in the Lega are also found among Bembe, Songola, Zimba, Bangubangu, Nyindu, Komo, Kanu, and even Nyanga, and vice versa. Many linkages among groups and individuals cross tribal lines. Correspondingly, ideas, material objects, and institutions are dispersed over wide areas. Associations similar to bwami are common among the groups mentioned, and an actual transfer of certain ritual complexes is acknowledged. Tribal boundaries are not so rigid and clear-cut as they appear to be on Western maps. Any serious stylistic and morphological study must take these factors into account, as Olbrechts (1946) anticipated when he referred to the gradual transition from Zimba work to Lega work or to Bembe work.

The origins and the age of Lega art remain a mystery. One is inclined to think that the art of wood carving is older than sculpture in ivory and bone. I am not saying that wooden objects in art collections are older than ivory and bone objects, but that the tradition of wood sculpture is older. Ivory and bone carvings are invariably connected with the highest grade of bwami, occurring only occasionally in scattered rites of the lower grades. There is a tradition in many ritual communities about the gradual growth of the bwami hierarchy, including the introduction of kindi and the "mother" carvings in ivory. There is also a firm tradition that the Lega knew bwami before they were chased southeastward from the Congo River to their present habitat. In the subsequent dispersal, according to some traditions, only the Babongolo groups managed to maintain kindi. Kindi later spread from the Babongolo to other groups, and the process was concretized in the transfer of the "mother" statues.

These traditions have special significance for the understanding of the "transitional" character that many observers have found in Lega art. We may assume that the Lega had bwami at the time of their immigration, and that whatever art forms they then possessed were of the northern type. After arriving in Legaland, some groups of Lega and their Bembe offshoots were exposed to new traditions from local groups and from their immediate southern neighbors. The Babongolo, in particular, who are represented in several parts of southern Legaland, were subject to Zimba and Bangubangu influences. The Bembe were in direct contact with the traditions of the Boyo and of the groups established along Lake Tanganyika, particularly Homa, Ciba, and Holoholo. The interaction was sometimes very marked, since fragments of these groups were established within the boundaries occupied by the Bembe and southern Lega groups.

There are also indications of small remnant groups of matrilineal Luba stock in parts of southern Legaland. The round and fuller forms that are characteristic of some carvings, and the more or less lozenge-shaped faces found on some figurines, are certainly the result of these influences. It must be remembered that in the Itombwe region, on the loosely drawn boundaries separating Lega, Nyindu, and Bembe, several bwami traditions converged, one of which seems to have had very ancient roots in the entire area now inhabited by Bembe, Nyindu, and eastern Lega. It is also likely that the monopolistic tendencies of bwami permitted the welding together of distinct art traditions in the same way that they favored the fusion of different rites.

The study of uses, functions, and meanings of Lega art unearths many new and unexpected facts and issues concerning the cultural significance of African art. The multiplicity of usages, the plurality of functions, and the multivalence of meanings for any single artwork are truly astonishing. A multifaceted analysis places art objects in their sociocultural context of ritual performance, song, dance, dramatic action, and configuration.

The misinterpretations and misrepresentations to which African works of art are subjected when they are examined out of the cultural matrix are clearly illustrated by the Lega situation. Incredible speculations about Lega art objects, based on the scanty information provided by Delhaise and on other carelessly gathered data, have been repeated ad nauseam. It is not important to single out any particular sources of misrepresentation for criticism, for they all suffer from the same inadequacy of the raw materials. It should be pointed out, however, that speculation about African artworks has been encouraged by the simplistic conceptions that have developed over the years. These works of art cannot be reduced to simple stereotypes based on usage and function, nor can they be rigidly defined in terms of function and meaning. They cannot be studied outside their cultural matrix. The dimensions of meaning, transcending narrowly defined religious categories, cover all aspects of cultural activity. For example, Lega artworks are used, in the context of initiation and learning, as visual aids and mnemotechnical devices in teaching, as condensations of complex ideas, as representations of characters, and as devices to enhance the dramatic efficacy of the rites. By the manner in which these works of art are owned and transferred, groups and individuals of different rank manifest their unity, solidarity, continuity, or opposition.

Little attention has been given in the study of African art to these other dimensions. There are many indications, however, that where artworks are connected with initiations of various types (boys' and girls' initiations; men's and women's associations), complex systems of learning about activities, moral and philosophical principles, myths, and history prevail. In such contexts the artworks are not simply used for the external purposes of dance, social control, and spirit control; they serve as devices of learning and as symbols of knowledge.

The usages, functions, and meanings of Lega artworks could fruitfully be compared with the initiation systems of East, Central, and South African populations, for which well-documented data are available. The close association and interchangeability of art objects, natural objects, and manufactured items are striking features of Lega initiations, but they are not surprising for an African people living in close communion with the environment. Further study is required for full understanding of relationships and of patterns of permutability.

The exceptional placidity and serenity of Lega art are in conformity with the extraordinary loftiness of Lega thought. Certain pieces that deviate from the Lega canon of goodness and beauty are deliberately made so as to express ugliness and to reaffirm through negative contrast the high-flying aspirations of bwami initiates. The forms are as inscrutable and mysterious as the initiations themselves, but learning through initation permits one to "climb the slopes of the sky" and transforms Ngonze (the shoulder bag; i.e., the One-without-a-Heart) into Katima (the One-with-a-Heart).

Appendixes

APPENDIX I

Lineages of Banasalu Clan

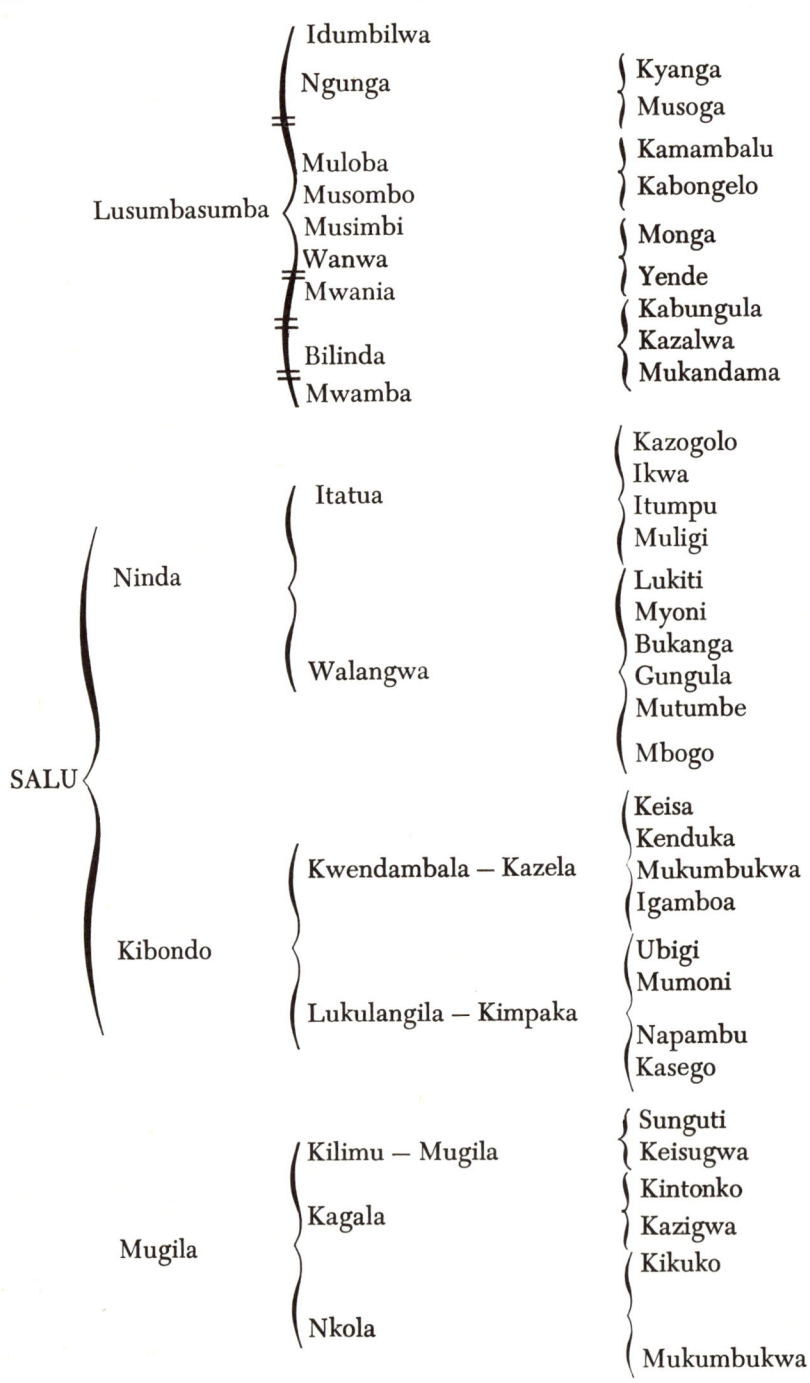

SALU
- Lusumbasumba
  - Idumbilwa
  - Ngunga
    - Kyanga
    - Musoga
  - Muloba
  - Musombo
    - Kamambalu
    - Kabongelo
  - Musimbi
  - Wanwa
    - Monga
  - Mwania
    - Yende
    - Kabungula
    - Kazalwa
    - Mukandama
  - Bilinda
  - Mwamba
- Ninda
  - Itatua
    - Kazogolo
    - Ikwa
    - Itumpu
    - Muligi
  - Walangwa
    - Lukiti
    - Myoni
    - Bukanga
    - Gungula
    - Mutumbe
    - Mbogo
- Kibondo
  - Kwendambala — Kazela
    - Keisa
    - Kenduka
    - Mukumbukwa
    - Igamboa
  - Lukulangila — Kimpaka
    - Ubigi
    - Mumoni
    - Napambu
    - Kasego
- Mugila
  - Kilimu — Mugila
    - Sunguti
    - Keisugwa
  - Kagala
    - Kintonko
    - Kazigwa
    - Kikuko
  - Nkola
    - Mukumbukwa

238

APPENDIX II

Initiations into Lutumbo lwa kindi in Banasalu Clan

1.	Kamambalu	Ninda/Walangwa/Gungula
		He derived it from Beigala with whom he stood in *buyukulu* (joking)
2.	Kinda	son of 1
3.	Kibisama	Lusumbasumba/Musombo
4.	Mungana	Ninda/Itatua/Ikwa
5.	Kokonyangi	Lusumbasuma/Bilinda/Kabungula
6.	Mulingwa	son of 2
7.	Bikenge	son of 5
8.	Kilungulungu	Ninda/Itatua/Ikwa/Koka
9.	Ntambwe	Lusumbasumba/Wanwa/Monga
10.	Lukinga	Lusumbasuma/Ngunga/Kyanga
11.	Luyukia	Kibondo/Kwendambala/Mukumbukwa
12.	Milabio	Kibondo/Kwendambala/Kenduka
13.	Byankula	Mugila/Kagala/Kintonko/Munyemu
14.	Bikenge	Mugila/Kilimu/Keisugwa
15.	Sakisala	Mugila/Nkola/Kikuko/Wampene
16.	Nsamba	Mugila/Nkola/Mukumbukwa/Kyanga
17.	Kingalingali	Mugila/Nkola/Mukumbukwa/Yango
18.	Musanga	Lusumbasumba/Muloba/Kabongelo
19.	Kitunda	Mugila/Nkola/Mukumbukwa/Kitunda
20.	Biganangwa	Mugila/Kagala/Kazigwa
21.	Kisubi	Lusumbasumba/Bilinda/Kabungula
22.	Kakoku	Mugila/Nkola/Mukumbukwa/Lukinga
23.	Kanyungu	Lusumbasumba/Ngunga/Musoga
24.	Lubungania	Mugila/Nkola/Kikuko/Kasanda
25.	Samyaka	Lusumbasumba/Wanwa/Monga
26.	Kikanda	Lusumbasumba/Bilinda/Kabungula
27.	Kalimu	Mugila/Kagala/Kazigwa
28.	Kangali	Lusumbasumba/Bilinda/Kabungula
29.	Kalingwa	Ninda/Walangwa/Gungula
30.	Kyamusage	Mugila/Kagala/Kintonko/Munyemo
31.	Kansilembo	Mugila/Kagala/Kazigwa/Muzinguzi
32.	Kyabonga	Ninda/Walangwa/Myoni
33.	Malonga	Lusumbasumba/Bilinda/Kabungula
34.	Munkina	Lusumbasumba/Wanwa/Monga
35.	Tubunda	Mugila/Nkola/Mukumbukwa/Kyanga
36.	Kimambi	Lusumbasumba/Muloba/Kabongelo
37.	Mindo (living)	Ninda/Itatua/Itumpu
38.	Kimimma (living)	Mugila/Nkola/Kazigwa/Mubigi
39.	Kandolo (living)	Lusumbasumba/Wanwa/Monga
40.	Kisubi	Mugila/Nkola/Kikuko/Wampene/Lubungania

41. Ikangamina (living)   Mugila/Kagala/Kintonko/Munyemo
42. Numbi   Lusumbasumba/Wanwa/Monga

Number of kindi per primary lineage:
    Kibondo, 2; Mugila, 16; Lusumbasumba, 16; Ninda, 8

Number of kindi per secondary lineage:
    Lusambasumba: Musomba, 1; Bilinda, 6; Wanwa, 5; Ngunga, 2; Muloba, 2
    Ninda: Walangwa, 5; Itatua, 3
    Mugila: Kagala, 6; Kilimu, 1; Nkola, 9
    Kibondo: Kwendambala, 2

Bibliography

GENERAL WORKS

Altman, Ralph. *Balega and Other Tribal Arts from the Congo.* Los Angeles: University of California, Dickson Art Center, 1963.

Anciaux, L. *Le problème musulman dans l'Afrique Belge.* Brussels: Institut Royal Colonial Belge, 1949.

Annaert, J. *Contribution à l'étude géographique de l'habitat et de l'habitation indigènes en milieu rural dans les Provinces Orientale et du Kivu.* Brussels: Académie Royale des Sciences d'Outre-Mer, 1960.

Aurez, A. T. "Etude sur les Bakota des Benia Mituku." Archives Province Orientale, 1930. Manuscript.

Bailly, M. A. *Dictionnaire Grec-Français.* Paris: Hachette, 1929.

Baumann, H., and D. Westermann. *Les peuples et les civilisations de l'Afrique.* Paris: Payot, 1948.

Beaver, Stanley, and L. Dudley Stamp. *A Regional Geography for Advanced and Scholarship Courses.* Part II: Africa. New York: John Wiley and Sons, 1961.

Beghin, J. "Enquête sur la nutrition et l'état de santé des enfants warega (Congo Belge)," *Annales de la Société Belge de Médecine Tropicale,* XL, 2 (1960), 253–288.

Bequaert, J. C. *Studies in the Achatinidae. A Group of African Land Snails.* Cambridge: Harvard University Press, 1950.

Biebuyck, Daniel P. "De vorming van fictieve patrilineaire verwantschapsgroepen bij de Balega," *Band,* XII, 4 (1953a), 135–145.

———. "La monnaie musanga des Balega," *Zaïre,* VII, 10 (1953b), 775–786.

———. "Mubela: een epos der Balega," *Band*, XII, 12 (1953c), 68–74
———. "Répartition et droits du pangolin chez les Balega," *Zaïre*, VII, 8 (1953d), 899–934.
———. "Signification d'une statuette Lega," *Revue Coloniale Belge*, no. 195 (1953e), 866–867.
———. "Some Remarks on Segy's 'Warega Ivories,'" *Zaïre*, VII, 10 (1953f), 1076–1082.
———. "De sociale instellingen der Babembe." Ph.D. dissertation, State University, Ghent, 1954a.
———. "De verwording der kunst bij de Balega," *Zaïre*, VIII, 3 (1954b), 273–278.
———. "Function of a Lega Mask," *Archives Internationales d'Ethnographie*, XLVII, 1 (1954c), 108–120.
———. "Maternal Uncles and Sororal Nephews among the Lega." In *Report on the Second Joint Conference on Research in the Social Sciences in East and Central Africa, 1953*. Pp. 122–133. Kampala: East African Institute for Social Research, 1954d.
———. "The Idego-Payments among the Lega." In *Report on the Second Joint Conference on Research in the Social Sciences in East and Central Africa, 1953*. Pp. 161–171. Kampala: East African Institute for Social Research, 1954e.
———. "Superstrukturen of geheime genootschappen? Het probleem van sommige gezelschappen in Kivu," *Folia Scientifica Africae Centralis*, I, 3 (1955), 6–8.
———. "L'organisation politique des Nyanga: la chefferie Ihana," *Kongo Overzee*, XXII, 4–5 (1956), 301–341; XXIII, 1–2 (1957a), 59–98.
———. "La société kumu face au Kitawala," *Zaïre*, XI, 1 (1957b), 7–40.
———. *Les Mitamba: système de mariages enchaînés chez les Babembe*. Brussels: Académie Royale des Sciences d'Outre-Mer, 1961.
———. *Rights in Land and Its Resources among the Nyanga*. Brussels: Académie Royale des Sciences d'Outre-Mer, 1966a.
———. "On the Concept of Tribe," *Civilisations*, XVI, 4 (1966b), 500–515.
———. "Effects on Lega Art of the Outlawing of the Bwami Association," *Journal of the New African Literature and the Arts*, I, 3 (1967), 87–94.
———. "The Didactic Function of African Art," *African Forum*, III, 4 (1968), 35–43.
———. "The Seniority Principles in Bembe Social Organization." 1969. Manuscript.
———. "The Art of the Kindi Aristocrats." In *Art and Leadership*, ed. D. Fraser and H. Cole. Pp. 7–20. Madison: University of Wisconsin Press, 1972a.
———. "Bembe Art," *African Arts*, V, 3 (1972b), 12–19, 75–84.
———. "The Problem of the Function of African Art." In *Présence Africaine: Proceedings of the First World Festival of the African Arts (Dakar)*. 1972c. In press.
Biebuyck, Daniel P., ed. *Tradition and Creativity in Tribal Art*. Berkeley and Los Angeles: University of California Press, 1969.
Biebuyck, Daniel P., and Kahombo Mateene. *Anthologie de la littérature orale Nyanga*. Brussels: Académie Royale des Sciences d'Outre-Mer, 1970.
Bohannan, Paul. *Social Anthropology*. New York: Holt, Rinehart and Winston, 1963.

Bibliography

Boone, Olga. *Carte ethnique du Congo. Quart sud-est*. Tervuren: Musée Royal de l'Afrique Centrale, 1961.

Borms. "Reconnaissance du pays Bango-Bango et d'une partie de l'Uzimba," *Belgique Coloniale*, VIII (1902), 255–257, 268–270.

Bronchart, A. T. "Le Luhuna." Archives Province du Kivu, 1931. Manuscript.

Bryan, M. A. *The Bantu Languages of Africa*. London: Oxford University Press, 1959.

Burk, Ellen. "The Lega School of Circumcision," *Zaïre*, X, 4 (1956a), 375–377.

———. "Proverbes Lega," *Zaïre*, X, 7 (1956b), 711–715.

Burton, Maurice. *Systematic Dictionary of Mammals of the World*. New York: Thomas Y. Crowell, 1962.

Cameron, Verney. *Across Africa*. New York: Harper and Brothers, 1877.

Ceulemans, R. P. P. *La Question arabe et le Congo (1883–1892)*. Brussels: Académie Royale des Sciences Coloniales, 1959.

Clarke, A. Stanley. "The Warega," *Man*, XXIX, 49 (1929), 66–68.

Cleire, R. "Talen van het Kivu-meer," *Aequatoria*, V, 2 (1942), 44.

———. "Talen en taalunificatie in het Vicariaat Kivu," *Kongo Overzee*, XVII, 1 (1951), 32–37.

Colle, R. P. "L'organisation politique des Bashi," *Congo*, II, 2 (1921), 657–684.

Comhaire, Jean. "Sociétés secrètes et mouvements prophétiques au Congo Belge," *Africa*, XXV, 1 (1955), 54–58.

———. "Sociétés secrètes et mouvements prophétiques au Congo Belge," *La Revue Coloniale Belge*, no. 230 (1955), 292–294.

Corbisier, F. "Les Bashi," *Bulletin des Juridictions Indigènes*, XX, 7 (1952), 197–205.

———. "La propriété foncière et le paysannat indigène," *Problèmes d'Afrique Centrale*, XIX, 1 (1953), 6–15.

Cordella, Ernesto. "Ricognizione nel Bacino dell'Elila (Stato indipendents del Congo)," *Bolletino Societa Geographica Italiana*, VII (1906), 864–878, 963–978.

Cornet, René. *Maniéma: Le pays des mangeurs d'homme*. Brussels: Editions L. Cuypers, 1952.

Cory, Hans. *African Figurines: Their Ceremonial Use in Puberty Rites in Tanganyika*. London: Faber and Faber, 1956.

Cresson, André. *The Essence of Ancient Philosophy*. New York: Walker, 1962.

Dartevelle, Edmond. *Les "N'Zimbu": Monnaie du Royaume de Congo*. Brussels: Société Royale Belge d'Anthropologie et de Préhistoire, 1953.

De Heusch, Luc. "Autorité et prestige dans la société tetela," *Zaïre*, no. 10 (1954a), 1011–1027.

———. "Eléments de potlatch chez les Hamba," *Africa*, XXIV, 4 (1954b), 337–348.

———. "Valeur, monnaie et structuration sociale chez les Nkutshu (Kasai, Congo belge)," *Revue de l'Institut de Sociologie*, no. 1 (1955), 1–26.

De Jonghe, Edouard. "Les sociétés secrètes en Afrique," *Congo*, II (1923), 394.

———. "Formation récente de sociétés secrètes au Congo Belge," *Africa*, XIX, 1 (1936), 36–56.

De Kun, Nicholas. "L'art Lega," *Africa-Tervuren*, XII, 3–4 (1966), 69–99.

Delachaux, Theodore. "Ethnographie de la région du Cunène," *Bulletin de la*

Société Neuchâteloise de Géographie, XLIV, 2 (1936), 5–108.
Delhaise, Le Commandant. "Moeurs des peuplades du Tanganika," *Belgique Coloniale,* XI (1905), 184–186, 195–198, 206–208, 220–222.
———. *Les Warega (Congo Belge).* Brussels: Albert de Wit, 1909a.
———. "Chez les Wasongola du Sud, Bantu ou Ba-Bili," *Bulletin de la Société Royale Belge de Géographie,* XXXIII (1909b), 34–58, 109–135, 159–206.
Demos, Raphael. *The Philosophy of Plato.* New York: Charles Scribner's Sons, 1939.
De Rop, A. "Lilwa-beeldjes bij de Boyela," *Zaïre,* no. 2 (1955), 115–123.
De Wildeman, E. "Notes sur les plantes largement cultivées par les indigènes en Afrique tropicale," *Annales du Musée Colonial de Marseille,* 2d ser., XVII, 7 (1909), 238–317.
Duchesne, Fl. *Les essences forestières du Congo Belge: Leurs dénominations indigènes.* Brussels: Ministère des Colonies, 1938.
Eloy, J. "Etude politique et foncière des Benia Lusanga." Bukavu: Archives du district du Maniéma, 1952. Manuscript.
———. "Les lotissements agricoles et le paysannat dans le District Maniéma," *Bulletin Agricole du Congo Belge,* XLIV, 6 (1953), 1249–1289.
Fagg, William, and Margaret Plass. *African Sculpture: An Anthology.* New York: Dutton/Vista Picturebacks, 1964.
Fortes, Meyer, and Germain Dieterlen, eds. *African Systems of Thought.* London: Oxford University Press, 1965.
Gaillez, L. "Monographie Forestière du Maniéma," *Bulletin Agricole du Congo Belge,* XLVI, 2 (1955), 281–318.
Galdermans, G. "Crimes et superstitions indigènes," *Bulletin des Juridictions Indigènes,* II, 10 (1934), 221–222.
———. "Fiançailles et mariage chez les Bakumu," *Bulletin des Juridictions Indigènes,* IV, 11 (1936), 284–286.
Gérard, J. "La grande initiation chez les Bakumu du Nort-Est et les populations avoisinantes," *Zaïre,* X, 1 (1956), 87–94.
Glorie, Lieutenant. "La marche du Lieutenant Glorie contre les révoltés de l'Est," *Belgique Coloniale,* IV (1898), 605–606, 616–617; V (1899), 3, 5, 7.
———. "L'expédition Glorie de Riba-Riba au lac Kivu," *Le Mouvement Géographique,* XVI (1899), 61–64.
Gluckman, Max, ed. *Essays on the Ritual of Social Relations.* Manchester: Manchester University Press, 1962.
Gould, John. *The Development of Plato's Ethics.* New York: Cambridge University Press, 1955.
Guthrie, Malcolm. *The Classification of the Bantu Languages.* London: Oxford University Press, 1948.
———. *Comparative Bantu: An Introduction to the Comparative Linguistics and Prehistory of the Bantu Languages.* Vols. I, III. Westmead: Gregg Press, 1967, 1970.
Hallet, Jean-Pierre. "Ethnographical Notes on the Traditional Organization Bwami of the Balega Tribe." Los Angeles: University of California, Museum and Laboratories of Ethnic Arts, 1963. Manuscript.
Hance, William. *The Geography of Modern Africa.* New York: Columbia University Press, 1964.

Bibliography

Hargot, F. "Monographie agricole du Maniéma," *Bulletin Agricole du Congo Belge*, XLVI, 1 (1955), 1–56.

Heymans, V. "Les noms vernaculaires des essences forestières du domaine forestier-colonie du district du Maniéma." Bukavu: A.I.M.O., n.d. Manuscript.

Hiernaux, Jean. *Analyse de la variation des caractères physiques humains en une région de l'Afrique centrale: Ruanda-Urundi et Kivu*. Tervuren: Musée Royal du Congo Belge, 1956.

Institut Géographique du Congo Belge. *Province du Kivu: Cartes des Territoires*. Léopoldville: Gouvernement Général, 1956.

Institut Royal Colonial Belge. *La Force Publique de sa naissance à nos 1914. Participation des militaires à l'histoire des premières anneés du Congo*. Brussels, 1952.

Jacobs, John. "La vannerie, la poterie et le tissage dans les proverbes Tetela," *Kongo Overzee*, XXI, 3–4 (1955), 272–288.

———. *Tetela-Grammatica (Kasayi, Congo)*. Ghent: Wetenschappelijke Uitgeverij en Boekhandel, 1962.

Kaufmann, Robert. *Millénarisme et acculturation*. Brussels: Institut de Sociologie de l'Université Libre de Bruxelles, 1964.

Lebrun, J. *Les essences forestières des régions montagneuses du Congo Oriental*. Brussels: Institut National d'Etudes Agronomiques au Congo, 1935.

Lecoste, Beaudouin. "Bangengele et Wasongola: Contribution à l'établissement d'une carte des groupes ethniques du Congo Belge," *Bulletin des Juridictions Indigènes*, XXII, 10 (1954), 241–243.

Lenaers, C. "Chez les Warega," *Grands Lacs*, LXI, 4–6 (1945–1946), 65–69.

Lewis, Phillip. *The Social Context of Art in Northern New Ireland*. Chicago: Field Museum of Natural History, 1969.

Liétard, L. "Les Warega," *Bulletin de la Société Royale Belge de Géographie*, III, 1 (1924), 133–145.

Linton, Ralph. *The Study of Man: An Introduction*. 1936. Student's ed. New York: Appleton-Century-Crofts, 1964.

Livingstone, David. *The Last Journals of David Livingstone in Central Africa*. New York: Harper and Brothers, 1875.

Loir, Hélène. *Le tissage du raphia au Congo Belge*. Tervuren: Musée du Congo Belge, 1935.

Lowie, Robert. *Primitive Society*. London: Routledge and Kegan Paul, 1921.

———. *Social Organization*. London: Routledge and Kegan Paul, 1950.

Luthala, A. "Mariage coutumier chez les Warega du clan Banyagabo, secteur des Bakisi," *La Voix du Congolais*, IX, 88 (1953), 468–469.

Maes, J. "La Société des Mwami," *Pro Medico* (Paris), X, 4 (1933), 109–111.

Maes, J., and Olga Boone. *Les peuplades du Congo Belge: Nom et situation géographique*. Brussels: Musée du Congo Belge, 1935.

Maesen, Albert. *Umbangu: Art du Congo au Musée Royal du Congo Belge*. Brussels: Cultura, 1960.

Mair, Lucy. *An Introduction to Social Anthropology*. Oxford: Clarendon Press, 1965.

Masson, P. *Trois siècles chez les Bashi*. Tervuren: Musée Royal de l'Afrique Centrale, 1960.

Masui, Lieutenant. *Guide de la section de l'Etat Indépendant du Congo à l'ex-*

position de Bruxelles-Tervuren en 1897. Brussels: Imprimerie Veuve Monnom, 1897.

Meeussen, A. *Esquisse de la langue Ombo (Maniéma)*. Tervuren: Musée Royal du Congo Belge, 1952.

———. "De Talen van Maniema," *Kongo Overzee*, XIX, 5 (1953), 385–391.

———. *Linguistische Schets van het Bangubangu*. Tervuren: Musée Royal de l'Afrique Centrale, 1954.

———. "De Talen van Kongo," *Congo-Tervuren*, I, 4 (1955), 147–150.

———. "Aktiespreuken bij de Lega," *Kongo Overzee*, XXV, 2–3 (1959), 73–76.

———. "Een en ander over Lega-muziek," *Africa-Tervuren*, VII, 3 (1961), 61–64.

———. "Lega-Teksten." In *Africana Linguistica*. Annales, Sciences de l'Homme, no. 42. Pp. 75–97. Tervuren: Musée Royal de l'Afrique Centrale, 1962.

———. *Eléments de grammaire Lega*. Tervuren: Musée Royal de l'Afrique Centrale, 1971.

Merlot, A. T. "Notes complémentaires sur les Warega du territoire de l'Elila." Bukavu: Archives, n.d. (1931). Manuscript.

Merriam, Alan. "The Concept of Culture Clusters Applied to the Belgian Congo," *Southwestern Journal of Anthropology*, XV, 4 (1959), 373–395.

Michelson, Alex. *Liste des essences forestières du domaine, identifiées au 30 juin 1944. Nouvelle classification*. Bukavu: Comité National du Kivu, n.d.

Ministère des Colonies. Arrêté no. 21,247 of August 6, 1948. *Bulletin Administratif du Congo Belge*, September 25, 1948, p. 2660.

———. *Recueil à l'usage des fonctionnaires et des agents du service territorial au Congo Belge*. Brussels: Société Anonyme M. Weissenbruch, 1925.

Moeller, A. "L'Adaptation des sociétés indigènes de la Province Orientale à la situation créée par la colonisation," *Bulletin de l'Institut Royal Colonial Belge*, II (1931), 52–66.

———. *Les grandes lignes des migrations des Bantous de la Province Orientale du Congo Belge*. Brussels: Institut Royal Colonial Belge, 1936.

Monheim, Ch. "L'organisation sociale d'une tribu congolaise, les Waregas," *Bulletin d'Etudes et d'Informations*, no. 5 (1931). 26 pp.

Mulyumba, Barnabé. "La croyance religieuse des Lega traditionnels," *Etudes Congolaises*, XI, 3 (1968), 1–14; 4 (1968), 3–19.

Murdock, George. *Africa: Its Peoples and Their Culture History*. New York: McGraw-Hill, 1959.

Musée Royal de l'Afrique Centrale. *Africana Linguistica*. Annales, Sciences de l'Homme, no. 42. Tervuren, 1962.

Pilsbry, Henry. *A Review of the Land Mollusks of the Belgian Congo, Chiefly Based on the Collection of the American Museum Congo Expedition, 1909–1915*. New York: American Museum of Natural History, 1919.

Piron, Pierre. *Codes et lois du Congo Belge*. 2 vols. Brussels: Ferdinand Larcier, 1954.

Préaux, G. "La parenté, race mrega," *Bulletin des Juridictions Indigènes*, XXI, 6 (1953), 248–252.

Province du Kivu. Affaires Indigènes. "Recensement de la population Congolaise du Kivu." Bukavu, 1954. Manuscript.

Raucq, P. *Notes de géographie sur le Maniéma*. Brussels: Institut Royal Colonial Belge, 1952.

Bibliography

Richards, A. I. "Pottery Images or Mbusa used at the Chisungu Ceremony of the Bemba People of North-Eastern Rhodesia," *South African Journal of Science*, XLI (1945), 444–458.

———. *Chisungu*. London: Faber and Faber, 1956.

Richards, P. W. *The Tropical Rain Forest: An Ecological Study*. Cambridge: Cambridge University Press, 1952.

Robert, Maurice. *Le Congo physique*. 3d ed. Liège: H. Vaillant-Carmanne, 1946.

Roumeguere, P., and J. Roumeguere-Eberhardt. "Poupées de fertilité et figurines d'argile: leurs lois initiatiques," *Journal de la Société des Africanistes*, XXX, 2 (1960), 206–223.

Rouvroy, V. "Le Lilwa," *Congo*, I (1929), 783–798.

Sacleux, Ch. *Dictionnaire Swahili-Français*. 2 vols. Paris: Institut d'Ethnologie, 1939, 1941.

Salmon, Jacques. "La polygamie en chefferie Wamuzimu," *Bulletin du Centre d'Etudes Politiques et Sociales Indigènes*, XVI (1951), 114–147.

———. "Le droit matrimonial des Warega," *Bulletin des Juridictions Indigènes*, XXI, 6 (1953), 121–148.

Sanderson, Ivan. *Living Mammals of the World*. Garden City: Hanover House, n.d.

Schouteden, H. *De Zoogdieren van Belgisch-Congo en van Ruanda-Urundi*. Tervuren: Musée du Congo Belge, 1947.

Schumacher, Peter. *Expedition zu den Zentralafrikanischen Kivu-Pygmäen*. II. *Die Kivu-Pygmäen (Twiden)*. Brussels: Institut Royal Colonial Belge, 1950.

Segy, Ladislas. "Warega Ivories," *Zaïre*, V, 10 (1951), 1041–1045.

Shaw, E. M. "Fertility Dolls in South Africa," *Nada*, no. 25 (1948), 62–68.

Slade, Ruth. *English-Speaking Missions in the Congo Independent State (1878–1908)*. Brussels: Académie Royale des Sciences Coloniales, 1959.

———. *King Leopold's Congo: Aspects of the Development of Race Relations in the Congo Independent State*. New York: Oxford University Press, 1962.

Stamp, L. Dudley. *Africa: A Study in Tropical Development*. New York: John Wiley and Sons, 1967.

Staner, Pierre. "Les paysannats indigènes," *Revue Coloniale Belge*, no. 241 (1955), 709–711.

Stayt, Hugh. *The Bavenda*. Oxford: Oxford University Press, 1931.

Stuhlmann, Frantz. *Mit Emin Pasha ins Herz von Afrika*. Berlin: D. Reimer, 1894.

Thilmany, R. "Chefferie Bango-Bango," *Bulletin des Juridictions Indigènes*, VII, 6 (1939), 185–188.

Troupin, M. "Carte de la végétation du Congo Belge." Bukavu: Institut pour la Recherche Scientifique en Afrique Centrale, 1956. Manuscript.

Turner, Victor. "Three Symbols of Passage in Ndembu Circumcision Ritual." In *Essays on the Ritual of Social Relations*, ed. M. Gluckman. Pp. 123–173. Manchester: Manchester University Press, 1962.

———. "Ritual Symbolism, Morality and Social Structure among the Ndembu." In *African Systems of Thought*, ed. M. Fortes and G. Dieterlen. Pp. 79–95. London: Oxford University Press, 1965.

———. *The Forest of Symbols: Aspects of Ndembu Ritual*. Ithaca: Cornell University Press, 1967.

Van Bulck, Gaston. *Les recherches linguistiques au Congo Belge.* Brussels: Institut Royal Colonial Belge, 1948.

———. *Manuel de linguistique bantoue.* Brussels: Institut Royal Colonial Belge, 1949.

———. *Les deux cartes linguistiques du Congo Belge.* Brussels: Institut Royal Colonial Belge, 1952.

———. "Nota bij de Talenkaart van Belgisch-Kongo en Ruanda-Urundi." In *Algemene Atlas van Congo.* Brussels: Institut Royal Colonial Belge, 1954.

Vansina, Jan. *Introduction à l'ethnographie du Congo.* Kinshasa: Editions Universitaires du Congo, 1966.

Vermoesen, C. *Manuel des essences forestières de la région équatoriale et du Mayombe.* Brussels: Ministère des Colonies, 1923.

Viaene, L. "L'organisation politique des Bahunde," *Kongo Overzee,* XVIII, 1 (1952), 8–34; 2 (1952), 111–121.

Wankenge, P. "Du mariage chez les Warega," *La Voix du Congolais,* IV, 29 (1948), 332–333.

Willame, J. *Les provinces du Congo: Nord-Kivu, Lac Léopold II.* Kinshasa: Institut de Recherches Economiques et Sociales, 1964.

———. *Les provinces du Congo: Lomami-Kivu Central.* Kinshasa: Institut de Recherches Economiques et Sociales, 1964.

STUDIES ON AFRICAN ART

Note: In addition to pertinent and valuable illustrations, the books listed below present information on the forms and styles of Lega art. They are a representative sample of the many catalogs, books, and articles that provide visual documentation relevant to this study. Several of them are also listed in the first part of the bibliography.

Altman, Ralph. *Balega and Other Tribal Arts from the Congo.* Pls. 1–22. Los Angeles: University of California, Dickson Art Center, 1963.

Art Primitif: Collection J. Van Der Straete. October 6 to November 11, 1956. Pls. 102, 104. Mechlin: De Zalm, 1956.

Baltimore Museum of Art. *The Alan Wurtzburger Collection of African Sculpture.* Pl. 98. Baltimore, 1954.

Bascom, William. *African Arts: An Exhibition at the Robert H. Lowie Museum of Anthropology of the University of California, Berkeley, April 6–Oct. 22, 1967.* Pls. 182–185. Berkeley: University of California, 1967.

Brooklyn Museum. *Masterpieces of African Art.* Pl. 211. Brooklyn, 1955.

Brussel, Algemene Wereldtentoonstelling. *Kunst in Kongo.* Pls. 16, 33. Antwerp: VTK, 1958.

Brussels. Centre d'Information et de Documentation du Congo-Belge. *Les arts au Congo belge et au Ruanda-Urundi.* Pls. 52–53. Brussels, 1950.

Chernova, Galina A. *The Art of Tropical Africa in the Collection of the Soviet Union.* Pls. 156–157. Moscow: Moscow Soviet Artists, 1967.

Christensen, Erwin O. *Primitive Art.* Pl. 52. New York: Thomas Y. Crowell, 1955.

Clouzot, H., and A. Level. *Sculptures africaines et océaniennes: Colonies françaises et Congo Belge.* Pl. 46. Paris: Librairie de France, n.d.

Bibliography

De Kun, Nicholas. "L'art Lega," *Africa-Tervuren*, XII, 3–4 (1966), 66–99. Pls. 11–32.

Delange, Jacqueline. *Arts et peuples de l'Afrique noire: Introduction à l'analyse des créations plastiques.* Pls. 165–167. Paris: Gallimard, 1967.

Delhaise, Le Commandant. *Les Warega (Congo Belge).* Pls. 23, 103, 129, 133. Brussels: Albert de Wit, 1909.

De Rachewiltz, Boris. *Introduction to African Art.* Pls. F, 68. London: John Murray, 1966.

Elisofon, Eliot, and William Fagg. *The Sculpture of Africa.* Pls. 305–311. London: Thames and Hudson, 1958.

Fagg, William. *Tribes and Forms in African Art.* Pl. 108. New York: Tudor Publishing Co., 1965.

———. *African Sculpture.* Pl. 151. Washington: National Gallery, 1970.

———. *African Tribal Images: The Katherine White Reswick Collection.* Pls. 270–278. Cleveland: Cleveland Museum of Art, 1968.

Fagg, William, and Margaret Plass. *African Sculpture: An Anthology.* Pls. 37–38, 50, 82, 144, 151. London: Studio Vista Limited, 1964.

Frobenius, Leo. *Kulturgeschichte Afrikas.* Pls. 78a–b, 101a–b. Zurich: Phaidon-Verlag, 1933.

Fröhlich, W., ed. *Exotische Kunst im Rautenstrauch-Joest Museum.* Pl. 135. Cologne: Greven und Bechtold, 1967.

Gabus, Jean. *Art nègre: Recherche de ses fonctions et dimensions.* Pl. 24. Neuchâtel: Les Editions de la Baconnière, 1967.

Gaffé, René. *La sculpture au Congo Belge.* Pls. 24–26. Paris and Brussels: Editions du Cercle d'art, 1945.

Himmelheber, Hans. *Negerkunst und Negerkünstler.* Pls. 330–331. Braunschweig: Klinkhardt and Biermann, 1960.

Hôtel Drouot. *Collection G. De Miré: Sculptures anciennes d'Afrique et d'Amérique.* December 16, 1961. Pl. 86. Paris, 1961.

———. *Ancienne Collection: Paul Guillaume, Art Nègre.* November 9, 1965. Pls. 80, 83, 91, 96, 102. Paris, 1965.

Kjersmeier, Carl. *Centres de style de la sculpture nègre africaine.* Pls. 54–56. New York: Hacker Art Books, 1967.

Kochnitzky, Leon. *Negro Art in Belgian Congo.* Pls. 61, 76–78. New York, 1948.

Krieger, Kurt. *Westafrikanische Plastik I.* Vol. I, pl. 245. Vol. III, pls. 348–354. Berlin: Museum für Völkerkunde, 1965, 1969.

Krieger, Kurt, and Gerdt Kutscher. *Westafrikanische Masken.* Pls. 74, 76. Berlin: Museum für Völkerkunde, 1967.

Lake Forest College. *African Art: The Herbert Baker Collection.* April 12–22, 1962. Pls. 12–15. Lake Forest, 1962.

Laude, Jean. *Les arts de l'Afrique noire.* Pls. 125–127. Paris: Librairie Générale Française, 1966.

Leiris, Michel, and Jacqueline Delange. *Afrique noire: La création plastique.* Pls. 135, 420, 422–423. Paris: Gallimard, 1967.

Leuzinger, Elsy. *African Sculpture: A Descriptive Catalogue.* Pls. 200–205. Zurich: Atlantis Verlag, 1963.

Maes, J. *Aniota-Kifwebe. De Maskers uit Belgisch Congo en het Materiaal der Besnijdenisritussen.* Pl. 49. Antwerp: De Sikkel, 1924.

Maesen, Albert. *Arte del Congo.* Pls. 54–56. Rome: De Luca Editore, 1959.
———. *Umbangu: Art du Congo au Musée Royal du Congo Belge.* Pls. 39–41. Brussels: Cultura, 1960.
Meauzé, Pierre. *African Art: Sculpture.* Pls. 214, no. 2; 215, no. 3. Cleveland and New York: World Publishing Co., 1968.
Muensterberger, Warner. *Sculpture of Primitive Man.* Pls. 33, 35, 45. London: Thames and Hudson, 1955.
Museum of Primitive Art. *The Lipchitz Collection (Jacques, Yulla and Lolya).* Pl. 25. New York, 1960.
———. *Traditional Art of the African Nations.* Pl. 74. New York, 1961.
———. *The John and Dominique de Menil Collection.* Pl. 34. New York, 1962.
———. *The Robert and Lisa Sainsbury Collection.* Pl. 21. New York, 1963.
———. *African Sculpture from the Collection of Jay C. Leff.* Pl. 5. New York, 1964.
———. *Masterpieces in the Museum of Primitive Art: Africa, Oceania, North America, Mexico, Central to South America, Peru.* Pl. 30. New York, 1965.
———. *Masks and Sculptures from the Collection of Gustave and Franyo Schindler.* Pls. 25, 29, 32. New York, 1966.
———. *African Tribal Sculpture: Collection of Ernst & Ruth Anspach.* P. 8. New York, 1967.
National Gallery. *Exhibitions on the Occasion of the First International Congress of African Culture.* August 1 to September 30, 1962. Pl. 115. Salisbury, Rhodesia, 1962.
Nelson Gallery–Atkins Museum. *Ethnic Art from the Collection of Mr. and Mrs. Herbert Baker.* December 17, 1966, to January 29, 1967. Pls. 111; 118; 123B, F, H; 124A, B. Kansas City, Mo., 1966.
Olbrechts, Frans M. *Plastiek van Kongo.* Pls. 177–179, 198. Antwerp: N. V. Standaard, 1946.
Olderogge, Dmitry, and Werner Forman. *The Art of Africa: Negro Art from the Institute of Ethnography, Leningrad.* Pls. 135, 139–140. London: Paul Hamlyn, 1969.
Parke-Bernet Galleries. *Primitive Art: Pre-Columbian, African, Oceanic.* April 22, 1965. Pls. 63–65, 70. New York, 1965.
———. *African Art: Property of a French Private Collector.* December 4, 1965. Pls. 76, 78–79. New York, 1965.
———. *African Art from the Collection of Jay C. Leff.* April 22, 1967. Pl. 110. New York, 1967.
———. *African-Oceanic, American Indian and Pre-Columbian Art from the Collection of Allan Frumkin.* January 27, 1968. Pls. 36–40. New York, 1968.
———. *African and Oceanic Art: Property of Dr. Sam Raeburn.* May 25, 1968. Pls. 143–145. New York, 1968.
———. *African and Oceanic Art: Property of Henri Lecler.* December 7, 1968. Pl. 100. New York, 1968.
———. *African and Oceanic Art.* Pls. 93–95, 98–99. New York, 1970.
Perier, Gaston D. "Artisanats et arts populaires." In *Encyclopédie du Congo Belge.* III, 800, 806, 807–808.
Plass, Margaret. *African Tribal Sculpture.* Pls. 40B–D. Philadelphia: University Museum, n.d.
Radin, Paul, and James Sweeney. *African Folktales and Sculpture.* Pls. 33, 98,

Bibliography

151–157. New York: Pantheon Books, 1964.

Robbins, Warren. *African Art in American Collections*. Pls. 267–273. New York: Frederick A. Praeger, 1966.

Roy, Claude. *The Art of the Savages*. Pp. 12, 15–16, 64. New York: Arts Inc., 1958.

Schmalenbach, Werner. *African Art*. Pl. 138. New York: Macmillan, 1954.

Segy, Ladislas. *African Sculpture*. Pls. 153–161. New York: Dover Publications, 1958.

———. *African Sculpture Speaks*. Pls. 19–20, 43, 76, 271. New York: Hill and Wang, 1952. 3d ed., 1969. Pls. 17–18, 406–422.

Sieber, Roy, and Arnold Rubin. *Sculpture of Black Africa: The Paul Tishman Collection*. Pl. 124. Los Angeles: Los Angeles County Museum of Art, 1968.

Sotheby and Co. *A Highly Important Collection of African Art, Chiefly from the Belgian Congo*. Pls. 100–106, 123–131. London, 1960.

———. *Catalogue of Important African Sculpture, Pre-Columbian, Oceanic and Indian Art*. Pls. 12–13. London, 1965.

———. *Catalogue of Indian, Tibetan and Nepalese Sculpture; Tibetan and Nepalese Scroll Paintings; African, Oceanic, Pre-Columbian and Pacific North-West Coast Art*. Pl. 154. London, 1968.

Sweeney, James J. *African Negro Art*. Pls. 446–447, 455, 462, 465, 472, 514. New York: Museum of Modern Art, 1935.

Syracuse University School of Art. *Masterpieces of African Sculpture*. Pl. 34. Syracuse, N. Y., 1964.

Trowell, Margaret, and Hans Nevermann. *African and Oceanic Art*. Pp. 42, 93. New York: Harry N. Abrams, n.d.

Van Geluwe, H. *Art Africain. Afrikaanse Kunst. J. Van Der Straete Collection*. Pls. 40–41, 44. Brussels: Musée d'Ixelles, 1967.

Von Sydow, Eckart. *Afrikanische Plastik aus dem Nachlass Herausgegeben von Gerdt Kutscher*. Pls. 121B–123. New York: George Wittenborn, 1954.

Walker Art Center. *Art of the Congo: An Exhibition Organized by Walker Art Center*. Pls. 27.1, 27.2, 27.11. Minneapolis, 1967.

Wassing, Rene S. *African Art: Its Background and Traditions*. Pls. 13–15. New York: Harry N. Abrams, 1968.

Wingert, Paul S. *The Sculpture of Negro Africa*. Pls. 106–108. New York: Columbia University Press, 1950.

———. *Primitive Art: Its Traditions and Styles*. Pl. 42. Cleveland: World Publishing Co., 1962.

Index

Aardvark, 5 n. 11, 15, 28 and n. 6, 81, 96, 145, 164, 199–200, 207, 222, 226, and pl. 93
Administrative divisions, xviii, 3–4, 13, 22–24, 46 n. 18. *See also* Kivu; Mwenga; Pangi; Shabunda
Adultery, 105, 125, 137, 151–161 *passim*, 169, 190–195 *passim*, 202–203, 216–220 *passim*, 223, 226, 228
Adzes, 33, 106, 120, 187–188, 228
Africa, 15, 21 n. 31, 71, 138, 170, 234
Agriculture, 29–33 *passim*, 227
'*a'inga*, 72
'Alenga, 24
Ancestors, 53, 136, 140, 211
Anciaux, 67 n. 1
'Angele, 69
Animal husbandry, 26, 31
Animals, 9 n. 13, 15, 27–28, 38, 42, 48, 54–55, 69, 95–96, 99–107 *passim*, 116, 118, 123, 124 n. 17, 126, 128, 132, 138–141 *passim*, 144–147, 151–152, 156, 162, 164, 171, 174, 176, 178, 180, 182, 186, 192–193, 195, 202, 207, 209–210, 216, 222–223, 225
Anklets, 33, 43, 112, 147, 160
Anteater, 94 n. 11, 101 n. 11, 163. *See also* Pangolin
Antelopes, 27, 100, 105, 109, 115–122 *passim*, 145, 147–148; black, 29; blue, 119; bongo, 15, 28, 33, 96, 112, 145, 148, 153, 169, 179, and pls. 1, 7; chevrotain, 119–120; duiker, 75, 120, 145; dwarf, 81, 226; figurines, 149; *lungaga*, 164, 169, 222; *mpombi*, 147; *nkenge*, 179; *ntundu*, 226
anthropismos, 131 and n. 21
Ants, 161; red, 63, 145, 190
Anvil, 172
Aphorisms, v–vi, *passim*, xix–xxii *passim*, 2 n. 5, 8 n. 13, 12, 23, 34, 39–42 *passim*, 44, 47–50 *passim*, 52–57 *passim*, 65–67 *passim*, 72, 74–83 *passim*, 85, 90–91 *passim*, 93–94 *passim*, 99, 103, 105, 114, 117, 122–130 *passim*, 132–133 *passim*, 136–142 *passim*, 144, 146–147 *passim*, 151–226 *passim*
Apron, 99, 112, 132, 160, 162, 169, 173, 203, 206, and pl. 1
Arabs, xvi, 12–13, 27 n. 2, 30–31, 46 and 47 n. 18, 50, 58, 61, 177
Architecture, 33–37 *passim*, 67, 140
Armlets, 100, 147, 149
Arrows, 50, 58, 82, 148, 211
Art, xxi, 54, 57, 61, 66, 132, 157, 177, 178, 229–230, 233; decline of Lega, 226–227; study of African, 233–235
Artist, 173, 177, 179, 184, 214, 226–230
Art objects, 18, 33, 35, 51–53, 55–56, 67, 74–78, 80, 103–106, 137, 141, 157, 164–166, 179–184 *passim*, 229, 231, 234; display of, 81, 90–95 *passim*, 102, 105, 121, 124, 131, 136–145 *passim*, 151, 157, 167–180 *passim*, 193, 203–217 *passim*, 221, 231, and pls. 23–28, 34–35, 46, 48; functions of, 169–181, 184–227, 232, 234; meanings of, 184–226; ownership of, 90, 166, 170–171, 178–184, 220, 228; usage of, 166–169, 171, 179–

253

180, 193–218, 228–231
Artworks, 27, 142–157 *passim*, 164–169 *passim*, 174–178, 183, 188, 193–194, 206, 208, 227, 231, 234
Ashes, 137, 139, 145
Assemblage, 147, 160, 162–163, 165, 167, 207, 211, 214, 223, 226, and pls. 47, 110
Associations, 18–20, 22, 28 nn. 4 and 6. *See also* Bwami
Aurez, 82 n. 5
Axes, 30, 32–33 *passim*, 56, 74–75 *passim*, 77, 100, 112, 120, 122, 140, 147, 149, 164–165, 182, 185, 187, 189, 205, 209, 216, 225, 228, and pl. 105

Babene, xviii, xxi, 3, 23, 25, 83, and pls. 56, 64, 73, 75, 79, 82, 85–87
Babeya, 24 n. 35
Babila, 19–21 *passim*
Babongolo, xviii–xix *passim*, 10, 11 n. 6, 25, 50, 71, 73, 82–83 *passim*, 111, 143, 169, 233, and pls. 59, 72
Babundu, 24
Baenda, 68
Bagalia, 25
Bagezi, 24
Bagilanzelu, xviii–xix *passim*, 25, 73, 151, 156, and pls. 56, 75, 79
bagingi (*banyambala*), 70
Bagunga, 24
Bahwinja, 16
Bailly, 131 n. 21
Bainyindu (Banyindu), xix, 68–69 *passim*, 72. *See also* Nyindu Bakabango, xvii–xix *passim*, xxi, 4 n. 7, 7, 10, 16, 23–25 *passim*, and pls. 72, 100
Bakabondo, 25
Bakasila, 25
Bakasyele, 25
Bâki (Baki), 1, 2
bakikulu, 38
Bakila, 25
Bakinkalo, 25
Bakisi, 3, 23–25 *passim*, 83, and pls. 67, 84, 90, 101
bakule, 53
bakulu, 128
bakungu, 70
Bakusa, 25
Bakusu, 12. *See also* Kusu
Bakuti, xvii, xix, 24, 73
Bakwalumona, 21 n. 32
Bakwame, 19–20
Bakyunga, xvii, xix, 25, 73, 83 n. 6, and pl. 101
Balambia, 25, and pl. 100
Balambo, 25
Balégga, 58
Baleka-Mitoko. *See* Mitoko
Balenge, 25, 68–69
Baliga, xvii, xix, 25, and pl. 67
balimu, 171
Balinji, 24
Balinzi, 24, 25

Balls, 147, 148
Balobola, 24
balubungu, 128
Baluzi, 21 n. 30
Balyanga, 7, 21
Bambote, 25. *See also* Pygmies
Bamishungwe, 25
Bamugamba, 24
Bamuguba, xvii, xix, 25, 73
Bamulinda, 24
Bamuzimu, 72. *See also* Wamuzimu
Banagabo, xix, 4 n. 7, 11 n. 16, 25, 73, 164, and pls. 84, 90
Banakagela, 25, 45, and pls. 71, 85
Banakasyele, 25, and pl. 84
Banakazigwa, 45
Banakeigo, xviii–xix, 25, 73
Banakinkalo, 25
Banakubunga, 24
Banalia, 221
Banalila, 25
Banalulimba, 25
Banalyuba, xviii–xix *passim*, 25, 32 n. 10, 73, 101 n. 10, 134, 172, and pl. 76
Banameya, 25, 83, 134
Banamilunga, 83
Banamombo, 25
banamombo, 128
Banamugila, 45
Banamugomba, 87
Banamugulu, 50, 87
Banamuningi, 25, 50, 212, and pl. 102
Banamunwa, xviii–xix *passim*, 25, 73, 83, 151, 156, and pls. 73, 82, 86
Banamunyaga, 50, 87
Banamusiga, 25, 50, 87, 109, and pls. 59, 69, 78
Banamwenda, 87
Bananas, xviii, 14–15, 22, 26, 29–31, 34–36, 53, 65, 67, 76–79 *passim*, 103–106 *passim*, 109, 116, 124 n. 17, 126–127, 143–144, 147, 159, 163–168 *passim*, 178, 191, 193, 200, 202, 205, 217, 226
Banangoma, xvii, xix, 11 n. 16, 25, 73, 164
Banangumbu, 134
Banankamba, 126
Banantandu, 25
Banasalu, xviii–xix *passim*, 25, 82, 88–89 *passim*, 156, 238–239, and pls. 61, 62
Banasunguli, 25
bandirabitambo, 70
Bangubangu, xix, 4–5 *passim*, 9–10 *passim*, 17–19 *passim*, 21–22 *passim*, 33 n. 11, 43, 52, 67, 82, 232–233
Bangwana, 30
Banibilila, 25
Banikinga, 25
Banikozi, 25
Banisanga, xix, 25, 33, 73, 82
Bantu, interlacustrine, 21; language, 3–4; equatorial, 21 n. 31
Banyarwanda, 31. *See also* Rwanda
Banyemganga, 25
Baraka, 12

Index

Barhinyi, 16
Barimi, 140
Bark, 29, 33–35, 140, 143, 147, 168, 226, and pls. 7, 34
Bark beaters, 33, 77, 147, 150, 165–166, 183, 207
Bark Cloth, 15, 33, 42, 57, 78–79, 99, 102, 112, 139, 148, 150, 160, 162, 166, 177 n. 9, 187, 199, 211, and pl. 20
Barundi, 31. *See also* Rundi
Basango, 71
Basi'asumba, 7, 24–25, 69
Basibucuma, 25
Basikasa, 24
Basimbi, 24, 25
Basim'minje, 25, 68–69, 71
Basimnyaka, 25
Basimwabi, 73
Basimwenda, xv, xvii–xix *passim*, 7, 9, 17, 24, 37, 70–72 *passim*
Basisunge, 24
Basitabyale, xix, 25
Basi'umbilwa, 24
Baskets, 32, 35, 43, 74–80 *passim*, 87–89, 95–97, 99–104 *passim*, 113–123 *passim*, 133–134, 143–151 *passim*, 158–159, 163–174 *passim*, 179, 181–185, 210, 229, and pls. 6, 8, 13–14, 23–24, 63, 67, 70, 110; *kaluba*, 78–79; *kampunzu*, 101–102; *kansilembo*, 181–182; *kasisi*, 78, 87, 101–102, 169, 181, 183–184; *kindi*, 87–88, 134, 163, 172, 183; *lutala*, 76, 95–98; *luzuka*, 101–102; *mulama*, 79, 101–102, 158; *musutwa*, 72, 87, 95–98; *mutulwa*, 78–81 *passim*, 87–89, 92, 95–96, 99, 101–102, 158, 201–203, 215–217; yananio, 87, 134, 150–151, 183
basula, 117
Basumbu, 82
basumbu (bakwa), 53, 171
Basyamakulu, 25
Bat, 181, 193, 209, 213, 219, 225
Batali. *See* Zimba
Batoba, xviii–xix, 25, 73
Batukya, 9, 10
Batumba, 25
Baudouinville, 63
Baumann, 21 n. 31
Bausa, xxi, 221
Bayoma, 10, 11 n. 16, 25
Baziri, xviii–xix, 25, 73
Bazyoga, 25
bazyoga, 70
Beads, 69, 76, 101 n. 11, 106, 119–120, 122, 145, 147–148, 160, 169, 220, and pl. 10
Beaks, 99, 101, 144–145, 150–152, 155–156, 159, 164, 169, 189, 191, 208, 216, 222, 225, and pl. 27
Beards, 199, 211–213
Beaver, 14 n. 17
Beer, 34 and n. 12, 112
Bees, 145, 171, 212
Beia, xviii–xix, xxi, 2–3, 23–25, 83, and pls. 57, 59, 60–63, 65, 68–71, 74, 76–78, 80–81, 98, 102, 107

Beiamisisi, xviii–xix, 25, 50, and pl. 77
Beiamunsange, xviii–xix, 10, 25, 51, 73, 87, 97–98, 101 n. 10, 134, 138, 172, and pls. 63, 65, 68, 70, 80, 107
Beianangi, xviii–xix, 25, 73, 82–83, 134, and pls. 59, 98
Beiankuku, xviii–xix, 25, 87–88, 108–109, and pls. 57, 59–60, 69, 74, 88
beidande, 44. *See also* Kinship
Beigala, xvii, xix, 25, 50, 73, 164, and pls. 84, 96
Beikalantende, xviii, xx
bele muno, 81, 167–168, 170, 174, 204, 211, and pl. 26
Belgian, 31, 61; administration, 13–14, 16, 24; administrators, xvi, 31, 60; colonial government, 47 n. 18; troops, 59
Bells, 33–34, 74; dog, 139, 147, 163–164, 205, 222
Belts, 33, 81, 91, 112, 147–148, 160–161, 163, 167, 169, 173, 175, and pls. 1, 7
Bemba, 17–18, 21 and n. 31
Bembe, xv–xvii, 2–5 *passim*, 7, 10, 12, 16–18 *passim*, 20–25 *passim*, 28, 34 n. 12, 37, 42–44 *passim*, 52, 61, 63–64, 67–69 *passim*, 71–72, 82, 93, 112, 160, 232–233, and pl. 104
Bequaert, 144 n. 2
biga (mubigo), 113
bigagazi, 141
bigulugulu, 129
bikulo bya kitampo, 114
bikuwe, 189
bilondo, 159
bimpa, 157
bingonzengonze, 159–160
Binja. *See* Songola; Zimba
binkungankunga, 159
binumbi, 159
Bira-Komo, 4 n. 9. *See also* Komo
Birds, 28, 156, 169, 176, 198, 202, 216, 219, 225; *bubulcus*, 179; *kakulikuli*, 144, 163, 191, 201–202, 226. *See also* Chicken; Eagle; Hawk; Hornbill; Ibis
bisaba, 97
bisinga, 104
bisukusuku, 78
bita bya ngabo, 50
bitondi, 228
bitondo bya kisi, 52, 138. *See also* Aphorisms
bitugu, 48
bituka, 35
bitungwa, 159, 160
bituzi, 77
biziki, 113
Blacksmith, 7, 33, 106, 111, 158, 187, 228
Blacksmithing, 26
Bloodsuckers, 128
Boar, wild, 76, 79, 144, 164, and pls. 23, 110
Bohannan, 90 n. 8
Bombwa, 72–73, 76, 85 and n. 7, 121, 160
Bone, 22, 26, 33, 73–75, 106, 140, 147–149, 158, 162–166 *passim*, 169, 175–176, 179–181, 183, 188, 191, 193, 198, 205, 218,

226, and pls. 26, 38–39, 66, 71, 99, 103–104, 106
Borms, 17 n. 20
Bouse, 7, 12, 21, 24–25
Bows, 50, 82, 148, 211
Boyo, 4–5, 17 n. 20, 19 n. 28, 23, 67, 232–233
Bracelets, 33, 42–43, 101 n. 11, 106, 112, 115, 147, 149, 165
Brooms, 147–148, 189
Bryan, 1 n. 1
bubake, 85 n. 7, 159
Bubundu, 11 n. 15
Buffalo, 15, 27, 144
Bufuliru, 21 n. 30. *See also* Furiiru
buganga, 54, 105. *See also* Sorcery
bugila, 86. *See also* Divination
Buise, 2
Bukavu, xvii
bukindu, 117
bukota, 82 n. 5, 130
bukumbu, 117
Bukutu, 11
bulago, 144, 167, 179. *See also* Perfume
bulema, 130
Bull-roarer, 52, 56, 75
Bulonda, 62, 77, 85 and n. 7, 101, 107, and pls. 8, 15–16, 50
Bulrush, 120, 128, 147–148, 189, 208
bulungila, 107, 123
bunene, 53, 129, 140
bunenekisi, 124. *See also* Master of the land
bungoli, 85
bungulu, 109
buninabo, 45
bunumbu, 130
Bunyamwa, 62, 73, 81–82, 85, 101, 105, 123, 163, 175, and pl. 51
bunyemu, 130
Burhinyi, 25. *See also* Rhinyirhinyi
Burk, 52, 55 n. 19
Burton, 144 n. 2
Burundi, 17 n. 20, 20 n. 30, 31, 68
Bush baby, 212
busikila, 130
busoga, 124, 129–132, 177
Busts, 160, 217
Buta, 221
Buttons, 148, 169, and pl. 10
buza, 130, 176
buzonga, 177
Bwa, 221, 232
bwali, 57
Bwami: defined, 66–71, 90–91, 126–127, 132–141 *passim*, 146, 156, 185, 206, 210, 233; eligibility to, 85–86, 89, 122, 151; foreign attitudes toward, xvi–xvii, 58, 60–64, 124, 126, 226; Lega definition of, 66–67, 74, 82, 91, 93, 125–127, 141, 206; membership in, xvi–xvii, xx, 44, 48, 51, 54, 59–61, 64–66, 85–92, 96, 99, 116, 124–127 *passim*, 132–142 *passim*, 160, 167, 224–227 *passim*; prescriptions, 90–91, 95, 114, 116, 148; privileges, 28, 44, 49, 89–94 *passim*, 103, 106, 123, 134, 141, 169, 173, 175, 180–181, 184, 210; regional variations of, 72–74, 82–85, 93–96, 105, 116, 162, 169, 181–182, 186, 221, 229–230; secrecy, xvi, 90–91, 113, 146, 207, 231; social functions, 131–141, 170–173, 178, 180, 193, 231; special statuses, 95–107, 114–117 *passim*, 123, 141, 163, 169, 175, 180–184 *passim*, 191, 209, 229; structure and organization, 72, 89–107, 172, 193, 231; varieties, 68–73, 82–85, 93–94, 181, 233
bwanya, 129, 140
Bwari, 18, 21 n. 32
bwenge, 127, 131
byambila, 80
byanda, 203, 204
byenze, 189

Calabash, 76, 144
Cameron, Verney, 58
Camwood, 15, 32 and n. 10, 33, 69, 104, 229
Candidate, 36, 74–79 *passim*, 86, 89–90, 93, 96, 99, 101–102, 107–110 *passim*, 113–127 *passim*, 136–137, 152–156 *passim*, 166–168, 172–177, 184, 192, 196–199, 202–209 *passim*, 222, 225, and pls. 8, 11, 12, 42–43, 54, 86, 104
Canes, 33, 77, 155, 164, 173, 189, 195. *See also* Staffs
Canoes, 7, 11 n. 16, 95, 138, 147, 153, 155, 164, 189
Carapaces, 27, 36, 79–80, 99, 101 and n. 11, 140, 145, 151, 155, 159, 189, 199, 226
Carved arms, 79, 102, 150, 154, 164, 188
Carved hands, 79, 102, 150, 154, 188
Carver, 33, 106, 111. *See also* Artist
Carvings, xvii, 17, 26, 35, 54, 78, 103, 107, 134, 136, 138, 144, 149, 155, 160, 163–164, 175, 178, 183, 191, 201–203, 215, 217, 221, 225–228, 233. *See also* Art objects; Artworks; Sculptures
Caterpillars, 26, 29
Cattle, 21 n. 30, 31
Ceulemans, 12, 67 n. 1
Centipedes, 55, 128, 145, 149, 163, 224–225
Chairs, 33, 35, 76, 105, 129, 147, 149, 163–165, 182, 186–188, 191, 211, 221, and pls. 9, 50. *See also* *kisumbi*; Stools
Chameleon, 153, 163, 223
Characters evoked: by anthropomorphic figurines, 77, 158, 161, 162, 169, 179, 186, 191, 201–205 *passim*, 215–221, and pls. 28–31, 33, 63 69, 70–77, 79, 81–87; in aphorisms, 152, 154—156, 158, 162, 166, 167, 170, 173, 174, 176, 178, 181, 185, 188, 195, 198, 207, 235; in assemblages, 163, 203, 209–210; by manufactured objects, 167, 186–190, 194, 196–198, 204, 230, 235; by masks, 76, 170–171, 174, 199, 200, 212–214, and pls. 42–45; by natural objects, 162, 189–191, 197, 198, 201, 204, 206, 217; by non-Lega carvings, 217, 221; by spoons, 96, 209, 226; by zoomorphic figurines, 191, 201, 210, 222–225
Charcoal, 144, 229

Index

Chickens, xix, 26, 29, 31, 43, 65, 109, 118, 120, 122, 144, 146, 152, 189, and pl. 17
Chimpanzee 15, 36, 79, 81, 99, 101, 104 n. 13, 144, 146, 150, 155, 164, 177, 201–203, 207–208, 212, 226, and pls. 23, 49
Ciba, 21 n. 32, 232–233
Circumcision, 7, 17–22 *passim*, 27, 38, 44, 48–52 *passim*, 56–57, 63, 66, 74, 85, 95, 98, 141, 155, 163, 167, 169, 177, 182, and pls. 100, 105
Civet, 29
Clan, xviii, 22, 28, 32, 37, 41–51 *passim*, 55, 60, 66, 70–73 *passim*, 82–88 *passim*, 92, 97–109 *passim*, 114–115, 120–121, 132–134, 145, 171–172, 181, 184, 186, 198, 214, 232; chiefs, 49, 71; genealogical groupings, 23–24, 44; groups, xviii, 71, 84, 171–172, 230; linked, 2, 22, 45–46, 50, 87–88, 92, 172; named, 17, 45, 50–51, 70–73, 82–83, 87–89, 97–98, 101 n. 10, 108–109, 134, 138, 151, 156, 164, 239–240; royal, 70; segmentary structure of, 24, 39, 88, 134, 172; subdivisions, 45–51, 87, 97; unity, 71, 87, 88, 172. *See also* Lineages
Clarke, Major, 62
Claws, 27, 81, 96, 106, 140, 145–146, 154, 162, 189, 199, 207, 219, 224–226, and pl. 110
Clay, 33, 73, 138, 148, 183; white, 26, 29, 145, 208, 229, and pl. 34
Cleire, 4 n. 7
Clitoridectomy, 50
Cloth, 38, 57, 99–100, 112, 115–120, 122, 145, 160, 167, 188
Collaret, 80, 106, 168, 176, 193–194
Colonial, xvi, 31, 62–64; administration, xvi, 3, 14, 16, 22, 27 n. 3, 37, 60, 64–65, 67; administrators, xvi, 47, 60–64, 177; government, xvi, 47 n. 18, 60–61; system, xviii, 124 n. 17
Comhaire, 67 n. 3
Configurations, 79, 81, 85, 91, 93, 124, 142, 145–146, 151, 155–156, 160, 167–168, 171, 175, 177, 180, 185–191, 193, 207–211, 214–217, 231, 234
Congo, 14–16 *passim*, 19 n. 28, 63–64, 68, 174, 177 n. 10; Democratic Republic of the, 2; eastern, 14, 21, 47 n. 18, 52, 61, 67 nn. 1 and 2, 68, 82; Free State, 12–13, 47 n. 18, 61; northeastern, 21 n. 31, 221, 230; northern, 21 n. 31, 232; southern, 21 n. 31
Copper, 76, 115, 147
Cordella, 2 n. 3, 58
Cornet, 13
Cory, 170 n. 6
Cowries, 32, 69, 71, 106, 112, 145, 147–148, 160, 169, 189, 230, and pls. 1, 10. *See also* Shells
Crabs, 29, 136, 145, 226
Crafts, 32, 33
Cresson, 129 n. 19
Crocodile, 28 n. 6, 96, 144–152 *passim*, 155, 163–164, 217, 223–226, and pl. 90
Cross-cousins, 20, 40–43 *passim*, 70, 103, 106.

See also Kinship
Curing, 26, 137, 145
Cwa, 7. *See also* Pygmies

daimonion, 171
Dance, 27, 50, 54–57 *passim*, 66–67, 74–82 *passim*, 90, 92, 95, 102, 105–106, 110, 124 and n. 17, 127–128, 131, 138, 140, 142, 145–148 *passim*, 151, 153, 157, 159–160, 167–171 *passim*, 179 n. 11, 185, 187–188, 192–201 *passim*, 205–206, 210–212, 215–217, 234, and pls. 15, 18, 22, 28–33, 36–37, 40–46, 51, 53–54
Dartevelle, 32, 110 n. 16
Death, 18, 28, 42, 50, 53–55, 64–67 *passim*, 70, 103–106, 126, 135–137, 140, 146, 152–156 *passim*, 162, 164, 171–176 *passim*, 183–197 *passim*, 202, 207–219 *passim*, 224–225
De Heusch, 82 n. 5
De Jonghe, 67 n. 5
De Kun, 169 n. 5, 180 n. 13, 215 n. 19, 230
Delachaux, 170 n. 6
Delhaise, Commander, xvii, 1–2 *passim*, 7 n. 12, 12–14 *passim*, 17 n. 20, 26–28 *passim*, 30 n. 7, 32–34 *passim*, 36–37 *passim*, 46 n. 18, 49, 55 n. 19, 58–61 *passim*, 104 n. 13, 130 n. 20, 169 n. 5, 173 nn. 7 and 8, 179–180, 215 n. 19, 228, 231, 234
Demos, 129 n. 19
Dendrohyrax, 15, 144, 169, 205, 226, and pl. 110
De Rop, 82 n. 5
Descent system, 17–18, 37–38, 43, 113, 184. *See also* Inheritance; Kinship; Succession
Design: circle-dot, 161, 183, and pls. 82, 92; decorative, 163, 183, 186, 192, 195, 201, 212, 221, 223, 228–230
De Wildeman, 143 n. 1
Dhanis, 13, 59
Diadem, 69, 71, 148, 160, 203, and pl. 3
Dice, 33, 165, 180
Diet, 26–30 *passim*. *See also* Foods
Disease, 79, 129, 137, 154–155, 174, 177, 213
Display of objects, 81, 90, 121, 124, 131, 138, 142, 145. *See also* Art objects, display of; Configurations
Divination, 26, 48, 53, 104, 193
Division of labor, 28–34 *passim*
Divorce, 42–43, 57, 118, 176
Dogs, 28, 31–32 *passim*, 42–43, 155, 163–164, 222
Doors, 77, 80, 99, 147, 164, 189–196 *passim*, 219. *See also* keibi
Drum name, 55–56, 156, 163, 175, 204, 224
Drums, 53, 56, 71, 75, 78, 102, 104, 137–138, 142, 158, 162, 166, 168, 221, and pls. 5, 16; slit-, 102, 147, 164

Eagle, 28 and n. 6, 15, 96, 145
Economy, 26–34, 84, 91, 96, 99–101, 107–123, 132–136 *passim*, 173
Education, 50, 52, 57, 63, 66, 68, 86, 132, 138–140, 177, 184, 187, 210, 234

Eggs, 29, 173, 190
Elaeis, 1 n. 2, 15 n. 18, 27 n. 2
Elephant, 15, 27, 33, 56, 65, 77, 81, 95, 101 n. 11, 109, 111–112, 117, 127–128, 144–145, 148–149, 151, 159, 162–163, 165–166, 169, 173, 177, 180, 186, 189, 192–193, 196, 207, 213–214, 216, 220, 224–229 *passim*, and pls. 2, 4, 10, 23; ears, 159, 173
Elila, 61–62
elungwano, 50
esombanya, 12
Ethiopia, 20 n. 30
Europeans, xxii, 27 n. 3, 30, 59–60 *passim*, 64, 88, 111, 124 n. 17, 157, 166 n. 4, 177, 182, 221
Evangelization Society Africa Mission, 15
Exchange, 29–34 *passim*, 42, 57, 73–75, 84–90 *passim*, 95, 107–123, 132, 142, 159, 170, 173, 193. *See also* Gift giving
Explorers, 12, 58–59, 61

Family, 171, 181, 184, 227; extended, 47, 88, 97, 114, 175, 182
Fang, 232
Fangs, 144, 147, 165, 225, 226, 232, and pl. 110
Feathers, 56, 65, 69, 75–80, 104, 106, 109, 144–145, 148, 151, 160, 169, 175–177, 189–190, 194–196, 200, 208, and pl. 17
Fence, 34, 171, 195, 200, 203, 211–213, and pls. 38–39
Fibers, *lukusa*, 33, and pl. 1
Fieldwork, xv–xxii *passim*
Figurines, 33, 72, 76, 81, 92, 99, 104–105, 137, 145, 155, 157–158, 160–163, 170–186, 191, 201–207 *passim*, 215–222 *passim*, and pl. 26; anthropomorphic, 33, 73, 87, 101–102, 147, 160–165 *passim*, 172–175 *passim*, 191, 204–205, 214–221, 229–230; anthropomorphic, bone, 169, 175, 179, 181, 183; anthropomorphic, clay, 183; anthropomorphic, ivory, 80, 101, 169, 172–185 *passim*, 195, 214, and pls. 74–79, 80–87; anthropomorphic, *ntutu*, 102, 177, 183; anthropomorphic, resin, 177, 183; anthropomorphic, wooden, 79, 81, 101, 150, 155, 161, 169, 179–185 *passim*, 201–202, 206, 214–215 and pls. 23–24, 28–29, 31–33, 63–72; zoomorphic, 33, 73, 80, 102, 149, 153, 155, 162–164, 169, 180, 182, 193, 195, 202, 215–216, 221–226, 229; zoomorphic, bone, 182, 201, 203, 224; zoomorphic, clay, 183; zoomorphic, ivory, 80, 163, 182, 207, 224–225, and pls. 90–94; zoomorphic, *ntutu*, 177, 183, 224–225; zoomorphic, resin, 177, 183; zoomorphic, wooden, 79, 81, 103, 150–151, 155, 163, 167, 182, 201, 206, 208, 224–225, and pls. 23, 25, 27, 63, 88, 89
Fire drill, 81, 147, 176, 196–198, 208
Firewood, 30, 35, 100, 112–117 *passim*, 199
Fish, 26, 29, 31, 43, 79, 95, 112, 122, 144; catfish, 29, 136, 152–153, 226; Kwale, 152; *nkamba*, xix, 67, 95, 126, 128, 204; *nkomo*, 191; *nsamba*, 101, 128, 153; poison, 29, 153

Fishing, 26, 29, 35, 140, 174; camps, 35; nets, 29, 32–33, 43, 112, 120; traps, 32, 35, 191
Fizi, xxii, 3, 63–64
Flyswatter, 78, 147, 160, 166, 169, 182, 208
Foods, xviii, 14–15, 26–32, 34 n. 12, 53, 55, 59, 74, 76, 92, 95, 98–100, 103, 107–109, 112–116 *passim*, 119–123, 126, 128, 180, 200, 212, 217, 221. *See also* Diet
Force, 53–54, 75, 137, 173–174. *See also* Religion
Forms, 160–165, 170, 179–180, 220–221, 228–229, 232–233
French, 2 n. 5, 5, 54, 68 n. 4
Friendship, 93, 117, 133
Frogs, 149, 163, 219, 224, 225
Fruits, 104, 126, 140, 143–144, 150–151, 159, 209, 213
Furiiru, xv, 17, 21 and n. 30, 34 n. 12, 68, 70

Gaffle (gaff), v, 143, 147, 150, 154, 163, 217. *See also igobo*; Sticks, forked
Gaillez, 14 n. 17
Galdermans, 19 n. 27, 82 n. 5
Game, 121, 122; meat, xviii, 26–28, 31, 100, 107–108
Game boards, 131, 153, 164
Gathering, xviii, 7, 26, 29, 33, 49
geibamba, 49
geisambe, 50
Genets, 27–28, 75–79 *passim*, 95, 106, 112, 145–147, 163, 169, 191, 207–208, 226, and pls. 1, 53
Genya, 4, 7, 17 n. 20
Gérard, 19 n. 27, 82 n. 5
Gift giving, 39, 112–123 *passim*, 131–137 *passim*, 151, 168, 173, 178 n. 11, 192, 206, 221, 228. *See also* Exchange
Glorie, Lieutenant, 13, 58
Glue, 147, 162, 165, 226
Goats, xviii, 26, 31–33, 38–39, 42, 46, 67, 98–99, 105–106, 109, 116, 119–122 *passim*, 141, 145–146, 148, 154, 163, 177, 189–196 *passim*, 208, 213, 226
Goods, 89–123 *passim*, 131–136 *passim*, 141–146 *passim*, 152–159 *passim*, 180, 187, 192–200 *passim*, 206, 210, 224; initiatory, 36, 42, 44, 86, 133, 136, 157–165
Gould, 129 n. 19
Grades, xviii, 39, 43, 48, 61–63, 71–82, 85–88, 91–137 *passim*, 145–148, 151–215 *passim*, 218, 221, 224, 227–228, 231, 233–234, 239–240; lower, 28, 35, 39, 50, 52, 69, 73, 82, 87–89, 91, 94, 110, 114, 117, 121, 124–126, 146, 156, 159, 161, 166, 169, 172, 175, 178, 181–183, 206, 210, 224, 227, 233; origin of, 68–70, 82–84. *See also* Bulonda; Bunyamwa; Kansilembo; Kindi; Kongabulumbu; Ngandu; Yananio
Greeks, 129–131 *passim*
Guinea fowls, 128, 209
Guthrie, 4 n. 10

Hallet, 169 n. 5
Hamlet, 35, 75, 98–99

Index

Hammers, xxi, 33, 165, 171, 180–182, 205, 211, and pls. 26, 99, 104, 107
Hance, 14 n. 17
Hargot, 14 n. 17
Hassani, 58
Hats, 11, 33, 69, 71, 75–76, 81, 91, 105, 147–148, 160–161, 167, 169, 173, 175, 182, 189, 191, 201–204 *passim*, and pls. 1–4, 7, 10, 17, 36, 47
Havu (Buhavu), 4 n. 10, 11, 17, 20, 21 n. 30, 68, 70
Hawks, 146, 154
Heads, anthropomorphic, 149, 160, and pl. 98
Hedgehogs, 27
Hides, 27, 33, 56, 69, 75–81 *passim*, 102, 105, 109, 112, 139, 141, 145–148, 151, 153, 160–169 *passim*, 187, 189, 191, 204, 206–209, 218, 225–226, and pls. 1, 7, 53
Hingwi, 181
Hippopotamus, 229
Hoes, 30
Holoholo, 4–5, 232–233
Homa, 18, 21 n. 32, 232–233
Honey, 145, 193, 213
Hornbill, 15, 55, 99, 101, 144, 150–156 *passim*, 164, 191, 208, 217, 226
Horns, 75, 137, 145, 164, 189–191, 222–223, 226
House, 34–37, 115, 127–128, 137, 146, 148, 166, 195, 220, 225; construction, 26–27, 33–35, 107, 114, 224–225
Hunde (Buhunde), 4 n. 10, 11, 20–22 *passim*, 52, 68, 70, 101 n. 11
Hunting, xviii, xxi, 7, 15, 22, 26–29, 33, 35, 53, 59, 65, 111, 114–115, 119–121 *passim*, 138–140, 144 n. 2, 146, 151–152, 159, 164, 174, 193, 195, 217; camps, 35, 120, 138–139; nets, 28, 32 n. 10, 43, 53, 138–139, 148; nomadism, 7; traps, 27, 42, 65; with bow and arrow, 27
Hwinja, 3. *See also* Bahwinja; Luindja
Hyena, 145

ibago lya nzogu, 81, 117, 198
ibamba, 88
ibeza, 36
Ibis, 128, 155, 163–164
ibonga, 129
ibugebuge, 81, 168, 200
ibungakwanga, 121
ibuta, 57
Idega, 1, 140. *See also* Lega, name
idigo, 38, 123
idimu, 164, 177, 183, 211, and pls. 42–43. *See also* Masks, wooden
iduli, 174
idumba, 209
idumbi, 190
idumbu, 192
igambia, 42, 113, 118
iginga, 160–162, 181–183. *See also* Figurines, anthropomorphic
igobo (Igobo), v. 154, 189. *See also* Gaffle (gaff)
igu, 117
Iguana, 69, 145, 152
igulu, 140
iima, 68
ikaga, 224. *See also* Pangolin
Ikama, 2
ikangamina, 189
ikaso, 113
ikunza lyane, 112
Inheritance, 37–38, 40, 43, 51, 96, 105, 107, 155, 162, 171, 173, 176, 181, 183, 192–193, 210–211. *See also* Descent system; Kinship; Succession
Initiates, xviii, xx, 8, 32, 35–36, 54–57, 61, 63–65, 67–68, 75–81, 83, 85–97, 99–104, 106–108, 110, 112–148, 151, 154–156, 158–162, 166–182 *passim*, 187, 190–202, 205–214, 217, 219, 222, 224, 226–230, 232, 234, 239, and pls. 7–8, 10, 12, 14–15, 46, 51
Initiation, xvi, xviii-xx, 27–41 *passim*, 45–46, 50–68 *passim*, 71–79, 81–85 *passim*, 86–127, 129–148, 150–159, 161–178 *passim*, 181 and n. 14, 183–190, 193–206, 208–216, 219, 221–227, 231, 234–235, and pls. 8, 15, 22, 42–43, 48, 52; hut, xviii, 36, 56, 74–81 *passim*, 91, 106, 117, 119, 128, 138, 141, 165–168 *passim*, 174–181 *passim*, 190–192, 195–199 *passim*, 201, 204, 207, 213, 217, 225, and pls. 19, 49; village, 35–36
Insects, 26, 29, 92, 127–128, 171, 173, 191, 212
Insignia, xx, 32, 61, 63, 69, 71, 90–91, 103–106, 145, 147, 150, 159–173 *passim*, 181–185 *passim*, 203, 206, 228, and pls. 1–14, 46, 48
Institut pour la Recherche Scientifique en Afrique Centrale (IRSAC), xvi, xxii, and pls. 56, 72
Institut Royal Colonial Belge, 13
Iron, 18, 26–27, 32–33, 42–43, 106, 112, 116–118, 120, 147, 225
isabukilo, 75
Isamwati, 2, 8
isandi, 189
isasamuna, 139
isengo, 75, 157–159, 173, 177. *See also* Objects, initiatory
Ishile, 4 n. 7, 24 n. 35
ishungwe, 69, 71
isigi, 38
Islam, 67 and n. 1
isula, 34
itima, 175
Itombwe, 69, 71, 233
itungulu, 189
itutu, 80–81, 176, and pl. 19
Ivory, 17, 22, 26, 27 n. 3, 33, 53–54, 72–81 *passim*, 92, 95, 102–105 *passim*, 136–137, 140, 144, 147, 149, 158, 162–164, 166, 169–170, 172–175, 178 n. 11, 179, 180, 181 n. 14, 182–185, 188, 191, 193, 195, 198–201, 203–205, 207, 209, 211, 213–214, 218, 224–227, 229, 233, and pls. 26, 38, 39, 47, 58, 66, 71, 73–87, 90–92, 97–99,

102, 107
Iwanyabaale, 4 n. 7, 24 n. 35
izombo, 50
izu, 127, 129

Jacobs, 82 n. 5
Jars, 119, 148
Jaws, 95, 191, 225–226, and pl. 110

kabamba, 105
Kabambare, 12, 59, 67
kabanga, 223. See also Pangolin
Kabangila, 67
Kabango, 2, 10. See also Bakabango
Kabare, 21
kabi, 104, 135, 180, 226. See also Ordeals
kabobela, 77, 78
kabubi, 75, 80. See also Lianas; *lububi*
kabukutu, 225
kafyondo, 222. See also Figurines, zoomorphic
kagoli, 75
kagumo, 187
kakenge, 105, 173
kakengelezio, 170
Kakola, 11 n. 15
kakunde, 200
kakusa, 36, 74, 100–101, 103, 108, 116, 119–120, 136, 146, and pls. 42–43. See also Tutors
Kalaga, 8, 9 and n. 13, 52–53, 140. See also Religion
kalamo, 174
Kalehe, 21
kalemba, 208
kalenganio, 177
Kalima, 14, 16
kalimbangoma, 160, 162, 169, 182, 222, and pls. 88, 100. See also Figurines, anthropomorphic; Figurines, zoomorphic
kalinganya, 93, 102. See also Preceptors
kalokagathia, 124, 129, 139
Kalole, 4 n. 7
kalolesia, 170
Kalonda, 77, 103. See also Bulonda
Kaluba, 11 n. 16, 78–79
kalukili, 164, and pl. 95. See also Spoons
kalumba, 37
Kama, 3, 23–26
kamangu, 130
kaminankya, 74–75, 137, 166
Kamituga, 13–14, 16
kamondo, 73–74, 77–78, 193, and pl. 15. See also Dances
Kampene, 14, 16
kampumba, 76
kampunzu, 101–102
kanganza, 107
kangwondo, 35
kaninkwa, 113
kankenda, 98
kankunde ka kindi, 81
kankutungwa, 191
Kansilembo, 36, 73, 75–76, 95–98, 121, and pls. 100, 104
kansimba, 37

kantamba, 34–35
kantangantanga, 93, 102. See also Preceptors
Kanu (Kano), 4–5, 20, 22, 68, 82, 232
Kanyamwa, 103, 106–108, 116, 123, 137, 161, 169, 175–176, 181–186 *passim*, 192, 194, 198–200, 203, 206, 214, 219, 221, and pls. 3, 6, 11, 14–15, 17, 72, 80, 99; ka idulu, 81; ka lwemba, 81. See also Bunyamwa
kaongama, 149
kapiya (*kabiya*), 228
kasabalala, 114, 117
kasanganwa, 122
Kasambulu, xix
kasele, 102
kasenga, 113
Kasese, 4 n. 7
kasili, 49
kasimba, 74, 102
kasina, 137, 171
kasisi, 78–79, 87, 94, 101–102, 113, 168, 177, 225, and pl. 20; *kampunzu*, 79. See also Rites
kasonge, 37
Kasongo, xxii, 12–13, 19 n. 25, 67
Kasuku, 12
kasuku, 78, 114, 190
kasumba, 81
katanda, 75, 168, 190
katati, 130
kate, 158
katimbitimbi, 160, 163, 169, 175–176, 181, 183, 203, 205, 214, and pls. 80, 99. See also Figurines, anthropomorphic; Phallus
Katinti, 83 n. 6
Katundugulu, 12
Kaufmann, 67 n. 2
kayamba, 126, 164, 183, 214, and pl. 37. See also Masks, horned
kazombolo, 105–107 *passim*, 159, 167, 173
keibi, 80, 189, 191, 195. See also Doors
keitula, 76
kibabulilo, 95–96, 99, 182
kibagilo, 35
kibala, 30
kibazonga, 129
kibembelo, 99
kibengelo, 189
kibindi, 109
Kibombo, 67
kibunga, 137
kibuti, 47
kidande, 44, 186. See also *beidande*; Kinship
Kidasi, 181
kigela, 122
kigogo, 74, 85
kikalasa, 228
kikuko, 189
kikuni, 167
kilamba, 191
kilego, 74, 100
kilemba, 19
kilembo, 189
kilezi, 36, 100–101, 116, 120. See also Tutors
kilimo, 30

Index

Kilimono, 7, 51, 88, 97
kilimu, 102, 211
kilimungenda, 109
kilinkumbi, 80, 164, 182, 183, 195, 224. See also Figurines, zoomorphic; Pangolin
kilisio (*kililo*), 113, 114
kiloba, 103
kilolo, 94
kiluba, 75
Kilundu, 11 nn. 15 and 16
kilungubalo, 34
kimazenze, 78
kimbilikiti, 104
Kimbimbi, 11 and n. 16, 83
kimini, 128
kimonano, 49
kimpilinda, 120
Kindi, xviii, 37, 48, 61, 66, 73, 77, 79–141 *passim*, 148, 160–161, 163–164, 167–170, 172–176, 178 and n. 11, 181–184, 195–201, 203, 205, 207, 214–216, 218, 221, 224, 225, 228, 231, 233, 239–40, and pls. 3, 9, 13, 17–19, 23, 24, 28–31, 33, 41, 48, 53, 55, 58–60; *kyogo kya*, 73, 80, 143, and pl. 1; *lugumbo lwa*, 174; *lutumbo lwa*, 40, 51, 73, 80, 81, 87–121 *passim*, 136, 170, 172, 174, 181–182, 186, 190, 192, 194–207, and pls. 2, 4–6, 10, 14, 26–27, 38–39, 44–45, 56–57, 63–65, 67–82, 84–87, 90–91, 96, 98, 102, 107, 161, 167; *musagi wa*, 40, 51, 73, 80, 87, 88, 92, 94, 97, 101, 111, 134, 162, and pls. 21–22, 47, 64, 79
Kindu, xvii, xxii, 7, 21, 64, 67
King, 69–71
kingungungu, 76
Kingwana, 5
Kinkunga, 8–9 and n. 13, 52–53, 140. See also Religion
kinkutu, 128
kinkwankondo, 130
kinsamba, 80–81, 167, 168, 170, 175, 179, 183, 205, 218. See also Rites
Kinship, 18, 20, 27, 38–42, 45, 48–49, 51, 54, 57, 64, 66, 70, 72, 82–136 *passim*, 146, 152–230 *passim*; nomenclature, xix, 37–41, 44, 70. See also Cross-cousins; Maternal uncles; Sororal nephews
Kinsmen, 28, 33, 55–57, 74, 80, 86, 88–90, 94–96, 100, 105, 108–109, 114–115, 121–125, 130–136 *passim*, 142, 152, 166, 172, 182–184, 197–198, 211–227 *passim*
kipopolo, 94
kirunga, 71
kisakulo, 75
kisanda kya mbili, 122. See also Fish, poison
Kisangani, 7, 11 n. 15, 19, 221
kisapupa, 130
kisesa, 130
Kisi, 2, 4 n. 7, 9, 23–24 *passim*, 48, 67, 131–132. See also Bakisi
kisulukutu, 99, 159
kisumbi, 79, 149, 182, 186–188, 191. See also Chairs; Stools
kisyenge, 130

kitampo, 48, 83, 137, 172
kitandala, 130
Kitatente, 11 n. 14
Kitawala, 67 and n. 2
kitindi, 126. See Aphorisms
Kitumba, 69
kitumbilwa, 130
kitunda, 165, 167
Kitutu, 4 n. 7
Kivu, xvi, xxii, 3, 7, 16 n. 19, 21, 63, 70, 157
Knives, 32–33, 35, 44, 49, 51, 79, 81, 95, 98–99, 104, 106, 112, 119–120, 122, 147, 149, 153, 164–165, 180–185 *passim*, 191, 193, 208–209, 223, 226, 228, and pl. 102; billhook, 30, 112, 169, and pl. 103; hornbill, 32–33, 147, 149, 153, 180
-*koma*, 129
Komo, 3, 4 n. 10, 10–11, 17 and n. 20, 19–22 *passim*, 28, 67–68 *passim*, 82 and n. 5, 232
Kongabulumbu, xix, 51, 74–75, 85–105 *passim*, 121, 124–126, 137, 146, 148, 160, 164, 172, and pls. 5, 54, 59, 95, 106
Koninklijk Museum van Centraal Africa, pls. 56–78, 80, 87, 90, 96, 98, 100, 102, 107, 109. See also Musée royal de l'Afrique centrale
Konjo, 10, 17, 20–21, 25, 68
kuboko, 154
kubonga, 129, 158
kubongia, 179; *masengo*, 167
kuigula idumba, 105
kuingilila, 86
kukambula, 94
kukana, 114
kukandoa, 86
kukinduzia bana ba tata, 117
kukonga, 129
kukukula, 114, 121
kulaga mwino, 104
kumoko, 77
kunanula, 137
Kunda, 7
kupupa makila, 53
kusoma, 68
kusomba, 118
Kusu, 17 n. 20. See also Bakusu
kusuluka kitumba, 103
kuswaga, 129
Kuta, 232
Kuti, 10
kutongania, 94
kutunda, 86
kuye, 101
kwa magala, 86
Kwame, 5, 17, 21, 25, 68, 82
kwandizia, 206
kwanga, 104, 129
kwangia mwino, 103
Kwele, 232
kwengia, 129
kwima, 68, 69
kwimana, 68
kyage, 34–36
kyako, 113, 114

kyandanda, 66
kyembe, 228
kyombi, 207
kyumo, 34

Ladders, 147, 176, 196, 197
Ladles, 33
Lakes: Albert, 11 n. 14; Kitatente, 11 n. 14; Kivu, 20 n. 30, 68; Tanganyika, xv, 13, 17–18, 21 n. 32, 68, 145, 232–233
Lala, 10
Last, Dr. Jay T., xxii, and pls. 66, 83, 89, 91–94, 103, 105, 106
Leather, 147
Leaves, 29–36 *passim*, 52, 56, 76–81 *passim*, 94, 100, 104, 110–112, 127, 137–147 *passim*, 158, 159, 174, 193, 197, 204, 207–208, 211, 213, and pl. 12; *lubenga*, 186; *lukenga*, 179, 228; *lukumbulwa*, 173; *matungulu*, 176, 196; *nkumbula*, 104; phrynium, 176, 189, 190, 196, 209–210, 224
Lebrun, 143 n. 1
Lega: administrative groupings, 16, 24–25; attitudes toward Europeans, xvii, 13–14, 27 n. 3, 59–60, 150, 157; cluster, 21–22; contacts with West, 12–14; cultural differences, xx–xxi, 84–85; cultural relations, xv, 2–3, 5, 10, 17–22; cultural subdivisions, xxi, 2–5, 8, 10, 22–24, 68–70; demography, 16; eastern, xv, xvii, 7–10 *passim*, 17, 20, 23, 34 n. 12, 37, 42–43, 46–47, 52, 54, 71–73, 77, 93, 111–112, 233; environment, 14–15; European attitudes toward, 58–64, 227; genealogy, 8–11, 18–19; language, xv, 3–5, 24, 185; linguistic relations, xv, 4–5; location, 2–3; migrations, 11–12; name, 1–2; and neighboring groups, xv, xix, 2, 3, 17–22, 43, 50, 52, 71–73, 229, 232–233; northeastern, xvii, 7, 10; northern, xvii–xviii, 3, 9–10, 23; northwestern, xvii; origin, 11; southern, xviii, 7–10 *passim*, 18, 70–73 *passim*, 93, 233; southwestern, xviii, xxi, 8, 10, 64; territory, 5–8; unity, 1, 3–14, 43; western, xvii–xviii, 7–11 *passim*, 18, 23, 32–33, 44, 45, 52, 70–73 *passim*, 93
Leka, 1, 4
Lenge, 20. *See also* Balenge; Renge
lenge, 71
Lengola, 4 and n. 9, 11 n. 16, 17, 82, 232
Leopard, 15, 19 n. 22, 28, 33, 67, 69, 79, 81, 96, 102, 105, 127, 141, 144, 146, 148, 149, 154, 165, 169, 177 n. 9, 196, 201–203, 226, and pls. 1, 2, 4, 7, 20
Lewis, 188 n. 17
Lianas, 153, 154, 187, 190, 196, 197, 200, 208. *See also kabubi; lububi*
Liétard, 19 n. 25, 55 n. 19
lilwa, 82 and n. 5
-limbo, 129
Lineages, 17, 19, 22, 28, 37–38, 42–46, 51–52, 55, 60, 66, 71, 74, 75, 82–92 *passim*, 97–99, 102–108 *passim*, 114, 119–123 *passim*, 132–134, 164, 171–172, 181–190 *passim*, 202, 225, 228, 230, 232, 238; council, 40;

linked, 50, 51, 97–98, 134; primary, 43–49, 51, 83, 87, 89, 97–101 *passim*, 115, 134, 151; secondary, 43–47, 51, 74, 87, 88, 97–101 *passim*, 115, 121; segmentary structure of, 39, 46 and n. 18, 49, 60, 87, 88, 114, 132, 134, 173; tertiary, 45, 46, 51, 74, 87, 92, 97, 98, 115, 121, 123
linyo, 158
Lion, 33, 144, 214
Livingstone, 58
Lizards, 149
Loir, 33 n. 11
Longangi, 24
Los Angeles, xxii, and pls. 66, 83, 89, 91–95, 97, 99, 103, 105, 108, 110
Lowie, 90 n. 8
Luba, 7, 18, 52, 67, 230, 233; cluster, 17, 21 n. 32; complex, 4 n. 10; northern, 18; Province, 21 n. 31; riverain, 11 and n. 16, 83 n. 6
lubala, 190
Lubero, 67
lububi, 196. *See also kabubi*; Lianas
lubungu, 36
Lubutu, 67
lugono, 130
lugumbo, 204
luhuna, 82 and n. 5
Luindi, 25
Luindja, 25. *See also* Hwinja
lukambu, 228
lukenye, 78, 80, and pl. 12
lukiri, 72
lukugo, 78
lukungu, 104, 164, 169, 181, 211. *See also* Masks, ivory
lukwakongo, 78, 164, 168, 169, 181–184, 193, 208, 209, 211–213, and pls. 34–36, 42, 43, 60–62. *See also* Masks, wooden
Lumbeku, xviii, xx
lunkulu, 84
lusaga, 80
lusasa, 35
lusembe, 69, 71
lusolo, 153
lusu: lwa bakikulu, 32; *lwa gamulungu*, 34; *lwa mukikulu*, 35; *lwidega*, 34
lutabe lumozi, 89, 94
lutala, 44, 51–52, 75–76, 95–98 *passim*. *See also* Baskets; Rites
lutangu, 36
lutende, 52
luzanzia, 206
luzelu, 36
luzuka. *See* Baskets
lwanza (lwanza), 73, 95, 131, 136
Lwiro, pls. 56, 72
Lyuba, 88. *See also* Banalyuba

Makumbi, 78, 80
malebo, 130
malimu, 75, 228
malinga (Malinga), 23 and n. 33
malonga, 130

Index

malumba, 164, 212
Mambila, 67
Mangbetu, xxi, 221, 232
mangele, 35
Maniema, xxii, 4, 13, 17 n. 20, 24 n. 35, 59
Manyuema, 58
manzoko, 54
mapuka, 50
Markets, 27 and n. 3
Marriage, 14, 20 n. 29, 24, 32, 37–47 *passim*, 62, 85 and n. 7, 91, 100, 106, 110, 111, 114, 115, 117–119, 122, 123, 130, 132, 133, 158, 176, 197, 206
masandi, 78, 114
Masanze, 13
masengo, 38, 157, 159. See also Objects, initiatory
Masisi, 67
Maskers, 97, 116, 171, 199–200, 211, 226, and pls. 36, 37, 40–45
Masks, 33, 81, 97, 101–102, 116, 127, 147, 157, 164–168 *passim*, 170–172, 182 and n. 15, 185, 199, 210–214, 228–229, and pl. 58; bone, 149, 164, 169, and pls. 38, 39, 57; horned, 150, 151, 155, 164, 183, 214, and pl. 37; ivory, 80, 81, 92, 104, 105, 149, 164, 169, 173, 181 and n. 14, 195, 200, 211, 213, and pls. 38, 39, 47, 56; wooden, 76–80 *passim*, 149, 151, 164, 168, 169–171, 177 and n. 9, 181–183, 195, 199–200, 208, 209, 211, 213, 221, and pls. 34–36, 38, 39, 40–45, 49, 59–62
Master of the land, 104, 123, 125, 131, 152, 157, 204, 209, 215, 225, and pl. 38. See also *nenekisi*
Masui, 17 n. 20
matakale, 36, 164, 195
Materials, 149, 160, 162, 165, 179, 181, 205, 214, 221–226, 228, 229. See also Bone; Clay; Ivory; *ntutu*; Resin; Stone; Wood
Maternal uncles, 18, 38–46 *passim*, 73, 83–84, 90, 100–109 *passim*, 113–125 *passim*, 154–157 *passim*, 184, 189–190, 196, 222. See also Kinship
Mats, 32, 35, 43, 77, 112–113, 116, 147–148, 159, 161, 167, 168, 185, 190, and pl. 8
Mauss, 232
mbale, 115
mbilu, 174
mbiso, 113, 118
mbisulile byasigile tata, 105
mbogimbogi, 131
Mbole, 17, 82, 232
Mbote, 7, 68. See also Pygmies
mbuntsu, 82
Mbuti, 68. See also Pygmies
mbuto, 158
Meat, 28, 43, 55, 59, 92, 105, 108, 139, 192. See also Exchange
Meeussen, 4 and nn. 7 and 10, 18 n. 21, 19 n. 24
Membranophones, 33, 76, 140, 207. See also Drums
Men's house, 28, 34, 35, 74, 76, 158, 218

Merlot, 169 n. 5, 215 n. 19
miaka, 36
Michelson, 143 n. 1
Micici, 13
mikeke, 34
milunda, 224
Mingalangala, 12, 83
minganangana, 114, 117
Mining, xvi, xxi, 8 n. 12, 13, 14, 16, 27 n. 3, 227
Mirliton, 51, 56, 75, 104, 229
Misisi, 8 n. 12
Missionaries, xvi–xvii, xxii, 12, 13, 64, 227
Mitoko, 4, 9–11 *passim*, 17, 18, 21, 22, 82 and n. 5, 130, 132
mitume, 159
mitumwa, 113
mizegele, 56, 80, 190, 194, 204, and pls. 14, 48
mizombolo, 80
M'minje, 7, 20. See also Basim'minje
Moeller, 11, 13, 19 n. 26, 28 n. 6, 62, 63, 82 n. 5
moko, 212. See also Bush baby
mokota, 47
Mole, golden, 79, 145, 151, 163, 200, 207
Moligi, 10
Money: Congolese, xviii, 14, 111, 119, 122; shell, xviii, 18, 29, 32, and n. 9, 33, 35, 42–43, 98, 100, 103, 106–110 *passim*, 111–123 *passim*, 190, 206, 228, 229, and pl. 109
Mongo, 4 n. 10, 11, 17, 19, 21
Monkey, 14, 27, 33, 75, 95, 102, 120, 127, 145, 146, 148, 154, 215, 218; *ambela*, 202; *kagelia*, 164, 190, 212, 226, and pl. 110
Moral philosophy, 49, 52–58, 65, 68, 85, 91, 93, 101, 120, 122–141 *passim*, 145–148, 151–157, 160, 161, 170, 177, 178, 185–190, 193–213 *passim*, 215–222, 231, 234
Mortars, 33
Moss, 163, 207
moza, 74, 148, and pl. 54
mpala, 142, 153, 157, 158; *za makeno*, 94
mpeneziginga, 84
Mpimbi, 141
mpita, 105
mpolo, 42
mpombi, 108
mpombo, 30
mpunju, 82 and n. 5
mubazi wa nkondo, 106, 228
mubigo, 42, 118
mubiko, 137
mubumbi, 52
mubuto uzinda, 46
mugila wa mulende, 50
Mugomba, 87
mugugu, 153, 223
mugugundu, 163, 168, 182, 193, 208, 222, 223, and pls. 88, 89, 92
mukingo, 34
mukomi, 36, 99–101, 106, 120, 123, 184. See also Tutors
mukondekonde, 151, 223. See also Crocodile

mukondi, 105; *we idumba*, 103
Mukoniama, 13
mukota wa kabilundu, 128
mukulumizi, 228. See also Artist
mukulu wibondo, 189, and pl. 1. See also Canes
mukumbi, 36, 78, 94, 121, 174, 178, 207–210, and pls. 49, 61
mukunga, 52
mulama, 101, 102, 151–158, 213. See also Baskets
mulamba, 158
Mulima, 80
mulombe, 79, 200
mulonga, 228
mulondosa, 139
mulongeki, 49
mululo, 113, 121. See also Exchange
mulumbilwa, 128
mulungi, 190
Mulungu, 13
mulungu, 34
muluta, 36
Mulyumba, 52
mumabi, 102
mumbilumbilu, 151, 223
muminia, 164, 199, and pls. 42–43. See also Masks, wooden
munana, 148, 189. See also Ropes, feather
mundala, 98
munene we idimba, 127
Mungininigini, 11–12
mungu mumenywa wa basoga, 128
Munie Chabodu (Shabudu), 12–13
Munie Mtoro, 12–13
Munsange, 87–88
munsembele, 80
Muntita, 83 n. 6
muntute, 49
Munyaga, 87
mupalia, 28
Murdock, 21 n. 31
muruta, 71
musanganano, 88
Musée royal de l'Afrique centrale, Tervuren, xvii
Musée royal du Congo Belge, Tervuren, xxii
musekelo we isengo, 113
Museme, 7 n. 12
Museum and Laboratories of Ethnic Arts and Technology, University of California, pls. 95, 97, 99, 108, 110
Mushrooms, 99, 140, 144, 150, 151, 174, 178, 179, 193, 205
Music, 26, 51, 54, 56, 75, 79, 90, 131, 138, 140, 142, 148, 151, 157, 168, 170, 174, 177, 193
musigo, 111–120 *passim*
musile, 105, 173
musimbi, 44, 50–52, 95–96, 98
musoga, 128, 154
musombo, 116
musumba, 35
musumbililo, 49

musungu, 113
musunguzi, 49
musutwa, 51, 87, 96–98. See also Baskets
mutandi mulazi, 66
mutanga, 52
mutende, 99
mutima, 47–48
mutondo, 128
Mutton, 26, 29, 109
mutu, 156, 189
mutula, 47
mutulwa, 78, 81, 87, 89, 92, 158, 215, 217, and pl. 27. See also Baskets
muyolelo, 114, 117–118. See also Exchange
Muzigi, 154
muzigi, 153
Mwenda, 87
mwene, 96, 99; *we ikaga*, 95–98 *passim*. See also Knives
Mwenembumbano, 12, 68
Mwenga, xvii, xxii, 3, 9, 16 and n. 19, 21, 23, 68
mwikalizi, 101 and n. 10, 116–117, 121. See also Tutors
mwikio, 113–114, 121
mwizakyumo, 47
mwizamulemba, 99
myabi, 75
myambalo, 122
myanga, 129

nabaganda, 70
Nails: animal, 27, 137; copper 149, 186
Nande, 11, 68
Ndembu, 185 n. 16
nduma, 129
Necklaces, 105, 110, 111, 112, 148, 160, 167, 169, 173, 221, and pls. 1, 2, 4
Needles, 33, 75, 112, 147, 159, 190, 191, 228
nenekisi, 44, 47, 48 131, 170, and pls. 38, 41. See also Master of the land
Nests 128, 145, 191
Nets, 35, 174, 189, 205, 209, 223
New Ireland, 188 n. 17
ngana, 130
Ngandu, 18, 20, 48, 51, 73, 76–110 *passim*, 121, 122, 160, 169, 181, 228, and pl. 105; *kyogo kya*, 77; *lutumbo lwa*, 77; *musagi wa*, 77
ngoli, 85 n. 7
Nicknames, xvi, xix, 156
nina, 170, 175
nkeka, 187, 188
nkiko, 34, 36
nkinda, 139
nkindo, 113
nkoko, 152
nkola za bwali, 51
nkondo, 187. See also Adzes
Nkulu, 10, 83 and n. 6
nkumi, 82 and n. 5
nkumu, 82
Nkundo, 82. See also Mongo
nkunda, 79, 168

Index

Noninitiate, 91, 102, 124, 127, 140, 159, 166, 177, 186, 189–191, 205, 208, 210, 227, 229
nsago, 190. *See also* Shoulder bags
nsingia, 74, 93, 102. *See also* Preceptors
nsombi, 206
ntata, 22, 23
ntundu, 47
ntutu, 33, 79, 102, 139, 144, 177, 181 and n. 14, 183, 214, 225, 229
Nuts, 77, 143, 144
Nutshells, 95, 143–145 *passim*, 148, 160, 169, and pls. 3, 10
nyagwamana, 56, 107, 108, and pl. 16
nyakabundi, 106
nyakambunda, 106
nyamalembo, 107
Nyanga, 4, 7, 11, 17, 19 n. 27, 20–22 *passim*, 28 and n. 4, 52, 68 and n. 4, 70, 71, 82, 157, 232
nyange, 129
Nyangwe, 12, 19 n. 25, 58
Nyindu, xv, 3, 5, 10, 12, 16, 20–25, 34 n. 12, 43, 68–70, 72, 82, 112, 160, 232, 233; Bunyindu, 21 n. 30; southern, 78. *See also* Bainyindu.
nzogo, 30

Objects: European origin, 150, 165, 179, 205, 217, 231; initiatory, 27, 29, 38, 51, 57, 69, 72–82 *passim*, 84–113 *passim*, 120, 124, 134, 137, 142–151, 158–178, *passim*, 184–187, 193, 218, 222–224 *passim*; manufactured, 27, 36, 52, 75–81 *passim*, 95–102 *passim*, 106, 112–122 *passim*, 137–172 *passim*, 178–234 *passim*; natural, 27, 32–33, 36, 52, 54, 69, 71, 74–82, 95, 99, 101–102, 106, 112, 122, 137–170 *passim*, 177–184 *passim*, 189–198, 204–215 *passim*, 218, 222–228 *passim*, 234, and pls. 49, 108, 110
Oil, 26, 27, 29, 32, 33, 43, 100, 104, 108, 111, 115–122 *passim*, 144, 145, 148, 192; castor, 167, 179, 185; palm, 27 and n. 2, 32 and n. 10, 110, 144; peanut, 27 n. 2
Ointments, 179
Olbrechts, Professor Frans M., xxii, 233
Ombo. *See* Songola
Oracle, 180. *See also* Divination
Oral literature, 27, 54–56, 61, 67, 68 n. 4, 123, 124, 138–142 *passim*, 157, 168, 177 n. 10, 193, 202, 231. *See also* Aphorisms; Songs
Ordeals, 75, 79, 103, 104, 135, 136, 180, 193, 226. See also *kabi*
Otters, 145, 147, 163, 223
Owl, 99, 159

Paideia, 132
Palm wine, 34
Pangi, xvii–xxii *passim*, 3, 4 n. 7, 8 and n. 12, 15–18 *passim*, 21, 23, 25, 64, 83, and pls. 56, 57, 59, 60–65, 68–82, 85–88, 98, 100, 102, 107
Pangolin, xix, 15, 28 and nn. 4 and 6, 35, 80, 95, 98, 99, 103, 106, 128, 138, 145, 147, 148, 150, 151, 163, 164, 182, 189, 190, 193, 195, 208, 212, 223, 224, 226, and pls. 93, 110
Paraphernalia, xx, 38, 56, 73, 84, 90, 91, 103–106 *passim*, 142–150 *passim*, 159, 160, 165, 168, 172, 173, 185, 200–206 *passim*, 211, 228, and pls. 17, 41, 47
Parrots, 65, 69, 82, 144, 208
Pathos, 129
Paulis, 221
paysannats, 14, 36 and n. 8
Pegs, 33, 165
Pende, 177 n. 10
Penemisenga, Omari, xix, xx
Pere, 68, 232
Performances, dramatic, 54, 56, 66, 90–92, 94, 102, 138, 140, 141, 167–171 *passim*, 176, 185, 186, 200, 207, 210, 234
Perfume, 144, 167, 179. See also *bulago*
Pestles, 33
Phallus, 155, 163, 164, 175. *See also* Yango; *yango*
Pheasant, blue, 55
Pigs, wild, 27, 121, 204
Pilsbry, 144 n. 2
Pincers, 145, 226
Pipes, 35, 75, 148
Piron, 24 n. 36
Plaiting, 26, 32
Planks, 80, 99, 147, 154, 189, 190, 195
Plants, 9 n. 18, 14, 15, 29, 30, 32, 35, 36, 52, 54, 75, 77, 102, 104, 127, 128, 140, 144, 147–149
Plates, 32, 33, 69, 76, 112
Pods, 143, 145, 158, 159, 190
Poles, 34, 35, 104, 127, 139, 200, 209, 211, 213
Political organization, 18–22, 37, 38, 46–50, 60–61, 67–71 *passim*, 91, 101 n. 11, 132–135 *passim*, 173
politique indigène, 60, 61
Ponthierville, 9, 11 n. 15
Porcupines, 79, 81, 99, 102, 126, 145, 147, 175, 176, 180, 190, 193, 205, 207, 208, 222, 226, 228
Potlatch, 136
Pottery, 26, 32, 33, 35, 43, 53, 75, 77, 95, 110, 112, 117, 119–121, 147–149
Potto, 71
Powder, red, 144, 145, 160, 179
Praise names, 140, 141, 168, 179, 198
Preceptors (*nsingia*), xx, 151, 159, 163, 164, 167–169, 174, 176, 180, 182, 190–192, 194–197, 199–201, 204–206, 209–211, 216, 217, 226, 228, and pls. 5, 12, 24, 31, 37, 39–43, 89, 98, 110. See also *kalinganya*
Pregnancy, 105, 139, 158, 161, 169, 201, 202, 207, 216, 218, 220, 225, 228
Pring 131 n. 21
Provincial: capital, 2; government, xvi, 1; governor, 60
Punga, 67
Punia, 21
Pygmies, 5 n. 11, 7, 12, 20, 68, 126, 140, 213.

See also Bambole; Cwa; Mbote; Mbuti; Twa

Quills, 79, 82, 99, 102, 145, 147, 160, 162, 175, 176, 180, 207, 222, 226

Raffia 15, 32, 33 n. 11, 48, 67, 75–80 *passim*, 95, 106, 109, 112, 127, 148, 180, 190, 191, 193, 207, 209, 213
Rats, 146
Rattles 32, 56, 80, 81, 104–107 *passim*, 148, 160, 166, 168, 169, 173, 182, 190, 193, 194, 199, 201, and pls. 14, 48. See also *mizegele*
Razors, 33, 75, 76, 112, 120, 147, 159, 191
Reed, 160, 166, 169, 182
Religion, 52–54, 67, 91, 124, 126, 128, 136–140 *passim*, 164, 171–175 *passim*, 234
Remnant groups, 10–12, 21, 233
Renge, 7, 12. *See also* Balenge; Lenge
Resin, 33, 95, 99, 112, 115, 116, 119, 141, 144, 147, 149, 162, 167, 177, 181 and n. 14, 183, 184, 190, 229
Rhinyirhinyi, 3. *See also* Barhinyi; Burhinyi
Ribariba, 12
Richards, A. I., 14 n. 17, 170 n. 6
Rites, 28, 31, 35, 55–57, 64, 65, 72–87 *passim*, 90, 92–110, 112, 113, 115–126 *passim*, 136, 139, 141–146, 150, 151, 155–157, 160, 163–170, 172–181, 183, 186, 188, 191–211, 215–218, 222, 229–231, 233, 234, and pls. 5, 11–51, 53–55
Ritual communities, xviii, xix, xxi, 11 n. 14, 46, 56, 71, 72, 80, 84, 85, 87, 89, 91, 94, 99, 101, 105, 114, 122, 132, 136, 151, 155, 159, 171, 172, 181–184, 205, 207, 222, 226, 230, 233, and pls. 23, 25, 59, 63, 65, 67, 79, 80, 88, 100, 104
Riverains, 7, 10, 11, 17 n. 20, 18, 21, 232
Rivers, 9 n. 13, 33 n. 11, 55, 66, 77, 124 n. 17, 127, 153–155, 220, 221, 223, 225; Congo, 15, 233; Elila, 3, 13, 15, 17 n. 20, 29; Kalumange, 122; Kama, 29; Lowa, 12, 17 n. 20; Lualaba, 11 and nn. 15 and 16, 12, 15, 124 n. 17; Lugulu, 29; Lwindi, 152; Semliki, 11; Ulindi, 3, 7, 12, 13, 15, 17 n. 20, 29, 33 n. 11, 62
Robert, 14 n. 17
Rodents, 15, 166 n. 4; *nsongi*, 207
Roots, 140, 143, 159, 187
Ropes, 32, 33, 75, 76, 78, 104, 147, 189; feather, 180, 195, and pls. 39, 47, 54. See also *munana*
Roumeguere, 170 n. 6
Rouvroy, 82 n. 5
Rubber, 148
Rundi, 17 n. 20
Ruzizi Valley, 17 n. 20
Rwanda, 20 n. 30, 31, 68, 83 n. 6

Sacleux, 68
sakania, 47–48
Sakuzinda, 47–49
Salmon, 42 n. 15

Salt, xviii, 26, 32–33, 43, 100, 108, 110, 115–122 *passim*
Sanderson, 144 n. 2
Sandpaper, 228. *See also* Leaves, *lukenga*
sansaga, 168
Sanze, 5, 18, 21 n. 32
Sawasawa, 67
Scales, 27, 74, 95, 101 n. 11, 103, 140, 145, 147–150, 163, 167, 182, 190, 208, 223–226, and pls. 49, 110
Scepters, 33, 56, 75, 95, 140, 149, 165, 180, 182, and pls. 23, 104
Schouteden, 144 n. 2
Schumacher, 20 n. 30
Sculptures, 22, 66, 79, 139, 141, 160, 163, 166, 169–177, 180–184, 214, 223, 227, 230, 232, 233
Seeds, 69, 102, 143, 147, 160, 223
Sengele, 25
Seniority, 38–39, 44, 47, 55, 86, 88, 92–93, 117, 133, 170. *See also* Kinship
Shabunda, xvii, xxii, 3, 4, and n. 7, 9, 11 n. 16, 13–25 *passim*, 64, 67, 83 and n. 6, and pls. 67, 84, 90, 96, 101
Shaw, 170 n. 6
Sheath, 190, 191
Sheep, 26, 29, 31, 67, 109, 127, 146, 148, 196
Shells, xxi, xxii, 23, 27, 29, 53, 69, 71, 79, 81, 101, 106, 110–112, 122, 137, 145, 167, and pls. 7, 19; disk, 160; *kikoku*, 154, 182, 190, 204, 208; *lubumba*, 169, 190, 197; mussel, 169, 182, 190, 191, 196, 197, and pls. 4, 110; *nkola*, 191; snail, 150, 154, 155, 169, 190, 204, 208, 226, and pls. 26, 49. *See also* Money
shemwami, 70
Shi, 2, 4 n. 10, 7, 11, 16, 17, 20, 25, 34 n. 12, 52, 68, 70, 112
Shields, 50, 99, 147, 150, 164, 189, 190, 191–193, 213
Shile, 2, 4 n. 7, 9, 10
Shoulder bags, 8 n. 13, 33, 35, 74, 76–78 *passim*, 95, 97, 105, 115, 127, 159, 166–168, 173, 185, 190, 191, 205, 229, 235, and pls. 8, 46; *lutala*, 76, 95, 96, 98; *musutwa*, 95–98. *See also* Baskets
Sieber, Professor Roy, xxii
Skulls, 29, 36, 71, 79, 81, 99, 101, 104 and n. 13, 140, 144, 146–147, 150, 151, 153, 155, 159, 164, 171, 174, 177, 178, 189, 195, 201, 203, 208, 210–215, 223, and pls. 23, 49, 63, 110
Slade, 12, 13
Slave raiders, xvi, 12, 50, 58–61, 67
Slit-drums, 33, 54–56, 76, 102, 140, 147. *See also* Drums
Snails, 15, 23, 79, 95, 101, 110, 145–146. *See also* Shells
Snakes, 28 and n. 6, 79, 102, 140, 145, 147, 163, 225, and pl. 110; *igilima*, 224; *kamitende*, 96; *mpoma*, 28, 146, 165, 226; Mulinde, 152, 224; *ngimbi*, 202, 203, 224, and pl. 94; *sanda*, 224

Index

Soapstone, 33, 141
Social Science Research Council (Joint Committee on African Studies), xxii
Songola, 1–5 *passim*, 11, 17 and n. 20, 19 and n. 28, 21 and n. 31, 22–33 *passim*, 43, 54, 82, 232
Songs, 27, 54, 56, 74, 79, 90, 92, 95, 102, 106, 108, 110, 113, 121, 122, 124, 129, 131, 136, 138–140, 142, 157, 162–170 *passim*, 174, 185, 193, 200–202, 219, 222, 234. *See also* Oral literature
Songye, 17–18, 21 n. 31
Sophrosyne, 129
Sorcerer, 153, 154, 159, 188, 203
Sorcery, 53–55, 59, 67, 103–105, 124, 137, 139, 146, 157, 190, 204, 213, 219, 220
Sororal nephews, 18, 38–46 *passim*, 84, 103–125 *passim*, 133, 173, 176, 181 n. 14, 186–187, 190, 222. *See also* Kinship; Maternal uncles
Spears, 7, 27–29, 32–33, 35, 50, 67, 80, 99, 127, 130, 147, 150, 155, 164, 180, 189, 193, 217, 221
Spoons, 33, 72, 75–76, 79, 81, 149, 164–165, 169, 179–180, 185, 191, 198–199, 205, 209, 226, 229, and pls. 26, 92, 95–97
Squirrels, flying, 15, 71
Staffs, 147, 160, 182, and pls. 1, 9, 48, 54–55. *See also* Canes
Stamp, 14 n. 17
Staner, 31 n. 8
Statues, 53, 54, 102, 128, 137, 157, 191, 233. *See also* Figurines, anthropomorphic
Stayt, 170 n. 6
Sticks, 48–50, 56, 67, 74, 76, 104, 127, 140, 141, 147, 149, 189, 191, 207, 211; forked, 101, 143, 164; *kizingio*, 147; *kyombi*, 114, 121. *See also* Gaffle
Stimson, Mrs. Grace H., xxii
Stones, 29, 33, 76, 79, 145, 147, 229; quartz, 79, 101 n. 11, 102, 145, 177; red, 229; smithing, 128
Stools, 69, 70, 77, 79, 147, 149, 162, 164, 182, and pls. 18, 99–101. *See also* Chairs; *kisumbi*
Straps, 148
Stuffed skin, 178
Stuhlmann, 2 n. 3
Styles, 232–233
Submerged groups, 5–8
Succession, 38–39, 47. *See also* Descent system; Inheritance; Kinship
Swahili, 1 n. 1, 5, 54, 68

Tails, 27, 81–82, 95, 140, 144–147 *passim*, 151, 153, 169, 224, and pl. 10
Tali, 17
Tanzania, northern, 68
Taxonomies, 157–165
Technology, 26, 27, 52, 132, 227
Teeth, 27, 29, 32, 69, 71, 101 n. 11, 105, 140, 141, 144, 148, 149, 151, 155, 160, 162, 165, 169, 177, 225, 226, and pls. 1, 2, 4, 7, 110
Tembo, 17, 20, 68, 70, 232

temeteme, 130
Termites, 23, 26, 29, 53, 145, 166 n. 4, 181, 183, 193, 201, 214, 216, 225
Tesserae, 182
Tetela, 17, 82 and n. 5, 232
Thompson, Professor Robert F., xxii
Tibias, 95, 144, and pl. 110
Tippo Tib, 12
Tomb, 174, 175, 183, 195, 209, 210, 212
Toni Toni, 67
Tools, 18, 32, 33, 42, 43, 112, 118, 120
Toothpick, 213
Torches, 33, 75, 99, 100, 104, 112, 115–117, 119–122, 159, 167, 177, 190, 196, 197
Trade, xvi, xxi, 12, 13, 19 and n. 25, 27 and nn. 2 and 3, 32 and n. 10, 58, 59, 111
Trapping, 27, 35, 140, 193, 205, 233; camps, 35
Trees, 14, 15, 30, 33–35, 55, 56, 75, 77, 91, 99, 104, 126–130 *passim*, 139, 140, 143–145, 147, 166 n. 4, 170, 171, 180, 209, 214, 216, 225; *Allstonia*, 228; fallen, 152, 188, 223, 224; *ibulungu*, 203; *kabi*, 226; *munkugu*, 201; *muntonko*, 187; *nkungu*, 186; parasol, 15, 77, 80, 99, 127, 144, 147, 154, 188, 189, 193, 195, 228, 229; *Raphia*, 213. *See also* Wood
Trident, 76
Troughs, 33
Troupin, 14 n. 17, 143 n. 1
Trunk, 159
Tubala, 213
tulimu, 79, 164, 171
tumbukutu, 92
Tumbwe, 232
tuminimini, 44
tungeningeni, 206
Turner, 185 n. 16
Turtles, 15, 36, 48, 55, 79–81, 96, 99, 101 and n. 11, 128, 145, 149, 151, 155, 164, 171, 189, 193, 199, 200, 207, 212, 226
Tusks, 27, 74, 79, 81, 95, 144, 146, 163, 165, 166, 174, 183, 190, 225–226, 229, and pl. 110
tutendela, 113
Tutors, 151, 153, 156, 157, 168, 172, 183, 184, 187, 196, 197, 200, 221, 222, 225, 228, and pls. 21, 42, 43, 54, 86, 105
Tutsi, 20 and n. 30
Twa, 7, 10. *See also* Pygmies

Uganda, 11; southern, 68
Ugoma, 17 n. 20
Ulegga, 58. *See also* Lega
Unerga, 14
University of California, Los Angeles, pls. 95, 97, 99, 108, 110; African Studies Center, xxii; Press, xxii
University of Delaware, xxii
Uregga, 17 n. 20. *See also* Lega
Uvira, 12, 17 n. 20
Uyttebroeck, 47 and n. 18

Values, xix, 49–58 *passim*, 67, 86, 91, 93, 101,

117–137 *passim*, 155–157, 175–180, 209, 215–222. *See also* Moral philosophy
Van Bulck, 4 nn. 7–9, 24 n. 35
Vermoesen, 143 n. 1
Viaene, 101 n. 11
Village, 34, 35, 37, 45–48, 60, 78, 80, 83, 87, 91, 96–99 *passim*, 105, 106, 114, 117, 118, 120–125 *passim*, 132–138 *passim*, 146, 154, 158, 173, 184, 187–189, 192, 202–210 *passim*, 218, 227, 229, and pls. 11–14, 51; headman, 44, 47, 98, 135, 148, 152, 157, 189, 190
Vines, 32, 187, 191, 209, 223, 229, and pl. 108. *See also* Lianas
Violence, 36, 49–50, 98, 111, 122, 127–129, 135, 154, 155, 168, 169, 188, 193, 195, 201, 210–217 *passim*
Viper, 144, 146, 147, 163
Vira, xv, 5, 17, 20, 21 n. 30, 34 n. 12, 68, 70, 71

wabume, 131, 186
Walikale, 21, 28, 67
Wamuzimu, 23, 24, 37. *See also* Bamuzimu
Wankenge, 42 n. 15
War, 50, 111, 122, 127, 135, 158, 193, 198, 201, 212, 214
Warega, xvii, 1 and nn. 1 and 2, 13, 59, 62. *See also* Lega
Warthog, 15, 74, 95, 144, 146, 190, 226, and pl. 110
Wax, 147, 213
Weapons, 101 n. 11, 226
Weaving, 33 n. 11
Westermann, 21 n. 31
Wickerwork, 26, 56, 69, 80, 81, 99, 104–106, 112, 145, 147, 148, 160, 166, 169, 173, 180, 182, 189, 190, 193, 194, 199, 201, 204, 206, and pls. 10, 48, 55, 84, 110
Wildcats, 112, 145, 169, 204, 226
Witchcraft, 53, 204
Wood, 17, 22, 26, 33, 56, 73, 76, 78–81, 101, 103, 140, 141, 147, 149–151, 155, 161–164, 167–171, 174, 176, 177 and n. 19, 179, 181–183, 185, 187, 188, 195, 199–202, 204, 206, 208, 209, 211, 213–215, 217, 221, 222, 224, 225, 233, and pls. 26, 27, 32, 33, 35–43, 58, 59, 61, 63–66, 70–72, 88, 89, 92, 100; *Allstonia*, 147, 187; *ibesebese*, 51, 95; *katamba*, 154; *munsemunsemu*, 163; *muntonko*, 33, 187; parasol, 33, 36, 80, 99, 147, 164, 190; red, 144. *See also* Trees

Yaka, 177 n. 10
Yananio, xviii, 51, 59, 73–103 *passim*, 122, 134, 152, 160, 161, 163, 164, 167, 168, 173, 181–184, 191, 194, 224, 228; lutumbo lwa, 73, 78, 79, 88–106 *passim*, 118–121, 134, 150, 151, 154, 162, 169, 178, 181, 182 and n. 15, 184, 206, 207–210, 222, and pls. 7, 8, 12, 20, 21, 25, 34, 36, 37, 40, 42, 43, 46, 49, 53, 60–62, 88, 89, 100; musagi wa, 73, 78, 94, 121, 151, 152, 161, and pls. 7, 14, 15, 50, 105
Yango, 83, 166, 191, 207
yango, 77–79, 147, 150
Yela, 82 and n. 5, 232

Zande, xxi, 221, 232
ziko, 74, 167, 168, 207
Zimba, 2–7 *passim*, 10, 17–25 *passim*, 38 n. 11, 82 and n. 5, 232, 233
zumbi, 19
Zyoba, 5, 18, 21 n. 32

Plates

1.

2.

3.

4.

Plate 1. Lukuku, a kyogo kya kindi, wears a belt of bongo antelope, an apron of genet hide, a necklace of leopard teeth, and a hat of woven, blackened *lukusa* fibers. He holds a *mukulu*, "staff of greatness."

Plate 2. Lusolo, a lutumbo lwa kindi, wears an unusual hat of black goat manes with giant cowries. The necklace is made of imitation leopard teeth carved from elephant bone.

Plate 3. Mindo, a lutumbo lwa kindi, and one of his wives initiated into the kanyamwa grade. Mindo wears a most unusual hat made of *maseza* nutshells; his wife wears the diadem typical for a kanyamwa.

Plate 4. An initiate of lutumbo lwa kindi rank, wearing a hat made of elephant's ear and decorated with polished mussel shells. In his necklace are both real and imitation leopard teeth.

Plate 5. Kandolo, a lutumbo lwa kindi and a great preceptor, beats a suspended drum in one of the kongabulumbu rites.

Plate 6. A kanyamwa, in the typical dress of her grade, carrying an initiation basket that contains sculptures and other initiation objects of lutumbo lwa kindi.

5.

6.

PLATE 7. A group of initiates of lutumbo lwa yananio and musagi wa yananio awaiting the arrival of other invited participants. The initiates wear hats made of black goatskin or black goat manes. Those of the lutumbo level have a polished mussel shell attached to the front of the hat. Not all the initiates wear leopard teeth, but all possess them and have the right to wear them. The loincloth is made of reddened bark. The lutumbo may wear belts of bongo hide, but here most of them are wearing loincloths with a rope belt because they are in a relaxed mood awaiting the beginning of the initiations.

PLATE 8. An initiated woman of bulonda grade and her husband, a member of the lutumbo lwa yananio grade, arriving in the candidate's village for initiation ceremonies. She carries a sleeping mat and a basket; he carries his shoulder bag with assorted initiation objects.

PLATE 9. A large gathering of kindi and their initiated wives. High-ranking initiates, each holding a "staff of greatness," are seated on small wooden chairs.

PLATE 10. Two initiates. The one on the left is a lutumbo lwa kindi, as evidenced by his hat made of canvas covered with buttons and surmounted by an elephant tail. The initiate on the right wears a hat of wickerwork with only a few rows of buttons, indicating that he is still at the lower levels of kindi. Kindi hats studded with buttons are a recent development; older kindi hats are made of wickerwork studded with nutshells, cowries, or beads.

8.

9. 10.

PLATE 11. Women of kanyamwa rank conducting the wife of the male candidate into the village. She comes in humility wearing a minimum of attire.

PLATE 12. A long row of lutumbo lwa yananio making a ceremonial entrance (*lukenye*) into the candidate's village. The row is led by several preceptors. The initiates are swirling the midribs of banana leaves.

PLATE 13. A group of kindi leading an initiated woman carrying an initiation basket through the village.

PLATE 14. A group of kanyamwa women carrying initiation baskets of lutumbo lwa kindi being led into the village by an initiate of yananio rank. As messenger for a relative of kindi rank, he carries the *mizegele* rattle which is a symbol of kindi, a musical instrument, and an object used to transmit secret messages.

12.

13.

14.

PLATE 15. Yananio initiates and women of bulonda and kanyamwa taking part in a dance performance *(kamondo)* which preceded the actual initiations.

PLATE 16. A group of drummers and singers. The woman standing is of bulonda grade. She holds the title of *nyagwamana* because of her special training in strident singing. As the only female in the orchestra, she receives the tongue and esophagus of all game distributed in certain rites.

PLATE 17. A procession of kanyamwa women in a rare rite that permits women to wear the hats of their kindi husbands. All women wear bunches of chicken feathers, which are dancing paraphernalia, around their buttocks and hips.

PLATE 18. Two kindi dancing with wooden stools in the center of a circle of other kindi dancers. The dance illustrates a contemptible quarrel between high-ranking men over a boundary, represented here by the sticks on the ground.

16.

17.

18.

PLATE 19. A kindi performing the rooftop ritual *(itutu)* on the roof of the initiation hut. He is showing to those below a polished mussel shell which represents the moon crescent. The song reference is, "Crescent-of-the-Moon, those far away look up at him in awe."

PLATE 20. Two initiates dressed as leopard men in large robes of whitened bark cloth. The rare appearance of leopard men is connected with *kasisi,* one of the culminating rites in lutumbo lwa yananio.

PLATE 21. A musagi wa kindi acting as tutor for a relative being initiated into lutumbo lwa yananio holds him firmly in a protective gesture: "Those in charge of the candidate love him."

PLATE 22. An old musagi wa kindi being gracefully led to the row of dancers by two close agnatic relatives. The song reference, "The Old-One-of-the-Hat has come for the dances from far away," celebrates the special luster that very old initiates add to the occasion by merely attending initiations, without directly participating or becoming involved in them.

19.

20.

21.

22.

PLATE 23. Display on the village floor of the contents of an initiation basket linked with kindi initiations. Included are wooden figurines of both human and animal shapes, skulls of chimpanzee and young wild boar, and scepter-like objects made of elephant bone. Similar baskets have variable contents. The baskets, which are symbols of the social solidarity and ritual autonomy of specific kinship groups and ritual communities, change hands as the cycle of initiations evolves, passing always to the most recent initiate. Each object is carefully interpreted in sung aphorisms.

PLATE 24. Wooden figurines displayed on the village ground during kindi initiations. The two statues on the left are extremely rare examples of Lega art. These objects are sometimes individually owned by senior kindi or by preceptors, but usually they are among the contents of collectively held initiation baskets.

PLATE 25. A lavish display of animal figurines, called *mugugundu,* during lutumbo lwa yananio initiations. In some ritual communities the objects are individually owned only by members of the lutumbo lwa yananio grade.

PLATE 26. A display of ivory, bone, and highly polished wooden figurines during preliminaries to the *bele muno* rite of lutumbo lwa kindi. There are bone hammers and spoons, as well as a giant snail shell and a Western-made equestrian figurine. On this occasion each kindi present at the initiations is ordered to produce the art objects that he owns or holds in trusteeship.

24.

25.

26.

PLATE 27. Display of individually owned wooden carvings during the *mutulwa* rite of lutumbo lwa kindi. The collection includes stylized bird beaks and necks. The three objects on the extreme right are commercially produced outside Legaland.

PLATE 28. Four kindi dancing with three Katanda figures displayed in plate 27. A common way of handling the statues is to oil the objects, then display them, and finally dance with them category by category, singly or several at a time, while the exegesis is given in aphorisms.

PLATE 29. Four kindi dancing with three wooden figurines of the same functional type, called Wayinda. The dancers hold little sticks between the legs of the carvings to illustrate the administration of an enema to an adulterous pregnant woman.

PLATE 30. Five kindi dancing with a representation of Sakimatwematwe, Mr. Many-Heads, during the *mutulwa* rite of lutumbo lwa kindi. The proverbs sung in the context speak about equity based on wisdom, which marks the life-style of high-ranking initiates.

28.

29.

30.

PLATE 31. A kindi dancing with a representation of Wayinda, the adulterous pregnant woman. The face of the dancer-preceptor expresses the pains the adulterous woman suffers during childbirth.

PLATE 32. Detail of plate 31. The figurine is awesome in its ugliness and so is the woman who, by committing adultery during pregnancy, causes ritual pollution and destruction of her family.

PLATE 33. A kindi dancing with the representation of Nyabeidilwa, the woman who likes to run around to different places and is overcome by night.

31.

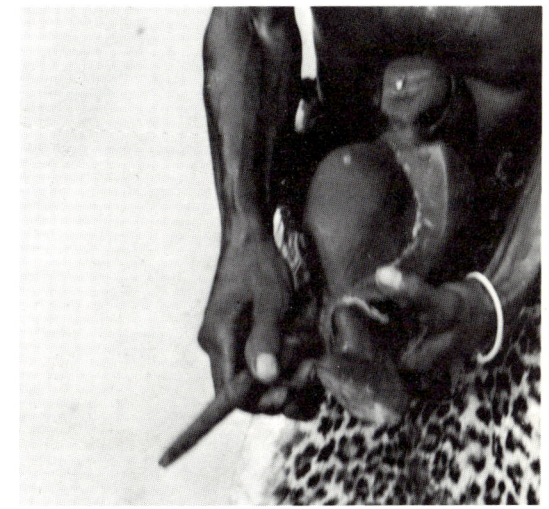

32.

33.

PLATE 34. Display of wooden masks of the *lukwakongo* type. These masks, covered with white clay, are used in the *lukwakongo* rite leading to membership in lutumbo lwa yananio. Each member of bwami in that grade owns a mask of this type. Much symbolic significance is attached to the beards, which are made of *lukusa* fibers, of fine strips of banana tree bark, or, more recently, of raffia.

PLATE 35. Display of wooden masks of the *lukwakongo* type (see legend for plate 34).

PLATE 36. Incumbents of lutumbo lwa yananio dancing with wooden *lukwakongo* masks. Note the characteristic way in which a mask is fastened to the temple or to a hat. These masks may also be placed against a fence, dragged over the ground, carried in the hands, worn on the face, displayed on a little mound, and so on, depending on the specific ritual sequence in which they are used.

PLATE 37. Two preceptors of lutumbo lwa yananio dancing with the rare horned wooden *kayamba* masks in a yananio rite.

35.

36.

37.

PLATE 38. Masks of ivory or bone fastened to a pala fence around a large wooden mask during a lutumbo lwa kindi rite. Each kindi of the highest level owns a mask of this type. The wooden mask is considered to be the *nenekisi*, master of the land, with all his children around him.

PLATE 39. Masks in ivory or bone attached to a pala fence by a *munana* feather rope, together with a large wooden *muminia* mask, during a lutumbo lwa kindi rite. Owners of the masks are squatting behind the fence. The large mask is owned by a preceptor of kindi grade.

PLATE 40. Members of lutumbo lwa yananio, wearing small *lukwakongo* masks fastened to the temples, are led in the dance by a preceptor to whose forehead is attached a larger whitened mask made of wood.

PLATE 41. A kindi preceptor, dressed in feathered paraphernalia, dancing with the large wooden *nenekisi* mask illustrated in plate 38.

39.

40.

41.

PLATES 42, 43. Two different scenes in the *nkunda* rite of the lutumbo lwa yananio initiations. The preceptor wears the wooden *muminia* mask, together with two wooden *lukwakongo* masks and a whitened wooden *idimu* mask. With his helpers he impersonates people in search of honey. The rite, called *nkunda* after the queen bee, is meant to illustrate the activities of the *kakusa* tutor who constantly searches for candidates whom he can help through the initiations and thereby gain material benefits and prestige.

PLATES 44, 45. Two scenes in the *ibugebuge* rite of lutumbo lwa kindi, illustrating the disastrous consequences of acts of disrespect and of quarrelsomeness. Plate 44 suggests the dangerous situations that follow destructive actions; plate 45 suggests the acts of seducing the wife of a co-initiate and of fighting.

43.

44. 45.

PLATE 46. Display, during the *nsago* rite of lutumbo lwa yananio, of shoulder bags in which initiates keep their personal insignia.

PLATE 47. An assemblage called *kitunda kya kindi* or *kizumba*, representing some of the attire of a musagi wa kindi. The paraphernalia are attached to a banana stipe by means of a feather rope *(munana)*. An ivory mask may be fastened to the hat. This particular assemblage is known as *kikuni*.

PLATE 48. Display of wickerwork rattles during kindi initiations. These *mizegele* rattles are used as musical instruments, as insignia of rank, and as a means of transferring secret messages hidden in knotted raffia fibers. Among the rattles is a rare wickerwork staff *(matakale)* imitating the structure of the rattles.

PLATE 49. Display inside the initiation hut of objects used during the *mukumbi* rite of lutumbo lwa yananio. The configuration includes chimpanzee skulls, wooden masks, giant snail shells, pangolin scales, and other objects contained in a small pit underneath the little mound in the foreground.

47.

48.

49.

PLATE 50. Enthronement rite of a woman recently initiated to the female bulonda grade. Her husband, who is musagi wa yananio, is seated in front of her. The woman stands on the *kisumbi* chair normally reserved for initiated men.

PLATE 51. Two high-ranking initiates performing a bunyamwa dance near the forest rim on the outskirts of the village.

PLATE 52. Three men of low bwami rank setting out on a net hunt organized in connection with the initiations, while a crowd of women of high rank wait for an early morning masked dance to be performed.

50.

51.

52.

PLATE 53. A kindi dancing with a genet hide during the *kabungulu* rite of lutumbo lwa yananio. Genet hides are used in contexts that stress respect for elders and warn against thievery, quarrelsomeness, and interference.

PLATE 54. A tutor and a candidate, leaning on their *mukulu* staffs, leave a house to attend the rites in the lower kongabulumbu initiations. The tutor carries the *moza* pot, around which the *munana* feather rope is tied. The candidate holds the ends of the feather rope.

PLATE 55. A kindi resting on the extremely rare wickerwork staff in a typical attitude before giving a speech: the kindi is old and weak but possesses great strength of the word.

54.

55.

Plate 56. *Lukungu* mask (4⅞" high) in ivory (collected by Daniel Biebuyck; deposited in Koninklijk Museum van Centraal Afrika, no. 55.3.135; transferred to the IRSAC collections at Lwiro, Democratic Republic of the Congo). The mask, received in 1953 after the *lukungu* and *kinsamba* rites leading to lutumbo lwa kindi from Kabondo, a kindi of the Bagilanzelu clan, chefferie Babene, Pangi territory, is one of the insignia of the kindi grade. The *lukungu* (skull) mask conceptually represents the "skull of my father" and is a symbol of the continuity that binds father and son, or different kinsmen, through bwami. During the dances these small masks are carried in the hand, fastened to a fence, or placed on the ground in a configuration that includes figurines and natural objects.

Plate 57. *Lukungu* mask (4⅜" high) in bone (collected by Daniel Biebuyck; deposited in Koninklijk Museum van Centraal Afrika, no. 55.3.14). The mask was received in 1952 after the *kilinkumbi* and *ibugebuge* rites leading to lutumbo lwa kindi from Kilolo, a kindi of the Beiankuku clan, secteur Beia, Pangi territory. Elephant bone and ivory are functionally interchangeable materials. Masks made of these materials are reserved for incumbents of the highest grade (kindi).

Plate 58. *Lukungu* mask (4⅞" high) in polished wood (collected by Daniel Biebuyck; deposited in Koninklijk Museum van Centraal Afrika, no. 55.3.65). The mask has the same meanings as those illustrated in plates 56 and 57. On rare occasions a well-polished wooden mask may be substituted at the kindi level for an ivory or bone mask.

56.

57.

58.

PLATE 59. *Muminia* mask (10¼" high) in wood (collected by Daniel Biebuyck; deposited in Koninklijk Museum van Centraal Afrika, no. 55.3.1). This unusually large mask was received in 1952 from Wakenga, a yananio of the Banamusiga, a small kinship unit incorporated with the Beiankuku clan, secteur Beia, Pangi territory. This Lega mask is so rare that several ritual communities, like Beianangi, Babongolo, and Beiankuku, used it for their initiations. Although primarily connected with yananio, the mask was also used in the lower kongabulumbu and the highest kindi initiations. As far as memory goes, the mask was inherited through the last four generations in an extremely close agnatic line of descent from Igulo to his son, to two of his grandsons (the senior first, and later the junior), and to his great-grandson by a third grandson. The mask symbolizes the ritual autonomy and social unity of a small kinship unit as well as of a larger ritual community. The rites in which the mask is used underscore concepts of seniority, greatness, power, authority, dignity, and immunity. (For further interpretation, see Biebuyck, 1954c.)

PLATE 60. *Lukwakongo* mask (7⅜" high) in wood (collected by Daniel Biebuyck; deposited in Koninklijk Museum van Centraal Afrika, no. 55.3.2). The mask was obtained in 1952 at the end of the yananio initiations from Mulyabantu, a lutumbo lwa yananio who had already achieved the lower level of kindi, of the Beiankuku clan, secteur Beia, Pangi territory. Traced back over four generations, it passed from a junior lineage in the clan to a senior lineage, and then from a man to his senior brother's son. In most ritual communities every incumbent of the second highest grade (lutumbo lwa yananio) possesses a *lukwakongo* mask as a token of his rank.

PLATE 61. *Lukwakongo* mask (6⅛" high) in wood (collected by Daniel Biebuyck; deposited in Koninklijk Museum van Centraal Afrika, no. 55.3.29). Obtained from Bikenge, a lutumbo lwa yananio of the Banasalu clan, secteur Beia, Pangi territory, the mask is traced back over five generations from Kyanga to his son, to his grandson, to two great-grandsons by another grandson, and to a great-great-grandson. It was used in the *bakumbonga, lukwakongo,* and *mukumbi* rites leading to lutumbo lwa yananio. These masks are used in a wide variety of rites that lead to full membership in lutumbo lwa yananio.

PLATE 62. *Lukwakongo* mask (6" high) in wood (collected by Daniel Biebuyck in 1952). This exceptionally beautiful mask was obtained from Kamundala, a lutumbo lwa yananio of the Banasalu clan, secteur Beia, Pangi territory. It is traced back over five generations within a close line of descent. All *lukwakongo* masks are used in several rites of lutumbo lwa yananio in a variety of ways: they are worn on the face or attached to the forehead so that the beard covers the face; they are sometimes fastened to the temple, to the back of the head, to a knee or an arm; they are placed in a row or in a circle on the ground or piled up together; they are attached to a fence or to the central pole of the initiation hut; they are carried in the hand or swung around or dragged over the ground; they are held under the chin, and so on. (See Fagg and Plass, 1964, p. 151; Fagg, 1970, pl. 151.)

59.

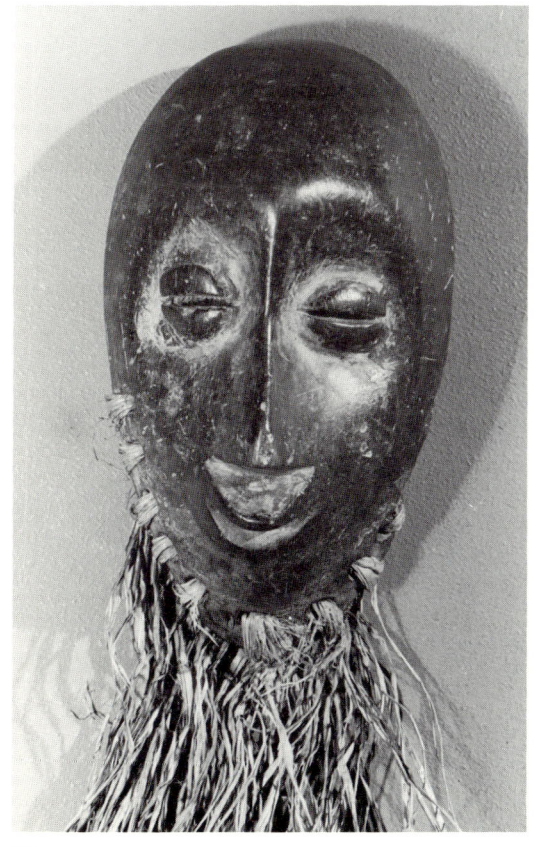

60.

61.

62.

PLATE 63. Human figurine (12⅛″) in wood, called Katanda (collected by Daniel Biebuyck in 1952; deposited in Koninklijk Museum van Centraal Afrika, no. 55.3.40). Obtained from the Beiamunsange clan, secteur Beia, Pangi territory, this small carving forms part of a *mutulwa* basket containing initiation objects (natural items as well as objets d'art) used in musagi and lutumbo lwa kindi rites. The basket, with its contents, is an expression of the unity and autonomy of the ritual community. The key aphorism referring to the figurine states: "I used to love you; fondling destroys good ones; it has destroyed Katanda." The figurine represents Katanda. Although literally meaning "mat," the term also connotes "something bad"; a wild dispersal of red ants, for example, is referred to as *katanda ke ibazi*. The holes in the body of the figurine suggest the dispersal of ants and signify evil. The statue is used in a context of human figurines and other objects (e.g., *Cercopithecus* skulls and rudimentarily carved birds' necks) to stress the positive and negative aspects of the bwami code of ethics. (See Fagg and Plass, 1964, p. 82.)

PLATE 64. Human figurine (6½″) in wood, called Kakulu kamwenne ku masengo (collected by Daniel Biebuyck in 1952; deposited in Koninklijk Museum van Centraal Afrika, no. 55.3.150). This small object was acquired from Kisula, a lutumbo lwa kindi of the Batoba clan, chefferie Babene, Pangi territory. It was used in rites of the musagi and lutumbo lwa kindi initiations, in a display of many objects, to represent the aphorism, "The Great-Old-One has seen many initiation objects; he goes bent under them," which refers to an old initiate who has helped many people go through the initiations and who, when some of them die, takes over the trusteeship and guardianship of their initiation objects. The display of the object in conjunction with other figurines tells the candidate that he should take good care of old, seemingly insignificant initiates because they are loaded with powerful things. (See Delange, 1967, pl. 165.)

63.

64.

PLATE 65. Human figurine (17″) in wood, called Bakwampego (collected by Daniel Biebuyck in 1952; deposited in Koninklijk Museum van Centraal Afrika, no. 53.3.52). Acquired from Nzogu, lutumbo lwa kindi of the Beiamunsange clan, chefferie Beia, Pangi territory, the figurine was used in a context of other artworks and simpler objects during the ritual display of the contents of the lutumbo lwa kindi basket. This rite is known throughout Legaland, but each ritual community makes its own special arrangements. The wooden figurine is one of the specialties, not merely because it is rarely found in Legaland, but also because it is not a part of the initiation basket even though used in that context. The statue is kept by a kindi of "keen intelligence" on behalf of the total membership of a ritual community which, in this instance, encompasses three linked primary lineages within the large Beiamunsange clan. The name Bakwampego (lit., "those who suffer from cold") suggests the aphorism, "Those who suffer from cold, there where a fire is being laid they refuse [to be]," which is interpreted as a complaint by an old initiate, who takes good care of the children of his deceased senior, that these children have come to despise him. Conversely, the aphorism is also interpreted as the complaint of a young man who, after his father's death, looks after an old relative. The latter, however, indulges in the same old quarrels he had with the young man's father.

PLATE 66. Human figurine (10″) in wood with raised arm. (Dr. Jay T. Last Collection, Los Angeles). Similar well-carved and well-polished statues in the possession of kindi are functionally equivalent to ivory and bone carvings. Carvings with one or two raised arms illustrate the kindi's privilege of serving as arbiter in quarrels and feuds. The figurine is called Kasungalala and the appropriate aphorism is: "What shoots up straight; I have arbitrated Igulu [lit., the sky]; I have arbitrated something big."

PLATE 67. Human figurine (12¾″) in wood (collected by Daniel Biebuyck in 1952; deposited in Koninklijk Museum van Centraal Afrika, no. 55.3.75). The object was used in the *kitange* rite of lutumbo lwa kindi among the Baliga, secteur Bakisi, Shabunda territory. It belongs to the collectively held initiation basket and thus is one of the material symbols that establish and foster the unity of the ritual community. The statue represents Wayinda, a woman found guilty of adultery during pregnancy, an act that causes ritual pollution, misery, and death in her own family group.

PLATE 68. Human figurine (10⅝″) in wood (collected by Daniel Biebuyck in 1952; deposited in Koninklijk Museum van Centraal Afrika, no. 55.3.41). Obtained at the end of the *kunanuna masengo* rite of lutumbo lwa kindi among the Beiamunsange, secteur Beia, Pangi territory, the object is part of the collectively held initiation basket. It expresses the same meanings as the figurine shown in plate 67. The frequently quoted aphorism is: "Wayinda died because of ritual pollution, [while] the enema funnel was still between the legs." The Wayinda character is the prototype of the ugly woman who destroys the harmony of the family. In the carving of these rudimentary images the Lega cultivate an aesthetic of the ugly.

65.

66.

67.

68.

PLATE 69. Human figurine (14¾″) in wood, called Kakulu ka Mpito (collected by Daniel Biebuyck in 1952; deposited in Koninklijk Museum van Centraal Afrika, no. 55.3.5). The object, received after the *kunanuna masengo* rite of lutumbo lwa kindi, belongs to the collectively held initiation basket of the Beiankuku and Banamusiga clans, secteur Beia, Pangi territory. It is used in a configuration with other items, which usually include representations of Wayinda (woman guilty of ritual pollution because of adultery during pregnancy) and Mukobania (the frivolous rowdy who causes division and dissension among people). Several meanings are ascribed to the object (see Biebuyck, 1953a), but the image is invariably said to represent Kakulu, the Old-One who falls victim either to Wayinda (adulterous behavior by his wife) or to Mukobania (the frivolous rowdy who caused trouble by calling together for a beer party several people whom he did not know well).

PLATE 70. Human figurine (14⅝″) in wood, called Mutu Nyabeidilwa (collected by Daniel Biebuyck in 1952; deposited in Koninklijk Museum van Centraal Afrika, no. 55.3.42). This object, which was in the collectively held initiation basket of lutumbo lwa kindi among the Beiamunsange clan, secteur Beia, Pangi territory, represents Nyabeidilwa, a woman who again and again abandons her husband to go back to her people, according to the aphorism: "Mutu [lit., Hornbill] who likes to be overcome by night, each time she goes, it is each time to be called back." (See Walker Art Center, 1967, p. 54.)

PLATE 71. Human figurine (5½″) in wood (collected by Daniel Biebuyck in 1952; deposited in Koninklijk Museum van Centraal Afrika, no. 55.3.34). The object was received from Lukinga, a lutumbo lwa kindi of the Banakagela clan, secteur Beia, Pangi territory, after the *bele muno* rite of lutumbo lwa kindi. This small, well-carved, finely polished statue functionally replaces a carving in ivory or bone. It was hanging on a string and was identified as representing the aphorism, "May I die today; may the little neck be cut by a claw." This aphorism has many possible applications: to the candidate who wishes his initiations were finished today; to the father who complains of receiving evil treatment from his child; to the Lega man who, although he knows he will soon die, still wants to achieve kindi.

PLATE 72. Human figurine (5⅝″) in wood, called Nkumba or Mulima (collected by Daniel Biebuyck in 1952; deposited in Koninklijk Museum van Centraal Afrika, no. 55.3.101; transferred to the IRSAC collections at Lwiro, Democratic Republic of the Congo). Received from Kyanga, a lutumbo lwa kindi of the Babongolo clan, secteur Bakabango, Pangi territory, this statue is sometimes called Nkumba, meaning literally a short piece of vine wrapped in wickerwork which is fastened onto a small woven disk and adorned with chicken feathers. This object, called *muzombolo*, is worn on top of the head by all kanyamwa women, who are frequently referred to as *bankumba*. In this sense the figurine represents an initiated woman of high rank. In another context the figurine, displayed hanging from a string with the head downward, is called Mulima (lit., bat): "Bat hangs with the head downward because of the bad word spoken by Sun." (See Fagg and Plass, 1964, p. 38.)

69.

70.

71.

72.

PLATE 73. Human figurine (7¼″) in ivory with four faces, called Sakimatwematwe or Nawasakwa nyona (collected by Daniel Biebuyck in 1953; deposited in Koninklijk Museum van Centraal Afrika, no. 55.3.123). The piece was obtained at the end of the *kinsamba* rite of lutumbo lwa kindi from Lutala, a lutumbo lwa kindi of the Banamunwa clan, chefferie Babene, Pangi territory. The meaning, in this instance, has nothing to do with the multifaced form of the head, which is the basis of most interpretations of similar pieces. The associated aphorism, "The one who had the signs of beauty engraved on the cheeks no longer is as he/she used to be," stresses the transience of people and things.

PLATE 74. Human figurine (5⅛″) in ivory with four faces, called Sakimatwematwe (collected by Daniel Biebuyck in 1952; deposited in Koninklijk Museum van Centraal Afrika, no. 55.3.8). This object was received from Mizeka, a lutumbo lwa kindi of the Beiankuku clan, secteur Beia, Pangi territory, at the end of the *kinsamba* rite of lutumbo lwa kindi. The associated aphorism, "Mr. Many-Heads has seen an elephant on the other side of the large river," emphasizes the quality of equity, based on wisdom and knowledge, which marks the high-ranking initiate. It also means that the kindi cannot easily be fooled.

PLATE 75. Human figurine (4⅝″) in ivory (collected by Daniel Biebuyck in 1952; deposited in Koninklijk Museum van Centraal Afrika, no. 55.3.118). Received from Kintimbuka, lutumbo lwa kindi, Bagilanzelu clan, chefferie Babene, Pangi territory, the figurine represents Katindili (one who has no strength to work): "Katindili calls for [people to work in] his new field; those of the dry season will refuse him in vain." The aphorism criticizes one who always talks about his plans for initiation but lacks the strength to persevere.

PLATE 76. Figurine (4″) in ivory, called Mulima (collected by Daniel Biebuyck in 1952; deposited in Koninklijk Museum van Centraal Afrika, no. 55.3.61). The carving was acquired from Penekenye, a lutumbo lwa kindi of the Banalyuba clan, secteur Beia, Pangi territory, at the end of the *bele muno* rite of lutumbo lwa kindi. It hangs from the ceiling in the initiation hut with the head downward: "Bat hangs with the head downward because of the bad word spoken by Sun." (See Delange, 1967, pl. 166.)

73.

74.

75.

76.

PLATE 77. Human figurine (3¼″) in ivory with double face, called Kakinga (collected by Daniel Biebuyck in 1952; deposited in Koninklijk Museum van Centraal Afrika, no. 55.3.28). The figure was received from Biganangwa, lutumbo lwa kindi of the Beiamisisi clan, secteur Beia, Pangi territory, at the end of the *bele muno* rite of lutumbo lwa kindi. The meaning attached to it is expressed in the aphorism: "The little maiden used to be beautiful and good; adultery is the reason that she perished."

PLATE 78. Human figurine (3⅜″) in ivory (collected by Daniel Biebuyck in 1952; deposited in Koninklijk Museum van Centraal Afrika, no. 55.3.10). The figurine, acquired from Kyenia, a lutumbo lwa kindi of the Banamusiga clan, secteur Beia, Pangi territory, after the *bele muno* rite, is called Nyaminia (lit., Mrs. Black). The aphorism is: "Nyaminia, my good and beautiful one; every man has his good and beautiful one."

PLATE 79. Human figurine (4″) in ivory (collected by Daniel Biebuyck in 1952). The object was obtained from Mulungilwa, a lutumbo lwa kindi of the Bagilanzelu clan, chefferie Babene, Pangi territory, at the end of the *kinsamba* rite of the musagi wa kindi initiation. In some ritual communities the initiate of musagi wa kindi (the level below lutumbo lwa kindi) possesses, in addition to other insignia, one human figurine in ivory or bone. These figurines, collectively called *kalimbangoma*, are usually smaller than those held at the highest level of bwami. The associated aphorism, "Nyaminia [Mrs. Black], my good and beautiful one; every man has his good and beautiful one," says that in all circumstances one can rely on people to give help and advice.

PLATE 80. Human figurine (2⅞″) in ivory (collected by Daniel Biebuyck in 1952; deposited in Koninklijk Museum van Centraal Afrika, no. 55.3.46). The carving was received from Mrs. Kabangwa, wife of a lutumbo lwa kindi and herself a kanyamwa of the Beiamunsange clan, secteur Beia, Pangi territory, at the end of the *kasumba* rite for women. These small ivory carvings, owned by women of the highest initiatory level, are rare and therefore are absent from most ritual communities. Classified as *katimbitimbi* (lit., little phallus), they are collectively referred to as "The little phallus, the penis that has not seen the circumcision ceremonies." In most regions the *katimbitimbi* are simple pieces of ivory, sometimes carved in a form suggestive of a phallus, worn by kanyamwa women on a ring hanging from a belt.

77.

78.

79.

80.

PLATE 81. Human figurine (5¼″) in ivory, called Beikalantende and Keitula (collected by Daniel Biebuyck in 1952). The carving, received from Musongelwa, a lutumbo lwa kindi of the Beianangi clan, secteur Beia, Pangi territory, at the end of the *bele muno* rite, is identified by the aphorism, "Those who think constantly ponder about many things," which celebrates the wisdom and the profound thoughts of the kindi. The figurine is also referred to in the context by the aphorism, "Keitula wa Yimbo [lit., what forges itself; son of the Famed Singer] is beautiful to look at," to stress the strength, beauty, and goodness of the kindi. (See Fagg and Plass, 1964, p. 144.)

PLATE 82. Human figurine (5⅛″) in ivory, called Nawasakwa nyona (collected by Daniel Biebuyck in 1952). Obtained from Kyelu, a lutumbo lwa kindi of the Banamunwa clan, chefferie Babene, Pangi territory, at the end of the *kinsamba* rite, the figurine illustrates the concept of transience of things and people, according to the aphorism, "The one who has the signs of beauty engraved on the body no longer is as he/she used to be."

81.

82.

PLATE 83. Human figurine (4¾″) in ivory (Dr. Jay T. Last Collection, Los Angeles). It is impossible to define with any certainty the precise meaning of this object; only the formulas gathered from the owners of figurines during kindi rites provide the clues for understanding the many Lega carvings that have no specific morphological features (such as several faces or heads, one arm, etc.) to correlate with a particular interpretation.

PLATE 84. Human figurine (4⅝″) in ivory (collected by Daniel Biebuyck in 1952). The carving was acquired from Nkasa, a lutumbo lwa kindi of the Banagabo clan, secteur Bakisi, Shabunda territory, after the *mizegele* rite. It was traced back to seven previous owners, some in the Banagabo clan, some in the Beigala and Banakasyele clans. The figurine represents Keitula, "the heart of the one who holds the wickerwork rattles."

PLATE 85. Human figurine (5½″) in ivory (collected in 1952 by Daniel Biebuyck; deposited in Koninklijk Museum van Centraal Afrika, no. 55.3.38). Received from Kyombi, a lutumbo lwa kindi of the Banakagela clan, chefferie Babene, Pangi territory, after the *kinsamba* rite of lutumbo lwa kindi, the statue represents "Mr. Little-Head-of-Hatred." Buttons are affixed to the head with resin to represent a bwami hat.

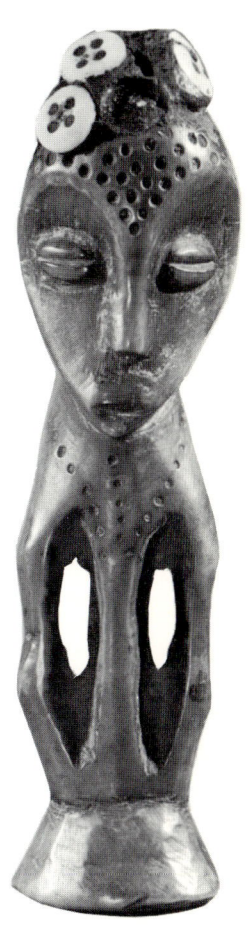

83.

84.

85.

PLATE 86. Double head (6⅛″) in ivory (collected by Daniel Biebuyck in 1952). The carving was received from Kibangala, a lutumbo lwa kindi of the Banamunwa clan, chefferie Babene, Pangi territory, at the end of the *kunanuna masengo* rite. Like all multifaced or multiheaded figurines, it represents the concept of Sakimatwematwe, Mr. Many-Heads, signifying the wisdom and the impartiality of the kindi. Additional interpretations of Kimatwematwe presented in the same area meant that a kindi cannot be taken for someone else and that he cannot be denigrated in his absence. In addition, two other aphorisms usually associated with other objects were sung in this connection: "Who will teach him, Bad-Heart, son of Whose-Heart-is-Dead" (referring to the bad person who does not listen to advice and whom nobody will continue to advise for fear that he may kill), and "What-Descends-with-the-Water has died without seeing the man to rescue him" (meaning that the bad swimmer will drown and that the candidate without a tutor will not succeed).

PLATE 87. Head on little stool (7⅜″), in ivory (collected by Daniel Biebuyck in 1952; deposited in Koninklijk Museum van Centraal Afrika, no. 55.3.145). The object was acquired from Kyabula, a lutumbo lwa kindi of the Banamukungwa clan, chefferie Babene, Pangi territory. Kyabula held it in trusteeship on behalf of the kindi of the Banambizu clan, with whom the members of his own group are intimately intermingled, because no lutumbo lwa kindi was available among the Banambizu. Massive figurines of this type are extremely rare in Legaland; they are usually held on behalf of a total ritual community by the most senior kindi (i.e., the first among the living to have been initiated to that grade in the group). The figurine is called Wankenge (lit., "of the bongo antelope"). The bongo antelope is a symbol of beauty, and Wankenge may signify the Good-and-Beautiful-One: the aphorism, "Do not kill Wankenge; Mwelwa [the Glittering-One] has many behind him," says that a kindi takes good care of his people. (See Maesen, 1960, pl. 39.)

86.

87.

PLATE 88. Animal figurine (4⅞″) in wood (collected by Daniel Biebuyck in 1952; deposited in Koninklijk Museum van Centraal Afrika, no. 55.3.6). The object was obtained from Mugeni, a lutumbo lwa yananio of the Beiankuku clan, secteur Beia, Pangi territory. The generic term for this type of animal figurine is *mugugundu*. In Mugeni's ritual community every lutumbo lwa yananio has such an object as part of the paraphernalia of his rank; functionally similar objects, which in other areas are small wooden human figurines, are identified as *kalimbangoma*. These generalized animal figurines may be interpreted as dogs, pangolins, or antelopes. Here the emphasis is on the object as a token of continuity in the kinship group.

PLATE 89. Animal figurine (12″) in wood with horns (Dr. Jay T. Last Collection, Los Angeles). Figurines of this type are rare; although connected with lutumbo lwa yananio, they are usually held only by preceptors. The generic category is *mugugundu*; specifically, the animal is referred to as a *lungaga* antelope or as *kilimba*, a billy goat.

PLATE 90. Animal figurine (7″) in ivory (collected by Daniel Biebuyck in 1952; deposited in Koninklijk Museum van Centraal Afrika, no. 55.3.72). Naturalistic animal figurines are rare among the Lega. Most of those made of ivory and bone are highly stylized and belong to lutumbo lwa kindi. The carving here illustrated was received from Kyelu, a lutumbo lwa kindi of the Banagabo clan, secteur Bakisi, Shabunda territory. It represents *kimena*, a crocodile, and is interpreted by the aphorism, "Who does not stop arguing will quarrel with what has the mouth widely distended."

PLATE 91. Animal figurine (6¼″) in ivory (Dr. Jay T. Last Collection, Los Angeles). This figurine is another unusual representation of *ikaga*, the giant pangolin, connected with lutumbo lwa kindi. In fact, any generalized animal carving, with or without suggestive additions such as scales, can be interpreted as a pangolin. The pangolin is a culture hero who is said to have taught people the technique for covering house roofs (phrynium leaves are arranged on the roof like the scales on the pangolin's body). It is a sacred animal whose accidental death creates ritual disequilibrium, which must be expiated by appropriate rituals and distributions.

88.

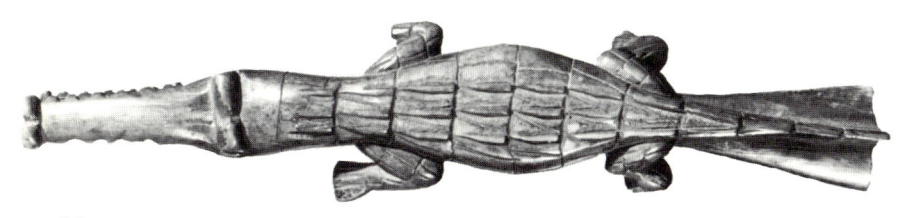

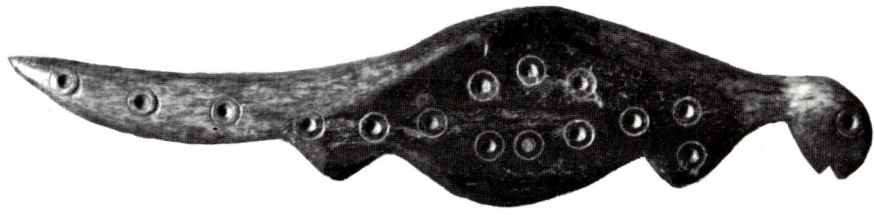

89.

90.

91.

PLATE 92. Animal figurine (4⅜″) in ivory, of the *mugugundu* type (Dr. Jay T. Last Collection, Los Angeles). These figurines have the same functions and meanings as the wooden *mugugundu* figurine illustrated in plate 88, but they belong to kindi. The circle-dot design, which is identified by the Lega as a tatoo or as a sign of beauty, is rare for figurines of this type. It is found most often on ivory and bone figurines and on spoons.

PLATE 93. Animal figurine (5⅜″) in ivory (Dr. Jay T. Last Collection, Los Angeles). This more realistic animal figurine may represent *ntumba* the aardvark, an animal of ritual significance which is of importance in Lega thinking. Aphorisms usually refer to the aardvark's claws, rather than to a representation of the animal. The aardvark is often contrasted with the pangolin as a junior is with a senior.

PLATE 94. Animal figurine (7⅛″) in ivory (Dr. Jay T. Last Collection, Los Angeles). This figurine is the representation of a *ngimbi* snake, which is frequently a symbol of death; the fangs of the snake are generally used to symbolize death. The associated aphorism, "The children play in shallow waters; the *ngimbi* snake kills," warns those who would think lightly about the sacred things used in bwami.

92.

93.

94.

PLATE 95. Spoon (6″) in ivory (Museum and Laboratories of Ethnic Arts and Technology, University of California, Los Angeles). Spoons of this kind, classified as *kalukili* or *kakili*, are used in various rites from kongabulumbu to kindi. They are not used for eating purposes, although occasionally masked dancers are symbolically fed with them. The spoons suggest sexual symbols and are sometimes interpreted as substitutes for knives.

PLATE 96. Spoon (8¾″) in elephant bone (collected by Daniel Biebuyck in 1952; deposited in Koninklijk Museum van Centraal Afrika, no. 55.3.92). This object was received from Mizege, a lutumbo lwa kindi of the Beigala clan, secteur Bakisi, Shabunda territory. The appropriate aphorism, "Kalukili [literally spoon, but here personified as Mrs. Spoon], you used to give me the lap; now you begin to give me the chest of ribs," is critical of a woman who neglects her husband.

PLATE 97. Spoon (7½″) in ivory (Museum and Laboratories of Ethnic Arts and Technology, University of California, Los Angeles, no. 378–106). Spoons symbolize respect or disrespect: "The buttocks of the elephant are flat; they have no regard for other people's things." A spoon is placed in the mouth of a person to whom the poison ordeal, real or mock, is administered. Spoons are also used as substitutes for knives in the "skinning of the elephant" rite, during which the initiation hut is demolished.

95.

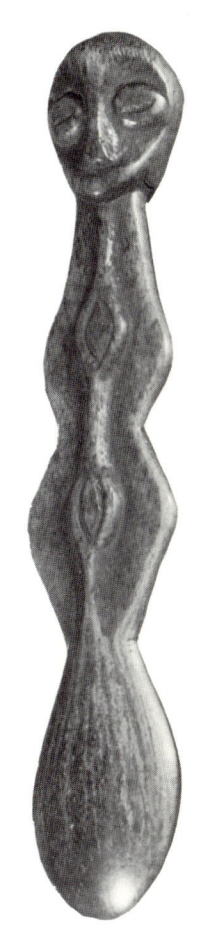

96.

97.

PLATE 98. Head (2⅜") in ivory, called Kankubungu (collected by Daniel Biebuyck in 1952; deposited in Koninklijk Museum van Centraal Afrika, no. 55.3.15). This object was received from Balumya, a lutumbo lwa kindi of the Beianangi clan, secteur Beia, Pangi territory. Objects of this type are extremely rare. Functionally they are identified as belonging to the broad category of *iginga,* carvings in human shape which are used in kindi. Similar objects are frequently owned by preceptors only.

PLATE 99. Group of four small carvings in ivory and elephant bone (Museum and Laboratories of Ethnic Arts and Technology, University of California, Los Angeles, nos. 378–46, 378–48, 378–50, 378–51). These objects, one suggesting a hammer, one a pestle, and the two others suggesting phalli, are fastened to a ring that is attached to a belt worn by a woman of kanyamwa grade. Called *katimbitimbi* (little phallus), they symbolize the social manhood of high-ranking women. The objects are marks of inalienability when placed around the neck of a goat or the leg of a stool.

98.

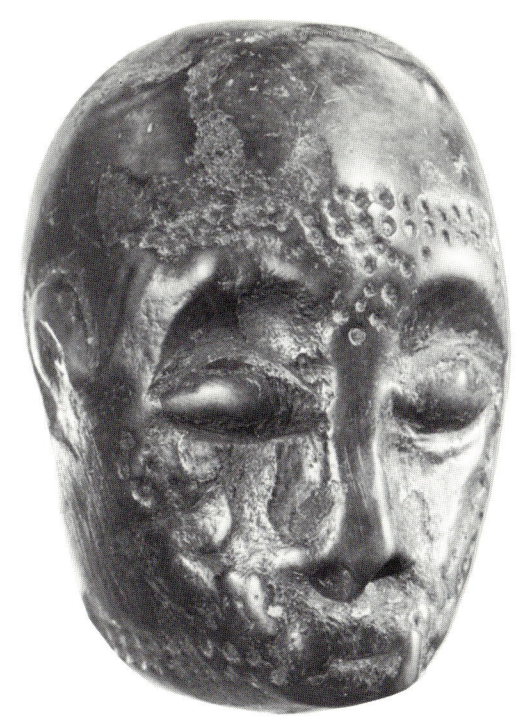

99.

PLATE 100. Miniature stool (1⅜″ high) in elephant bone (collected by Daniel Biebuyck in 1952; deposited in Koninklijk Museum van Centraal Afrika, no. 55.3.48). Received from Kwasola, a lutumbo lwa yananio of the Balambia clan, secteur Bakabango, Pangi territory, this little stool *(kisumbi)* is normally the emblem of one who possesses the privileges of kansilembo (second lowest grade in bwami which is also connected with the right to organize circumcision cycles). In this instance the object was functionally identified with the group of small *kalimbangoma* wooden carvings used by some ritual communities in the *mulama* rite of lutumbo lwa yananio.

PLATE 101. Stool (7½″ high) in wood with copper nails (collected by Daniel Biebuyck in 1952). This object was acquired in the area of the Bakyunga clan, secteur Bakisi, Shabunda territory. Stools of this type, called *kisumbi,* are used in a variety of rites throughout bwami initiations. The Lega have two other types of chairs—a tripod made of aerial roots against which one sits in a reclined position, and a heavy plank chair in which one lies down—but they have no ritual significance. The intricate symbolism of the stool concerns its form, its specific features (e.g., four legs and a protuberance in the center), the wood of which it is made (usually *Alstonia),* the tools used in making it, the location of the tree, and the life-forms associated with the tree. The most frequently stated aphorism, "Give me a stool; the stranger does not go with his one [chair]," emphasizes the value of hospitality.

PLATE 102. Knife (8⅜″) in ivory (collected by Daniel Biebuyck in 1952; deposited in Koninklijk Museum van Centraal Afrika, no. 55.3.22). This object, classified as *kabemba,* was acquired from Muloba, a lutumbo lwa kindi of the Banamuningi clan, secteur Beia, Pangi territory. The piece is used in *ibago lya nzogu,* the ritual skinning and cutting up of the elephant (symbolized by the initiation hut) at the end of the kindi initiations. Ownership of *kabemba* knives is also connected with *kibabulilo,* the right to skin and distribute sacred animals (pangolin, crowned eagle, *kamitende* snake, *izezekumbe* turtle) in one's own village.

100.

101.

102.

PLATE 103. Hornbill knife (9″) in elephant bone (Dr. Jay T. Last Collection, Los Angeles). Classified as *mugusu*, this object is a miniature representation of the large hornbill used to clear away forest undergrowth. One of the key concepts expressed with the *mugusu* is that without the help of many people it is impossible to finish the initiations promptly: "He who has not many [people] cannot clear the tangle of lianas."

PLATE 104. Scepter (8¼″) in elephant bone (collected by Daniel Biebuyck in 1951). This object comes from an area where Lega and Bembe cultures overlap. In the ritual communities where it occurs, the scepter (called *kituta* or sometimes *nondo*, literally, a hammer) is used to beat the chest of the candidate while the preceptor is teaching him the principles of bwami: "Put down your heart; you are being beaten by your own hammer." As part of the contents of the shoulder bag in *kansilembo* rites, the scepter also conveys the idea that the head of the lineage has his own hammer with which the petty work can be done, thus eliminating the need for a blacksmith. The scepter must not be confused with smaller, similar objects that are inserted into the soil to support the sacred fence, made of a feather rope *(munana)*, within which initiation objects are displayed.

PLATE 105. Ax blade (6⅝″) in elephant bone (Dr. Jay T. Last Collection, Los Angeles). The ax blade, called *isaga*, is used in various rites, particularly of the ngandu and yananio grades. It is also a symbol of the honey harvester and of the circumciser. It is given by the candidate to his *kilezi* tutor as a symbol of strength. It is associated with aphorisms that stress certain ideas: objects that are too often borrowed are lost or destroyed ("Kakuma [Little Ax] is the Great-One of the tangle; Isaga [Ax] has died [deteriorated] in being borrowed"); people are destroyed by those who are closest to them ("On the parasol tree grows the ax [handle] that will cut the forest"); and the individual who does not follow the counsel of his father and his seniors will destroy himself.

PLATE 106. Piece (8⅝″) of carved elephant bone (Dr. Jay T. Last Collection, Los Angeles). In certain rites, particularly at the level of the kongabulumbu initiations, pieces of carved elephant bone are beaten two by two, instead of drums and rattles, to accompany the songs. The key aphorism reads: "Where the hammer sounds, at the blacksmith's forge, that is where we are scheduled to meet."

103.

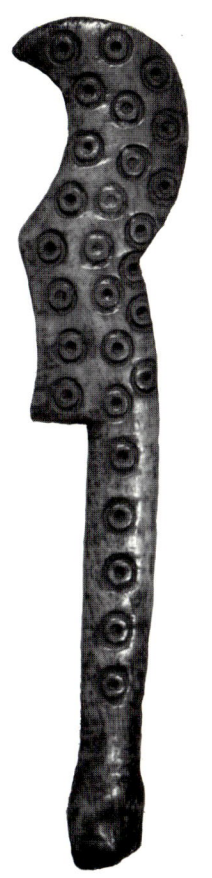

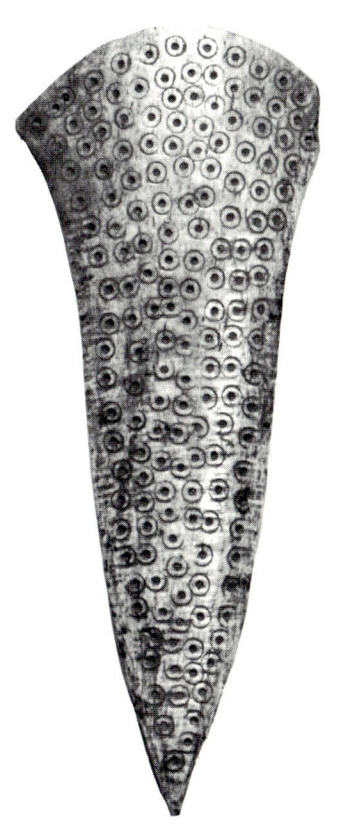

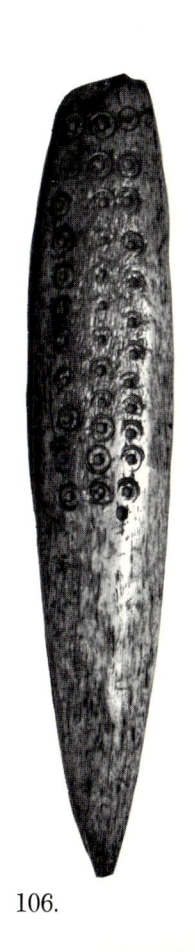

104.

105.

106.

Plate 107. Hammer (5⅜″) in ivory, classified as *nondo* (collected by Daniel Biebuyck in 1952; deposited in Koninklijk Museum van Centraal Afrika, no. 55.3.51). This hammer, acquired from Lusolo, a lutumbo lwa kindi of the Beiamunsange clan, secteur Beia, Pangi territory, is used with figurines in the *bele muno* rite of lutumbo lwa kindi. It is a symbol of continuity.

Plate 108. Excrescence (15¼″) of a vine (Museum and Laboratories of Ethnic Arts and Technology, University of California, Los Angeles). Well-patinated natural objects are sometimes substituted for carved figurines.

Plate 109. Strings of shell money, called *musanga* (collected by Daniel Biebuyck; deposited in Koninklijk Museum van Centraal Afrika). These fragments are derived from giant achatina shells. The shells are strung on raffia fibers; many different lengths are recognized, with specific lengths prescribed for specific rites. Shell money is used as a means of exchange throughout bwami initiations and also in daily Lega life.

Plate 110. Group of natural objects, some of them slightly modified, used in bwami initiations (Museum and Laboratories of Ethnic Arts and Technology, University of California, Los Angeles). The objects here shown are an extremely small sample of the immense variety of natural items used in the initiations, very often in conjunction with objets d'art. They include a warthog tusk, a pangolin claw with wickerwork, a *kagelia* monkey skull, a polished *lubumba* mussel shell, a pangolin scale, the snout of a young boar, an assemblage with snake fangs, an unidentified jawbone, an assemblage of dendrohyrax teeth, a tibia of a *kagelia* monkey. These objects, and hundreds of others from the animal and vegetal worlds, are interpreted by means of aphorisms that emphasize different aspects of the bwami moral code. Many of them are also distinctive insignia and paraphernalia connected with certain levels and grades of bwami. Some are owned by all incumbents of a certain grade; others are kept in the collectively held initiation baskets; others are owned only by preceptors or other titleholders.

107.

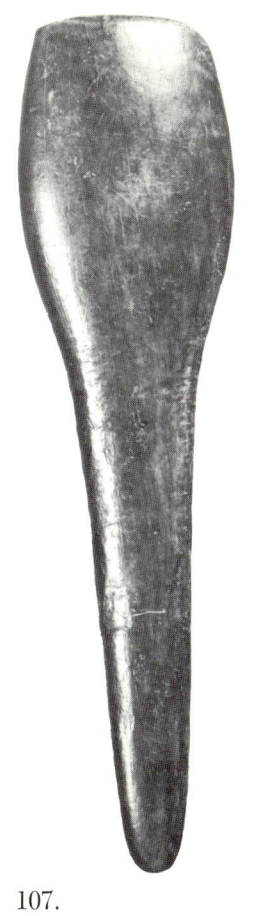

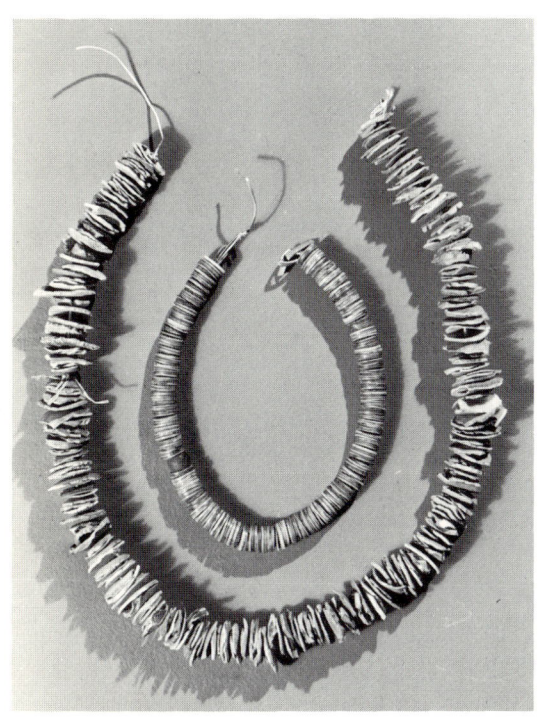

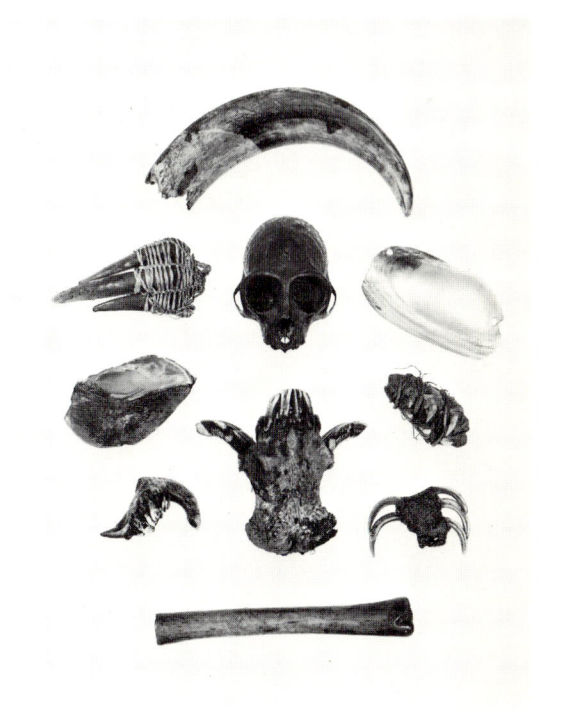

108.

109.

110.